VICARS
OF
CHRIST

VICARS
OF
CHRIST

POPES, POWER,
AND POLITICS IN
THE MODERN WORLD

MICHAEL P. RICCARDS

A Crossroad Book
The Crossroad Publishing Company
New York

1998

The Crossroad Publishing Company
370 Lexington Avenue, New York, NY 10017

Copyright © 1998 by Michael P. Riccards

Printed in the United States of America

Library of Congress Cataloging-in-Publication Data

Riccards, Michael P.
    Vicars of Christ : popes, power and politics in the modern world
/ Michael P. Riccards.
      p. cm.
    Includes bibliographical references and index.
    ISBN 0-8245-1694-X
    1. Papacy – History – 19th century. 2. Papacy – History – 20th
century. I. Title.
BX1386.R53 1998
282′.092′2 – dc21
  [B]   97-33160
                                           CIP

To Barbara

Dal primo giorno ch' i' vidi suo viso
In questa vita, infino a questa vista,
Non m' è il seguire al mio cantar preciso.

The Church has nothing to gain
from the propagation of vain legends,
and nothing to lose
from the manifestation of the truth in history.
— Pius XII

If you cannot give up everything of this world,
at least keep what belongs to the world
in such a way that you yourself
are not kept prisoners of the world.
— St. Gregory the Great

CONTENTS

PREFACE

In my recent work, I have explored very different types of leaders and leadership mystiques. My *Ferocious Engine of Democracy* is a two-volume history of the American presidency and the enormous changes that have taken place in the Republic since 1789. This volume is obviously very dissimilar in its cast of characters and concerns, but it examines men who were in some cases important leaders bestriding the world stage — the contemporary popes of the Roman Catholic Church. Adherents of the Catholic faith, my faith, have been taught that there is a continuous line of succession from St. Peter to the present, that the Church, with all of its faults, is God's imperfect home here on earth, and that the pontiffs are not the first among equals among the bishops, but actually possess a unique and very special ecclesiastical authority.[1] Many accept that formulation, and many depart from it. But it is accurate to say that the papacy is the oldest continuous elective office in the Western world.

If the American presidency has changed enormously over the past two centuries, imagine how the papacy and the Church have altered over two millennia! From the early and primitive beginnings of a Jewish sect later called Christianity, through the heroic missionary work in the Roman Empire and beyond, to the triumph of the Christian Church under Constantine the Great, to the Dark Ages and its waves of barbarians, through the confusion and splendor of the Middle Ages, the growth of the papacy was truly remarkable. The Church, though, has always been greater than its popes, and at times even the most sympathetic observer must acknowledge the venal, overbearing, and even heretical figures who have led this most traditional of ecclesiastical unions.[2]

And later, through the assorted schisms and the wrenching Protestant Reformation, the very fabric of the Church — one, holy, catholic, and apostolic, as it calls itself — was continually rent asunder. The more creative minds of the Church had in the past reached into its deep spiritual reserves for self-cleansing and self-reformation. It was in this way that the defensive and compelling Counter-Reformation was born. But as the Church settled in for a midcourse correction, it found that the enormous forces unleashed by revolution, nationalism, individualism, progress, science, and industrialization all seemed to work against its interests and its authority. Partially as a consequence of those battles, the upheavals destroyed the patterns of deference, of class structure, of personal restraints that had been prominent in the West since the Middle Ages. This volume explores the modern papacy with an introduction that begins oddly but correctly with the long, eventful, and at times tragic papacy of Pius IX (Pio Nono). That pope, Giovanni Maria Mastai-Ferretti, whose reign extended from 1846 to 1878, sought initially to bridge the deep chasm between the authority of his Church and the tumultuous world in which he lived. They cheered him in the beginning, and then threw mud at his casket at the end. Such is the fate of moderate men in an immoderate world.

My focus here is on leadership — its skills, its burdens, its contexts, and its exercises. I have not written a history of the Catholic Church as an institution or as a community of believers. Nor have I written a history of the last two centuries through the eyes of the papacy and its court. Rather, this study looks at a unique institution administered by human beings who seek to live in the world of God and in the world of man — which St. Augustine warned us against in the fourth century.

ACKNOWLEDGMENTS

The origins of this book lie in repeated exhortations from Rev. Ralph Sodano that I follow up my history of the presidency with a study of the papacy. I am grateful for the encouragement of a variety of people including Rev. Richard Lewandowski, Harry Semerjian, Joseph Hagan, James McManus, and Mary Keesecker. Dean James F. Brennan of Loyola University of Chicago and Wilton Wynn were kind enough to review my work. The librarians at Shepherd College and Fitchburg State College have been involved in assisting me over the years in tracking down sources. Cheryl Flagg has been meticulous in her review of the manuscript and in insisting on the highest editorial standards. Lastly, my appreciation to the editors of Crossroad Publishing Company for their confidence.

INTRODUCTION

In his classic essay on leadership, Max Weber identified three types of authority: traditional, charismatic, and legalistic, the last with its rules, regulations, and bureaucracies. In religious institutions, including those that are old and established, one can still see elements of each type in ways that are often not apparent in the secular realm.[1] This is especially true in the papacy. The popes sit on top of one of the most rigid and formal bureaucracies in the world, one whose very structure goes back in part to the Roman administrative practices of Emperor Diocletian. It is hierarchical, generally predictable in its rulings, paper or record driven, and edict bound. In its deliberations it is legalistic — even having its own courts and judges. And lastly, it should be remembered that the very word "charismatic" is religious in origin. It meant those who possessed "charism," or a gift of grace from God to preach, to heal, and to bear witness to the Gospel and to the Almighty's ways. The descent of the Holy Spirit on the faithful on Pentecost is seen as the defining event of charismatic presence. Today we have debased the word, using it to characterize rock stars, good looking politicians, and assorted individuals who are halfway presentable on television. But once the word meant what it defined.

The fusion of those leadership types gives the papacy many of its strengths and some of its weaknesses, for popes endure without set terms in office, and sooner or later they become bored and weary, just like all of us. The leadership of the popes in this century, and quite possibly before, exhibits some characteristics that would limit their ability to succeed in the outside world. Indeed the ones who have the best historical reputations in this period are Leo XIII and John XXIII, traditional men who reached out to change the Church in order to adapt it to the ways of the world, rather than vice versa. The great limiting factor on the papacy, however, is the perception of the faithful and, more importantly, of the ecclesiastical elite that runs the Church that its central mission is to preserve an ancient God-given faith. Popes can alter the method of delivery, change the nuances a bit, seem pleasant and accessible, but the office is one that places the occupants often at variance with the prevailing trends and moods of the secular societies around them.[2]

Popes are characterized as "liberals" or "conservatives," as "progressives" or "reactionaries." They are portrayed as captives or rebels in their dealings with the ambitious Roman Curia — the ecclesiastical bureaucracy of the Church that administers its programs, its agencies, and its diplomacy. But the core preoccupation of the office is one that stresses safeguarding the faith. No pope is or can be fashionable. Also, by the time most popes ascend to the papacy, they have been socialized in the ways of the Church hierarchy, been rewarded by their predecessors with appointments, rank, and prestige, and been proven to be reliable. Most systems of advancement have as their primary purpose to weed out dissidents, crackpots, and rebels. This is especially true in a organization that binds people together by ideas, ideology, and faith, for orthodoxy is extremely important in religion. One can contrast that to corporations and businesses which are run for profit and in which the innovator has a key role to play and can often change the organization and its behavior patterns.

But by the time a man becomes pope, he is usually fairly old and is at a stage in his life in which he and most individuals wish to leave something behind, something that transcends the inevitability of death. Psychologist Erik Erikson has said that at this time the elderly desire to pass on their views and their achievements to the young before they become disengaged from the hubbub of the world.[3] A sense of mortality and transcendence is even more heightened in a faith that is preoccupied with notions of certain death and hopeful resurrection. And quite probably these men of the cloth are like all of us. They too wonder if there is anything beyond this world, if in a sense they have wasted their lives promoting an illusion. Faith means that one overcomes doubts, not that doubts do not exist. As the father of a possessed boy in the Gospel of Mark once implored, "Lord, I believe; help my unbelief."

In dealing with the popes in this century, there is another human factor that we must take into account, a factor that is unique to this office as compared to other positions of high leadership. Popes have been celibate, or at least single men, born and raised, except for John Paul II, in the culture of nineteenth- or early twentieth-century Italy. There is a marked tendency generally for older men living alone to become crotchety and rigid in their final years. It may be that without the vibrant and annoying presence of the young they become even more sealed off from the currents and the tempo of change. There is something remarkable about Pope Paul VI sitting in his study listening to the rock musical *Jesus Christ Superstar.*

The rigidity of men of this age may also be due to the increasing physical deterioration that often results in minor circulatory incidents or tiny strokes which change the personalities of people and make them less flexible in terms of ideas and habits. Such is the argument made to explain why Woodrow Wilson, normally an extremely astute political operator, could not compromise in the end on the Versailles Treaty.[4] It is not just that one cannot teach an old dog new tricks; sometimes the old dog has learning impediments in the very opposite way that young children with their less formed brain patterns acquire foreign languages more easily than the middle-aged.

Also, the cutting off of men from the comforts and affections of women must surely have an effect that one can acknowledge without falling into the crude stereotypes of the male-centered bureaucracy called the Catholic hierarchy. Studies show that married men live longer than unmarried ones. (The opposite is true for women!) There apparently are real benefits in terms of companionship, sexuality, and personal bonding that pay off in greater longevity. Popes live in a pampered environment, it is true, so one cannot say that they are denied the labors of women keeping house or showing deference. But the absence of wives and children and grandchildren must make one's work and one's position in an ecclesiastical hierarchy even more lonely and more important to popes. At that stage of one's life — the sixties, seventies, and even eighties — popes are unlikely to embark on a sea of uncertain change. They wish to keep and preserve rather than to innovate and reform. That is what made seventy-six-year-old John XXIII so out of the ordinary. In him we could appreciate the real distinction between authority and leadership. Authority generally involves protecting and preserving the status quo. Leadership, however, often implies the need to change the direction of an institution — to engage at times in behavior that upsets the current equilibrium.

The world in which all but one of these men grew up was the Baroque epoch of nineteenth- and turn-of-the-twentieth-century Italy. It was then a nation that had just completed unification under a hostile anti-Catholic regime, that knew the plagues and ravishing diseases of the late 1800s, and that eventually shared in the devastating destruction that visited Europe in World Wars I and II. Those happenings are remote in history for most Americans, but not for Europeans.

The revolutions of the last two centuries have generally been antichurch and often antihumanity. The popes may seem to be reactionaries at first glance, but the millennial secular religions of modern times — Revolutionary France, the Bolshevik, the Fascist, the Nazi, the Maoist — have been terrible experiences for humankind. Historians of the Enlightenment and their successors like to write about the abuses of the Inquisition and the decadence of the Renaissance Church. The criticisms are indeed valid, but in comparison to the experiences of the twentieth century they pale in terms of brutalities. The most serious criticism of Pius XII was not that he did not hate Fascism and Nazism, but that he did not directly confront those ideologies with the traditional strength of the Church, even if it would have added Catholic casualties to the Holocaust. He failed, it is said, to be a visible witness against the greatest calamity of our time. On the other hand, the Polish pope, John Paul II, probably used his good offices and influence to undermine the Soviet empire. After he observed the end of the Marxist regimes, he was asked by a reporter what his judgment was on those developments. The pope calmly remarked that Marxism was "just another Tower of Babel." The perspective of two thousand years of papal tradition provides the right analogy.

Thus, if one wants to assess the leadership of popes in this century, one must understand the common and the unique influences that play upon them. Like all of us, they live in a very specific time and place, make their way in an environment of critical peers, and accept the compromises necessary to succeed. But they reach the pinnacle of an organization that holds its leaders to an even more demanding yardstick than corporate success or failure. At the end they will be judged, they believe, by an exacting standard of a demanding God who asks what they did with their spiritual stewardship. Not to recognize those dynamics is to misunderstand the unique nature of leadership in this powerful institution.

CHAPTER ONE

PIUS IX:
THE FIRST
MODERN POPE

The Catholic faithful like to believe that the inspiration of the Holy Spirit
guides the secret deliberations of the conclave that elects the pope. Skeptics brush away that reassurance as romantic nonsense. But in the conclave
of 1846, it must have seemed remarkable that a College of Cardinals,
appointed mainly by a rigidly conservative pope, would reject the reactionary candidates and choose one of its more liberal members to succeed
to the chair of St. Peter. The deceased pontiff, Gregory XVI, had reigned
for sixteen years (1831–46). He had denounced even the railroad as an
instrument of the devil. The Italian historian Adolfo Omodeo wrote, "reactionary, stubborn, and inert, opposed to every sort of innovation, even
to the building of railroads, Gregory XVI died after sixteen years of bad
government, leaving a difficult heritage to his successor."[1]

In his time, Gregory XVI had established himself as a close political
ally of the brilliant diplomat Klemens von Metternich, chancellor of the
Austro-Hungarian Empire. Metternich sought to establish a conservative
balance of power in Europe, restore the stability of the old order, and
chase away the nightmares of the Napoleonic reign. In the process, he
guaranteed the continuation of the temporal rule of the popes over the
Papal States, which after 1815 included the Patrimony of St. Peter (most
especially Rome and its environs), the Marches, the Umbria Region, and
Romagna (or Legations).

Originally the Catholic Church in the eighth century had taken over control of the central part of Italy after the Byzantine rulers left the West, and
the popes were compelled to look to the French princes for protection from
the invading Lombards in the North. At the height of its temporal power in
the thirteenth century, the papacy controlled most of the peninsula, includ-

ing at times even Naples and Sicily. And later, in the sixteenth century, the
papacy was occupied by warriors, diplomats, and builders who helped restore Rome and further extend the papal sway. But as the glory increased,
so did taxes and administrative problems, and by the time of Gregory XVI,
the Papal States — once celebrated for their learning, mild government, and
lenient rule — were seen as clerical monopolies riddled with corruption,
nepotism, and unenlightened leadership. Gregory, however, proved to be
a faithful ally of Metternich and consequently denounced any evidence of
democracy in France, Germany, and Italy. But as he left to meet his Maker
for whom he so labored, his position was taken by a man with a different background, one who was thought to have a very different orientation
toward the world.

THE "LIBERAL" POPE

Giovanni Maria Mastai-Ferretti came from a mildly liberal home with parents from the lower nobility who were termed "enlightened" within the
context of those times. As a boy he had suffered an epileptic seizure, but
later seemed cured. After being educated by the Jesuits, Mastai-Ferretti was
ordained, became deeply involved in pastoral activities, and worked for
an orphanage. He then went to Latin America as an auditor and became
personally committed to missionary work. After he returned to Rome, he
headed up a hospice, later was chosen archbishop of Spoleto, and finally
was appointed to the more important bishopric in the diocese of Imola.
    One critical historian has bitterly concluded that while at Imola

> he lived an easy, pleasant life and gained a reputation as an eloquent,
> emotional preacher after the fashion of the sugar-sweet practices of
> modern Italian devotion. The doctrinal liberalism of his neighbor,
> Count Pasolini, suited the Bishop's sentimental, shallow nature, while
> the spectacle of the misgovernment of the Papal States confirmed his
> political views. His liberalism had no real aim, no intellectual founda-
> tion; it was as much a reaction of the senses as his later conservatism.
> His weak goodness of heart was joined to a curious vanity, a van-
> ity which always claimed for itself a knowledge of a higher kind that
> was open to his fellows; as pope he "felt" his own infallibility. He
> was never cynical because he never saw the consequences of his acts,
> just as he never seemed to regret his friends or servants after they
> were dead. He was always greedy for adulation; his emotional nature
> needed excitement, and this excitement was gained most easily under
> the stimulus of applause from the crowd.

But the opinion of the time was much more positive from those who
knew him best. In fact, he proved overall to be a well regarded Church

leader and in 1840 was named a cardinal, although the pope himself probably talked to him about his criticisms of the administration of the Papal States. At a two-day conclave in 1846 he was elected pope in part because he was seen as a moderate progressive, especially when compared to the powerful reactionary cardinal Luigi Lambruschini. His predecessor, Gregory, had sarcastically remarked once that even the cats in Mastai-Ferretti's house seemed to be liberals. And Metternich lamented, "We have foreseen everything except a liberal pope." The master of Balliol in Oxford, however, called him "a capital fellow," while more conservative Englishmen called him "a radical pope" and "a pontifical Robespierre."[2]

Taking the name of Pius IX (Pio Nono, as he was called), the new pope seemed at first to live up to his liberal reputation. He signed an amnesty degree that released one thousand captives held in the Papal States and allowed hundreds of exiles to return home. On July 17, 1846, the decree was placarded on the walls of Rome, and it marked a new beginning. Metternich observed in disgust that such an amnesty was a change of principles, and he counseled, "God never grants amnesty, God pardons."

Previously, the Papal States had been run by an oftentimes harsh group of ecclesiastics and their sympathizers. More importantly, those areas were seen as a battleground in the political hostilities between France and Austria which dated back to the medieval rivalry of the Hapsburgs and the Valois in Italy.[3] Now, though, the creation and the maintenance of the Papal States became a European issue, and it invited outside intervention. Some leaders of the revolutionary movements had designs on creating a unified Italy, and those attentions were accentuated by the beginning of a fervent nationalist consciousness called the Italian "Risorgimento," under the dedicated and fiery leadership of Giuseppe Mazzini, which sought to bring all of the peninsula under one government.

Pius IX had not learned a basic fact of political life — that liberalization generates agitation more than it pacifies. It makes the unhappy more disenchanted, recharges their negative enthusiasms, and reinforces their agitations. Moderate reform is more often killed by the extremes of liberalism than by the lumbering weight of conservative or reactionary sentiment. That is why the ways of reform are perilous and the careers of reformers short. But Pius IX surely saw that the intransigence of Gregory XVI had not made matters better; if anything, that form of repression had run its course. And so Pio Nono began his turn at moderate change — at first. He appointed Pasquale Tommas Cardinal Gizzi as secretary of state and followed up with a commission on railroads — striking a very different pose from Gregory. The pope received plans for establishing gas lighting in the streets, creating a gas distillery, and supporting an agricultural institute. He enjoyed promoting scientific congresses in the Papal States and was genuinely interested in school and prison reforms. By the end of the year, he had introduced tariff reform and established commercial ties with other

Italian states, excused Jews from the onerous obligation of having to listen to weekly Christian sermons, reformed the criminal code and its courts, and supported the idea of guaranteeing the writ of habeas corpus. He even accepted a new law relaxing press censorship. It was an extraordinary performance, especially by a pope.

Conservative Catholics, especially those in the Roman Curia, believed that the pope's spiritual power and autonomy were absolutely dependent on temporal control over a nation-state. Thus, the Papal States took on an importance that is now difficult for us to comprehend. The Papal States were in part a consequence of the long history of disunion that characterized Italy for centuries. That peninsula was a collection of independent republics, duchies, and kingdoms which had resisted the centralizing monarchies that unified such disparate nations as Great Britain, France, Spain, Portugal, the Austro-Hungarian Empire, Sweden, and czarist Russia, among others. Only Germany was as fragmented as Italy. The major components of Italy in 1846 were Piedmont with Sardinia and Savoy; Lombardo and Venetia; Parma; Tuscany; Modena; Lucca; San Marino; the Kingdom of the two Sicilies (the Naples region and Sicily); and, in the geographic middle, the Papal States.[4]

Clearly, the new pope was a decent and amiable man, one who seemed to be a liberal at heart — but so did his predecessor, Gregory, who initially had come into office as a tolerant scholar and monk. The nature of the Papal States required that the popes and their diplomats protect their temporal possessions, which were seen, as noted, as essential to the integrity of the Church. The sovereignty over the Papal States was an outgrowth of the pope's spiritual primacy, even though he was also concerned with the policies of governments all over the world, especially in the areas of education, marriage regulations, and compulsory military service.[5]

THE PAPACY BEFORE PIUS IX

To comprehend this position, one must understand the world that preceded Gregory and Pius IX. The great traumatic event of the previous century had been the French Revolution. A spirit of emancipation led to frontal assaults on the Ancién Regime, and the Church in all its splendor and all of its corruption was one of the props of that way of life. As the Revolution became more radical and more mindless, however, it ate its own children and created instead a "Religion of Humanity" replete with new rituals, priesthoods, feast days, and calendars. The new faith became a caricature of the old rather than a substitute. Finally, the chaos was stanched by Napoleon, a son of the Revolution, who became emperor, dictator, and demagogue.

Actually the French Revolution began as a moderate affair to curtail the powers of an autocratic Bourbon king. But with each successive wave of leadership, the Revolution became progressively more radical. At first even the Catholic clergy supported the goals of constitutional liberty and economic freedom. The Catholic Church, of course, was part of the Ancién Regime, so all recognized that the Revolution would bring some unfavorable consequences, but few expected the brutalization by the revolutionaries of the clergy, especially of local parish priests. The Revolutionary Assembly enacted a Civil Constitution of the Clergy, which paid pastors a salary, eliminated control by the pope over the French Church, and provided for the election of bishops and priests. Then, however, the new regime insisted that all the clergy take an oath of compliance. That demand split the Church into two factions, led to the deportation of uncooperative priests into exile, and eventually helped to spread violence against the clergy across the nation.

But most critically, the radicals of the French Revolution attempted to destroy Christianity and substitute in its place a new secular religion. It all seems now so absurd, but the new republic became in the eyes of Christian peoples everywhere a frightening abomination.

Priests left the clergy in droves — a loss of an estimated twenty thousand. Others were killed, and some four thousand married for a variety of reasons. Finally the French radical Maximilien Robespierre abandoned the pagan theology of his predecessors and established on May 7, 1793, a new cult of the Supreme Being to replace the worship of Reason. From that point forward, there was a republican sign of the cross, a new Lord's Prayer, new feast days, and assorted imitations of the rituals of the old Roman Church.[6]

After Napoleon Bonaparte took control of the Revolution, he saw the need to reach some reconciliation with the papacy. In 1801, he signed a concordat with Pius VII, which mandated that all bishops in both factions submit their resignations to the pope, that Napoleon could name new bishops, and that the pope had the ultimate right to install them canonically. The Church in turn agreed that it would not seek to restore its lost property and that the clergy were to be put on a state salary. Later Napoleon unilaterally added the Organic Articles to the agreement. Those so-called police regulations constituted a code of laws controlling the activities of the Church and revived some of the restrictions of the Gallican days.*

The seventy-seven articles of the Organic Articles were divided into four titles. The first required that all Roman Church acts, decrees, and briefs, all synodal decrees, and even pronouncements of ecumenical councils had to be submitted to the *placet,* or approval of the state. The government had to approve the holding of national, metropolitan, and diocesan synods, and papal nuncios, legates, and vicars apostolic had to get the authorization of the government to exercise their functions on French soil or anywhere else

---

*The Gallican, or French, Church was in communion with the Church in Rome, but it historically opposed control over its operations and rituals.

in dealing with the French Church. Appeals of the decisions of the clerical administration would go to the Council of State.

Title two dealt with the clergy and ended exceptions from episcopal jurisdictions. It allowed bishops with government authorization to set up seminaries and cathedral chapters, but prohibited other ecclesiastical establishments. Also bishops could not leave their dioceses without the first consul's permission, and seminary professors were required to consent to the Gallican decree of the French clergy formulated in 1682.

Title three mandated a single catechism and single liturgy, and regulated preaching, the ringing of church bells, and the introduction of new religious feasts. Nuptial blessings could not be given to couples unless they had been previously married in a civil ceremony. Priests at Mass had to pray for the prosperity of the Republic and its consuls. Title four dealt with the size and number of dioceses and reimbursement for clergy, religious foundations, and church properties. Although the papacy vigorously protested those unilateral regulations, they remained in effect until 1905, when the concordat was terminated at the initiative of the French government.

Characteristically wearing his commitments lightly, Napoleon continued to seek greater control over the Church than he had at first acknowledged. But the pope refused to compromise, most pointedly on the traditional neutrality of the Papal States during the emperor's war against Great Britain. An angry Napoleon seized the Papal States, and the pope summarily excommunicated him. Napoleon, by then a self-crowned emperor, had Pius VII arrested in 1808 and shipped to France. For six years the pope faced his captivity with dignity, prayer, and composure. And then when Napoleon was defeated in his campaigns in Russia, he allowed the pope to return to Rome. On May 24, 1814, Pius VII entered the Eternal City to wild cheers and prayerful supplications. When Napoleon himself was sent into exile, Pius was acknowledged as a symbol of resistance to tyranny and a patron saint for conservative elements in European society. Later, Napoleon said of his attempt to control the pope, "If I had succeeded in this, what a lever to world power it would have been! . . . I would have had the spiritual world in my hands as well as the political. . . . The control of the spiritual power was the object of all my thoughts and desires. Without it, one cannot rule."[7]

After Napoleon was deported to Elba, the powerful reactionary forces of Europe met and sought to restore the old order at the Congress of Vienna. There sitting by the side of diplomats was the astute and charming papal agent Ercole Consalvi, who with Foreign Minister Charles Maurice de Talleyrand of France, Lord Castlereagh of England, and Metternich of Austria sought to obliterate the effects of the French Revolution in Europe. Consalvi was a protégé of Cardinal York (Henry Benedict Stuart), the last legitimate successor of James II and younger brother of "Bonnie Prince Charlie." As Consalvi grew up he socialized in a circle of exiled aunts of

Louis XVI. Although he was never ordained a priest, Consalvi became secretary of the conclave at Venice that elected Pius VII, was made secretary of state by that pope, and negotiated the original concordat with Napoleon.

In October 1814, he presented his proposal for the reestablishment of the papal territories, including the old site at Avignon, France. These bargaining positions were impossible demands, but his skill and perseverance marked the beginning of Consalvi's successes. Thus was born the restoration of the temporal power of the papacy.

At that time, the conservative Roman Curia also continued its support for the Index of Forbidden Books and in 1815 forbade all political books. In the Congregation for the Inquisition, in one brief period there were 724 charges of heresy pending. In one edict, 1824 monasteries and 622 nunneries were restored. Freemasonry and even Bible societies were condemned as Pius VII concluded that "the translations of Holy Scripture in general will do more harm than good, and none is to be tolerated which is not sanctioned by the Holy See and furnished with explanations by the Church Fathers."[8]

There were other developments which underscored a more aggressive papacy, most importantly the restoration of the once banned Society of Jesus and the signing of concordats with foreign governments. The Jesuit order had been banned by Clement XIV on July 21, 1771, in part as a response to enormous political and ecclesiastical pressures about the alleged abuses of the order and its supposedly unethical dealings. But the Jesuits were seen now as the skilled foot soldiers in the war against the French Revolution and its pervasive influence throughout Europe.

The second major offensive was the proliferation of concordats or treaties between foreign governments and the regime of Pius VII. The objective was not just to strengthen the papacy in its temporal activities and firm up control over the Papal States. These concordats were also meant to help the Roman pontiff and the Curia stifle the power and practices of the national and local churches and their clergy. The leaders of Protestant states who strengthened the pope by signing these agreements did not seem to realize that outcome, or just did not care.

The model for the concordats was ironically the first such document, which was signed, as noted, by that great opportunist Napoleon Bonaparte, and which had crushed the rights of the pre-Revolutionary Church, disposed of legally chosen bishops, and made new bishops in effect subject to the pope. Napoleon was untroubled by his concessions, saying that "the concordat is a religious vaccination; in fifty years there will be no more religion in France." Still, he felt that at that time people needed faith, myth, and mystery to keep law and order in the state. In the restored world after the Congress of Vienna, the papacy sought to encourage more treaties of understanding as it continued to expand its control in ways that princes and prime ministers could not comprehend. While the latter two groups fought for dynasties and elections, the papacy sought to intertwine religious orthodoxy and political power as it had during its flowering in the Middle Ages.[9]

THE PERILS OF REFORM

The papacy and its enemies shared the same view about the necessary ties between politics and religion. Nearly a half century after the French Revolution, the Italian nationalist Giuseppe Mazzini would still view politics as a continuance of religious concerns. And Napoleon III, Camillo Cavour, and Otto von Bismarck may all have talked about the separation of church and state, but in fact they meant the subordination of the former to the latter. They continued to flirt with control over clerical appointments and Church pronouncements, closed convents, and in 1871 even launched a major attack upon the Catholic Church in Germany called the *Kulturkampf.* Thus, it is not that the popes had an obsolete view of the desirability of the union of church and state, which was a mistaken retread of the glory of the Middle Ages. The pontiffs understood all too well that many of the major secular states and their leaders also preferred dominance in the relationship, and they could not agree to that.

In those battles the papacy was rather flexible in achieving its objectives. As Pio Nono said, he was indifferent to "the forms of government." At times the papacy supported conservatives, but in France the Holy See embraced the so-called Ultramontanists, who were anti-Gallican. The Ultramontanists (believing that the power of the papacy extended beyond the Alps, thus the name) were generally liberal and opposed the Gallican or nationalist French Church leaders who in turn supported the conservative authorities. Back in 1682, the hierarchy in France insisted that the Holy See had no right to interfere in civil and political matters in that nation, that the general councils had authority over the popes, that the apostolic power in France had to be exercised in conformity with the laws and customs of their Church, and that even on questions of faith, the pope was not infallible without the concurrence of the Church. For over two centuries, this nationalistic doctrine represented to the papacy one of the most serious challenges to its authority, and it looked forward to ways of triumphing over its own fellow churchmen.

Support for the Papal States thus was a part of a larger strategy which had religious as well as political implications. Criticisms of that regime, however, had intensified over the years, even from the new pope, Pius IX, when he was bishop. Between the death of Pius VII in 1823 and the election of Pius IX in 1846, there were three other pontiffs: Leo XII (Annibale Sermattei della Genga), who ruled from 1823 to 1829; Pius VIII (Francesco Saverio Castiglione), whose term extended for only eighteen months, and Gregory XVI (Bartolomeo Alberto Cappellari), who was pope from 1832 to 1846. All of those men were preoccupied with the problems of papal restoration and the increasing difficulties in administering the Papal States. In 1831 some of the great powers of Europe formally asked the papacy to begin to liberalize some of its restraints in the States, and in the spirit of compromise the popes had tried to do just that.

The reign of Gregory XVI, however, was still seen by its critics as repressive, corrupt, inefficient, and undemocratic. Surely his regime encouraged a clerical monopoly of offices and had made use of spies, a not uncommon practice for governments in Europe. Corruption and political patronage were rampant in the Italian states, but that was not unusual even in Britain. The actions of the police force, the so-called Civic Guard, were also extensively criticized. Originally formed to guarantee law and order and to make the papacy less dependent on foreign troops, it contained too many thugs and brigands.

In choosing the role he was to play, Pius IX was influenced, it was said, by the large tome of Abbé Vincenzo Gioberti titled *Primacy* or *Ile primato morale e civile degli Italiani.* That priest from Turin saw the papacy as the center of what would be a new unified Italy, which would govern with the rulers of the Piedmontese monarchy. Under the presidency of the pope, the new state would embrace a federation of "consultative monarchies." In the end, the Risorgimento moved to accept a king, but abandoned the papacy as the nationalists embraced the revolutionary calls of unification, pushed by Mazzini, Cavour, and Giuseppe Garibaldi — the agitator, the diplomat, and the general, who finally created the new state.

In the beginning, the pope was viewed as a liberal. In April, one witness recorded seeing a colorful procession with the approving citizens in Rome chanting "Viva Pio," just one expression of his great popular support. The conservative statesmen were clearly uncomfortable with him, especially in Austria — a nation that had proven such a loyal son in protecting the papacy and its temporal claims over the years.

One of the major reforms of the Papal States was the introduction of some laymen into positions of authority. Obviously, the clergy were by their very nature and training generally more literate and more worldly than many of the lay people, but there was increasingly a sentiment — especially among the Roman populace — that their problems would be dealt with more effectively if the role of the churchmen was limited. In June 1847, the pope in response formed a Council of Ministers, but made no mention of lay Ministers of State, which some had hoped for.

However, in April 1847, he had invited lay representatives from the provinces to meet with him and to discuss the formation of a Consultative Assembly at Rome. The announcement was greeted with great enthusiasm in the streets of the city. Much later, on October 14, the pope finally announced the formation of a council of twenty-four individuals to be elected indirectly. Although it was as the name implies only consultative, the Assembly could bring matters to the attention of the Council of Ministers. In addition, prohibitions on a free press were loosened and a municipal government for Rome was established. The new Council of Ministers would have only one position guaranteed to a cleric: the secretary of state, who would be responsible for foreign affairs. In all the other positions, lay people would be eligible to be ministers.[10]

The progress seemed remarkable, but what the populace did not realize was that in Pio Nono's view these were the limits of his flexibility. And he was clear on that point. He insisted on retaining the final power in his hands and on being the real head of the Papal States that he had inherited. Like many modern secular statesmen, he came to realize that the least traveled road is often the middle one — especially in the explosive Italy of the late 1840s where the political universe was divided into two groups: committed reactionaries and revolutionary liberals.

Crowds that were marching and singing the pope's praises initially were also demonstrating against the Bourbons, or the Austrians, or whomever. Some of these individuals simply wished to participate in the great liberal reforms that were sweeping across the English-speaking world, and some were still at heart liberal followers of the first Napoleon; others like the Italian Carbonari or the Mazzinians, wished for genuine revolution and forcible union of the Italian states.

The conservative prime minister Metternich continued to worry about the state of affairs in Italy, and on July 17, 1847, his forces moved into Romagna, Italy, without notifying his ally. The pope regarded that offensive as an insult and a hostile act directed both at him and at Italians in general. Then, rather remarkably, Pius appealed directly to the peoples of Europe against the outrage. When the Austrians would not yield, he threatened to break off diplomatic relations with them, to excommunicate Catholic Austrians, and to exhort the Italians to expel the invaders!

Suddenly it was the pope — the "Patriot Pope" — who was being hailed throughout the peninsula. Mazzini, who was anticlerical and hated the papacy, wrote from England an obsequious open letter to Pius. "There is no man I will say in Italy, but in Europe, more powerful than you. You have, therefore, Most Blessed Father, immense duties: God measures them in accordance with the means which he gives to his creatures. . . . Humanity cannot live without heaven. The social idea is none other than a consequence of the religious idea. We shall, therefore, have sooner or later, religion in heaven." He then argued that the pope must believe in the nationalist cause and unify Italy in order to "achieve great, holy, and enduring things." Later, when the pope did not obey his prescriptions, he would unleash his effective, vitriolic rhetoric on the pontiff. In the end Mazzini would be hailed as a liberator of Italy, while Pius would become a prisoner in the Vatican.[11]

But for a time Pio Nono seemed to encourage many in the Italian nationalist movement. On December 16, 1847, the Austrians left, and the pope emerged in triumph. Metternich, observing the situation, wrote to his ambassador in Paris,

> Each day the pope shows himself more lacking in any practical sense. Born and brought up in a *liberal* family, he has been formed in a bad school; a good priest, he has never turned his mind toward matters of government. Warm of heart and weak of intellect, he has allowed himself to be taken and ensnared, since assuming the tiara, in a net from which he no longer knows how to disengage himself, and if matters follow their natural course, he will be driven out of Rome.

As harsh as it seems, he was correct in his prophesy. Metternich further concluded,

> A *liberal* pope is not a possibility. A Gregory VII could become the master of the world, a Pius IX cannot become that. He can destroy, but he cannot build. What the pope has already destroyed by his liberalism is his own temporal power; what he is unable to destroy is his spiritual power; it is that power which will cancel the harm done by his worthless counselors. But to what dangerous conflicts have not these men exposed the man and the cause they wanted to serve.

Later, Metternich was to say in a similar vein that the realities in 1848 had lifted the many veils that people had hidden behind, and of Italy, "The veil is liberalism; it will disappear in Italy, as in every other country, before radicalism and action."[12] To Metternich and his fellow believers, political revolution would lead to social revolution which in turn would result in immense catastrophe for all involved.

The pope came to accept the view that he could play a prominent role in a modest federation that could lead to a united Italy. In August 1847, he actually proposed a customs union similar to that in the German states. Major opposition to those initiations, however, came from King Charles Albert of Piedmont, who decided to wage war against the Austrians and thus unite at least northern Italy under his aegis.

In early January 1848, revolution broke out in Sicily; soon Naples followed suit, and the pope was being cited as a supporter of liberation. In February, he issued a statement proclaiming the papacy as a rock of stability during tempestuous times, and the next month he came forth with a constitution for Rome. The document established what was in effect a limited monarchy under the pope and protected the rights of the Church and its officials.[13]

In March, Metternich was toppled from power in Vienna, and later the population of Milan rose up and drove the Austrians out of their city. King Charles Albert declared war on March 24, and the papal army moved toward the northern frontier to defend the state against any Austrian counterinvasion. Pio Nono, however, stopped any aid to the Piedmontese and insisted that his forces would not be involved in belligerent actions against the Austrians — a defensive policy traditionally held by many of his predecessors. He was the ecclesiastical head of a Church that embraced a variety of nationalities, and it was the position of the papacy that force could be used only for self-protection.

Although he had been proclaimed a blossoming revolutionary, Pio Nono was quick to distance himself from the radical ideas of Mazzini's adherents. He formally criticized the extremists in 1848 and dismissed any allegiance to what was becoming the Risorgimento. Consequently, he was seen not as a breath of fresh air, but as another reactionary pope. Now he had alienated the traditional protector of the papacy — Austria — and also disillusioned the liberals by refusing to go to war. Meanwhile, Charles Albert suffered defeat, and the dream of Piedmontese domination vanished, at least for the moment. To many it seemed that only the Mazzini radicals could deliver on the struggle for Italian unification.

After several false starts, the pope chose Count Pellegrino Rossi as premier for his new government, a one-time radical who was determined, however, to protect the Papal States. He believed in the pope's vision of a federal league with the pontiff as president. That policy ran headlong into the ambitions of the "Young Italy" partisans and Mazzini's revolutionary objectives. As for the pope, only a year after his much celebrated ascendancy, he was himself disillusioned and also disillusioning to the nationalist elements who saw him at first as a beacon of secular reform, and also as an ally in their anti-Austrian foreign policy. As Rossi sought to wind his way through the thickets of ambition, nationalism, and personal hatreds, he approached the chamber in Rome on November 15.

Like Julius Caesar, he had been warned to stay away from the legislative body that day, and as he walked up the steps to the council chamber, he was murdered by Luigi Brunetti, the son of a Mazzini adherent. The rabble began to mingle with the carabinieri, which led some to conclude that the beginnings of this revolt were carefully planned. Even the noble Garibaldi praised the act of treachery, comparing it to the assassination of Caesar by Marcus Brutus.[14] In the cause of revolution all can be forgiven.

The radicals subsequently sought to call a gigantic demonstration the next morning, and then to demand that the council declare war and establish also the separation of spiritual and temporal authority in the Papal States. But the pope stood in the way and instead quickly called the Chamber and the high council together and named a new prime minister. Soon the crowd forced the Swiss guards to disband and installed the Civic Guard in the Quirinal. The pope became a prisoner of the radical elements in his own Papal States.

The Bavarian Ambassador, Charles Spaur, prepared to spirit Pio Nono away to Gaeta, where a Spanish ship would take him to the Balearic Isles.

Dressed in the garb of a simple priest and carrying the Sacred Host, the pope escaped out of a secret passageway to a waiting carriage, which traveled past the Lateran gate — the site of the first great church of Catholicism before St. Peter's Basilica was constructed — to a modest hotel in Gaeta, and then to a royal palace. There he remained, waiting for support from the Catholic monarchs and the Catholic populations in Europe.

THE END OF THE PAPAL STATES

Meanwhile in Rome the nationalists voted to establish a republic and end the temporal power of the pope. On February 12, Mazzini, who was actually born in Genoa, was made a Roman citizen and his motto "for the name of God and the people" was promulgated. For a brief time, this revolutionary became one of the triumvirate chosen to rule the new state. Supporting the republic was the general of the armies, Giuseppe Garibaldi, one of the last of Europe's truly romantic figures, who arrived mounted on a white horse and dressed in a tattered red shirt, the symbol of his fighting men.

From November 24, 1848, when the pope took refuge in Gaeta in the Kingdom of Naples, until April 12, 1850, when a French expeditionary force and European diplomacy prevailed against the revolution, the republic floundered. On February 18, 1849, the pope appealed directly to the Catholic regimes for assistance. The Spanish were ready, but Piedmont and Austria were opposed to Spanish intervention. Naples was also prepared to assist, as was Austria, but on its own terms. France, however under the duplicitous leadership of Bonaparte's nephew, Louis Napoleon (later Napoleon III), was not supportive. The Catholic regimes were more concerned about each other having an advantage in Italian affairs than in restoring the pope to his temporal authority. As noted, Charles Albert had abruptly sent his Piedmontese army into battle against the Austrians, but on March 23 at Novara his forces were decisively defeated. Eventually he abdicated in favor of his son Victor Emmanuel II, who ironically would become initially an ally of the pope and then the first king of a unified and secular Italy.

But the consequence of Austria's victory was that France now feared the former's strength in Italy; thus the French government on April 20 dispatched a force of nine thousand men aimed at restoring the pope to power. The French troops, led by General Nicolas Oudinot, marched toward Civitavecchia and did battle with Garibaldi's legions, and later after a series of deadlocks prevailed when more French forces were introduced into combat. The republic however continued, and soon outrages were reported against the clergy, along with sacrilegious treatment of Catholic rites and rituals. It seemed to some as if it were the French Revolution all over again. Even Queen Victoria sent the pope a note of sympathy, and the English, who loved Garibaldi and allowed Mazzini sanctuary in their land, now praised the so-called *liberal* pope.

But the telling issue was the genuine sympathy of the French Catholics, many of them leftists, who pressed for a restoration of the Papal States. Consequently, the French moved to occupy Rome, staying until 1870. In the process of exile, restoration, and beyond, the pope seemed to turn more to the Jesuit order as the years passed. He beatified Jesuit Peter Claver on July 16, 1850; John de Britto on May 18, 1852; Andrew Bobola on July 5, 1853; and Peter Canisius on August 2, 1864.[15]

By April 1850, the Italian Republic was routed and the pope was restored to his see in Rome, and also to his throne as the virtual monarch of the troubled Papal States. The pope returned as he left — through the Lateran gate — at 4:00 p.m. on April 12, 1850. His main advisor was a cardinal who had stood by him through his turmoil — the shrewd and calculating Neapolitan peasant Giacomo Antonelli, who became his trusted secretary of state.

Eight months had ensued between the collapse of Mazzini's republic and the pope's triumphal return, and in the interval the state was run by three cardinals and the French army. After some difficult decisions were made and some punishments meted out, the pope came in and carried out some modest reforms. He created a Council of State, pushed for elected provincial and municipal councils, introduced more laymen into the administration, and allowed only a small army to be maintained. Eventually, the pope's ministers cut the public debt, pushed for railroad connections in the Italian peninsula, and held down taxes.[16]

Still, some of the causes of the turmoil remained. In the late 1840s and beyond, Italy and other parts of Europe faced grain shortages, hunger, price gouging, hoarding, and speculation. In addition, the pope's difficulties were compounded by the beginning of a more aggressive administration in the Piedmont kingdom, with its new master, Camillo Cavour.

Cavour through guile and duplicity would establish himself as a totally unscrupulous and extremely able diplomat who struggled to force another war in Europe so as to consolidate the hold of Victor Emmanuel's House of Savoy over all of northern Italy. Remarkably though, by 1860, he came to see that Garibaldi, who controlled southern Italy, could be persuaded to relinquish his dictatorial title and pledge his fealty to Victor Emmanuel as king. Thus, the stage was set for the control of virtually all of Italy, except for Venice and Rome. Soon the Papal States, with the exception of the Eternal City, fell to the Risorgimento. And by 1860, the pope was once again a prisoner in the Vatican — a king without a kingdom, a religious leader who insisted on calling down God's intercession on temporal politics. But that was all ahead of the pope as he returned to power in 1850, with a more guarded attitude toward liberalism and what he saw as its inevitable allies — secularism and anarchy.[17]

During his eventful and extraordinarily long reign, Pio Nono laid the groundwork for the modern papacy. His initial embrace of liberalism, his exile and triumphal return, his long battle against the forces of the Italian Risorgimento are all dramatic historical events, especially when played against the contrasting and colorful backgrounds of Mazzini, Garibaldi, Cavour, Napoleon III, Victor Emmanuel, and other nineteenth-century historical giants.* But Pio Nono was pope, and it was in his critically important ecclesiastical changes that his leadership was most apparent. His critics later said that Pio Nono learned his lesson and turned bitterly reactionary, both in politics and in his expressions of theology. But in fact neither was true. As has been seen, the pope never posed as a friend of secular liberalism; as a reformer in temporal matters, he would go only so far, which is where he went during his first year in office. And this pope was a genuine Italian nationalist who shared many of the resentments about foreign occupation, especially against the Austrians. Years later, he was to remark admiringly that he and Garibaldi were the only two people who had not gotten anything out of the Risorgimento.[18]

Still, it must be admitted that he returned from exile far less likely to dally with the agendas of reform — progressive or moderate — than he was in the early months of his pontificate. His enemies, and later most historians, would see his condemnations of modern ideas and his support of the doctrine of papal infallibility as examples of a severe turn to the forces of reactionary politics. But to a large extent, those orientations were a long time in the making, both for this pope and for the Catholic Church. Like him or spurn him, Pio Nono was the father of the modern papacy, and not since the Council of Trent (1548–63) had the Church appeared more at peril and yet also more influential.

Even after his restoration and with all the spiritual reserves of authority he embraced, the pope's undoing became the nearly irresistible urge of the educated populace for Italian unification. As noted, in this great battle he came especially into direct conflict with the designs and diplomatic skill of the Piedmontese prime minister. Camillo Cavour was born of Swiss, French, and Italian background, raised in an aristocratic family, and made wealthy by inheritance and his wise management of the family estates. At the age of thirty-eight, he became a political figure, and within five years he was named prime minister of the Piedmont-Sardinia kingdom called the House of Savoy. His overall objective was to extend Piedmont's control over most of northern and central Italy, and he used in fits and starts the strengths and the weaknesses of his state to encourage, instigate, and

---

*It should be noted that Napoleon Bonaparte (1769–1821) had a son by Marie Louise named Napoleon II (1822–32), who was called Emperor of the French and King of Rome. Bonaparte's nephew was Louis Napoleon (1808–73), who became president of the Second Republic of France (1848–52) and Emperor Napoleon III of the Second Empire (1852–70). It was the last who dealt with Pius IX.

scheme for a major European war to destroy the advances of the Austrian Empire. He would both meet clandestinely with Garibaldi and publicly attack Mazzini's radicalism in order to encourage Napoleon III to support the Piedmont cause as the more moderate and dependable way to guarantee France's influence in Italy.

As a young man, Cavour had indulged occasionally in revolutionary European rhetoric, but his real heroes were conservative English statesmen such as Robert Peel and especially William Pitt the Younger. He attacked the Church relentlessly, was excommunicated by the pope, but made sure that when he faced death he would have a sympathetic priest there to give him the last rites of the Church.

Over the years, Cavour argued that the Church controlled too much of the property and riches of the kingdom. There were ten thousand priests in Piedmont and almost as many monks and friars, one for every two hundred people. In Sardinia the ratio was 1–127. There were ten thousand religious foundations, and the state contributed an additional one million lire a year for clerical incomes. Cavour's response was to end the subsidies, abolish any monastic orders not devoted to education or charity, end mendicant orders that begged for their upkeep, and foster other anticlerical measures.[19]

Key to his policy on unification was the need to court the fickle Napoleon III, the only hope Cavour had to break both Austrian and papal control over the upper part of the peninsula. He even convinced Victor Emmanuel to give his fifteen-year-old innocent daughter, Clotilde, to a profligate nephew of the emperor Napoleon. When an associate demanded to know how he could justify sending her to such a voluptuary, Cavour simply observed, "Oh, what scoundrels we would be, if we did for ourselves what we do in the name of Italy."

In general, the king, Victor Emmanuel retained a personal affection and regard for the pope, and his family respected the Holy Father and the tenets of the faith. But it was Cavour who would set the tone of the House of Savoy and its foreign policies from 1852 to his death in 1861. One of Pio Nono's major biographers, E. E. Y. Hales, has concluded that the pope's hostility toward the onslaughts of the Piedmont regime and the broader Risorgimento laid the groundwork for his hostility toward what was defined as "progress" and resulted in his controversial *Syllabus of Errors*. Hales further argues that Pius's reign was a study of the relations between politics and religion and that "the defeat of Mazzini's Roman Republic in 1849 was a check to the political aspiration of Mazzini and Garibaldi, but it was also a (temporary) victory for the papacy over Mazzini's religion of the people. Cavour's victory in closing the Piedmontese monasteries was the prelude to his assuming political sovereignty over the Papal States. Napoleon's planned withdrawal from defending Rome in 1864 provided the occasion for the issue of the notorious religious-political document —

the *Syllabus of Errors*. The errors of that *Syllabus* were largely Cavour's, Mazzini's, and Napoleon's errors."[20]

Cavour's policies would result in both the end of the Papal States and belligerent attacks upon the prerogatives of the Church. It is easy to sympathize with his slogan of "a free Church and a free state," but the premier more often advocated a campaign of anticlericalism, ad hominem attacks on the religious orders, and a genuine denigration of the spiritual worth of the ecclesiastical way of life. The pope saw the Papal States as a part of the heritage that he was sworn to uphold, and he was committed to protecting church property. To him, it was "the robe of Jesus Christ," a part of the Passion of the Lord that he was pledged to guarantee. He wrote Napoleon that he must defend "My sacred character, and the consideration which I owe to the dignity and to the rights of this Holy See, which are not the rights of a dynasty, but rather the rights of all Catholics."[21]

By 1860, though, Austria had lost its ability to influence greatly the situation in Italy, especially in the middle section of the peninsula, and Napoleon was not willing to challenge Piedmont and protect the Papal States any longer. Thus, the major Catholic powers and also Spain, Portugal, Belgium, and Bavaria were reluctant to get involved. Protestant England summed up the new policy best: nonintervention should prevail in Italy.

The pope and his major advisors sought at first to place their wary confidence in Napoleon rather than create a large standing army of their own. But, by 1860, they entertained the notion of a volunteer army of Catholics from all over Europe to protect the Papal States. In the south, Garibaldi had moved from Sicily across the straits toward Naples and was bringing his forces north, while the papacy faced an aggressive anticlericalism coming down from Piedmont and elsewhere. Cavour insisted that he and the Piedmont regime were the real bulwarks against revolution, against Mazzini's radicalism, while in fact he was in contact with Garibaldi and with Mazzini partisans. Napoleon both counseled restraint publicly on the part of the Piedmont region and also let them know clandestinely that he would allow the dismantling of the Papal States.[22]

Cavour in turn had promised Napoleon Nice and Savoy for his cooperation. The French emperor was also growing unsympathetic toward the Church, fearing the strength of strong Catholic groups hoping for a Bourbon restoration in his own land. Napoleon, however, genuinely believed that Cavour was a check upon Mazzinism as the premier had claimed. Thus the emperor would defend the pope's claims around Rome as the old Carolingian kings had once defended the popes in their time, but he was not willing to intervene beyond that limited objective.

Both Napoleon and Cavour were counting on the death of the aging pope to ease the situation. Indeed, on Holy Thursday in the Sistine Chapel, the pope had collapsed and remained unconscious for several minutes. But he was to outlive by years Cavour, who contracted an intestinal infection on May 29, 1861, and died several weeks later. The minister was received into the Church, although his confessor was later berated for giving Cavour the last rites without him having exhibited much repentance for all the troubles he had caused the pope and the Church.

Still the pope in a characteristic display of generosity remarked, "My God, be merciful with the soul of this unhappy man." And he then said Mass for his powerful foe. Later, in a rare moment of candor the pope seemed to observe admiringly, "Ah, how he loved his country, that Cavour, that Cavour. That man was truly Italian. God will assuredly have pardoned him as we pardon him."[23] Later, in the same spirit, the pope near his own end graciously sent his confessor to minister to the dying Victor Emmanuel, who had so betrayed him and the cause.

The pope had to face the duplicity of Napoleon III, who publicly had pledged his support of papal claims — to a large extent because of the power and influence of French Catholics who respected the pontiff and were concerned about his safety and welfare in the midst of the turbulence of the Risorgimento. Events were in the saddle, however, and outdistanced even Cavour's genius or Napoleon's duplicity. Garibaldi, the dictator now of the Kingdom of the Two Sicilies, gave over control of that region to Victor Emmanuel, and Italy was coming into unification in a way few had thought possible. By January 1861, the whole peninsula, except for Venetia and the Patrimony of St. Peter, were a part of this new domain. Without Cavour, the king, however, lost a valuable ally in working with the uncertain Napoleon III. Indeed the latter wearily remarked, "Italy, with her unlimited pretensions, has ended by tiring even her friends."[24]

However, Napoleon decided to maintain the pope in Rome so as to satisfy Catholic concerns both at home and abroad and to continue some French influence in that region, especially after Garibaldi began his celebrated march to Rome in August 1862. The pope through his advisors, however, insisted that the Papal States had to be fully restored, but that bargaining position was gone forever. Pio Nono had come to recognize that he could not put his faith in the French or the emperor, but only in God. As for the lame suggestion that the emperor wanted him to reach some agreement with the new Italian government, the pope responded that he did not need foreigners to intervene on that score: "When all is said and done, we are Italian!"[25] Indeed, the pope exhibited throughout much of his adult life many of the attitudes that Italians of his class and era had concerning Italy and the pernicious influence of foreign elements.

The papacy with its weak standing army was dependent on foreigners — on France, Austria, Spain, and Bavaria — over the decades. The temporal states required the pope and his agents to bargain with and cajole other states to protect the papal territories. Those territories, however, were central in the battle over a unified state. The pope insisted that the Papal States must be maintained for the good of the spiritual mission of the Church, but for the Italian nationalists the maintenance of a separate regime in the central region would destroy the dream of one Italy. And the romantic vision of a pope heading a united Italian confederacy was an early casualty of intrigue, anticlericalism, and the pope's own reservations.

Looking at the loss of the Papal States, it is easy to judge that somehow Pius IX made grave judgments that led to disaster. But if one examines his real options, that judgment is somewhat flawed. He could have pursued the reactionary policies of Gregory XVI, made minor adjustments in the administration of his regions, and hugged closer Metternich's Austria. But Gregory had done just that, and there is little dispute that that path, though well worn, had not solved any of the papacy's problems. Besides, Metternich himself would be cast out of power in 1848, despite his preeminence in the world that followed the Congress of Vienna.

The pope could have embraced more vigorously the Risorgimento, but could he really have become any ally with such a violent, secular, anticlerical movement and still claim spiritual leadership? He could have tried the diplomatic approach, but no diplomats were more subtle and able at playing the European court games than the Vatican secretaries of state in this period — and still they could not accomplish their one major objective, which was to hold on to their wavering ally, Napoleon III, as guarantor of the Papal States. The only option for the pope was to create a large, powerful army, and then he would have had to become a very different sort of religious leader — a Julius II, who was a priest warrior during the Renaissance. Consequently, he would have lost some of the valuable support of the Catholic princes and also had to raise taxes in a territory honeycombed with agitators and traitors, thus accelerating the level of complaints that were already high for a variety of reasons. It just may be that in life one can fail just because the circumstances and odds are overwhelming.

ATTACKING THE ERRORS OF THE WORLD

By 1864, the pope decided to turn his focus on the whole catalog of the world's problems, some of which he had experienced in the most personal and intense ways. In that mood, if not in that spirit, he issued a statement of a syllabus of modern errors of thought and opinion and an encyclical *Quanta Cura*, which were sweeping and harsh denunciations of the times. The *Syllabus* and the accompanying statements cast the pope, the papacy, and the Roman Catholic Church in the popular eye as totally reactionary institutions, opposed to reason, freedom, and progress across the world. The pope's statements became grave embarrassments to the Church, especially in democratic states, and set the tone for the Curia and the promoters of orthodoxy that lasted until Vatican II and even beyond. In one sad sense the *Syllabus* did what Napoleon I and Cavour were never able to do: it helped to severely undermine the intellectual credibility of the Church.

Pius's secretary of state, Cardinal Antonelli, in his introduction said that the document was sent out so that "the bishops may have before their eyes all the errors and pernicious doctrines which he has reprobated and condemned."[26] Apologists then and now have said it was a technical theological document, but it was also a catalogue of eighty propositions which attacked such assorted errors as pantheism, naturalism, moderate rationalism, indifferentism, latitudinarianism, socialism, communism, secret societies, Bible societies, and liberal societies. It dealt with the rights of the Church, the limits on civil society, natural and Christian ethics, matrimony, the pontiffs' "civil princedom," and the relationship of certain errors to contemporary liberalism.

In a much-quoted sentence it attacked the expression that "the Roman Pontiff can and should reconcile and harmonize himself with progress, with liberalism, and with recent civilization." It has been said the *Syllabus* was a specific attack on the Piedmont regime's definition of progress and civilization, but to many it was an assault upon the nineteenth century's liberal tradition. As noted, the biographer Hales has seen the specifics of the *Syllabus* coming from the Italian situation with its Mazzini and Cavour, with its new nationalist, atheist, and pantheistic propaganda; thus, "progress, liberalism, and recent civilization" really meant the closing of monasteries and convents in Italy and the imposition of secular education in the new state.

Perhaps, but it also reached beyond those experiences to call into question the Church's position on the democratic American state, the toleration practiced in Great Britain, and the acceptance by many French of the revolutionary changes of 1789. What the *Syllabus* called the "pest of indifferentism" was actually called elsewhere religious toleration and personal respect; what the *Syllabus* denounced as "the corruption of manners and morals," others saw as freedom of speech, press, and assembly.[27] Almost immediately, progressive clerics sought to explain away what the pope had said, and the bishop of Orleans, Felix Dupanloup, in fact wrote a widely circulated pamphlet (which had the approval of the pope) that sought to tone down the encyclical by explaining away what the effects of the tenets would be in the real world.

But clearly to liberal Catholics, especially those living in pluralistic societies, it became a terrible burden. It gave credence to the view that the pope believed that there was no salvation outside the Church and that errors should not be allowed to be spread among Catholic peoples. For the pope, it was perhaps a revenge for the ill treatment he had received after being forced into exile, after the violent death of his prime minister, after the duplicity of Napoleon III and Cavour, after the aggressiveness of the Italian nationalist movement, and after the overall betrayals of the world. But for the Church in Europe, its enemies received more ammunition in their anticlerical crusades.

Pio Nono seemed even more extreme than his predecessors, more prone to a siege mentality and a defensiveness that moved beyond logical safeguards to simple intransigence. Added to that impression was the very real fact that his problems increased as Rome was occupied, as the pope declared himself to be a virtual prisoner in the Vatican, as the anticlerical campaign intensified during Victor Emmanuel's reign, and as Bismarck in the German Reich began in his *Kulturkampf* the blunt and vicious attack on Catholicism.[28]

When the increasing assault against the papacy began, Pio Nono turned to a bold reassertion of papal authority within the Church, where he could count on his authority to prevail. On a personal level, the clergy and some of the faithful celebrated with enthusiasm his anniversaries as priest (1869), pope (1871 and 1876), and bishop (1873). Despite the intrusion of secular events, Pius IX was characterized as the "pope of prayer," as a patriarch who encouraged audiences to meet with him, who favored extensive missionary work in Africa, Asia, and America, and who restored the Catholic hierarchies in Protestant England and Holland.

Like many modern popes, he developed a strong attachment to the Blessed Virgin Mary and was instrumental in furthering what some critics called the cult of the Virgin. Of all the mainstream Christian denominations, Catholicism has been more committed to such a veneration of Jesus' mother than any of the others. Some have ascribed the Church's devotion to a conscious or subconscious affection for the earth mother or old pagan fertility goddesses. Mary is the linear descendant of those female guideposts in that simplistic anthropology. Others argue that a Church run by celibate men seems fascinated by female beauty and virtue, by feminine charms, and by the need of all men to replace mother with another woman. It is love and passion by another name.

Perhaps there are such manifestations in the cult of the Virgin, but it is more likely that orthodox Christianity remains bewildered and fascinated by its central theological tenet — that God could become man to save humankind. And so the vessel of this remarkable occurrence is even more revered than one's mother. For centuries the exact relationship of Mary to God and to the common person had been debated, discussed, theorized, and proclaimed. By the reign of Pio Nono, there was some demand, which he eagerly recognized, to define the dogma of the Immaculate Conception of Mary.

As all knew, the pope had a special high regard for the Mother of God, and on June 1, 1848, he appointed a commission of twenty theologians to deal with the issue. The final dogmatic statement was that the Virgin Mary, at the moment of her conception, was exempted from original sin. The Bible really did not deal with the issue except in the Angel Gabriel's salute, "Hail, Mary, full of grace." But the Church Fathers had speculated that God could not have been conceived and carried in a mortal body with such a taint — as all of us have. In the Church Council of Ephesus in 431, the participants recognized her special sanctity, and later councils had acknowledged a concept of the Immaculate Conception. In any case, the pope asked for comments on the draft concerning the dogma; nine-tenths of those responding were supporters, with only a few opposing any such definition. Pio Nono released the proclamation and ordered a column erected at the Piazza de Spagna, which celebrated the Virgin's appearance to Catherine Labouré in Paris. Most importantly, the pope issued the proclamation on his own authority, not jointly with the bishops. In 1950, Pius XII would in a similar way proclaim the dogma of the Assumption of the Blessed Virgin, body and soul, into heaven.[29]

Even with his secular troubles, his contemporaries again and again commented on Pio Nono's winning personality, kind wit, and patience during his troubles. Most significantly, he decided in 1867 to call a general Council of the Church for the end of 1869 to deal with the climate of adversity that the papacy and the Roman Catholic Church found itself in. It was expected by some that the Council would be focused on reasserting the temporal power of the papacy and that it would make the *Syllabus of Errors* Church doctrine.

In fact, the Council and its major document *Dei Filius* emphasized doctrines of accepted faith concerning God and revelation and did not deal with some of the major parts of the *Syllabus of Errors* such as political liberty and freedom of expression. But its most important claim to history is that Vatican I was the Council that defined the dogma of papal infallibility.

ESTABLISHING INFALLIBILITY

The history of that dogma is a complicated one. Some historians (including several Catholic ones) have argued that some of the early popes promulgated what were later and are still regarded as heretical positions. How then can papal infallibility be seen as a guarantee of the purity of the faith deposited in Rome by St. Peter himself? Others maintain that it is the Church Council or the congregation of bishops that should have the final say on what constitutes articles of faith. Still others hold that the Church itself is not spared the opportunity to be in error even on basic dogmas, but that the *ecclesia* (the Church) is infused with the Holy Spirit, which in turn guarantees that *overall* the Church persists in the truth of Jesus Christ.

What Pius IX and his ardent followers wanted was a very strong definition that when the pope speaks *ex cathedra* on matters of faith and morals he is infallible, that he is unable to be in error. There is no requirement that he has to speak in accord with the Council or with the bishops; rather he is granted that very specific divine guarantee. Although papal infallibility had some articulate critics during and after the Council, most notably Lord Acton in England and some clergymen in Germany and especially France, it is clear that the overwhelming majority of the hierarchy supported the assertion. Even if one admits that the pope had appointed a good many of these men to their bishoprics and that there was enormous social pressure to move along with the authority in the Church, papal infallibility was a tacit assumption on the part of very many clergy in very many ways.

It has been charged that Vatican I was in a sense hoodwinked by the Jesuits or the Roman Curia and even that the pope was not above campaigning before some groups such as the American clergy in Rome. Actually, some of the Curialists, such as Secretary of State Antonelli, were concerned about the summoning of a council in the first place. They feared it would bring to Rome dissident German and French theologians who would challenge Rome's authority. There was also a worry that Napoleon III would be displeased by any such Council, and he was after all the protector of what was left of the pope's temporal realm. Indeed, Garibaldi had not given up on his final quest in that region, and his forces were crying, "Rome or death" on their marches. By late 1866, the last of the French troops had left the city, although Garibaldi, who had continued his invasions in October, suffered a major defeat at Mentana in November 1867, when French troops were reintroduced.[30]

Added to the triumph of the extreme papal cause was the pleasant personality of the pope himself. He was not a great Vatican diplomat or a fine intellect or a distinguished theologian as some of his fellow popes were and have most recently been, but he was a man of deep sensitivity, genuine spirituality, and personal kindness. His reign of thirty-one years was the longest in history, and in his appointments he had reached out to create a large number of non-Italian cardinals, thus underscoring the Church's claim to universality. Still, some of the Church Fathers felt that it was inopportune to define papal infallibility at that time. Napoleon actually sent a very blunt warning that the Council should not dare make the *Syllabus of Errors* Church dogma — a position probably taken at the urging of some of the French hierarchy. As for the pope, he faced the beginning of the Council philosophically observing, "The Council always passes through three phases. First, there is that of the devil; then comes that of men, finally that of God."

After the defeat of Garibaldi in 1867, the Italian government was reluctant to antagonize Napoleon, and there was a lessening of pressure on the papal government in Rome. Thus, in December 1869, on the feast of the Immaculate Conception of Mary, Pio Nono finally opened the Vatican Council with about seven hundred bishops from all over the world in attendance. Critics of the Council claimed that deliberations were crudely stacked and influenced by the pope. Even Pius IX's decent attempt to find suitable lodgings and provide some subsistence for bishops from poor dioceses or with little means was cast in a bad light.[31]

Critics asserted that the pope named the presidents of the special congregations or commissions, and in the general congregations the right to speak could be denied. In the public sessions, discussions were to be excluded and members could only vote *placet* or *non placet*. The rule of unanimity which had previously prevailed where dogma was concerned was not honored, and a simple majority was all that was required. The acoustics were poor, so people could not hear each other, and the propositions were distributed singularly and piecemeal so that participants could not see the full range of what was being discussed and in what context.

Very quickly a proposition on papal infallibility was presented and pushed along. The pope's position on the issue was clear to the bishops, and he promised them in turn more control over the lower clergy. When there was a reference to the ancient tradition of the Church, Pio Nono was supposed to have answered imperiously, "I am the tradition." The debate on infallibility lasted from June 15 to July 4, and it was maintained that speakers in opposition were interrupted and subjected to expressions of displeasure. However, of the 635 bishops who voted on the issue, only 2 voted no. Thus, papal infallibility was finally recognized.[32]

It is true that the pope abandoned his earlier position of neutrality on the subject and made it clear that he believed in the dogma, and also that he was frustrated with the attempts of some of the liberal minority to use their governments to influence the deliberations of the Council. He charged that that group did not believe that the "Council is governed by the Holy Spirit." And as the argument on infallibility progressed, the majority was indeed getting more and more impatient. Still it is obvious that the proposition had the overwhelming support of the bishops, even without the pope's views being expressed so firmly. In the general congregation, there was indeed endless debate with endless repetitions on the issue, but as with most deliberative bodies, few votes were changed by speeches.[33]

After the voting a great storm swept across the region and darkness enveloped the basilica. The pope stood by a large lighted candle, moved through the ceremony, and then blessed those before him. Most importantly, on July 15, Napoleon declared war on Germany, and the Franco-Prussian conflict began — a precursor and, some believe, a contributing cause to the more awesome conflagrations in the twentieth century. Preoccupied with this struggle, Napoleon moved his remaining troops out of Rome for the last time and gave up any semblance of protecting the papacy once and for all. On September 20, the forces of Victor Emmanuel entered Rome, and the Council was adjourned *sine die*. Victor Emmanuel, who had made mendacity into a regal style, wrote the pope as a son, a Catholic, and an Italian, he said, to announce that he felt responsible for keeping law and order in the Italian peninsula.

Pio Nono called his masters "white sepulchers and vipers" and ordered only token resistance to the king's forces. He insisted that a white flag fly high from the cupola of St. Peter's, and then almost whimsically the aged pope began to compose a riddle on the verb *tremare,* to tremble. Later the annexation of the Patrimony of St. Peter's to the kingdom was approved on October 2, by a vote of 133,681 to 1,507. The pope then withdrew into the Vatican and became of his own will a prisoner. In November 1870, the government issued a Law of Guarantees, as the unilateral agreement was called, which would regulate the rights of the papacy until the Lateran Treaty under Mussolini. The law recognized the pope's sovereignty, held him immune from arrest, and protected him under the treason laws. The pope could establish diplomatic relations with other governments, could keep his personal guard, and was given exclusive use but not ownership of the Vatican, the Lateran, and Castel Gandolfo. The papacy was also to receive an annual sum of 3,225,000 lire for the lost territories, but Pio Nono ignored the law and waived aside the subsidy. When the pope criticized Bismarck for his campaign against the Catholic Church in Germany, the chancellor sought to apply pressure on the Italian government to curb the pontiff. That government refused to act, thus upholding its guarantees to the papacy.

As will be seen, Bismarck's *Kulturkampf* began as an attack upon the religious orders in 1871 and sought to subject the training of priests to the directions of the state. Later, as opposition mounted to the chancellor's high-handed policies, he backed down in 1879. The key to Bismarck was his cold calculation of strength and his ability to know when to compromise. Still, his actions encouraged anticlerical campaigns in other German states, Austria, Switzerland, and even Italy. Despite the guarantees to the pope, the government in Italy later pushed for a "Clerical Abuses Bill," which would subject clergy to special penalties for criticizing the state. The government also insisted on interfering in the rights of bishops; thus, the rhetoric of a free Church and a free state was stripped bare.[34]

MATTERS SPIRITUAL

Still the pope continued on — preaching and living a life of prayer and devotion. He urged greater respect for the Sacred Heart of Jesus and the special recognition of the Blessed Virgin Mary. On February 7, 1878, he died, and the papal chamberlain who would be his successor tapped him on the forehead with silver hammer three times. Appropriately enough, the chamberlain called him by his baptismal name. The lengthy reign of Pius IX was over. Three years later his coffin was carried to his final resting place at San Lorenzo Fuore le Mure. Even at night a crowd surrounded the coffin, and chants and jeers were heard, and then mud was thrown at the remains of the longest reigning pope in history.

The papacy of Pius IX has been seen by its friends and by its critics as the beginning of the modern papacy. Clearly, the Ultramontanist position with its cult of papal personality, its strong Roman Curial bureaucracy, and its monopoly over dogmatic teachings had arrived. The pope was now outside the traditional constraints of the councils of bishops and even the ecumenical Council with his assertion of authority and control.

Pio Nono had been a participant and a victim in the great movements of revolution and nationalism. Even his staunchest supporters had to recognize that when he left, papal diplomacy with most of the great states was in shambles, and that his insistence on proclaiming the doctrine of infallibility and noncooperation with many secular states left Catholics isolated and vulnerable to their enemies. He had commanded an army, supervised sophisticated and often cynical diplomats, and enacted a program of moderate reform. But the Papal States were central to the unification of Italy, both in terms of location and history. And so the temporal power of the pope fell as did the collections of duchies and small kingdoms that once marked medieval Italy and later Germany. Both those states became like the rest of Europe — unified regimes. In one sense the loss of the Papal States was as logical as the loss of the power of the duke of York or the barons of France. It just happened in the 1860s and the 1870s, not earlier, as in Britain under the Tudors, in France under the Bourbons, and in Spain under Ferdinand and Isabella.

But he left the legacy of the modern papacy in a spiritual sense also. The pope, through incredible courage and Herculean effort, refused to be consumed by those monumental temporal events. He encouraged religious devotions, endorsed Scholasticism, and advocated papal infallibility as a guard against impurities creeping into the faith. In the end he was neither a typical reactionary pope nor a successful liberal reformer. He was essentially a pastor in thought and practice — blessed with wit, perception, and a generous spirit. It was his unfortunate destiny to be alive during unfavorable and yet momentous political and social events.

CHAPTER TWO

LEO XIII:
THE SOUL OF THE
INDUSTRIAL STATE

In September 1877, Joachim Cardinal Pecci, bishop of Perugia, was named by the Vatican to be the camerlengo (papal chamberlain) in the household of the aging Pius IX. When the pontiff died, Pecci, according to the rite of the Roman Catholic Church, tapped Pius's forehead thrice with a silver hammer and said his name each time, proclaiming, "The pope is really dead." He then took the Fisherman's Ring off Pius's finger and had it smashed, a symbol of the end of his authority. In the interim between the death of a pope and the selection of a new one, the papal chamberlain controls the temporal power of the papacy — whatever is left of it. The Sacred College of Cardinals represents the spiritual power of the Church.

Two days after Pius's temporary interment and three days before the conclave to choose a successor would begin, important political happenings were occurring. Henry Cardinal Manning of England and Alessandro Cardinal Franchi, Pius IX's prefect for the Propagation of the Faith, met with some other cardinals to discuss the critical question of choosing a new pope who could reconcile the Church and the Italian government on the so-called Roman Question. Apparently, they decided on the aged Pecci as their choice. Pecci had been a cardinal since 1853, but he had never been a part of the inner circle because of his early disagreements with the policies of Pius's cardinal secretary of state, Giacomo Antonelli. Pecci was now nearly sixty-eight, and it was expected that his papacy would be a short, transitional one. Instead, it lasted more than twenty-five years and has been judged to be one of the most significant reigns in the long history of the Church. On the third ballot Joachim Pecci was elected and chose the name Leo.[1]

THE CARDINAL OF ARTS AND LETTERS

Joachim (or Gioacchino) Vincenzo Pecci was born on March 2, 1810, not far from Rome in the mountainous village of Carpineto in the Papal States. His father and mother both came from illustrious families, although they were not wealthy. He was the sixth of seven children and studied at the Jesuit College in Viterbo and at the Roman College. He was interested in the sciences, theology, and law, received doctorates in both civil and canon law, and was later recognized by Gregory XVI for his courage during a cholera epidemic in 1837. In 1838 he was named governor of Benevento, where he vigorously sought to control banditry in the region and to curtail the excesses of liberalism — two favorite causes of Gregory, who prized order and theological stability. Pecci was transferred to Perugia in 1841; he proved to be a good administrator with a concern for economic improvements and established a savings bank for farmers.

In 1843, at the age of thirty-three he was sent to Belgium as papal nuncio and made archbishop of Damietta. But unfamiliar with the subtle arts of diplomacy and not knowing French, he seemed to some ill-prepared. His letters to his family show that he was less concerned with serving the Church and its spiritual mission than in bringing more distinction to the Pecci family. He wrote to his brother that he would "rise in the hierarchical branches of the prelacy, and thus ensure the just respect which our family enjoys in the land." He scrupulously sent every certificate of appointment and every other document that singled him out to the family archives. And after he was made an archbishop, he had a life-sized portrait of himself commissioned and sent home to be hung between the two portraits of his parents in their salon.[2]

It is interesting to record some of the observations made about him at different stages in his long career. In Brussels, the Austrian ambassador Count Dietrichstein said Pecci was "the best of good fellows, but young, passive, without initiative, without authority and altogether lacking in that adaptability which was necessary to keep the affairs of his office in order." Later, the wife of Italian premier Urbano Rattazzi said of Archbishop Pecci,

> I have seen few such expressive heads as his, on which firmness, resolution, and strength are so clearly stamped. He inspires alike fear, esteem, and sympathy; but fear is the predominant feeling. One would like to love him, but one is afraid to. One thing is certain — he is no ordinary person. His voice is sonorous and full. He has not the princely bearing of Pius IX, but he is equally imposing. His demeanor is majestic and full of dignity; the chief impression one gets is that of asceticism and sternness, but this is softened by a certain benevolence, especially when he unbends to children. In a word, Cardinal Pecci of Perugia is a grand and impressive figure, and...he may one day be our pope.

A biographer, René Fülöp-Miller, has observed, "He was a slight, nervous figure with long, slender hands, that infinitely clever head crowned with locks, the white locks, the dark piercing eyes, the massive nose, and a broad, strong-willed mouth."

Prince Bernhard von Bülow gave another vivid picture of the man, this time shortly before Leo's death:

> Everything about him had a spiritual aspect. He was very amiable, but in accordance with Italian *gentilezza* without too much emphasis on officiousness. His poise was perfect, particularly in the sense that no impression from without could shake his equilibrium, let alone endanger it. He had wonderfully fine eyes in which there shone the unassailable faith of the earthly representative of Christ.... He appeared to have transcended matter and, so to speak, to have reabsorbed it into himself.[3]

In Belgium, Pecci for the first time experienced the merciless ravishings of the new industrial society and the wreckage of workers and their families. With no protection from the state or labor unions, men, women, and children worked long hours, often endured hunger, and lived in hovels. Gone were the placidness and fresh air of peasant life; gone were the communities that nourished rich and poor alike.

Pecci at first got along well with King Leopold and even received the Grand Cordon of St. Leopold. He met Queen Victoria in London and King Louis Philippe in Paris, thus being exposed to two important monarchs and two great capital cities. But in a critical dispute, he supported the Belgian bishops and Catholic politicians who opposed Prime Minister Jean Baptiste Nothomb's proposal to have the government name members of "University Juries."

The king ordered the nuncio recalled by the Vatican because of his interference in local political matters. The Church had done fairly well under the liberal administration in Belgium, and the Vatican did not wish to get involved so directly in an academic controversy. In a sharp personal rebuff, Pecci was sent back home to Perugia, where he was to be banished in a sense for the next thirty years. His high-level career in the Curia bureaucracy was over, and it surely must have taken a toll on the bright and ambitious cleric. There in Perugia he stayed and ran a well-organized and caring diocese. In 1853, Pius IX rewarded his quiet successes with a cardinal's hat.[4]

Unlike the pope and much of his inner circle, Pecci was above all an intellectual — a man who loved and lived for ideas. What had set him off from the dozens of pastorally oriented clergy on the Italian peninsula was his deep commitment to learning, his fearless respect for intellectual curiosity, and his regard for the medieval theologian St. Thomas Aquinas. Together with his Jesuit brother, Joseph, he opened the Academy of St. Thomas and promulgated what would become the ascendancy of Neoscholasticism. Pecci was a fine classicist himself, possessing a beautiful Latin style. At the local diocesan seminary, he reversed the prohibition against reading Dante's *Divine Comedy,* a classic he admired and much of which he knew by heart. In addition to his initiatives in seminary and university training, he founded evening schools for the sons of working men and opened institutes which advanced money on corn.[5]

The bishop and then cardinal of Perugia stayed away from Curial politics and achieved a record as a social liberal who supported, however, the conservative Pius IX. Blocked by the powerful Antonelli, Pecci remained an illustrious provincial leader, but not a major figure in the papal court hierarchy. Later when he was pope, Leo observed that to talk of Antonelli still distressed him too much. He concluded, "I think if it had not been for him, the Pope today would not find himself in such a difficult position."[6] At the Vatican Council, he was an adherent of Pio Nono's views, but he left no real contribution to that short and turbulent time. Across the continent, the Church was swept up in the tides of anticlericalism, especially the *Kulturkampf* in Germany, tense relationships with France, and the unsettled Roman Question, which led to the self-imposed captivity of the papacy. In addition to those political and ecclesiastical disputes, the rise of industrial capitalism was bringing forth a new ideological movement — socialism in all its varieties.

Then as if touched by the hand of destiny, the obscure cardinal of Perugia seemed to come out of his library and publish a series of well-regarded pastoral letters on the Church and modern society. Unlike Pius IX, Pecci fought the ideas of nationalism and socialism, not just with authority, but with other ideas. In a famed Lenten message in 1877, he reminded his adherents that the Church and civilization were not enemies, but in fact were allies. It was the Church that had for so many centuries held back the forces of barbarism and darkness. He maintained that the Church wished that humanity should have a better material life on earth, and he went on to quote not the Bible or St. Augustine, but the French philosopher Baron de Montesquieu that the "Christian religion, which seems to have no other end but to secure our happiness in a future life, also ensures our felicity on earth."[7]

Pecci placed the Church on the side of decent working conditions, beneficial science, and true progress, but he still argued that the basic question before humanity was not politics or economics, but the relationship of individuals to nature, knowledge, and the Church itself. The cardinal thus turned the *Syllabus of Errors* upside down and made it not a defensive doctrine, but a powerful critique of man's inhumanity to man. Something very different was going on in those responses, and Pecci soon acquired fame and prominence. In November 1876, he was called to Rome after Antonelli's death, and in September of the following year named the new papal chamberlain, taking up residence in the historic Falconieri palace.

The Pecci family had acquired a contemporary luster to its old but worn nobility. Six months later, on February 28, 1878, he became pope.[8]

Thin and aesthetic-looking, the sixty-eight-year-old cardinal complained at his election that he was a feeble old man, who could not handle the burdens of the papacy. He was to live twenty-five more years, burying his friends and foes alike, proving that in life only God can set the measure of things — and that on a baser level longevity is the best revenge! Despite his initial inclination, he did not give his first blessing from the outside gallery of St. Peter's that overlooks the piazza — thus honoring the Curia's insistence that the pope must remain a prisoner in the Vatican. On March 28, Leo XIII professed his faith and took an oath to observe the Apostolic Constitutions, which included protecting the Church's lost territories.

DIPLOMATIC OVERTURES

The Roman Question and the establishment of an Italian state would bedevil Leo throughout his papacy. Although he would depart at times from the traditional wisdom on many issues, he backed away from repudiating Pius IX's legacy on the need for a separate state. Still, many Italian political leaders and even some Freemasons applauded at first his elevation as pope.[9]

Although Pecci's only foreign diplomatic assignment had ended in less than success, it was diplomacy that would lead to some of the major achievements of his papacy. Immediately after his coronation, he instructed the deputy secretary of state, Monsignor Vincenzo Vannutelli, to send out letters to the sovereigns and heads of states. The letters were remarkable for their reconciling tone. To the emperors of Germany and Russia, he underscored the importance of liberty of conscience for their Catholic subjects and also reassured them of his coreligionists submission to imperial authority and of their "scrupulous obedience." He wrote to each that while there was no official diplomatic ties between the Holy See and that nation, "We appeal to the magnanimity of your heart to ensure that peace and tranquility of conscience may be granted anew to so large a portion of your subjects." Later, in his encyclical on civil sovereignty, the pope said, "The Church of Christ *cannot* be either suspect to princes or disliked by peoples."

To the president of the United States, Queen Victoria, the kings of Holland, Sweden, and Norway, and the emperor of Austria, he wrote to thank each for what had been done in each nation to benefit Catholic citizens or subjects. On the issue of Switzerland, he acknowledged the estranged relations over the last two years and urged that "suitable and effective remedies would be found for those evils without delay." There were some complaints from the Curia that the pope had not consulted with its members on those overtures, but he simply moved along. It was time to reach out to the international order and to increase Catholic influence in those circles, he seemed to indicate. Even Pius IX had recognized the changing realities. Before his death, he observed, "Everything around me has changed: my system and my policy have had their day, but I am too old to revise my orientation. That will be the work of my successor."[10]

Later, critics were to say that Leo was autocratic, despotic, greedy for power, but to the larger world the aged pontiff seemed to be pushing early in tentative but distinct ways toward some reconciliation with the contemporary world. He would later be called the pope of the working class, but he loved to grant his benedictions from the regal gestatorial chair above the crowds of nobles and commoners alike. He enjoyed the liturgical pomp, but lived a personal life of frugality. Leo read extensively, approved of the introduction of modern electricity and communications, was usually affable, but did not have the easy humor of his predecessor. He was the first pontiff to be recorded on cinema and the first to allow electricity into St. Peter's Basilica. He had a deputy in the secretary of state's office prepare daily digests of newspaper articles across the globe and was well-read in the sciences as well as in theology and literature. Shrewdly he once concluded, "I want to see the Church so far forward that my successor will not be able to turn back." And he observed, "It is for me to sow, for others to reap."[11]

At first, Leo seemed to strike several different poses. He reaffirmed Pius's insistence that the spiritual power of the Church required a temporal state, condemned "enemies of the public order," and opposed Catholic associations participating in national elections in Italy. On the other hand, he reissued his earlier letter on the compatibility of the Church and modern civilization and mixed easily with intellectuals. The pope expressed an interest in anthropology and archaeology — tossing aside the fears of some that science of all sorts was a synonym for atheism. This new pope, an old man, was harder to categorize than his predecessors. He seemed committed to his papal prerogatives and to his predecessors' policies; yet he enjoyed ideas and was deeply concerned about the savagings of the new industrial order.

Immediately Leo sought to face the difficulties called the *Kulturkampf*. As has been seen, the Church had conflicts in Prussia with its chancellor, Otto von Bismarck, which then had spread to other German states, to Austria, and to Switzerland. A Prussian atheist and scientist, Rudolf Virchow, in the Prussian Landtag had called the disputes the *Kulturkampf* — or a struggle between different cultural value systems. The original points of contention had been over religious mixed marriages, increasing intolerance of Protestant rulers, growing Catholic demands for civil liberties, and a fear of papal power, especially after the Vatican Council's declaration of infallibility. In addition, since the Revolution of 1848, German liberals had become more hostile toward Catholicism, and they had advocated eliminating all religious influences from public and private life.

To add to suspicions, Catholics favored the inclusion of Catholic Austria in the new Germany — a proposal Bismarck opposed since it would threaten Prussian ambitions to become the leading state in the new Reich. In 1870, Catholics also took the initiative in forming the Center political party which became one of the major sources of opposition to the chancellor.

Bismarck, an astute and crafty politician, genuinely disliked Catholicism and also misunderstood its traditions and sources of power. He grew increasingly belligerent as Catholics tended to favor a more federal union, not a Prussian-run Reich, and when Catholic clergy in Silesia supported the use of Polish in religiously run schools, Bismarck argued that the Center Party with its advocacy of papal sovereignty in Italy was really a state within a state, more concerned with fostering Catholicism's power than with loyalty to the empire he was building. On July 8, 1871, the government ominously abolished the Catholic Bureau in the Prussian Ministry of Education and Public Worship. The *Kulturkampf* had begun.[12]

The chancellor then ordered all normal schools and school inspections in the Alsace-Lorraine region removed from the control of the Catholic clergy, where it had been previously housed. He also pushed for the Pulpit Law, enacted on November 28, 1871, which provided for severe penalties for those who used the pulpit to criticize the state. Tensions increased when Pius IX refused to accept Gustav Cardinal Hohenlohe as his nation's first ambassador to the Vatican, in part because the cardinal had opposed the Council's declaration on infallibility. Bismarck then publicly attacked the Church and proclaimed defiantly, "We shall not go to Canossa" — a reference to the humiliation of German Emperor Henry IV, who waited in the snow before Pope Gregory VII's door for forgiveness in the year 1077.

First, Prussian Minister of Education and Public Worship Adalbert Falk, prepared a law for the Prussian Landtag to subject all schools to state inspection. Then in June, religious orders were prohibited from participating in public education in Prussia. The German Reichstag ordered all Jesuits dismissed from the empire within six months, and in December 1872, Bismarck severed diplomatic relations with the Vatican after the pope protested his government's actions. In 1873, four other religious orders were also expelled. Then in the same year the Prussia Landtag passed the so-called May Laws, which placed seminary training under the auspices of the state and required students for the priesthood to go to a German university for three years and to submit to examinations in literature, history, and philosophy. The state also established restrictions on the Church's powers of excommunication and discipline and made episcopal decisions subject to an appeal before a civil tribunal.

The reaction was swift and strong among Catholics as they became more of a unified force after several influential bishops were arrested. In 1874, bishops and priests who opposed the laws were subject to exile, and nine out of twelve bishoprics in Prussia were vacant. Later, in February 1875,

Pius IX was to declare the May Laws null and void. In July 1874, a Catholic had attempted to assassinate Bismarck, and the chancellor used that attack to add fuel to the fire. In February 1875, civil marriage was made obligatory in Prussia, and soon other German states followed that lead. In April, the state suspended financial grants to dioceses where the laws were not being obeyed, and in June all church property was confiscated. Later a determined Pope Leo was to observe of the chancellor, "I shall have to continue to battle foot-to-foot against the man of iron."

Elsewhere in Germany other states emulated Prussia's policies. Baden had actually preceded Prussia in enacting restraints on the Church in 1860, controlling clerical appointments, and aiding those "Old Catholics" who had opposed the Vatican Council. In Austria, the government, using the papal infallibility decree as a pretext, broke its concordat of 1855. In 1874, the parliament restricted the rights of religious orders, curtailed Church control over its own finances, and sought to interfere with ecclesiastical appointments. Even in usually mild Switzerland, the monasteries had been closed earlier, and bishops who supported the Vatican Council were harassed. Religious orders were expelled in 1874, the papal nuncio was asked to leave, and diplomatic relations were severed until 1884. Civil marriage was required, and schools became interdenominational. That was the situation that Leo faced in the rest of the German-speaking world as he assumed the chair of St. Peter's.[13]

Meanwhile in Italy, Leo continued his predecessor's policy of Catholic noninvolvement in Italian government and political life, the so-called edict of *non expedit* — it is not expedient to participate. Leo was intelligent enough, however, to admit that such a declaration would eliminate the moderating influence of Catholic laity and parish priests in the civic life of the new state and consequently increase the power of radicals, anticlericals, socialists, and Freemasons, but still he would not change.

When in April 1880 the Chamber of Deputies in Italy was dissolved, prominent Catholics begged the pope to reconsider. He then convened a committee of cardinals to examine the issue, but they urged a continuation of the ban. The prospect for liberalization of the ban suffered another setback when in July 1881 a crowd attacked the casket containing the remains of Pius IX as he was being transferred to his final resting place. Horror was expressed by those both inside and outside the faith, and even by opponents of the Vatican. Deeply upset, Leo began to consider removing the papacy from Rome altogether.

Later, in 1886, loyal Catholics again pushed to end the ban. This time even the Italian government quietly asked the papacy to lift the prohibition, citing its own fear that a more radical and anticlerical element would end up controlling the Chamber of Deputies to the disadvantage of both the Church and the state. But the Holy See reiterated that prohibition and actually even tightened it. Leo concluded almost with a tone of resignation,

"As long as I live, the *non expedit* will be maintained; my successor will see what is best to do afterward." By 1900, the complete bankruptcy of the policy was obvious to all, yet the pope let it continue.[14]

In his diplomatic efforts, Leo XIII struggled to use the diplomatic leverage of the Vatican to persuade Italy to restore some of the Church's temporal power. The pope and his secretary of state tried for a decade to have Germany and Austria-Hungary convince Italy to make some accommodation on the issue. France, however, was now run by republicans who would not lend their services to protecting the Church. As Leo moved toward bettering relations with Bismarck, he tried to get him to pursue that policy toward Italy as well. Relations with the German Reich did improve, even to the extent that Bismarck urged that the pope serve as an international mediator in the dispute between Germany and Spain over possession of the Caroline Islands in the Pacific. He also quietly asked the Vatican to persuade the Catholic Center Party to support a military appropriations bill—which it did. Later Leo offered to make Bismarck a Knight of the Order of Christ and gave him the insignia of that order.

But on the divisive Roman Question, the "Iron Chancellor" did not wish to interfere in Italian policies, especially after 1882, when Italy became a German and Austro-Hungarian ally. Austrian Emperor Francis Joseph also welcomed some bettering of ties between Germany and the papacy, but he too did not choose to provide any help on the Italian problem. While Leo remained optimistic, his new secretary of state, Mariano Cardinal Rampolla, saw no real use in cultivating further the Reich and the Austro-Hungarian Empire and turned his attentions back to France. As anticlericalism and Freemasonry increased their hold on Italians, Leo faced even greater opposition in Rome and was looking for allies. The new Italian prime minister, Francesco Crispi, had made a career out of fiery, anticlerical rhetoric and let it be known that if Leo left Rome as a protest, he would not be allowed to return. He even encouraged the unveiling on June 9, 1889, of a statue of Giordano Bruno in the Campo di Fiori. Bruno was a philosopher who was burned in 1600 by the Church on that very spot as a heretic, and now he became a hero to Italian anticlerical elements. Leo in turn expressed often his fears of the Freemasons and tried unsuccessfully to foster counterrevolutionary activity.[15]

The pope did decide to stay in Rome, but the Vatican's foreign policy turned toward its traditional protector, France, which by now, though, was unsupportive of the papacy. Years later, a rapprochement was begun with Italy under Pope Benedict XV, and a settlement on the Roman Question was reached under Pius XI when the dictator Benito Mussolini agreed to the Lateran Accords of 1929. Those agreements codified much of what Leo had advocated decades before.

Leo had easier times with the English-speaking world. In 1850, the Roman Catholic hierarchy was reestablished in England, and the first cardinal archbishop of Westminster was named, Nicholas Wiseman. He was followed by Henry Edward Manning, who was instrumental in Leo's election and who blazed the path for greater concern for the worker in the Church. Almost immediately after his coronation, the pope honored former Anglican clergyman and Catholic philosopher John Henry Newman with a cardinal's hat, reestablished the Scottish hierarchy, and urged Irish Catholics to curtail their opposition to Her Majesty's government. As nuncio to Belgium, he had once dined with Queen Victoria and had met the prince consort, Lord Palmerston, and foreign minister, Lord Aberdeen. Throughout his life, Leo retained a respect for British achievements.[16]

On December 9, 1886, he conferred honors on fifty English martyrs who had been murdered for their faith under the regimes of Henry VIII and his daughter Elizabeth I. Two of the most famous of those figures were Sir Thomas More, chancellor of England, and Bishop John Fisher of Rochester, both symbols of Catholic courage and resilience, who were eventually canonized by Pius XI in 1935. Later, the pope was to name the ancient British ecclesiastical historian Venerable Bede (673?–735) as a doctor of the Universal Church, and on April 2, 1895, the intellectual pope also approved Catholics attending the universities at Oxford and Cambridge.[17]

With the renaissance of the Church in England, Leo, however, had to face two very difficult problems: the relations of the clergy with their hierarchy and the validity of Anglican orders in the eyes of the Roman Catholic Church. The absence of a hierarchy for so long resulted in an uncertain relationship between the lower orders of the clergy, who were used to doing things their own way, and their newly consecrated bishops. Added to that ambiguity were the conflicts between the hierarchy and the Jesuits in England. Under pressure from that hierarchy, especially Cardinal Manning, Leo agreed to deal with the basic issues under contention.

One of the principals in the dispute, Bishop Herbert Vaughan of Salford, argued that the Jesuits "attach great importance to this case because it will regulate America. And it is better to settle the case with the English Bishops than with the American Bishops, who are Irish and more violent."[18] Although Leo was under considerable pressure from a variety of quarters, he kept his own counsel and moved at his own pace. In the end, he sided with the hierarchy — as one would have expected — and enforced the authority of the Church over its own. It was after all a matter of discipline. The second issue was the controversy over whether Rome would accept the validity of Anglican clerical orders, that is, after all the centuries of division, was there still a clear line of succession from the Apostles down to the present? Could the Roman Catholic Church recognize as valid an Anglican priesthood similar to its own?

As so often happens, the episode began with a chance meeting, this time between Abbé Fernand Portal and Lord Halifax. Halifax argued that his views and those of many other Anglicans were theologically close to the Roman Church, and that many wished for a reunion of the two. Halifax, like Cardinal Newman, had been deeply influenced by the Anglican High Church spirit in the Oxford Movement, which emphasized ties to traditional Catholicism with some guarded problems over a strong papacy.

The abbé spread his views about the congeniality of both churches in a well-received pamphlet published under a pseudonym, arguing that Anglican orders "may be regarded as valid." In 1894, the Abbé Portal went to England and saw for himself the elements of the High Church that incorporated the vestiges of the Roman ways: vestments, Stations of the Cross, solemn Masses, Holy Souls chapels, Catholic literature, the Lady altars and the like. He then met the secretary of state, Cardinal Rampolla, and later the pope himself. One report of the meeting claimed that the pope was enthusiastic and foresaw the beginning of a reunion after centuries of estrangement. Recognizing the incredible opportunity for him and the Church, he surely saw it as a fitting capstone to his career. "You know I am eighty-five years old," he kept on adding, recognizing how little time he thought he had left. He even considered writing directly to the archbishops of Canterbury and York on the possibilities of such a reunion. The Catholic hierarchy in England obviously was dismayed, and its representatives hurried to Rome to meet with the pope and the secretary of state to talk about the "wild ideas in Rome."

The pope then ordered a scholarly examination of the validity of Anglican orders, and the archives included background material on Pope Paul IV's bull *Praeclara Charissimi*. Issued on June 20, 1555, the bull dismissed the validity of those orders and was cited in the current dispute. Leo again temporized and held his own counsel while the arguments were being made. Obviously, the issue of a possible reunion meant more than dealing with the problem of Anglican orders. The real roadblock was and remains the right of the pope to teach and govern the Church: the assertion of papal supremacy worldwide. A commission of six theologians was established to examine the question, and clearly Leo was excited and preoccupied with the possibilities. His own secretary of state supported the Anglican claims, and Leo was aligned with him.

But the pope finally received the argument against the claims, and on September 13, he issued his own bull, *Apostolicae Curae,* which concluded that the orders were null and void because of defects in form and intention. Among other issues, serious questions were raised about whether the Church of England itself had recognized the apostolic succession of the priesthood and the sanctity of the sacraments. Leo the scholar acknowledged the force of tradition, and Leo the pope kept the faith. But he still was human, and he was a proud Pecci. Leo probably deeply desired to be remembered in history as the pope who brought back the Anglican Church — or at least the High Church element — into the fold of Christ. In their own way, in their own times, old popes like young men can feel the tides of excitement, the sense of wild achievement, the flush of possible triumph that adds pinnacles of emotion above the flatness of life and routine. But in the end, duty and orthodoxy prevailed.[19]

In France, Leo seemed to face a complex of problems that rivaled those he had with Germany. There the turmoil continued as the Franco-Prussian War (1870–71) led to the destruction of the Second Empire and the ascendancy of the German Reich under Prussian aegis. As Napoleon III's armies went down to defeat, a self-appointed committee of Republicans established a Government of National Defense, which sought to keep up the fight. Paris fell and a new Assembly was necessary to meet and come to terms with the victorious Germans. A plebiscite to elect the Assembly led to a majority of Monarchists and not Bonapartists being elected. But Paris was taken over by a proletariat group with some republican bourgeoisie which created the Commune of Paris — a government separate from the rest of the nation. After a bitter battle and a repressive aftermath, the Commune was defeated by the armies supported by the new Assembly. Later, other uprisings took place in Marseilles and Lyons under the auspices of French anarchists opposed to the centralization of power in France, but to no avail. Now the world was to hear the name of the greatest socialist theorist and apologist Karl Marx, who praised what he called the civil war in France.

During all of this turmoil, the French Church continued to favor the restoration of the monarchy, however those who wished to reinstitute the royal line were divided in their allegiances. The Bonapartists were discredited by the war, but the Assembly still had factions divided between the Legitimatists, who wanted the Bourbons restored, and the Orleanists, favoring the descendant of Louis Philippe. Compromise was ruled out when the Bourbon heir, the count of Chambord, stubbornly refused to come to power unless the state used his white flag instead of the tricolor which commanded the allegiance of many of the French. The Monarchists' cause seemed to lose some of its luster as these disputes dragged on.[20]

The clergy's views ran counter to the Republican positions on education, marriage, and religious orders, even though they received financial support from the state. Leo at first tried to avoid taking sides, hoping that the French would somehow help him recover Rome just as twice in his lifetime popes had had their temporal power restored to them after European upheavals. Somehow the legacy of Pius IX still governed the Church. But by 1875, it was clear that popular sentiment in France had shifted to the Republicans, and Leo continued to contemplate the problem during the early years of his pontificate and beyond. Added to those dynamics, the pope named a new secretary of state, Lorenzo Cardinal Nina, following Cardinal Franchi's death five months after Leo's ascension. Nina had been the nuncio in Paris and understood the liability of continuing intransigence and following the Ultramontanist sentiment.

The influential cardinal archbishop of Algiers, Charles Lavigerie, also warned Leo XIII of the consequences of continuing to support the lost monarchical cause. On October 22, 1880, the pope wrote to the archbishop of Paris and reminded Catholics that the Church rejected no specific form of government per se, that citizens should obey those who govern, and that order is the foundation of public security.[21]

In late August 1883, the count of Chambord, or "King Henri V," as his followers wistfully called him, died. Who then was the legitimate heir to the throne for the Royalists, which included a good part of the Catholic clergy? Leo responded with a letter to the hierarchy of France in which he tactfully recalled the glory of their nation's Church and then rejected the desire of some to change the form of the established government in their divided nation. The pope in turn criticized the attacks on the Church — especially in the area of education — the institution of civil marriage, and military service for the clergy. The message to the Catholic hierarchy and to the populace was clear: they were not to be fellow travelers anymore in the monarchial cause.

In his encyclical *Immortale Dei* the pope also laid out general principles on the church/state issue. The Church, he maintained, lived in the world, but was not of it, and it could endure in a variety of nations with very different forms of government. He opposed popular revolution and treason against legitimate authority. Quoting the famous words attributed to Jesus, "Render to Caesar what is Caesar's and to God what is God's," he authoritatively supported such a policy of accommodation. Leo, however, opposed those who thought that liberty could survive without being allied with virtue and truth. But still, he separated himself from the view that any person should be forced to embrace Catholicism, quoting St. Augustine, who insisted, "Man cannot believe otherwise than of his own will."

But the anti-Republican sentiment continued its aggressive campaigns in French life, and Leo clearly feared the consequences for Catholics and his Church. Finally, on November 12, 1890, Cardinal Lavigerie gave a luncheon for the staff of the French Mediterranean Squadron and other distinguished guests. At the toast, a calculating cardinal saluted the legitimate authorities in France and urged national unity. He then had the White Fathers' band play the national anthem, the "Marseillaise."

The pope, who probably had encouraged the general overture, remained quiet as the monarchist Catholics reacted bitterly. Tensions increased, and even after a decade of effort, Leo still was not successful in normalizing the relationships between the aggrieved Church and the difficult French state. The Vatican continued to apply pressure on the French clergy to reach some accommodations with the Republic and the French cardinals reaffirmed that the nation "has need of governmental stability and religious liberty."

Then in a letter to the French people dated February 16, 1892, the pope proclaimed that Catholics were to support the Republic. Privately though, Leo assumed that Catholic political strength would prevail and that consequently the Constitution would be changed. He noted that the French could later establish a monarchy and revealed, "I am a Monarchist myself." There was strong rightist opposition, but the pope's authority ended for some at least the legitimacy of fighting the fruits of the Revolution. Leo insisted that French Catholics faced the inevitable triumph of the events of 1789, although many refused to comply. By then, however, the great ideological challenge to Catholicism was not from the remnants of the Revolution, but from secular socialism which was growing in the fertile fields of discontent in France.[22]

While the pope made considerable progress in opening up avenues of dialogue and accommodation with Germany and France, he continued to be wedded to the policies of Pius IX with regard to the Italian situation. Although he seemed at times to grope for some new ways of dealing with the so-called Roman Question, Leo was on that issue too much of a traditional cleric at heart and too much of a traditional pope in practice to accept closure on that controversial issue. In that rigidity he was surely influenced by the long, nasty, and threatening influence of anticlericalism that engulfed so many of the members of the Italian ruling class. They were still the heirs of Cavour, Mazzini, and Garibaldi, who defined the nationalist struggle, somewhat correctly, as opposition to the temporal and religious power of the Roman Catholic Church. Only when that generation of revolutionaries passed away and conservative Italians began to fear the advent of socialism did the quarrel begin to become more mute during the reign of Pius X.

As for Leo, though, this anticlericalism was fueled by the forces of Freemasonry — an international brotherhood that was bound together by secret rights, rituals, and its own hierarchy. It is in fact hard to overestimate the genuine fear and dislike that the normally open-minded Leo XIII had for that order. In part he was correct: it was an element of an international vanguard aimed at destroying the influence of the Church and the papacy, and the group had many adherents in Italy, a romantic land given to extremes of sentiment.

In his first allocution, or formal address, delivered on March 28, 1878, Leo dealt with the Roman Question. He supported, as all expected, the righteousness of Pius IX's position, but did so in remarkably mild terms. "The papacy and the church needed its temporal state in order to exercise its special mission," he argued. A month later, he reiterated that view and explained that a temporal government was necessary, for "the security and well-being of the entire human family is also in jeopardy." He pressed the Church's claims and yet seemed to try to strike some sort of an accommodation.[23]

A year later after his election, he explained that the Holy See needed only as much territory as would make it completely free. The new pope indicated that he was willing to renounce the former States of the Church and would accept something that approximated the "Leonine City," or the papal enclaves in the heart of Rome, with maybe a passage to the sea. Actually the Church generally enjoyed the complete use of those areas and edifices already, but what was being asked for was the juridical separation of the "Leonine City" from the kingdom of Italy. Even Pius IX had come to accept that formulation toward the end of his life. Unfortunately for the Church, that modest solution came to fruition some fifty-one years later.

There were other diplomatic endeavors in which Leo was involved: he urged the abolition of the African slave trade, restrained the king of Portugal's right to control the Goa area of India, established or reestablished the hierarchies in India (1886), North Africa (1884), and Japan (1891), and reorganized the missions in China. In addition, he had some hopes of reunion with the Oriental and Slavic churches and recalled the famous historic apostolic missions of Sts. Cyril and Methodius. The Eucharistic Congress in Jerusalem in 1893 and his apostolic letter on November 30, 1894, were meant to encourage a reunion with the East, which did not materialize. He did though reach some accommodations on church/state relations with Belgium in 1884 and Russia in 1894. And although Leo was seen as a political pope, he established 248 sees, 48 vicariates, or prefectures, and 2 patriarchates. He devoted eleven of his encyclicals to the Blessed Virgin Mary and respect for the rosary, established a feast of the Holy Family, and consecrated the human race to the Sacred Heart of Jesus at his jubilee in 1900.[24]

LEO AND AMERICANISM

Toward the other great English-speaking nation, the United States, Leo had a real fondness for the confusing pluralistic democracy which had just gone through a terrible civil war. He regarded it as one of the most promising missionary lands, a huge country with enormous possibilities and one that permitted full civil liberty. The growth of Catholicism, however, in the United States was due less to conversions of Protestants or nonbelievers than to the massive migrations of Irish, German, and later Italian and Slavic peoples. The hierarchy was basically Irish-born or first-generation Irish-American, and there was little in the way of ecclesiastical laws, especially as the new Church reached out into the hinterlands. In 1878 there was still no representative of the pope in the United States, and the American government had no minister accredited to the Holy See. Some American bishops had been especially vocal about the inopportuneness of the infallibility declaration at the Vatican Council, although, in the end, they fell into line. Still, the Curia had several concerns about the American Church, especially on the need for Catholic education for the children of immigrants and the organization of proper discipline between the bishops and the far-flung clergy.[25]

From the founding of the United States in 1789 to 1878, the number of Catholics had gone from thirty thousand to nearly six million. The number of bishops had climbed from one, John Carroll of Baltimore, to one cardinal, twelve archbishops, fifty-one bishops, and over five thousand priests organized into sixty-three dioceses or vicariates. The Catholic population included not just the immigrant masses coming after the Civil War and the old Anglo-Americans in the seaboard states, but also Spanish, Indian, and French missions dating back often to the sixteenth century.[26]

In 1875, the Curia moved to impose traditional canon law on the American Church. Some of the bishops in the western states had advocated a plenary council in the United States to discuss the problems that they were facing, and in 1884 one was held. The year before, the pope and the Curia sought to impose a series of broad-based rules covering seminaries, cathedral chapels, irrevocable pastorships, ecclesiastical garb, participation of Catholics in non-Catholic organizations, Catholic education, the care of immigrants, and Negro and Indian missions, among other items. Several of these proposals were opposed by the Americans, and there were some compromises. After the plenary council, however, canon law was effectively imposed on the American Church, and later a resident delegate was sent to the United States.

The Vatican hierarchy, however, retained some real reservations about the American Church, which were fueled in part by internal squabblings among the American clergy over issues of foreign-language churches and a so-called heresy, "Americanism." Unlike many Europeans, the American prelates were resounding patriots who celebrated the constitutional separation of church and state. They regarded such a development not as a pragmatic necessity as in Europe, but believed as a matter of principle in pluralism, toleration, and the sectarian peace imposed by the Constitution. While Pius IX and Leo were fighting their wearisome battles against nineteenth-century liberalism, nationalism, and anticlericalism, the American Catholics were exempt from much of that particular bitterness.

Like the early Catholic Church, the Americans recognized that there was a difference between society and the state. In Europe, the two had become thoroughly fused from the Middle Ages on into the nineteenth century, and Leo accepted the separation of church and state really to protect the Catholic faith from its enemies. Probably, if he had his choice, he would have liked to have seen church and state joined if his church could prevail. It is not that he was an intolerant man; he believed that freedom had to be grounded in a protection for truth and morality, which was the very essence of the Church's code of conduct. The new European philosophies came to celebrate instead the triumph of sentiment, of humankind freed from law or constraint. Their heroism was grounded in individualism, what was personal and particular to time and place. Leo lived in history, in an ancient network of natural laws and natural rights that were meant both to protect and to civilize people. And central to the advance of civilization was the influence of the Catholic Church.[27]

The Americans had their own problems with anti-Catholicism, which was linked in part to antiforeign nativism and usually anti-Irish feelings. But the wars of religious ideology, the Inquisitions committed by both Catholics and Protestants on each other and on themselves, the personal attacks on the papacy with its exiles, its humiliations, its reactions were residues of a past that did not wash up on their shores. It is not that Americans lived in a pristine, utopic state. It was that Europe was far away both geographically and intellectually. Besides, most American Catholics outside of the clergy did not care about theology, papal pronouncements, and Curial politics.[28]

The non-Irish parishes and congregations, however, resented the power, influence, and arrogance of their counterparts in the U.S. Church. Opposition built up especially in the Midwest among Germans, and in 1886 a petition went to Rome from a group of German priests asking for redress. Later, in 1891, a German merchant, Peter Paul Cahensly, and others renewed that petition for foreign representation in the American hierarchy and for special protection of foreign-language immigrants. The American Catholic establishment, led by Archbishop John Ireland of St. Paul and James Cardinal Gibbons of Baltimore, vigorously protested in part because of their preference for the assimilation of Catholics in order to underscore their allegiances to the new nationality being created. The pope ended up supporting his hierarchy.[29] But Ireland in particular had been criticized for his support of a proposed law in neighboring Wisconsin requiring the use of English in all public schools and for his ingenious proposal according to which schools supported by the state of Minnesota could have instruction led by Catholic teachers. In one sense, he was evading the Church's requirement that there be set up a separate and expensive Catholic parochial school system. Later, he had to defend himself both against Protestants in the United States who saw his proposal as another nefarious Catholic attempt to break down the wall of separation of church and state and also from traditional Catholics who accused him of abandoning the Vatican's directives.[30]

In 1891, Ireland went to Rome, this time to defend himself. Before, in 1886, he traveled to the Vatican to push for the establishment of the Catholic University of America, a proposal that the senior prelate, Cardinal Gibbons, had reservations about at first. The pope, though, loved learning and quickly agreed to the new institution. Leo had apparently asked Ireland, who spoke fluent French, to visit Paris and urge the Catholics to support his controversial encyclical of February 1892 calling on French Catholics to cooperate with the Third Republic. Ireland agreed and was well received there, although resistance continued. Later Leo sent Vatican-held documents on the explorer Christopher Columbus for the Columbian Exposition in Chicago in 1893, and he authorized Francesco Satolli, the archbishop of Lepanto, to be his representative to the fair. Satolli soon was named by the pope as the apostolic delegate to the United States — against the reservations of some Catholic prelates. He was to be the major source of information for Leo on that very confusing and yet bustling continent, and he generally supported the progressive hierarchy.

But all was not well for the progressives. In the Exposition was a World Parliament of Religions, which treated each faith in an ecumenical and equal way. Gibbons, Ireland, and other clergy participated in this friendly celebration and consequently left themselves open to bitter conservative criticism for not recognizing the special validity of Catholicism. In another controversy, they had stopped Leo from attacking the Knights of Labor in America, as he had done at the instigation of the Canadian hierarchy in their country. In that maneuver, Gibbons enlisted the powerful support of Cardinal Manning of England, who convinced the pope that the labor organization was not an anti-Catholic secret society. Later, though, Gibbons was not as successful when the Holy Office insisted on banning Catholic membership in the Odd Fellows, the Sons of Temperance, and the Knights of Pythias — generally benign secret organizations that probably reminded the Vatican of the hated Freemasons.

In September 1895, Leo in his encyclical *Loginqua Oceani* praised American Catholics and admitted that their progress was due to the toleration embedded in the federal Constitution and in the laws. Still he argued that separation was not the ideal formulation for the relationship of church and state everywhere. He also criticized divorce and civil disobedience in his letter and proscribed membership in societies dedicated to violence. In response to the critics of the Parliament of Religions, the pope mandated that Catholics had to hold their own congresses or meetings apart from others. The second rebuke came on the issue of Americanism.

In 1891, Walter Elliott published a complimentary biography of Isaac Hecker, a convert to Catholicism and founder of the Paulist Fathers. The volume was translated and published in France, where it became a major literary event. Hecker was portrayed as a role model for priests, a man who sought to reconcile the Catholic Church and democracy. French Catholic conservatives, however, bitterly attacked the volume, and the controversy went to the Vatican. Gibbons again asked for a delay before any condemnation of what was being called "Americanism." And Ireland again went to Rome, but arrived too late to stop the pope's letter.[31]

On January 22, 1899, in a papal letter to Cardinal Gibbons entitled *Testem Benevolentiae,* Leo criticized certain doctrines that had arisen on the occasion of the Hecker biography. Very gingerly the pope made it clear that he was not talking about those "characteristic qualities which reflect honor on the people of America." Instead, he was referring to the view that the Church should modify its doctrines to suit modern civilization in order to attract those outside the faith. He went on to enumerate some specific errors:

> that the Holy Spirit bestows more charisma in the present day than in earlier ages; that direct inspiration obviates the need for spiritual direction; that natural virtues are preferable to supernatural, because the former prepare the Christian better for action in the world; that, therefore, active virtues are preferred to passive ones like humility, meekness, and obedience; that the vows taken by members of religious orders inhibit liberty and are out of step with the imperatives of the present order; and that new methods, more in harmony with contemporary reality, should be employed to convert non-Catholic Christians.[32]

Ireland simply indicated that he did not hold such views; Cardinal Gibbons also agreed that no educated American Catholic had such opinions and other American Catholics blithely referred to it as a "phantom heresy." Clearly, Gibbons and other progressives were trying to sidestep the controversy, but the pope's admonition gave considerable strength to the conservative wing of the Catholic Church. Later, Leo was supposed to have insisted that the letter was meant to stop the controversy in Europe, and that Americans need not worry. But he was being disingenuous if he said that. For the letter was sent to Gibbons for a real purpose. It is doubtful if many of the faithful from the United States even knew of the controversy, but it surely led to a very cautious and timid hierarchy for generations to come. Later Catholic clergy avoided theology and Church history — except in the most celebratory modes. And as for their hierarchy, those men became preoccupied with building parishes, cathedrals, churches, schools, and colleges, but rarely would they be what Leo had been as a bishop — a man of ideas. After the appointment of William O'Connell as bishop of Portland, the pontiff told him that a bishop cannot afford to be a "near mystic," but had to be a "man of action."[33]

Indeed, Leo XIII was one of the few popes who could easily be called both an intellectual and a man of action. He not only read and respected the works of St. Thomas Aquinas, but in his *Aeterni Patris* he proclaimed Aquinas's theological system in effect the Church's official philosophy. To many it was an aged pope simply returning to the medievalism of the past. Indeed Leo added to that impression by building a splendid mausoleum in St. John Lateran in 1891 for the remains of Pope Innocent III (1198–1216), the epitome of powerful popes in the Middle Ages.

But, in fact, Leo was a broader scholar than that. In 1893, he urged Catholic experts to come to the defense of the Scriptures by studying Oriental languages and the techniques of biblical criticism. Against the opposition of the Curia, he opened up the secret archives of the Vatican to the year 1831 and commented, "We have nothing to fear from the publication of the documents." He showed a deep interest in the Vatican Library and in the Vatican Observatory, established a school of paleography and comparative history, funded or assisted in the establishment of national colleges in Rome, and pushed for a seminary in Ceylon for the training of priests.

He encouraged, subsidized, and approved of a variety of intellectual ventures, saying at one point, "Every newly discovered truth may serve to further the knowledge or the praise of God." He established the Thomist Academy in Rome and at his own expense gave it 300,000 lire for an edition of the works of St. Thomas Aquinas, he arranged for another 150,000 lire to go to the University of Louvain to help fund a chair focusing on scholastic philosophy and its relationship to the natural sciences, and he helped set up academic chairs at the Universities of Fribourg and Lille and in Washington. In his advanced years, Leo returned to an early love: he supported a public subscription for a statue of Dante in Ravenna and advocated a special chair in Dante studies at the Roman Institute. Yet at the end of his pontificate, his attitudes seemed to harden as he curtailed scholarship on the Scriptures (1893), set standards for censorship (1897), created another Index of Forbidden Books (1900), and agreed to set up a permanent Biblical Commission (1902).[34]

FROM JUSTICE TO THE SOCIAL GOSPEL

If the above were a summary of his papacy, he would be seen as a pope who concentrated much of his considerable effort on diplomatic maneuvers to protect the Church and educational endeavors to enhance its teaching mission. He would be a substantial figure in the papacy, one who tried skillfully to repair some of the damage caused by or at least manifested during Pius IX's long reign. But in fact these activities are overshadowed by the most famous encyclical ever issued by a modern pontiff — *Rerum Novarum*, the papal letter on the condition of labor.

The Industrial Revolution had started in the textile mills of Great Britain at the end of the eighteenth century and moved onto the European continent and into the United States. Great fortunes were made by the industrial leaders who created this new world. The very landscape changed, and so did the patterns of immigration as families left their farms and rural estates and went into the burgeoning cities. Railroads became increasingly important as arteries that moved material and production, not just in Europe, but in the United States. In the United States for example, the number of rail miles jumped from 70,000 in 1873 to 193,000 by 1900. Added to that was the rapid growth in population. In Europe, the figures went from 140 million in 1740 to 188 million in 1800 to 266 million in 1850 and then increased by another 130 million by the turn of the century. The reach of education and the sharp decline of illiteracy also followed in most of the northern and western European countries. And so, concomitantly, did the rise of newspapers and journals of opinion and the presence of broad-based democratic enfranchisement for many adult males.

The conditions of poverty grew more burdensome, however, and in the cities more visible. Factories and slums existed side by side, and men and their families worked twelve to fifteen hours a day for low wages. It was said that a whole generation of urban children rarely saw the sun rise or set.

The Catholic Church began to become more critical of the new industrial state and more sensitive to the so-called social question. The Church of Rome, of course, in the past had been committed in many ways to a more regulated guild-oriented commercialism, one ready to accept constraints on the use of property, on the exploitation of people, and on the need for religious holidays, vacations, and regulated workdays. In part, the medieval roots of the Roman Church allowed it to realize that capitalism was not the only economic order in the history of humankind — a balanced view not as prominent in some Protestant countries.

The major secular response to the social question came with the rapid growth of Socialist or Worker parties, many of them committed to the doctrines of Karl Marx. Socialist parties grew up in Germany by 1875, in Austria and Switzerland by 1888, in Sweden and Holland by 1889, and in Italy, Poland, and Finland by 1892. The Church then not only had to wage war against nationalism and the anticlerical spirit but also against disciplined Socialist parties and a compelling ideology that addressed the great social issue before the West. By 1880, the working class in France — the eldest daughter of Catholicism, as it was called — was lost to the Church.

In England, however, Cardinal Manning, who had been converted from the safe haven of Anglicanism and become a Catholic and later a prelate, brought his adopted Church into the battle for better working conditions. In December 1872, he appeared at a rally to support the cause of farmers. He urged Prime Minister William Gladstone to advocate legislation to end early child labor and regulate housing conditions. In 1874, he delivered an electrifying address on "the rights and dignity of labour" in which he supported the right of unions to organize and demanded legislation to regulate hours and control underage labor. Serving on a royal commission on housing, he pushed for town planning that was community oriented. In 1889, Manning supported the use of arbitration in the London dock strikes, and he was to be a major inspiration for Leo's encyclical.[35]

Rerum Novarum had two purposes: to thwart the advances of socialism and to lay out a social policy on the abuses directed against workers under the new industrial order. Thus, by the end of the nineteenth century, the greatest ideological challenge to Catholicism came from a counterideology, not nationalism or Freemasonry or a variety of hybrids of romantic individualism but the attractive philosophies of socialist theorists, reformers, and utopians. There were many variations in the age-old beliefs in economic equality and common ownership. But none exercised greater attraction than Marxism, which maintained that in the dialectic or movement of history there would be an inexorable triumph of the tough, disciplined dictatorship of the proletariat.

Karl Marx's ideology would meld or mix the humanitarian and utopian dreams of equality and brotherhood, the acceptance of conflict, turmoil, and violence for the greater socialist good, and the alliance of idealism and the power impulse that so fascinates elites and intellectuals. Much of nineteenth-century socialism was aligned to the romanticism of Jean Jacques Rousseau, the cult of violence, the celebration of naked reason, and the promulgation of atheism — a brew that was bound to capture the condemnation of Roman pontiffs.[36]

But to Leo, it was more than another heresy; it was a new coalition of forces that would be distinctly anti-Catholic. Soon conservative politicians and the upper classes were made to understand the powerful appeal of socialism and the organizational strength of Marxist cadres and agitators. The pope's encyclical began with a deeply moving analysis of the vast expansion of industry and science and the enormous fortunes of the few who cared little about the utter poverty of the masses and the prevailing moral degeneracy that resulted from such power and abuse.

Gone were the ancient workingmen's guilds which had been in operation up to the last century, and since then no other protective organizations had taken their place. "Working men have been surrendered, isolated, and helpless [left to] the hard-heartedness of employers and the greed of unchecked competition," the pope declared. A small number of very rich have "been able to lay upon the teeming masses of the laboring poor a yoke little better than that of slavery itself." The encyclical read as if it were written by Rousseau or Marx.[37]

Then Leo proceeded to make five basic points: first, he attacked socialism for its refusal to recognize the right of people to own private property, which promoted a sense of intelligence and independence and protected the family. Second, the pope outlined the important role of the Church in social affairs, noting its indispensable presence in a well-ordered society. Third, Leo talked of the importance of charity and justice to alleviate grinding poverty. Fourth, the pope departed from the fashionable argument for a laissez-faire state and presented a positive view that stressed not just the government's role in promoting public safety but also the need to regulate conditions of work, the guarantee of a just wage, and the encouragement of a wide distribution of private property. Then lastly, he emphasized the importance of voluntary organizations like trade unions and Catholic social action groups.

To us, those ideas are rather modest and dated, the language a bit archaic, but in 1891 it was an extraordinary document to come from the Vatican. Leo and other high-ranking clergy in Germany, the United States, the United Kingdom, and Ireland had explored for some time a recognition of the problems of labor and farmers. But this encyclical became a rallying cry for what was to be called "Social Catholicism." Later, after Leo's death, it was heralded as papal approval for the development of Christian Democratic parties in Europe — movements that checked socialist and communist governments even though Leo was not sympathetic to political parties.[38]

Leo thus had transformed the Church in many ways that his colleagues had never imagined. He was seen at times as imperious and to some a bit too intellectual, but he had lived a long time and had seen much foolishness and turmoil. He mixed very conservative theology with canny diplomacy and a strange curiosity toward new ideas. Whereas his predecessor fought the enemies of the Church with will power and courage, Leo tried to avoid confrontation with states and regimes. Sometimes against the admonitions of the Curia, he insisted on recognizing the realities of those states and did so occasionally with calculated abandon.

Above all, he sent his orthodoxy into battle against the ideas of secular ideologues, and in the great social challenges of his time he was not found wanting. In other pronouncements, Leo vigorously denounced the remnants of slavery, pressed for peaceful solutions of international disputes, and embraced in tentative ways the avant-garde views of a social gospel. In the first cause he sought to make the historic archiepiscopal see in Carthage a center for the antislavery campaign.

Still, he was a prisoner in the Vatican as was his predecessor. Leo would walk the Vatican gardens, sit and read under the old oaks, and occasionally welcome pilgrimages of working men. He once wistfully remarked concerning the developments of biblical scholarship at the end of his life, "I would like to have ten years to resolve this question in harmony with the words of the church and the exigencies of science."[39]

On July 3, 1903, at the age of ninety-three, he became very ill, and as he approached death, he asked about the proofs of one of his Latin poems. He then recalled his own role as papal chamberlain and warned that he should not be tapped too hard on the forehead for he might wake up! Two figures were carved on the either side of his tomb, the one a mourning woman representing the Church and the other a tradesman with his tools and characteristic dress, marking the passing of a prelate called the pope of the working man.

In his quarter-century reign, Leo remained true to many of the dogmatic statements and public pronouncements of his immediate predecessor. One of his biographers has argued that as a cardinal in Perugia he had actually encouraged Pio Nono to issue the *Syllabus,* call the Vatican Council to advance the infallibility decree, and promulgate the dogma on the Immaculate Conception. Thus, by all predictions, Leo should have been a keeper of Pio Nono's flame.[40]

But from the very first, Leo XIII charted a different path in two significant areas: the relationship with sovereigns and states and the perils of industrial capitalism. On the first issue, he simply abandoned Pius's orientations and diplomatic style, seeking to make the Church more protected from the adversities of the world by making peace with it, except on the Italian or Roman question. As has been seen, before Leo, the Church was constantly on the defensive, especially among the educated elites and the ruling classes. After Leo, the Church seemed to become intellectually respectable once again. Shorn of temporal possessions, the Vatican and the pope were able to assume more of an intellectual and moral force than in generations before.

Conservatives, after their first dismay over the labor encyclical, praised Leo as a major impediment in the way of secular socialism sweeping across Western Europe. There is some truth to the observation that the Catholic Church became a great fortress against Marxism, in the same way that the forces of the United States of America became the foot soldiers battling the advance of communism — the most virulent form of Marxist ideology.

But Leo and his advisors saw the labor encyclical as a genuine response to the evils of industrialization and a dehumanization of workers and their families. It is something quite remarkable to witness an eighty-one-year-old sheltered, religious prelate electrifying the Western world with a denunciation of exploitation and a call for justice and comity. No encyclical in modern times has had such a positive impact on people, and none has so added to the intellectual and teaching powers of the Roman Church.

Leo had his pastoral side, his personal commitment to piety and the religious customs of folk Catholicism. But at the core, he was a man who recognized the play of the intellect, although he occasionally embraced forms of censorship and doctrinal admonitions. But in his long papacy there was a remarkable confidence that the Church had the ability and resilience to face the advances of science and the critiques of philosophy and still prevail in fair debate and dissertation. At age sixty-eight Leo seemed to have learned the limits of authority and the need to persuade, cajole, and encourage the recalcitrants, the skeptics, and the unscrupulous. Some observers of his time said that as the pontiff aged, he began to look more and more like the French atheist and philosopher Voltaire. But appearances are deceiving. Leo drew strength from his beliefs, hope from his faith, and a sense of irony learned from the lessons that life on earth is but a trial and not the totality of human fate.

CHAPTER THREE

PIUS X: MOODS OF PIETY AND MOODS OF REPRESSION

On a hot July 25th evening in 1903, the fragile remains of Leo XIII were placed in a triple coffin, the first of cedar with the official seals of the Roman Catholic Church, the second of lead, and the third of wood. At the feet of the corpse were placed three small bags, one with twenty-five gold medals, one with twenty-five silver, and one with twenty-five bronze, corresponding to his years as pope. One of the observers of that scene, the patriarch of Venice, Giuseppe Cardinal Sarto, noticed how the *sanpietrini* gave the last coffin a final kick to shove it into the tomb. He ironically concluded, "That's how the popes finish."[1]

However, unlike the ignominious sight that disgraced the movement of Pius IX's final remains, Leo was honored by political heads and kings who came to respect the range of his intellect and the popular base of his moral authority. He had been very successful in his initial objectives, which were to open up the Church and make it more of a force in modern life. Leo's diplomacy had achieved major successes, but his critics argued that toward the end of his reign he had neglected to modernize the Curia and its departments, and that his style of administration seemed to focus more on his personal glory than on the Church itself. In the last years of his pontificate there seemed to be a need for greater attention to the pastoral aspects of the office, but by then Leo was too far advanced in age to change. In 1894, the devout Catholic Contardo Ferrini observed that Leo had improved the Church's position beyond all expectations, "But at the death of Leo XIII, the Church may have need of a supreme head who will more conspicuously lead it back to the evangelical virtues of the days of the apostles, to goodness, charity, poverty in spirit, meekness; and in this sense a most fitting choice might be Sarto, who has in the highest degree the reputation of such virtue."[2]

A LIFE OF PIETY

At the conclave held a decade later, the same judgment would be made: the cardinals after several confusing days would indeed choose the patriarch of Venice, Giuseppe Sarto, in an attempt to emphasize the papacy's spiritual orientation. Leo was the diplomat and the intellectual; Sarto was the parish priest and the humble man of deep piety. His election was clearly meant to restore the Church to its basic roots — the care of souls — even though at the time of his election he was one of the least visible members of the College of Cardinals.

Leo had appointed him first a cardinal and then three days later patriarch of Venice — a sign to the people of that city that he was rewarding the man before he was recognizing the see. Apparently, the perceptive Leo saw Sarto as his possible successor and had the highest regard for him, calling him the jewel of the Curia. However, once he did summon him to Rome to question why the patriarch of Venice had encouraged Catholics to participate in elections there in league with moderate liberals. The cardinal informed the pope that the liberals were in fact people who believed in the sacraments and in the faith, to which Leo observed, "Then they should be called Catholics," which pretty much settled the dispute in the days of the *non expedit*.[3]

Of all the popes of this century, none has acquired such a reputation for personal piety and religious devotion as Pius X. Indeed, no pope since Pius V (1566–72) had been canonized a saint — a person whose glory in heaven is sealed and who is worthy of veneration. And no modern pope before him, for as long as people could remember, came from such a poor and humble background. He was born on June 2, 1835, in a small village called Riese to a local village official — a sort of process server and messenger — and a seamstress twenty years younger. As a boy, Giuseppe Sarto would walk to school barefoot in order to save his shoes for when he really needed them. The family lived on a tiny plot of land and had little in the way of luxuries. The then patriarch of Venice, Jacopo Cardinal Monico, who himself came from a blacksmith's family in Riese, named Sarto as a scholarship student at the seminary in Padua.[4]

Upon graduation, Sarto was ordained a priest and sent to Tombolo, a rough town known for its cattle dealers and brokers. There the gentle and humble priest began to become popular for his charity and his simple but compelling sermons. Later he was transferred to Salzano, where he was at first not well received by the people, who were used to clergy from better backgrounds and breeding. But soon he became successful, concentrating especially on the need for greater catechetical instruction and proper liturgies. His charity, especially in the cholera epidemic of 1873, won the hearts of his parishioners, and already people were calling attention to his saintly virtues.

In 1875, Sarto became the diocesan chancellor and the spiritual director of the Treviso seminary. He quickly established himself as a strict but kind disciplinarian and a proud exponent of the glories of the priesthood. His activities apparently came to the attention of Leo, who was a keen judge of character and also of the ambitions buried in the human heart. Sarto consequently was named the bishop of Mantua, the Renaissance state of the Gonzagas. There he came face to face with the aggressiveness of liberalism and the Freemasons.

The diocese he inherited was desperately short of vocations to the priesthood, and he began a concerted campaign aimed at young men, which proved to be highly successful. Sarto remained, though, a parish priest at heart — teaching children the faith, visiting the sick and dying, and hearing confessions. For the first time in over two centuries, a diocesan synod was held, aimed at revitalizing the Church in his region and focusing on the sacraments, the liturgy, the rights of the Church, the first communion of children, and relations with the Jews, who were numerous in Mantua.

In his time in the diocese, one can see some precursors of the policies that would define his papacy: early communion for children, attacks against science and the concepts of progress that aimed at updating the faith, a strong assertion of the rights of the papacy, and a respect for the Gregorian chant and appropriate liturgical music. He also took on so-called Modern Christianity, later to be called "Modernism," which he saw as a formidable collection of heresies. In place of an excessive reliance on intellectual pride, he fell back on traditional piety and recommended meditation on the mysteries of the rosary. However, on one occasion he maintained, "Religion has no fear of science. Christianity does not tremble before discussion, but before ignorance." On another occasion he refused to follow the tradition of allowing a procession to go to his cathedral and the local synagogue on the marking of the king's birthday. Sarto's objection, though, was not that it honored the monarch, but that it created a public scandal by putting a church and a Jewish temple of worship on an equal plane.[5]

Throughout all these years Leo watched carefully the cleric's successes, and, as noted, on June 12, 1893, he named him a cardinal and then patriarch of the powerful see at Venice. However, the Italian government argued that it had a right to approve the appointment because Pius IV (1559–65) had given that concession to Austria. Indeed he had, but since 1866 Venice had been spared Austrian rule and was now a part of the kingdom of Italy. The claim was no more than harassment of the Church, and after sixteen months the government finally acceded on September 1894, after the

Vatican named an Italian to a post previously held by a Frenchman in the apostolic prefecture of Erythrae.[6]

From 1894 to 1903, the patriarch promoted his major objectives: organized religious instruction, appropriate liturgy, increased emphasis on vocations, and an upgrading of seminary education. He insisted on living simply, remembering his roots. He walked the streets in a black cassock greeting all and reminding people that he should not be called "Your Eminence" since he came from such a poor family in Riese. Even to the worldly and skeptical, it was clearly not a sham; he was what he seemed: a saintly and humble man in a position of high authority. After he became pope, he was advised by patricians in Rome that he should make his peasant sisters papal countesses. He dismissed the pretensions and remarked, "I have made them the sisters of the pope — what more can I do for them?"

Observing Sarto, French Minister of Education Caumie concluded, "He is a man of magnetic personality and splendid appearance, with an open face from which decision and firmness shine forth, but on the other hand, the mildness of his eyes tempers all severity. Every manifestation of dignity is contrary to his nature, but there is nothing vile in him; his manners are perfect; they are the manners of one who is completely master of himself."[7]

At the conclave, the cardinals at first leaned toward Leo's very capable secretary of state as a successor, Mariano Cardinal Rampolla. But then in a surprise move, the bishop of Krakow, Jan Kozielko Cardinal Puzyna, reported that the emperor of Austria wished to exercise his right of veto against Rampolla, who had headed up Leo's very pro-French foreign policy. Actually there is some evidence that the Italian government asked Austria to exercise that veto on its behalf.[8]

Historically, the veto was claimed by certain Catholic states to guarantee that no person could be elected pope who might be unacceptable to their interests. The right was maintained by the emperor of Austria and by the kings of France and Spain as successors of Charlemagne, who in turn as emperor of the West inherited the right which belonged to the Byzantine emperors as representatives of the Roman people. In fact, Austria had used the veto against Antonio Gabriele Cardinal Severoli at the conclave that named Leo XII (1823), and Spain against Giacomo Cardinal Giustiniani during the conclave that chose Gregory XVI (1831). Also it has been alleged that Baron de Chateaubriand was said to have formulated a veto against Cardinal Albani without awaiting instructions from Paris at the conclave of Pius VIII (1829), and that the conclave of Pius IX would have been deprived of his services if Gaetano Cardinal Gaysruck had not arrived too late to exercise Emperor Frederick's veto.[9]

The aged dean of the Sacred College, Oreglia DeSanto Cardinal Stefano, immediately declared the intervention invalid, and Cardinal Rampolla protested vigorously, but after several more ballots, the tides changed. Sarto emerged as the leading candidate, and then to the surprise of his fellow cardinals, he genuinely seemed unwilling to accept the office. It is not unusual for popes-designate to declare originally their unworthiness, but then they acknowledge God's will and move on. But Sarto truly wished to decline until the leaders of the conclave bluntly warned him of the consequences of disobedience to God's will and the plight of refusing the Church. Finally he accepted and announced his choice of a name — Pius — out of respect for those recent popes who had gone before him with that name.

On August 29, the pope arrived for his coronation in St. Peter's Square, not as Leo did in the Sistine Chapel. Over forty thousand people crowded into the square and sang the hymn "Behold a Great Priest," and cries of "Long live Pope Pius X" were heard in a variety of languages. The pope signaled for silence but the cheering continued, and handkerchiefs waved in the breeze from all over the basilica and the square. After acknowledging the pope, the master of ceremonies lit a small ball of hemp on top of a candlestick. Thus passes the glory of the world and all things temporal, Pius was reminded. The Mass began and the Epistle and the Gospels were chanted in both Latin and Greek; the choir sang Perosi's "Benedictus" at the consecration. At the end of the Mass Cardinal Rampolla, the archpriest of the Basilica, and two canons gave the pope the traditional offerings of twenty-five lire and said, "Holy Father, the chapter and canons of this basilica offer the usual stipend for a Mass well sung."

Already his contemporaries were calling him saintly. A French observer, Amelia Olivier, said of him that while he lacked the majestic appearance of Leo XIII, he had an irresistible kindness and pleasantness of manner. His answers were short and decisive, and he seemed calm and courageous, slow to condemn, but inflexible once he made up his mind. "He will prove himself a hero and a saint," Olivier concluded.[10]

There is in this century a strange and discernible pattern of papal behavior and conclave elections that swing almost as a pendulum from side to side. The Church, with all of its tradition, its constancy, and its institutional stubbornness, seems nonetheless to recalibrate itself with very different pontificates that revolve around the polar stars of popes who are inflexible, legalistic, pious, and inner-directed, and those who are more subtle, innovative, and outer-directed. Leo followed Pius IX, whose established reign ended with a hostile defensiveness toward the world, a firm policy of infallibility, and a highly centralized papal court.

But Leo sought to establish alliances with states and sovereigns, to recognize the aspirations of working men and women, and to encourage the Church to be a movement for social betterment. He said that he wished to so reform the Church that it would not return to what it had been before him. Yet he was to become the patron of a man who would succeed him and swing back in so many ways to Pius IX's attitudes and orientations. Some observers even said that Pius IX and Pius X looked alike, although the latter was more handsome and fairer. Still, the similarities are apparent, especially in their deeds and in their attitudes toward dogma and dissent.

Later Pius X's successors would in turn be more attuned to the skills of diplomacy and outreach. They would be international leaders and not just men of recognized saintly piety. Admirers of Pius XII also liked to emphasize his spirituality, but it never crested in the popular imagination the way Sarto's did so quickly. And then once again the Church seemed to be guided away from the aridness of the final years of Pius XII and moved into the short but eventful reign of John XXIII, a pope pledged to open up the windows to let in the light and fresh air. Still once more, the Church resorted to its same cycle with the election of another pastoral, pietistic pope, one given to powerful denunciations of doctrinal deviation and moral corruption: Karol Wojtyla, or John Paul II. It may be that the papacy lends itself to such oscillations and historic swings, because the terms are undefined and so long compared to secular positions that it is inevitable that the seed time and flowering will be followed by decay and atrophy. Thus, it is not the leadership but the final death rattle of an indefinite term in office which one's survivors are repudiating.

In any case, it is clear that not all the members of the Church's hierarchy were pleased with Leo's dallying with European powers, especially with his inconclusive diplomacy toward France. And at the end of his papacy, with or without his final informed consent, there was coming from the Curia an offensive ready to be unleashed against "Modernism," which Pius was to call a collection of heresies. Almost as soon as he was crowned, Pius X embraced the cause; this was to be his *Syllabus of Errors*. It would have profound repercussions not so much in the outside world but on the internal morale and comity of the Catholic Church. The pope's aggressive leadership gave rise to a series of wild, reckless attacks on distinguished churchmen — both the hierarchy and the lower clergy. It was thus another broadside aimed not so much at liberalism or the children of the Enlightenment as at the reformers in his own Church who sought to expand the fold and to reconcile the worlds of science and faith, a step which Catholic thinkers from Aquinas to Leo had welcomed.[11]

And there was a second affinity that marks Pius X and some people of faith, a sort of antiintellectualism that juxtaposes fallible reason and childlike faith. No church has produced more great giants of Western thought than Roman Catholicism, but there is always an anxiety that God-given reason must be viewed suspiciously. Since the major modern celebrators of that reason were men and women who fell in with the Enlightenment, the Reformation, and anticlerical liberalism, one could see how from the Vatican perspective such a method of knowledge was a twisting road fraught with dangers. But Leo entered on that path with a sense of security, wishing only that he had ten more years to reconcile biblical criticism with science and the words of the Church.[12]

Pius's tilting though was not just away from that confidence; it was toward catechism, communion, and doctrinal purity. Still, no matter how well the young are educated and inculcated, no matter how real their faith and devotion are, they and their elders cannot be sealed off from the world of indifference and temptation. Not all people are as pious as Pius, or as saintly in their ways. In the end, though, the young need inculcation and not armor to combat the diseases of the mind and soul. But for this new pope, the moods of piety and repression were not contradictions in his personality or in that of his Church, but one integrated response against a world that they did not fully comprehend or at least could not abide in.

THE MODERNIST CRUSADE

Pio Nono had his liberals, Leo his Freemasons, and now Pius X would focus on the Modernists. The roots of that last intellectual movement are rather confusing. Some scholars say it started with a critique of Neoscholasticism and the inadequacy of Aquinas's teachings in dealing with contemporary scholarship on the Scriptures and Church history. There was talk of how doctrines developed and faith unfolded, and that religion was not a fixed set of dogmas but a personal sentiment which must be lived or experienced. The notion of evolution or development was also linked intellectually with the powerful biological theories of Charles Darwin, which led some to argue that human destiny unfolded in the fabric of the physical universe. In addition, the Church was divided, especially in France and Germany, between conservative elements and those that urged a more aggressive agenda of social action and also viewed the Church as a cultural rather than a religious force.[13]

Actually, Modernism began in Western Europe as an attempt to rejuvenate the embattled Church. It was a reformation led by friends. One such liberal French priest, Alfred Loisy, advocated a well-known interpretation of the Gospels that presented Christ not as savior, but as a preacher who predicted the literal end of the world. Christ never conceived that the Church would come into being to preach his words later. In England, a Jesuit, George Tyrrell, in a similar vein attacked papal infallibility and minimized the role of Church dogma while laying out a complicated theory about the relationship of revelation and secondary dogmas. In Italy the Modernist movement was embraced in a novel, *Il Santo* (written in 1905 by Senator Antonio Fogazzaro), which advocated a return of the Church to evangelical simplicity and the end of legalism and authoritarianism.[14] There was also the development of Christian democratic movements, some of which sought to be independent of the Church and clerical control. And in Germany there was a greater emphasis on intellectual freedom coupled with an attack upon Scholasticism and papal power which seemed to remind some Catholics of Luther's earlier attacks on the Church.

Leo had serious reservations about these intellectual movements, but he decided not to take any specific action. His successor, however, immediately moved to place some of the major Modernist works on the Index of Forbidden Books, insisted that Catholic Action be subordinated to Church officials, and had some Modernist clergy dismissed. On July 3, 1907, he issued his own syllabus of errors called *Lamentabili Sane* — meaning "with truly lamentable results" that the age had pursued novelties and rejected the faith. A list of sixty-five beliefs were proscribed and condemned, including higher criticism of the Bible, the denial of divine authorship of the Old and New Testaments, skepticism about the divinity of Christ and his true ministry, the downgrading of the importance of the sacraments, an abandonment of the special teaching authority of the Church, and an advocacy of readjusting basic Christian doctrines in order to accommodate notions of scientific progress. The objective of these erroneous efforts was to turn Catholicism into liberal Protestantism, the Vatican claimed, which was somewhat true.[15]

On September 8, the pope issued an encyclical on the doctrines of the Modernists titled *Pascendi Dominici Gregis*. Pius argued that Modernism was "the synthesis of all heresies" and that its philosophical roots were grounded in agnosticism or the belief that human reason could not deal with questions beyond the world of phenomena. He asserted boldly, "The number of the enemies of the cross of Christ has in these last days increased exceedingly, who are striving, by acts, entirely new and full of subtlety, to destroy the vital energies of the Church, and if they can, to overthrow Christ's kingdom itself." He lamented that this heresy and its "partisans of error" were to be found not just among the laity but among the very ranks of the priesthood. The Modernists had many manifestations, the pope argued: philosopher, believer, theologian, historian, critic, apologist, and reformer. Thus the spread of these doctrines was found among biblical scholars, church reformers, classroom teachers, and even those who nominally acknowledge the teaching authority (or the magisterium) of the Church.

Then in a rare step for a papal encyclical, the pope offered very specific prescriptions on how to do battle against this heresy, which included the study of Thomistic or Scholastic philosophy; tighter restrictions on choosing directors and professors in seminaries and candidates for the priesthood; greater episcopal vigilance over publications and stronger censorship over books and newspapers; a general ban on secular priests editing newspapers or periodicals; and a severe limitation on congresses of priests' meetings. Concluding, the pope then asked for diocesan watch committees, or what he called "Councils of Vigilance," to expose any signs of Modernism in publications and teaching and to "combat novelties of words."[16]

Several years later, on September 1, 1910, the pope continued his crusade by requiring that all clergy take an oath against the Modernist heresy and reaffirm their belief that God can be known by natural reason, that miracles and the prophesies are reliable signs of revelation, that the Church was founded by Christ himself, and that there is a certain deposit of faith that is emitted not from the subconscious but from a real ascent of the will to seek truth. The second part of the oath required submission to the statement of errors, the *Lamentabili,* and to the encyclical *Pascendi.* Although there was some opposition, especially in Germany and France, only about forty priests refused to take the oath.[17]

Papal apologists liked to celebrate how the aggressive actions of Pius X, so different from the hesitations of his predecessor, Leo XIII, ripped up this synthesis of heresies root and branch, but in fact Modernism was never that significant a force except among some visible authors and theologians, and they were few and far between — known today only as a result of the pope's condemnation. The long-lasting consequence of the denunciations was that they created a period of genuine repression in the Church, which led to witch hunts and finger pointing even among orthodox and traditional Catholic clergy and hierarchy.

For example, in 1911 the bishop of Pisa, Pietro Cardinal Maffi, wrote to the Vatican complaining that he had been accused, attacked, and publicly insulted by several priests using the Modernist crusade as a rationale. Later, in 1915, the primate of Belgium, Désiré Cardinal Mercier, who had been suspected of Modernist tendencies, wrote publicly that these insidious personal controversies led to attacks on the authority of the bishops by "impetuous spirits." Such persecutions resulted in general mistrust and a paralysis of the will, he warned.[18]

There was not only a vigorous Supreme Congregation of the Holy Office (the old Inquisition), but also a new Consistorial Congregation and later a "thought police" headed by Monsignor Umberto Benigni called "Sodalitium Pianum" (the Fellowship of St. Pius V), which was under the control of the cardinal secretary of state with the approval of the pope himself. Investigations were initiated in a variety of locales under the euphemism of "apostolic visitations." In Italy when the pope decided to make a visitation to every diocese, his activities led to anxiety in some quarters. Indeed, Benigni's group employed spies to seek out possible culprits spreading unorthodox views. In fact when Pius X's canonization case came up in 1949, serious reservations were raised about his role in allowing these abuses to haunt the Church and intimidate the hierarchy. However, Pius XII pushed for a speedy beatification and canonization of his beloved predecessor and the objections were disposed of.[19]

When Pius X's successor was chosen, apparently several cardinals took him aside and told him that the Modernist crusade and its repressive techniques must end, which they did. Indeed the new pope, Benedict XV, had himself been under suspicion for alleged doctrinal deviation! It is one thing to condemn Protestants or isolate a liberal Jesuit or a Dominican theologian; it is another to destroy the morale of the Church hierarchy. Later, another young clergyman, Angelo Roncalli, was also accused of Modernist tendencies and had to fight to protect his reputation. He was to become John XXIII and was to be accused of having opened the Church up once again to the Modernist heresy in his instigating of Vatican II.[20]

It is difficult — at times incongruous — to link the Pius of such anti-intellectual repression with the genuinely humble parish priest who exuded a sense of serene spirituality. But the pope in fact was as intensely devoted to doctrinal purity as he was to personal piety. For him they went hand-in-hand — one believed fervently in dogma and served to keep it uncontaminated. It was certainly different from the approach of the more tolerant and aristocratic Leo.

Privately, though, Pius was even more unyielding. He called the Modernists "miserable wretches," who were more deadly than Luther in their pernicious effects. "Kindness is for fools," he counseled, and then said that they should be "beaten with fists. In a duel, you don't count or measure the blows, you strike as you can. War is not made with charity: it is a struggle, a duel. If Our Lord were not terrible, He would not have given an example in this too. See how he treated the Philistines, the sowers of error, the wolves in sheep's clothing, the traders: He scourged them with whips!"[21]

THE PASTORAL POPE

Still though, Pius overall was a genuine, amiable, down-to-earth priest who talked to everyone and who, unlike Leo, had the common touch and a sense of humor. He wore a modest wristwatch, while Leo wore none and kept the conventional etiquette. Pius allowed people to eat with him, another change from the practice maintained since Urban VIII (1623–44) that the pope had to dine alone, and he insisted that Catholics sit down often in his own chair, unlike Leo, who had Catholic lay people kneel in his presence. No one was allowed to kiss Pius's slipper, and he disliked being transported in the sedia gestatoria, saying it made him dizzy. Soon he returned to his old habits: every Sunday afternoon in the courtyard of St. Damascus he explained the catechism; and he once again led a reform of Church music, placing emphasis on the Gregorian chants and polyphonic music, thus laying aside the sounds of operatic and individual performers who seemed to be turning churches into common music halls.[22]

As before, he focused on reform of the seminaries and on the training of the young. He celebrated the virtues of the priesthood, established the Pontifical Biblical Institute, and instigated a major effort to codify canon law, a monumental task completed just after his death. Pius made headway in restructuring the Curia (the first major change since Sixtus V in 1587) and helped ban begging priests (called "scagnoizzi") from Rome, seeing them as unsightly and a scandal in his very diocese. Most far-reaching was his controversial decision to allow very young children — those above the age of reason — to receive communion and his encouragement to all to receive frequently the Eucharist. Pius was in part furthering personal piety by these actions, but also by allowing children to receive the sacrament he was in fact addressing directly another French heresy: Jansenism. That movement emphasized the gloomy dogma that human beings were so sinful that they could never be sure of the state of their souls and thus should be wary of taking communion. Pius saw the Eucharist not as a guaranteed reward to the saved, but as a powerful aid on the road to salvation.[23]

These pastoral concerns had all been anticipated by his previous experiences at the parish and diocesan levels. Unlike the experience of many popes, his formative years in the clergy were not spent in universities or in the diplomatic corps, but in ministering to the lives of families. Thus, as the Modernists and even some of the clergy were downplaying the importance of the sacraments and traditional rites and rituals, Pius was expanding the range and scope of such activities and sentiments.

PIUS X'S FOREIGN POLICY

In moving outside the Church, Pius sought ways both to balance the Church's strict demands for controls over its adherents and also to relax a bit Leo's admonitions about nonparticipation in Italian politics. On June 11, 1905, Pius published a statement on Catholic Action, calling for less timidity and more social activity to support God, the Church, and people. He told the faithful to "prepare themselves prudently and seriously for political life in case they should be called to it." In his own experience in Venice he had encouraged an alliance of Catholics with moderate liberals to oust the anticlerical regime there, and he was never very preoccupied with the Papal States and temporal power. He seemed at first willing to encourage Catholics to form a unified group for social reforms in Italy. Still the pope tried to prohibit Catholic popular action groups from embracing too closely an agenda of partisanship as occurred in Germany, fearing the counterascendancy of anticlerical political movements.

Pius did support political participation in achieving some reforms, but again he feared losing control, especially among his own clergy who might become involved in those activities. And in his mind the enemy was in his own household, as he linked some of them with Modernism. The Vatican was especially troubled with the French Christian Democracy movement, which started out trying to follow Leo's call for *ralliement* — or cooperation with the secular government. Pius agreed, and he ended up condemning the work of loyal Catholic Marc Sangnier and the Sillon group, which rushed to welcome non-Catholics and which formed alliances that the Vatican found troubling.[24]

Leo's policies toward France had been carefully crafted by himself and by his secretary of state Mariano Cardinal Rampolla, an astute Sicilian, who favored a tilting away from Austria, one of the traditional protectors of the papacy. Those policies ended up costing Rampolla the papacy at the conclave. But after Pius assumed that office, anticlerical sentiment in France increased under the ministry of former priest Émile Combes, who sought to prohibit teaching by religious communities and who interfered in episcopal nominations. After the conclave, the new pope appointed as secretary of state the thirty-eight-year-old Rafael Merry del Val, the son of a Spanish marquis and an English mother, who was educated in Belgium and England and who was also familiar with Germany, Austria, and Canada.

Although able and astute, Merry del Val was roundly criticized for his interference in French affairs. When the president of France visited the rulers of Italy, Secretary of State Rampolla wrote a dissenting letter to the Catholic governments, and it ended up being printed in a French socialist journal, *L'Humanité*. Intense criticism was directed at the Vatican, and the French government then had an excuse for breaking off diplomatic relations with the Holy See, which it did on July 30, 1904. A year later, the disagreement led to a unilateral annulment of the concordat of 1806 and the transfer of the Church's possessions to lay associations called "Associations Cultuelles." Pius was to have even less success with France than did Leo, and he left the Church there under siege and vulnerable.

Still Pius's policies toward France have to be seen in the long historical context of a century and a quarter of turmoil and ideological warfare.[25] The Catholic Church went from being a pillar of the Ancién Regime as late as 1789 to a target of persecution by the French radicals to being a partner in an uneasy detente with Napoleon Bonaparte. Napoleon at first signed a concordat with the Church, insisted that the pope be at his coronation in 1804, and five years later kidnaped and imprisoned Pius VII. During the Bourbon restoration (1814–30), Catholicism was declared "the religion of the state," Sunday was restored as a day of rest, divorce was struck out of the Civil Code, religious education was approved by the state, and criticism of religion by the press was curtailed. By 1830, the Bourbon line was ended, and Louis Philippe was chosen monarch. Increasing anticlericalism was apparent as more attacks against some churches and clergymen, especially the Jesuits, took place. These activities, though, were marked by the appearance of the beginnings of liberal Catholicism in that nation.

As has been noted, the Revolution of 1848 marked increasing anti-church agitation in France and in much of Western Europe. Louis Napoleon was elected president and then conducted a plebiscite which named him emperor. He moved from being protector of the papacy to co-conspirator against the temporal powers of the pope. Leo XIII began and ended his reign trying to reach a reconciliation with the French state and his own Catholics, but his attempts were only partially successful. In addition, in 1899, an army officer who had been convicted of treason five years earlier and then deported to Devil's Island was pardoned. Alfred Dreyfus was a Jew and a Republican, while the true culprit turned out to be an aristocrat, a Catholic, and a Royalist. The controversy thus revolved around those polar ideological opposites, and by 1905 the Republicans used that injustice to push for a separation of church and state, thus finally ending Napoleon's concordat.

Despite Merry del Val's antagonistic attitude toward the French regime, Pius started off in the spirit of conciliation saying, "I have to follow the lines of conduct of my predecessors." But after the Vatican's criticisms of the French president's visit and cancellation of a meeting by the French foreign minister, Théophile Delcassé, with Merry del Val, the situation deteriorated. The private note of protest which was sent to Catholic monarchs and which was published in *L'Humanité* led to an outcry all over France. The note specified that the French should be grateful for Vatican support over the years and that it expected that the current government would soon fall.[26]

As has been seen, these indiscretions gave the government the opportunity to end the concordat, which Republicans had talked about doing but never seemed to get around to. Under pressure from the new and strong working-class Socialist party, a law was passed which confiscated church property and abolished the *budget des cultes,* or compensation for the appropriation of ecclesiastical lands during the Revolution of 1789. Consequently, Associations Cultuelles — religious associations — were founded and put in charge of church buildings, and for a limited time presbyters and seminaries. Over a four-year period, the state would phase out its contributions to the salaries of clergy, although it did guarantee existing pensions. Bishops, though, were allowed to correspond freely with Rome and to adjust diocesan and parish boundaries as they saw fit, and religious insignias were allowed. But even the ringing of church bells, which some found both offensive and annoying, was to be regulated by local mayors.

On February 11, 1906, against the advice of a majority of the French hierarchy, Pius X condemned this act, the "Law of Separation," saying that it refused to acknowledge the hierarchical nature of the Church and the need for Catholics "to follow the lead" given to them. Some saw the pope's actions as a traditional assertion of papal authority, but he was probably also motivated by a fear of allowing the French hierarchy some say in major policy questions — a concern about reestablishing the spirit of the Gallican Church. Also, as in the Modernist dispute the pope again could show that the papacy could be counted on as a bulwark against such hostile innovations. In late May, the French bishops met and sought to reach some accommodation with their government, but in August the Vatican opposed compromise, saying it violated the sacred rights of the Church. The

Church followed its pope; one prelate glumly concluded, "They wanted an infallible Pope: they have got one."[27]

Although traditional Catholics praised the pope's heroic intransigence, the Church in France was not in good shape to begin with, having experienced a notable decline in the period from 1901 to 1907. One commentator at the time, Jean D. Bonnefon, observed, "The urban masses are becoming atheists, the royal masses pagan." In Limoges, for example, the number of births without baptism rose from 8 percent to 25 percent in that period, lay funerals from 6.85 percent to 22.9 percent, civil marriages from 18.5 percent to 48.5 percent. By August 1910, the pope had condemned the independence of Marc Sangnier's Le Sillon movement, charging that its democratic ways would lead to an end of Church discipline and to a new religion of humanity. It is only with the beginnings of World War I and the strong support of the French war effort by its Catholic clergy that much of the anticlerical spirit was diminished in that nation.[28]

Elsewhere, papal diplomacy faced similar problems. In Germany there was some criticism of the pope's encyclical *Editae Saepe*, issued on May 26, 1910, which was dedicated to St. Charles Borromeo, but which was critical of the Protestant Reformation. Also, in praising the Polish people, Pius drew the wrath of the Russian czarist government, which was used to controlling its neighboring state, and the pope's legate to Ireland was attacked in London for his sympathies toward Catholic people in that land under English domination. In Spain the Church was facing both an anticlerical crusade of the government and the hostilities of the Catalan Nationalists; in neighboring Portugal the government pushed for separation of church and state, which resulted in violent religious persecution. In 1911, in that nation mobs raided convents, priests were molested, church property was confiscated, and bishops were driven from their dioceses. The prime minister concluded, "Religious sentiment is a lie and every kind of church a farce." In another unfortunate flap, the pope refused a papal audience to former U.S. President Theodore Roosevelt because he was scheduled to speak at the Methodist church in Rome — thus carrying Vatican policies to a ridiculous extreme. On another occasion, though, the pope was to declare exuberantly to James Cardinal Gibbons of Baltimore, "I love these Americans. They are the blooming youth of Catholicism."

In his dealings with Latin America, Pius criticized antireligious legislation in Ecuador, expressed concerns over the maintenance of ecclesiastical laws in Bolivia, and had his agent serve as mediator in a dispute involving Brazil, Bolivia, and Peru. On June 7, 1912, the pope spoke out to Latin American bishops on the degrading plight of Indians on their continent. In Mexico, there was persecution of priests and religious, a rupture of diplomatic relations with Spain, and anticlerical and antireligious riots with churches destroyed and priests killed.[29]

But all of these occurrences paled in comparison to the rising war clouds moving over Europe in 1914. Pius had predicted just such a conflagration years before and lamented, "In ancient times, the pope with a word might have stopped the slaughter, but now I am powerless." On August 2, 1914, he pleaded in vain for peace and compromise. On one occasion he even refused to bless German army units, but extended his personal regards to the individuals in front of him who were pledged to the faith and were co-incidentally serving in uniform. Several weeks later, weary and depressed, he died from bronchial flu. The inscription on his tomb called him "poor and humble at heart."[30]

CREATING A SAINT

There is a tendency among certain types of Italian males to be quiet, diffident, and almost passive in the way they deal with the turmoils of the world. That presentation is at variation with the general stereotype of loud, boisterous, and gesticulating men who stand in piazzas drinking wine and commenting on the attributes of women. But this more mild, contained, and placid style is apparent, and it leads those individuals at times to be unwilling victims of the aggressive world and its ministers of ambition. It seems that in his early career, Giuseppe Sarto was just such a person: a priest uninterested in advancement and committed to Catholicism in its most pastoral and pietistic expressions. He was not the resolute martyr like Pius IX, or the wily, intellectual diplomat like Leo XIII. Yet he was promoted by Leo and others and was recognized early on for his saintly demeanor.

Usually the word "saint" is used in such a slack and easy way to define individuals who seem to be committed to religion and its salutary virtues, but in Sarto's case many contemporaries felt that they were in the presence of a special person with deep reservoirs of spirituality, more than even would have been normally expected of a clergyman or a man of God. When he became pope he surprised even his secretary of state with his tough determination to protect the faith. Merry del Val writes that Pius at times seemed tolerant and diffident as a person, and then almost as if changing his cassock to papal white, he still would steel himself up and remark that he had to act like a pope and make the decision for the good of the Church.[31] It is from such determination that the canon law code was reformed, the Gregorian chant officially reblessed, the question of communion for the young finally resolved, and compromise with the French government refused. And it is from such determination and rigid sense of stewardship that the pope lent his good offices, not just to a broad condemnation of Modernism, but also to the patterns of officially sanctioned abuses that resulted.

And yet much of that is now forgotten, for the image of Pius X is clearly set with his canonization as a true saint of the Church—a very rare honor for a pontiff in modern times. For while they all serve their Church conscientiously, popes are too much in the world to be regarded often as saintly. Some have said that such a designation was encouraged by Pius XII because he desired to further the cult of the papacy to his own advantage.[32] Perhaps there is some truth in that criticism, but the movement to canonize Giuseppe Sarto began almost immediately after his death, and in Italy he still today has a very strong following.

This study examines the varied styles of leadership that the papacy has embraced in this century: bureaucratic, political, legalistic, intellectual — we all understand those variations on a theme. But the idea that leadership can be grounded in saintliness seems to belong at best to the Middle Ages with its superstitions, its relics, its cults of enthusiasm. In fact, with Pius X his ability to govern and prevail was linked in some cases with the view that he was indeed a saint — a person whose behavior was not only good, but went beyond normal human expectations.

And although it may be unacceptable to the modern skeptical mind, Pius was linked in his lifetime and certainly afterward with alleged miracles. Some were more modest expressions of piety, as when on the day of his coronation he went to see a very sick Spanish cardinal, Herreroy Espinosa, archbishop of Valencia, who after the visit seemed to walk away from the door of death and then went back home again! Later the Vatican began to get special requests for assistance from people with incurable diseases and disabilities who asked for the pope's prayerful intercession. The afflicted would come hoping to see him at audiences or to touch him — shades of Jesus in the marketplace. From cities and backwaters would come tales of cures and relief in ways not common when speaking of other popes.[33]

Modern Christians feel inspired by the altruistic teachings of Jesus of Nazareth, but some are clearly uncomfortable if not scornful of miracles. But the Jesus of the Scriptures was a miracle man; his detractors called him a magician. He cured the sick, comforted the afflicted, and most extraordinarily on one occasion in the name of the Father raised up Lazarus, who had gone on the other side of death. The miracle stories are not just inserted for narrative color; they are an integral part of the definition of Christ and Christianity.[34] Today, though, miracles are often reduced to explanations involving illusion, psychosomatic confusion, or cures that can be explained by mathematical probabilities.

But there remains in fundamentalist Protestantism and in strands of pietistic Catholicism a very strong tradition of believing in miracles, prophecies, and holy people. Before the Church formally acknowledged Fatima and Lourdes and the stigmata of Padre Pio, those occurrences held the allegiances of many practitioners of the folk religion alive in the byways of Catholicism. They belonged to the people before they were acknowledged by the hierarchy. The respectable bureaucratic Church is always concerned about a scandal, especially among its own devotees. It is hard to control the excesses of passionate devotion.

But after Pius's death, rumors and then testimony began to tell the story of the faithful who claimed cures as miraculous happenings. The Church finally recognized some of those assertions in its cumbersome process of making a saint, and Pius XII canonized Sarto on May 29, 1954. Whether one believes in miracles and direct supernatural intervention in personal lives or not, and whether one attributes such to Giuseppe Sarto or not, there is no question that we are talking about a very different dimension of leadership. It is so rare and striking that in the modern eye it links the ecclesiastical and the bureaucratic office to something over the line of regular human expectations. And by doing so it adds to the prestige of the office and the legacy on which the papacy draws. It is one thing to have a saintly pope in the year 1500, and another at the dawn of our century — in the lifetimes of our grandparents, people who remembered this man walking on earth. Thus it was that the simple parish priest became a saint in the Church of his baptism.

CHAPTER FOUR

BENEDICT XV AND
THE MAD DOGS OF WAR

As the young and the romantic celebrated the beginnings of war, the old man in the Vatican pleaded for peace. But peace would not come. The conflict started in the miscalculation of diplomats, the timetables of military strategists, the purveyors of nationalistic hatreds. In the end, in the trenches of France, on the frozen tundra of Russia, and in a million hearts that lost the dreams of a single young man on the battlefield, the lessons of war were soon learned. When the war was relegated to the annals of history, it left four major empires destroyed and set in place the beginnings of the terrible totalitarian states that led to a second and even more destructive war. If Pius X approaching death saw the vast array of consequences that would visit the earth, it is little wonder that he seemed to grieve so heavily.

When the conclave met to choose his successor, the cardinals wanted a man who would combine personal piety with strong diplomatic experience. Some seemed to accept intuitively that his pontificate would be defined by the Church's reactions to the war that was just beginning. Still others realized that the preoccupation of Pius X with internal Church matters might not serve the faithful in this period of strife. They were correct. After that conflict was done, a disillusioned John Maynard Keynes was to conclude, "Never in the lifetime of man now living has the universal element in the soul of man burned so dimly."

As has been noted before, the formal "veto" of certain Catholic states over candidates for the papacy was ended by Pius X right after his election, but the French ambassadors in London and in Madrid were still instructed by their government to use their influence in this conclave to form a united bloc of English, French, Belgium, and Spanish cardinals to get a candidate who would be sympathetic to their cause. The favorite of France was Domenico Cardinal Ferrata, a former papal nuncio to that nation, who was seen as indeed friendly to those interests.

The issue of Modernism also played a role in the conclave as the zealots supported the young and brilliant Domenico Cardinal Serafini, a Benedictine monk, assessor to the Holy Office, and former apostolic delegate to Mexico. Opponents of the continuing Modernist crusade rallied around Pietro Cardinal Maffi, the popular and patriotic archbishop of Pisa. Later, the supporters of both Maffi and Ferrata were to throw their support to a compromise candidate. Thus in one sense the division seemed to be between the followers of Leo and the adherents of Pius X. But when all was said and done, the cardinals again chose one of their own: a conservative Italian, a reliable product of the Curia, a protégé of Secretary of State Rampolla, the archbishop of Genoa, Giacomo Della Chiesa, or "James of the Church" as his name could be translated.[1]*

THE MAKING OF A DIPLOMAT

A small, quiet person, he walked with a slight limp, spoke in a high-pitched voice, and seemed an unlikely successor to the strong-willed Pio Nono, the regal Leo, and the forceful saint, Pius X. As a youth Giacomo had heeded his father's advice and gone to a public institution, graduating with a doctorate of civil law from the University of Genoa and was associated with the Catholic Action movement. Having completed those studies, he was then free to follow the religious vocation that he felt in his heart and become a seminarian in Rome. After ordination and further study, he received a doctorate in sacred theology from Capranica College and another doctorate in canon law from the Gregorian University.

Della Chiesa boarded at the Accademia dei Nobili Ecclesiastici, a special training school for the diplomatic corps of the Church which included such distinguished alumni as the legendary Ercole Consalvi, Leo XIII, Rampolla, Merry del Val, and later Pius XII. There he was called to the attention of the rising Monsignor Rampolla, who in turn had been promoted by Leo XIII to become his nuncio in the difficult arena of Spain. Rampolla was permitted to bring a personal secretary with him, and he took the well-recommended student Della Chiesa.

It was Rampolla's responsibility as papal nuncio to unite Spanish Catholics and implement Leo's encyclical *Quam Multa,* addressed to the nation's hierarchy. Rampolla was to prove rather adept diplomatically and rather charming personally. When a cholera epidemic swept through the nation in 1885, he and his secretary tended to the sick and dying. In the best charitable traditions of Christianity, they organized the relief effort, cleaned soiled beds, prepared food and medicine, and seemed heroic and immune

---

*The name was supposedly given by St. Ambrose of Milan to the House of Della Torre in recognition of its stand against the Arians of their day. On his mother's side, Giacomo was also related to Pope Innocent VII (1404–6).

to the disease's ravishes. On March 14, 1887, Monsignor Rampolla was made a cardinal, and two months later he was chosen by Leo XIII to succeed Cardinal Iacobini as secretary of state.

Rampolla promptly recalled Della Chiesa to Rome to become his "minutante" (personal assistant) and later made him undersecretary in the Secretariat of State, where he remained for fourteen years. His contemporaries generally found him to be an unprepossessing and courteous colleague with a lively sense of humor, an incredible capacity for work, and a marvelous memory. In 1887 one Italian observer paid him the highest compliment: Monsignor [later Cardinal] Agliardi observed he was "a new Consalvi." The quiet undersecretary lived in Rome with his parents in rooms in the Arcione, and later the Palazzo Brascha.[2]

During that period, his career would parallel the handsome and brilliant Rafael Merry del Val, who would become for a time a sort of rival. Indeed Merry del Val was everything Della Chiesa was not; he was impressive, witty, engaging, and carried himself with a domineering presence that both inspired and pleased. Della Chiesa on the other hand was diffident, slight, and so small that he was nicknamed by some "Il piccoletto" — the dwarf. He said of himself, "I am but an ugly gargoyle on the beauties of Rome."[3]

When Leo died, Rampolla was cast out of power, and it was Merry del Val who assumed ascendancy as the thirty-eight-year-old secretary of state under the new Pius X. Rampolla's protégé had lost his patron, and it seemed that he was no longer the charmed staff person advancing in the Curia. For four difficult years, he remained in the Secretariat of State, while loyally visiting his old friend who was tucked away in the ecclesiastical corners of the sacred city.

Under Rampolla's guidance, he had been promoted in 1901 to the office of deputy secretary of state and given the title Secretary of the Cypher. There he acquired a profound understanding of Vatican diplomacy, the subtle workings of the Curia, and the intricacies of Church dogma and law, and in the process took the measure of the personalities who had moved past his desk and who would later become important during his reign.

Pope Leo, a shrewd judge of character, had actually considered him for the archbishopric of Florence in 1902, but apparently Leo informed him that Rampolla objected, fearing he would lose his most valued aide. Later, when Della Chiesa's mother complained to the cardinal secretary of state that her son deserved a higher position in the Church hierarchy, Rampolla countered, "Have patience, Lady Marchioness, your son will make a few steps forward, but they will be great ones."[4]

When Pius became pope, he replaced Rampolla as was the custom, but by 1907, he decided to advance Rampolla's protégé to archbishop of Bologna, although he did not name him a cardinal as many expected. Apparently, a wary Merry del Val had stopped Pius from making Della Chiesa the papal nuncio to Spain, seeking to end Rampolla's influence and diplomatic legacy there permanently. On the other hand, the pope claimed that God had inspired him to send Della Chiesa to Bologna rather than Madrid, and so it was done. It was only in May 1914 that Della Chiesa was named to the College of Cardinals, and that honor lasted for only three months, since he was soon elected pope. Della Chiesa knew well the men with whom he was dealing. He had, for example, close contact with Pius X, and early in his reign in 1903 had observed sardonically, "The new Pontiff is a sweet delicacy. If it were possible to sin by an excess of charity and amiability, then I think the new pope would be guilty of that fault."[5]

As for Della Chiesa himself, the observations of his contemporaries were often diverse. In 1913, one person wrote, "He has a high, pale forehead, crowned by the blackest hair; his eyes are black, vivid and penetrating; he has a large mouth with thin, drawn lips, but full of expression. He reminded me of Leopardi, and, in fact, his face and figure belong undoubtedly to the same type as those of the great poet."[6]

Still with his fastidiousness, his deep ties to his widowed mother, his tendency at times to be prissy and even surly, Della Chiesa seemed to be forbidding to some, even though he lacked the pretentiousness so often apparent in Roman clergy, especially those on the rise. Above all, though, he was in demeanor and bearing a natural aristocrat. Although Della Chiesa was strongly in accord with Pius's attacks on the Modernist heresy — indeed was called the pope's right hand in the cause — he appears to have disagreed with the controversial methods of Monsignor Benigni's Sodalitium Pianum. Although it was not generally known, apparently that group was investigating him at that time as well, probably because of his seeming approval of quasi-secular Catholic journalism.

Those "integral," or pure, Catholics, as they liked to call themselves, were obsessed with any signs of doctrinal deviation from their traditional views, and even casual friends of their critics were suspect. Cardinal Rampolla, then in retirement and living at the Palazzina Disanta Maria behind St. Peter's, denounced what he called the "sad impression that they made with their excessive zealism." Later his protégé, early in his pontificate, would criticize those who would split the Church into groups because of their mistaken crusade.[7]

Della Chiesa, however, safely tended to his archdiocese from 1908 to 1912 and did not visit Rome at all. In 1913, he led a major Italian pilgrimage to Lourdes; in December of that year he received news of the death of his great patron, Rampolla. As noted, the Vatican gossip was that the pope and Cardinal Merry del Val had removed Della Chiesa from power in Rome in order to guarantee a clear break with the progressive policies of Leo and his last secretary of state. Now that challenge and that presence were gone. Because a cardinal's hat was not granted to a see which had traditionally been headed by one, the message, however, was clear about the reservations that some in the Vatican, including the pope, apparently had about its current incumbent. Even the Bolognese were dismayed, and one group finally went to see the pope and bluntly declared that if Della Chiesa were not worthy to be a cardinal, then he was not worthy to continue to be archbishop of Bologna and should either receive the honor or be transferred. Even saints, it seems, can be petty at times and not above politics in their dealings with mere mortals. Finally after Rampolla's death, the archbishop of Bologna received the honor.[8]

The major and unintended consequence, of course, was that Pius had cleared the path for the emergence of a successor who would look back with favor on the progressive policies of Leo and on his diplomacy. At the conclave, the cardinals listened intently to the opening sermon of Monsignor Aurelius Galli, who warned that the Church in the midst of war must choose a man of superior intelligence, savoir-faire, and genuine holiness, and one who was especially imbued with Christian charity. Then in secret the cardinals voted; it has been speculated that Della Chiesa received only the minimal two-thirds vote necessary to be elected. Apparently, there was even a challenge, based on the rumor that he had voted for himself — which was not permitted — an accusation which proved to be groundless. Impassively, he accepted the office and then to the surprise of his fellow cardinals chose Benedict as his new name in honor of both the great monastic saint and church reformer, and also out of respect to the last bishop of Bologna to succeed to the papacy, the cultured Prospero Lambertini (1740–58), Benedict XIV.

It was said that in greeting one particular individual at the ceremony, the new pope quipped, "And We assure you the Holy Father is not a Modernist." Within earshot of Cardinal Merry del Val, the pope was also supposed to have remarked, "The stone which the builders rejected is made the headstone in the corner." The cardinal diplomatically responded, "It is the Lord's doing, and it is marvelous in our eyes." It was a tactful rejoinder, but his days were numbered, and he was given forty-eight hours to vacate the secretary of state's apartments. Thus, Benedict XV, the Church bureaucrat and the Curial spectator, inherited the manifold duties and the lengthy title of his office: Vicar of Christ, Bishop of Rome, Successor of St. Peter, Supreme Pontiff of the Universal Church, Patriarch of the West, Primate of Italy, Archbishop and Metropolitan of the Province of Rome, and Supreme Steward of the Temporal Possessions of the Holy Roman Church.[9]

In his first actions as pope, he seemed to be a traditional figure returning back to the clerical court he knew so well. Indeed, Benedict moved easily and comfortably through the familiar Vatican corridors where he was no stranger. He restored the custom that the pope would eat alone, permitted the faithful to kiss his slipper, and was crowned, not in St. Peter's Square, but as Leo had been in the Sistine Chapel. He replaced Merry del Val as secretary of state, choosing Cardinal Ferrata, who soon died of appendicitis; he then appointed Pietro Cardinal Gasparri, the son of a sheep raiser from the Umbria region. Gasparri was also a Rampolla protégé, a talented person who seemed, however, a bit disorganized as he surrounded himself with parrots who shrieked in his office while he did the Church's business.[10]

Without having the very close ties to his extended family that Pius had, Benedict withdrew into himself more — even avoiding the members of the Apostolic College. He made no special provision for his sister to visit him, although he did travel through the Vatican Gardens with his partially paralyzed brother. He rarely held public audiences, in part because of the restrictions on foreign travel for the faithful during the war, and he was punctual and businesslike in his dealings with subordinates. Appropriately, the new pope seemed to have a fetish for watches and for avoiding lost time.

The great and consuming issue before Benedict, of course, was the immensely gruesome and costly war. Soon, Europeans were to know that what some had mistakenly predicted would be a pleasant little engagement was reaching into still another year of terrible battles and untold tragedies. Later, the pope was rightly to condemn the war as simply "useless slaughter," and the "surrender of civilized Europe."[11] In late 1914, the pope issued his first encyclical, *Ad Beatissimi Apostolorum Principis,* which was roundly criticized as a disjointed and saccharine exposition on the importance of love and charity in the midst of the horrors of mechanized warfare.

But if one reads the papal letter, it is difficult to comprehend the vehemence of the criticism. There is no question that Benedict incorporated into *Ad Beatissimi* some brief observations, especially at the end, on Modernism, the need for an independent papacy, the role of bishops, and the desirability of unity among Catholics. It is clear, however, that his lamentations over the war set the real tone of the letter and indeed for most of his pontificate. It has been speculated that Benedict had in general an instinctive repulsion toward violence, which may have been connected with his physically weak condition, and that the repeated slaughters of the war moved him even more than most observers of the human condition.

He eloquently denounced the ruin, slaughter, and bloodshed, the increase in the number of widows and orphans, the disruption of economic life, and the general misery of the poor "All are in distress," he judged. It is true that Benedict did not give a sophisticated summary of the causes of the war, for he was not a historian, but a moral critic. Still, he focused on the absence of mutual love among humanity, the disrespect for authority, the injustice in relationships between economic classes, and the inordinate striving for material goods. Later chroniclers of the conflict would cite the importance of imperialism, nationalist envy, the overconfidence of the military, and a score of other "causes," which surely supplemented Benedict's initial diagnosis.[12]

THE CAUSES OF THE GREAT WAR

Indeed several generations of historians and countless other citizens across the globe have struggled then and now with the question of what caused the First World War. It is as if they sensed that it was too gruesome and far-reaching to have come about by accident or as a consequence of the murder of the Austrian Archduke Ferdinand and his wife on June 28, 1914. Authorities on the war still disagree, but in general there are probably four underlying causes that can be identified.

The most important was the development of a web of entangling alliances in the period following the Franco-Prussian War in 1871. As a result of that war, Germany annexed Alsace-Lorraine, and Otto von Bismarck, the Reich chancellor, created a series of alliances to isolate France and prevent retaliation from that humiliating loss. A second destabilizing factor was the rapid growth of huge national armies and armaments. The success of the Prussian armies made a profound impression throughout Europe, and those developments led to an increase in standing military forces. A third factor that led to the outbreak of war was the rapid rise of imperialism as a way of thinking and as a way of life. The great powers coveted colonies for their cheap raw materials and markets for manufactured goods over which they could have a monopoly. Added to these dynamics was the spread of nationalism among various groups, especially in the Balkans.

In December 1912, a secret memo of the German general staff predicted that in the coming war with France, it "would be necessary to violate the neutrality of Belgium." By early 1914, the Russians were meeting secretly to plan for action in the straits near Constantinople and laid out a military offensive in the West. In general, the European chiefs of staff expected a short war, one that would favor the first nation to strike. Their model was the German wars of unification; a more appropriate lesson would have been the long bloody civil war of attrition in the United States. Grant and Sherman would have been better reference points for the military strategists than the European generals Karl von Clausewitz or Helmuth von Moltke.

When Archduke Francis Ferdinand, the heir to the Austro-Hungarian or Hapsburg throne, went to the capital of Bosnia, he was aware of the threat of assassination in that region. At the alleged instigation of the head of the intelligence division of the Serbian chief of staff, three Bosnian men volunteered to kill the archduke. To the Hapsburgs, the assassinations of the archduke and his wife lent credence to a reckoning with Serbia and, with the support of Germany, they prepared for a localized war. The Austro-Hungarian regime issued a series of ultimata, nearly all of which the Serbians surprisingly agreed to. But the Austrians wanted war and severed diplomatic relations with Serbia as a prelude to military engagement. Concerned about these happenings and preoccupied with the fate of

Constantinople and the Bosphorus Straits, Russia supported the Serbians. As tensions increased, the British foreign minister, Sir Edward Grey, proposed a peace conference and a mediation of the dispute. To avoid any such mediation, the Austrians declared war on Serbia on July 28 and bombarded Belgrade the next day. Meanwhile, the Russian military had also been preparing for war, and on July 29 it mobilized against the Austrians. Soon France followed Russia and the war began.

Germany's success in the war depended on rapid action, while Russia, because of its vast areas and poor transportation, needed more time for mobilization. Now the system of entangling alliances fueled the fires of war. Great Britain insisted that the neutrality of Belgium and Luxembourg must be respected, but the Germans needed to defeat France quickly, and the corridor through those small countries was the fastest way to accomplish that objective. This "brutal" invasion of Belgium was used by some British leaders who wanted a war to defend their empire's interests. British public opinion was treated to detailed statements on "the rape of Belgium" by the Huns. In fact, British foreign policy had been historically committed to protecting the narrow seas across from the channel and to stopping any one nation from gaining hegemony on the continent. The British had gone to war in the past, partially for those reasons, against Louis XIV and Napoleon I, and would go to war again. The Germans protested that "necessity knows no law" and expressed shock that Great Britain would go to war over "a scrap of paper" — its treaty obligations with Belgium. But by August, even Japan and Turkey were in the conflict, and it had indeed become a worldwide conflagration. Foreign Minister Grey correctly summarized what was happening when he grimly prophesied, "The lamps are going out all over Europe. We shall not see them lit again in our lifetimes."

Europe had known war before, but never with the mechanized barbarity that this total war brought. The casualties were so high that their count even today numbs the mind. The official statements indicated that Russian casualties reached 1.7 million men — the true total, though, is probably double that; Germany lost 1.8 million, surely another underestimation; France, 1.3 million; the United Kingdom, 744,702 and the British Empire, 202,000; the Austro-Hungarian Empire, 1.2 million; Italy, 460,000; Turkey, 325,000 plus many more unaccounted for; and for the late-arriving United States, the count was 115,660 casualties. Probably not since the Black Plague in the Middle Ages, which killed one out of every three people, had death visited so many households in Europe.

Even more stark were the casualties in the major battles of the war. A few will suffice to give a frightening sense of the carnage. On the eastern front in September 1914, the Austrian chief of staff Conrad von Hotzendorf lost 350,000 of the 900,000 men in his army near the Galicia region. At Tannenberg, the German generals Paul von Hindenburg and Erich Ludendorff in August 1914 defeated Aleksandr Samsonov's Russian armies, took 120,000 prisoners, and decimated that fighting force. In September, they defeated the Russian First Army, inflicting 125,000 casualties in the battle of Masurian Lakes alone.

In the west, the first battle of Ypres resulted in the loss of 58,000 British officers and enlisted men — the virtual destruction of its regular volunteer army — and led to conscription to fill the new ranks. On the German side, the battle would be called by some "the slaughter of the children," a lament over the demise of so many young men of promise. In May 1915, at the battle of Ambers Ridge, the French suffered 100,000 casualties and the British lost 27,000, with negligible military results. In ten days in September, the French lost another 145,000 men, achieving no military objectives at all. By March 1916, the Germans suffered the loss of 81,000 and the French 89,000 at the battle of Verdun. After ten months, the total on both sides reached an incredible 700,000 killed or wounded. After four months at the battle of the Somme even more carnage resulted — 415,000 British Empire casualties, 195,000 French casualties, and German losses at least equal to the total of the allied nations they opposed.

In the Balkans, the Serbian army, with thousands of old men, women, and children following, retreated through the mountain snows. Only one quarter of the 400,000 people survived the march. After eighteen months of war, Serbia had lost over one-sixth of its total population. In June 1916, the Russian general Aleksey Brusilov attacked the Austrians in Galicia, taking 400,000 prisoners. Later in his last desperate offenses, Ludendorff's plans for victory cost the Germans over 350,000 men. And on it continued — staggering casualties for literally yards of disputed territory, incalculable civilian losses, new weapons of frightening efficiency, and the early introduction of gas warfare. Following on the heels of the terrible war was a frightening influenza epidemic that in 1918 killed more people than the armed conflict itself. It has been estimated that the influenza took more lives than any epidemic since the Black Plague, which decimated Europe in the fourteenth century.[13]

Thus, during nearly all of his papacy it was in this frightening context that Benedict would live and react. Initially, the British and the French press especially criticized his first encyclical. One author, Robert Dell, characterized it thus: "It is really difficult to believe that this was actually written in the year 1914; it sounds like the utterance of an elderly gentlewoman of about the year 1830." There also was the assumption that because the pope did not condemn the Central Powers by name, he was in effect showing his sympathy for Germany and the Austro-Hungarian Empire. The pope simply responded, "The Holy See has not been, nor wishes to be, *neutral* in the European War. It has, in turn, the right and duty to be *impartial*." Privately, he observed, "My appeals not only have gone unheeded, but have been scandalously misinterpreted."[14]

He regarded the attacks on him so early in his pontificate as a concerted campaign to prevent him from speaking out, and Benedict insisted, "They want to silence me, but they shall not succeed in sealing my lips; nobody shall prevent me from calling to my own children, peace, peace, peace."[15] In fact, there is some substantiation for Benedict's speculation. The Italian government, especially Foreign Minister Sidney Sonnino, had insisted that the Treaty of London, which was signed on April 26, 1915, contain a clause, number 15, that would require that members of the Entente bar the pope from participating in the crafting of a final peace treaty. That agreement became public only at the end of 1917, when the renegade Bolshevik government in Russia published it. Resorting to its anticlerical tradition, the Italian government had forced the article on the reluctant British and French governments who were anxious to have another ally at any cost.[16]

THE WAGES OF NEUTRALITY

During the war, Benedict would be accused of both remaining silent and of favoring one side or the other — usually of tilting toward the Central Powers, who were supposed to be closer in attitude to the historic authoritarianism of the papacy. In an interview with *La Liberté,* on June 22, 1915, the reporter Louis Latapié gave the distorted impression that Benedict was indeed an authoritarian prince with an aristocratic demeanor who seemed somewhat flippant about the German invasion of Belgium. Benedict was also supposed to have criticized the Italian government for its censorship of mail that was going to the Vatican, which in turn brought forth the predictable anticlerical Italian barrage and hindered the pope's ability to deal with the Roman Question.[17]

His secretary of state, Cardinal Gasparri, had to return from vacation quickly and conducted a press conference to control the damage, but the critics of the Vatican's diplomacy continued their work. Actually, Gasparri, in the name of the pope, had condemned the violation of Belgium neutrality on July 6, 1915, a public criticism that other neutral nations including the United States had not levied. When questioned about whether he was taking sides, he remarked quite correctly that even the German chancellor admitted the invasion was contrary to international law.[18]

In May 1915, three weeks after the torpedoing of the *Lusitania,* Benedict deplored "methods of attack both by land and sea, contrary to the laws of humanity and international law," but he refused to condemn specifically German submarine warfare.[19] Benedict insisted in that year that the pontiff "must embrace all the combatants in one sentiment of charity," and yet he censured without modification "every injustice by whatever side it may have been committed."[20] By May, Italy had joined the Entente against the pope's entreaties, and German and Austrian nationals were told to leave that nation.[21] For the Vatican and its basically Italian Curia, the war took on a new urgency and reality.

On January 10 of the same year the pope had asked for a day of peace, and he even composed his own prayer to be said until the war was over. In Italy some people denounced the peace prayer, and a socialist journalist by the name of Benito Mussolini criticized the invocation when it was circulated among the fighting men.[22] In France, the police actually seized newspapers that published the prayer and then released them the next day. Events were not going well for the combatants on either side, and the war leaders were not able either to bring victory or to stop the fighting. Benedict's appeals thus were a problem for them, for his insistence on peace again and again was seen as a hindrance to waging total war and promoting high morale for the cause. Indeed he even refused to let chaplains appear in military uniform in the Vatican, citing the need to be impartial.

To add to the pope's difficulties in trying to stay impartial, he was presented with evidence of treason against the Italian state by one of his high-ranking Vatican officials. In August 1916, the warship *Leonardo da Vinci* was blown up off the harbor of Taranto. The papal chamberlain and keeper of the wardrobe, Monsignor Rudolf Gerlach, was heard to say that that was the price Italy paid for her treachery toward Germany. What was suspect was that Gerlach made this observation several hours *before* the news had reached Rome about the explosion!

Gerlach had previously received permission from the pope to stay in the Vatican even after the Italian government had expelled all German and Austrian nationals, and he apparently led a life of luxury, including buying an expensive Lancia automobile. The pope at first defended his chamberlain, but it was soon clear that Gerlach had indeed received money from agents of the Central Powers and had been subsidizing pro-German newspapers. Benedict had no option but to confront him with the charges and then dismiss him. The Vatican simply recorded of Gerlach, "He did not respond as he should have done," and the monsignor was led by Italian officials to the Italian-Swiss border at Lugano. Quixotically, Benedict observed, "He was always so jolly and seemed so frank and loyal." Later Gerlach was tried in absentia and sentenced to life in prison at hard labor. But by then he was gone. The whole episode reflected poorly on the pope's judgment and surely did not help in his desire to settle the vexatious Roman Question.[23]

One of the most sensitive issues during the war was the relationship between the Holy See and Italy as the latter moved toward entering the fighting in August 1914. At first, Italy had stayed neutral in the conflict, since Germany and Austria entered the war without consulting Italy, as was required by the pact of the Triple Alliance, which all three states had signed. But some of the Italian leaders feared that their nation might be punished if its previous allies were victorious and Italy had deserted them, while others expressed concern that Italy might miss out on the fruits of victory if it ignored the entreaties of the Western allies. Businessmen in the banking community generally favored neutrality, as did the Socialists and some of the clerically oriented Italian Catholics. But the strong Nationalist element saw the war as the final chapter in the Risorgimento and pushed for an adjustment of Italy's northeast boundaries with Austria.

In fact Benedict had privately encouraged Emperor Charles of Austria to discuss the question of Trieste with Italy. At first Charles agreed, but after the Austrian and German victories in the Julian Alps, he refused to make any concessions. Still others, including the Freemasons, saw the Western nations as advocates of democracy and liberty, and the Central Powers as oppressors and autocrats. To them, the war was another chapter in trying to establish a society "without altars and without thrones."[24]

The Law of Guarantees mandated Vatican independence, but it never really dealt with the complexities of Italy going to war and the Vatican remaining neutral. What was the status of diplomats accredited to the Vatican by the Central Powers after Italy changed sides? Italy decided that while it would guarantee the diplomatic immunity of such ministers, the Vatican had to censor their correspondence. When the pope refused, the diplomats voluntarily retired to Lugano, making the question moot. Later, the Lateran Treaty of 1929 allowed such representatives to stay on Italian soil, even if Italy had severed relations with their nations during war.

There were discussions that the pope should remove himself from Italy during the conflict, and the Spanish government offered several times the Escorial as a papal residence, but Benedict XV, remembering the tribulations of some of his predecessors in exile, refused. As might be expected, there were some real tensions during the war years between the Vatican and Italy, such as when the Italian government seized the residence of the Austrian ambassador to the Vatican in late August 1916, after an air raid on the Palazzo Venezia. But generally the two sides were remarkably circumspect and correct.

And while the pope remained impartial as he so often said, Benedict and most of the Curia were still men of Italy in their sympathies. When there was some newspaper speculation early on that the Vatican expected to recover its Temporal States if Germany won the war, the Holy See was clear and to the point. Cardinal Gasparri indicated that the Holy Father regretted Italy's intervention in the war and had hoped for some Austrian concessions on the disputed border territories. However, with regard to the Roman Question, the pope did not desire to seek its solution through foreign intervention and arms. He expected that that controversy would be dealt with fairly by Italians as a sentiment of justice advanced. It was a fine and somewhat patriotic response.

During the war and after it, the pope's record was continually denigrated by the accusatory question: Why did Benedict remain silent? It would be asked later in a more inflammatory way of Pius XII's performance during World War II. In Britain a pamphlet was published entitled *The Silence of*

Benedict XV, containing a sweeping indictment of organized Christianity for its impotence and timidity, and especially focused on what it called the most organized and universal organization, the Roman Catholic Church. The pamphlet claimed that the pope "wields the greatest power in the world, for how do the greatest empires compare with the Roman domination over the hearts and minds of 240 millions of the human race?" The author concluded that Benedict could be "a trumpet call of hope and inspiration to the hearts of millions," but instead, he had exhibited a sphinx-like quiet because of fear or reasons of Vatican policy, thus exhibiting both silence and moral cowardice.[25]

The indictment focused on several general charges: (1) the pope had not spoken out to stop the war; (2) during the war he and his Church had done nothing; (3) he had not protested against the violation of the moral law; (4) he had taken up an attitude of neutrality which was cowardly and indefensible; and (5) by his silence, he had compromised not only his own Church, but Christianity in general. These charges were not unique to this one pamphlet. In fact, they were the general stuff that was repeated again and again in some of the anticlerical and even the mainstream presses. From a historical perspective it is remarkable to realize the number of adherents who held those views and to reread the intense censure that was directed at Benedict. Obviously, the pope should not have been immune from legitimate criticism, but the grounds of that criticism were generally baseless, which was obvious even at that time. Looking back, it seems as if some of the frustrations and anger over the bloodletting settled on the fragile pope — as if even non-Catholics seemed to feel betrayed by his inability to bring an end to the war. Ironically, some of the anticlerical elements and their allies that worked so energetically to cripple and destroy the papacy complained that the Holy Father lacked the moral power and authority to end the carnage. As Pius X observed early in the war, the days when the pope could force a truce or a settlement were long since over.

Later, when even the French hierarchy raised the issue of the pope's alleged pro-German sympathies, the cardinal secretary of state again responded. Gasparri laid out Benedict's views: Belgian independence, maintenance of the Austro-Hungarian empire; establishment of Poland within limits; guarantee of the traditional integrity of France and its role as a first-class power; and a settlement of the Balkan question which would exclude Russia from Constantinople and the Straits — a provision meant to protect Catholic interests in the Middle East. Those policy objectives were remarkably close to Britain's public statements.[26]

At that point in time, however, the pope did not put forth a peace proposal publicly, but was waiting for President Woodrow Wilson to take the lead. The Vatican instructed Cardinal Gibbons to present to the president and to Secretary of State Robert Lansing the Vatican's views, but the American government did not feel that it could pursue an offer of mediation since the belligerents had not really requested such a step. Thus, Benedict in this period concentrated on quiet but effective humanitarian efforts.

The pope in fact became a remarkable model of appropriate behavior in his salutary efforts at humanitarianism, which exceeded even those of the Red Cross and neutral states such as Spain and, initially, the United States. Benedict had learned the lessons of diplomacy well in the school of Leo and Rampolla, and he was not lacking in subtlety, in tact, or in understanding of the true nature of the international conflict. Indeed, out of his pontificate came the great Church diplomats who would become his successors — Pius XI, Pius XII, indirectly John XXIII, and Paul VI. They were men who were either schooled by him or by his associates and who helped shape the twentieth-century world and the Church in which they lived.[27]

In December 1916, the kaiser and the leaders of the other Central Powers, which included Germany, Austria, Belgium, and Turkey, suggested to the Entente, which then included Great Britain, France, Russia and Italy, that peace negotiations should begin. The Vatican did not comment on the proposal despite the pope's often repeated desire for an end to hostilities. Only later did it come to light that British leaders indicated to the pope that any intervention on his part would be poorly received by both their nation and France, and so Benedict did not abandon his posture of impartiality. In Britain, David Lloyd George summarily dismissed the Central Powers' proposal and committed himself to total victory; across the Channel, the French leader Aristide Briand simply called the proposal a "trap."[28] And so the war continued.

During all of this, the pope did not remain idle. Benedict decided to reach into the ranks of the Curia and appoint the young Eugenio Pacelli as his nuncio to Bavaria, so that he could have a listening post there and in the kaiser's court. Pacelli was quickly consecrated archbishop, then sent to Bavaria, and on May 26, 1917, he presented his credentials to King Ludwig III. Later he visited the chancellor of the German Reich, Theobald von Bethmann-Hollweg, and discussed four points as a basis for a possible settlement: a general limitations on armaments; establishment of international courts to handle disputes; restoration of the independence of Belgium; and the settlement of territorial disputes such as the Alsace-Lorraine by the agreement of those concerned.

The chancellor maintained that Germany was willing to restore Belgium if that nation did not fall under British and French domination, and indicated that he was willing to reconsider a readjustment of Germany's western frontier. On July 19, the Reichstag overwhelmingly passed a resolution embracing moderate peace terms introduced by Deputy Matthias Erzberger of the Catholic Centre Party. The German Socialists were also moving toward supporting a Swedish proposal for an international socialist conference in Stockholm aimed at achieving a peace "without annexation and without indemnities." Some Catholics proposed that the pope issue a peace proposal to upstage the Socialist plans before the Stockholm meeting. In the meantime, Pacelli had also met with Kaiser Wilhelm II, who, among other matters, insisted that the pope should have used his papal infallibility to denounce the Entente![29]

Unfortunately for the peace efforts, the kaiser in August 1916 appointed Paul von Hindenburg as field marshal and Erich Ludendorff as quartermaster, which consequently made the military increasingly autonomous from the civilian government. When Chancellor Bethmann-Hollweg pushed for a conciliatory peace plan, they insisted that he be removed, and he was replaced with George Michaelis on July 14. Michaelis at first seemed to support the Vatican's overtures, but quietly and effectively, with the support of the new military leadership, he strangled them in the cradle.

Not knowing Michaelis's true intention, Benedict was encouraged by the initial German response, and he contacted the British minister to the Holy See, Count John De Salis, asking him to present his peace proposal to His Majesty's government, France, Italy, and the United States. The papal note of August 1, 1917, began by reiterating his general policy of absolute impartiality, respect for people regardless of their backgrounds, and a firm commitment to end the war. Benedict then laid before the powers a very specific peace proposal revolving around the following principles: (1) the substitution of "the moral force of right" for the law of material force; (2) a simultaneous and reciprocal decrease of armaments; (3) international arbitration as a substitute for armed force; (4) true liberty and common rights over the sea; (5) reciprocal renunciation of war indemnities; (6) evacuation and restoration of all occupied territories; and (7) an examination "in a conciliatory spirit" of rival territorial claims.

The British reply formulated by its minister of foreign affairs, Anthony James Balfour, refused to accept or reject the note, but indicated that Germany had never pledged that it would restore Belgian independence. Meanwhile, there was some argument between Britain and France as to how to respond jointly to the pope's overture. Their dilemma was solved when on August 27, 1917, Secretary of State Robert Lansing, writing for President Woodrow Wilson, chastised the pope, concluding that in their judgment the war was a crusade to free people by stopping the vast military establishment that sought to dominate the world. Wilson thus refused to endorse the papal note.

To add to the pope's problems, the kaiser, under prodding from his new chancellor and his military, began to insist on the importance of having some presence on the coast of Flanders after all. The chancellor wrote to the pope that his government would support every effort to bring about peace if it were consistent with the interests of the German people; Ludendorff later complained that in his judgment the pope's plan was too favorable to the Entente. As for the Entente, France insisted that it really did not wish to pursue such peace efforts. Radical French Socialist deputy and later Premier George Clemenceau termed it a "German Peace Plan." Italy chose not to respond, although the Socialists favored the pope's plan, while the Nationalists and the Liberals generally did not. Emperor Charles of Austria-Hungary, however, supported the proposal, as did Ferdinand of Bulgaria, and the Sultan of Turkey, Mohammed V, expressed his approval of "the lofty thoughts of His Holiness."[30]

As the deliberations continued, Chancellor Michaelis refused to provide a conclusive answer on the critical question of Belgium, thus giving the Entente both a reason and an excuse not to pursue the pope's note seriously. A bitterly disappointed Benedict watched as his plan unraveled, and as he was once again subject to suspicious attacks from both sides. Later, on January 8, 1918, Woodrow Wilson presented to Congress his Fourteen Points, which contained propositions similar to parts of Benedict's proposals. But his address was meant to be a clarion call for victory and a blueprint for the expected peace, not an armistice and an early end to the bloodshed that the pope had insisted on.

Unlike his recent predecessors, Benedict, a seasoned diplomat, chose to abandon the defensive postures of the past and to get the Vatican directly involved in the most difficult arena of international politics — the attempt to end the war and guarantee peace. There have been different explanations offered for his failure. It was said that Michaelis was influenced by his ties to the anti-Catholic German Evangelical Alliance, which opposed in general working with the papacy. The secret Treaty of London, which prohibited the pope's participation, clearly presented another obstacle for the Vatican's attempt at peacemaking. When it became public, the British government tried to explain away the provisions by citing the Italian government's insistence on having such a veto. In Rome, Baron Sonnino, attempting to cover up his role in the prohibition, actually charged that the Bolsheviks had forged the text.[31]

These factors severely limited Benedict's ability to command a sympathetic audience, but they did not sidetrack an ongoing process. The war continued because neither side could imagine that it would not win. When czarist Russia collapsed in February/March 1917, it seemed that a war waged nearly totally on the western front would spell victory for Germany and its allies. When the United States entered on behalf of the Entente on April 16, 1917, that influx of supplies and fresh troops would eventually lend credence to the view that victory would belong to the other alliance.

Thus it appears that both sides fought on and on for their own honor, self-interest, patriotism, and folly. And following that intransigence, the upheavals in Russia and the United States' new military presence in Western Europe changed previous calculations of the war. People knew suffering at home but not the true condition of their armies out of sight. When Germany surrendered, a substantial portion of both the armed forces and the populace felt betrayed by its civilian leadership, charging that it had stabbed the military in the back. They thought all was going well, on the war fronts at least, despite their personal calamities.

Sadly, the pope addressed his cardinals on Christmas Eve, 1917, and lamented, "We do not deny that when we saw the effects of once flourishing nations given over to the paroxysm of mutual destruction, and feared the hourly near-approach of the suicide of civilized Europe...We sadly asked: When and how will this savage tragedy ever end?"[32]

While it is always dangerous to play the speculative game of "what if" history, one can still wonder what would have occurred if the pope's peace plan had been accepted. We do know that the war brought not only incredible destruction, but it ended four stabilizing empires: Austria-Hungary, czarist Russia, the Ottoman Empire, and the Second German Reich. In its place came fragmented nation-states, Communism, and eventually Nazism and Fascism. If the belligerents had reached an armistice when Benedict proposed it, the United States would not have deployed troops in Europe and would not have emerged as a world power that soon, for the forces of isolationism were strong and traditional in that nation.

France would not have been given the whole of the Alsace-Lorraine region and may not have antagonized so strongly the German people such that a Hitler could rise to power. An independent Belgium would have been restored, and Italy would have claimed only those modest gains and territories where populations truly desired Italian rule. Poland would have been smaller and perhaps less desirable as a target to both Russia and Germany. And perhaps the moderate provisional government in Russia would have staved off the Bolshevik coup d'état. Wilson in fact had warned Benedict that the pope's initial proposal would lead Russia to intrigue and counterrevolution. He was wrong; the crushing burdens of war led to Communism and to its later tragedies.

The Austro-Hungarian Empire might have been realigned eventually and maintained a much-needed mild authoritarianism in a region that seems sadly to need such a form of government to avert age-old nationalistic hatreds and genocide. And perhaps the peace plan would have allowed the Ottomans to maintain some organized control over most of its areas, with the exception of Armenia.[33]

This is all speculation, of course, but it is a speculation informed by the judgment that the world the war conceived and helped to deliver could not be any worse than what resulted. Opponents of the German Reich at the time argued that a negotiated settlement would allow the autocratic Wilhemite regime to continue, that it would not have learned any lesson from its aggressions. So it was taught that lesson, and the consequences were a worse regime with an even more disastrous war and a long, protracted nonpeace lasting until our time. One may not learn from history, but its muse is surely a terrible and harsh witness to human follies.

THE HUMANITARIAN AGENDA

Thus in the end, the pope could not bring peace. Instead Benedict had turned to important and good works during the war. Benedict had facilitated the exchange of prisoners, helped more than fifty thousand of the sick and wounded to get to Switzerland, repatriated those captured soldiers with tuberculosis, and proposed Sunday as a day of rest for prisoners. He intervened to see that the dead at the Dardanelles were cared for, photographed, and identified. His private donations were truly remarkable, as he gave away a considerable amount of the liquid assets of the Vatican and steered contributions in the direction of genuine need.[34]

The pope was instrumental in getting over $250,000 to Belgium to assist in the relief efforts, and he sent 40,000 lire to the archbishop of Paris, 10,000 lire to Luxemburg, 10,000 lire to Eastern Prussia, 25,000 lire to German captives in Russia, 10,000 lire to Poland, and then 145,000 lire to the same cause under various guises; 10,000 lire to the Lithuanians; 10,000 to the Ruthenians; the same sum to the Serbs; and 10,000 crowns to the Montenegrins. Benedict also authorized vast amounts of clothing, food, and books to concentration camp prisoners, and he earmarked another 140,000 lire for the war orphans of Italy. He gave other smaller sums to Italian captives at Sennelager, who had sent him a postcard appeal, and money to refuges and orphans affected by attacks on Italy. On occasions, the pope directly solicited for more donations for specific causes, and even clemency for particular individuals as well.

Then reaching back into the vocabulary of the Middle Ages, he tried to resurrect the *Treuga Dei,* or the prohibition of hostilities on certain days. He pushed for a Christmas truce in 1914, but France's general staff refused, saying the Germans could not be trusted to observe it. Another complexity in that disintegrating world was that Russia and Serbia, under the Julian calendar, did not observe the same day for Christmas as did the Western powers. There was still some criticism that the pope should have issued a statement blaming the war on one side or the other. Yet, as noted, he was the only head of state who had protested the violation of Belgium neutrality by Germany. Even Woodrow Wilson at that time stayed silent, as did Switzerland.*[35]

In addition, Benedict fostered the "Save the Children Fund" to alleviate the sufferings of the youngest and most vulnerable, and the Vatican also established an "Office of Prisoners," volunteers who took care of thousands of letters of inquiry and appeals. Eventually hundreds of thousands of such questions about prisoners were processed and researched, and repatria-

---

*The last time a pope issued specific instructions to combatants was in the Turco-Montenegrin conflict in 1862, when Pius IX forbade the Catholic tribes in Northern Albania from attacking the Montenegrin Christians.

tion was facilitated, although the office was eventually closed after critics persisted in calling it a facade for espionage.[36]

These actions were not one-time occurrences, but longstanding, systematic humanitarian efforts undertaken by one man in a tiny "city-state." These efforts and other direct gifts to beleaguered peoples, children, and cultural institutions, including the Louvain University Library, reached striking totals. Benedict's successor, Pius XI, was startled to read the summary of figures of how depleted the Vatican treasury was that he inherited; there was only £10,000 left. The Vatican actually had to borrow money to bury Benedict and undertake the conclave in 1920.[37]

At the end of the war, the pontiff had moved from being an easy target of anti-Catholic and anticlerical abuse, being characterized as a German or a French sympathizer or as a temporizer who feared making a moral choice in the war. He became instead "the pope of peace" — a voice of reason in the midst of incredible carnage. In the process of seeking that peace, he extended the Holy See's sway diplomatically as no pope, including Leo XIII, had done in recent memory.[38]

In January 1919, the pope and President Woodrow Wilson met at the Vatican. Wilson had abruptly turned down Benedict's original peace proposal and in his personal life was never an admirer of things Catholic. However, Cardinal Gibbons had previously told the president of the pope's high regard for him, which surely helped set the right tone. After his conversations, as the pontiff solemnly blessed Wilson's efforts, the president seemed genuinely touched by his kindness. Barred from being a part of the peace conference himself, Benedict seemed to put some confidence in this former professor who was the moralistic son of a Presbyterian minister. The pope asked for the president's assistance in protecting the Church's missionary efforts in German-controlled colonies, and Wilson agreed to be of assistance. Still the pope later sent Monsignor Bonaventura Cerretti to Paris to watch over Vatican interests at the peace conference and to protect the missionaries' freedom and the right of the Church to hold private property in those lands.

The pope later sent a letter of thanks to Wilson and also asked the president to speak out against any proposed trial of the kaiser and his military chieftains. Using research from a legal expert at the University of Bologna, the pope argued against war crimes trials. Wilson wrote back concurring, and Italy and then Japan and the United States dropped their support for any such efforts.

To those who criticized Benedict's alleged pro-German leanings, the pope quietly reminded them that Kaiser Wilhelm II had never been a friend of the Church; later, General Ludendorff, who had benefitted from the pope's direct intercession on the war trial issue, attacked the pontiff after his death for his alleged sympathies toward France. Gratitude is rarely a virtue for serious men of affairs. At the peace conference, Wilson presented again his Fourteen Points, which incorporated themes similar to the pope's peace note, and Benedict was on record favoring the idea of a league of nations and international arbitration, although he had serious reservations about what he saw as a harsh peace treaty and the role the new league would play in enforcing it.[39]

POSTWAR DIPLOMACY

There were, of course, other events besides the Great War during Benedict's pontificate. Although he was a protégé of Leo XIII and his secretary of state Rampolla, Benedict did not return to their rigidity on the Roman Question. Like Pius X, Benedict seemed to be unwilling to resume the bitterness of a new debate on the temporal power of the papacy. Quietly, he began to lay the groundwork for a solution with Italy which his successor finalized. In January 1919, he allowed the Sicilian priest Luigi Sturzo to organize a political party — Partito Popolare Italiano — although Benedict insisted on staying out of partisan politics. The People's Party, as it was termed, would support religious, civic, and social liberty, labor legislation, educational changes, agrarian reform, and even women's suffrage. In November of that year, the party carried over a hundred seats in the Italian Parliament. Thus, the *non expedit* was quietly abandoned.

In addition, Benedict directed that his secretary of state, Cardinal Gasparri, meet with Benito Mussolini, the one-time socialist editor and new leader of the Fascist party. The first steps toward a settlement on the Roman Question were being taken. Deep in his heart, Benedict was an Italian patriot, truly distressed by the havoc and wreckage that the war brought to his homeland, and he actually wept when Italy was defeated at the battle of Caporetto in December 1917 and three hundred thousand of its troops captured. Reports were transmitted that the retreating Italians had cried out, "Long live peace, long live the pope, long live Giolitti" (an antiwar politician). And some of the Italian military staff were supposed to have proposed that the pope should be hanged for his pacifist sentiments.[40]

For the first time a pope, though, referred respectfully in his correspondence to "the king of Italy," then Victor Emmanuel III. In the past, the Vatican had refused to acknowledge the legitimacy of the House of Savoy and also refused to see Catholic princes who had visited the king of Italy, or receive any head of state who visited the king of Italy first. The situation was an embarrassment to all involved as was obvious in the episode involving Merry del Val's response toward the president of France during Pius X's reign. Benedict simply dropped the policy citing "the changing conditions of the times and the dangerous trend of events." In fact, Cardinal Merry del Val wrote a protest criticizing the way Cardinal Gasparri was working so closely with the Italian government.[41]

Benedict also moved toward repairing ties with the French government, saying to his secretary of state, "If France gives me only her little finger, I will hold out both my arms." In that spirit, the pope decided to canonize that nation's legendary heroine, Joan of Arc, and expressions of admiration were made between the Vatican and the French hierarchy. In 1919, the French government proposed a resumption of diplomatic relations with the Holy See, a major accomplishment for the pope.[42]

In dealing with Catholic Poland, the pope recognized the newly found independence of that state, which had freed it from the crushing sway of czarist Russia and the threats of German and Austrian interference. He accepted from his secretary of state a surprise nomination for the apostolic visitor position there: Monsignor Achille Ratti, a fine scholar and well-known Vatican librarian. Benedict's odd choice proved to be remarkably astute. As papal nuncio, Ratti was generally well regarded and hardworking. He used his post also to establish some tentative contacts with Bolshevik Russia and to give the Vatican a better understanding of that new harsh regime.

However, when Ratti wrote a letter in German and Polish asking both nations to understand each other's point of view and to remember that they were Catholics first, he was bitterly denounced by both Germans and Poles and his recall was pressed. Benedict, the subject of much bitter abuse himself, initially rejected the demand. But Ratti was also involved in some very difficult territorial questions while serving on the Inter-Allied Commissions for the plebiscite areas in Upper Silesia, and his position as papal nuncio became untenable. He was eventually transferred and then consecrated cardinal archbishop of Milan; four months later he became Pius XI, Benedict's successor.[43]

Although Benedict had often stressed his impartiality during war, he clearly favored the Polish forces over the Bolshevik Russians who were moving west and threatening not only Poland but Germany and the rest of Western Europe. On August 15, 1920, Marshall Józef Pilsudski stopped the Soviets at the gates of Warsaw. Not since 1683 when the Polish King Jan III Sobieski destroyed the Turkish armies of Grand Vizier Kara Mustafa in the battle of Vienna had that nation played such a role in history. The pope clearly celebrated the victory in a most partial way. Three months before, on May 18, Pilsudski was received in triumph in Warsaw. And on May 18, 1920, in the much smaller town of Wadowice, a baby was born named Karol Józef Wojtyla, who would become the first non-Italian pope in nearly a half a millennium, John Paul II.[44]

Benedict, the trained civil and canon lawyer, was also able to celebrate the completion of the codification of the canon law and to acknowledge graciously Pius X's initiative. He also encouraged interest in the Scriptures and in the widespread dissemination of the Gospels, underscoring again his intense commitment to missionary efforts and to closer relationships with Eastern Orthodox Christianity. It was also during his pontificate that the apparitions at Fatima began. On May 13, 1917, three children in Portugal claimed to have seen the Virgin Mary in what would turn out to be one of the most persistent and powerful expressions of the folk religion tradition of modern Catholicism. As for the pope, he referred in his letter *Inter Sodalicia* to Mary as "the coredemptrix," and he also paid homage to Thérèse of Lisieux, the so-called Little Flower, another popular religious figure of the time. Then on April 24, 1920, a reasonably healthy pope called for his old rival Cardinal Merry del Val, the archpresbyter of St. Peter's, to accompany him while he visited the crypt of the tomb of Pius X. There near that spot he indicated he wished to be buried. A little over a year later, he predicted a new conclave soon. Then in January 1922, Benedict apparently caught cold, and he died of complications at the relatively young age of sixty-eight.

In his time, Benedict proved himself to be an expert diplomat, one who carefully advanced the interests of the Church and encouraged monumental humanitarian gestures during the war. At times he was criticized for not clearly denouncing the war guilt of the one side or the other. But it must be remembered that the final burden of such guilt was not as clear as it seems today. First, we tend now to link the blame of causing World War I with German responsibility for World War II, which is more obvious, seeing it thus as a historical continuum. And then too, it was only in the 1950s that the Italian historian Luigi Albertini presented a definitive analysis that clearly established the heavy weight of German and Austrian responsibility in creating the conditions that led to the World War I. Neither side was exemplary, of course, but it is now clearer to us than to Benedict and his counterparts that the military staffs and the diplomats of the Reich and the Austro-Hungarian Empire were the major architects of the First World War.[45]

In his attempt to broker a peace, Benedict maintained an impartial position and was denounced by both sides for his alleged sympathies to the other. It was said that he tilted toward France, was anti-Italy, was pro-German, that he leaned toward his native Italy, or was ready to welcome a German victory so as to restore the Papal States and stop Orthodox Russia. Many times his detractors cited the same incidents and examples to support their very divergent cases. Actually, his peace plan was scuddled by a West that wished victory, by an anti-Catholic German chancellor, and by an Italian government still feeding off anticlerical feasts. Still, his humanitarian record was simply unparalleled by anyone of his era, including the Red Cross, neutral Spain and Switzerland, and even the fine U.S. relief administrator, Herbert Hoover.

The intensity of criticism directed at Benedict was in part a legacy of the anticlericalism that plagued his predecessors. But the widespread denunciations of the pope also came from a sense of futility and despair — that somehow Benedict should have been able to stop the carnage and the killings and restore civility to the European community. The successors of the very forces that had cut the papacy down in the previous century, weakening its sway and range, now seemed at times to denounce the very successes that they had celebrated. In life it often seems that we come to regret the very world that we ourselves labor to create.

The war was a terrible conflagration, and it seems historically to over-shadow Benedict and his pontificate. Indeed, except for John Paul I, who was in office for only thirty-three days before he died, no pope in this century has vanished so quickly into obscurity. In 1919, just before his death, there was a fine statue done by the Italian sculptor Quattrini that memo-rializes the pope in his tiara and cope, standing in front of his throne and reaching out as if trying to help those in desperate need. In his left hand is a document, a list of names, and on his face are the etched marks of a tired man motivated by human sympathy.

The statue was not erected in the native Italy he so loved, or by the efforts of Catholics he labored for, or at the instigation of the Church he so protected all his adult life. Instead, it stands in Muslim Turkey, meant to remember one man's charity. On its base is the inscription:

> To the Great Pope of the World's Tragic Hour
> BENEDICT XV
> Benefactor of the People
> Without Discrimination of Nationality or Religion
> A Token of Gratitude from the Orient.[46]

CHAPTER FIVE

PIUS XI AND THE
NEW MEN OF VIOLENCE

The postwar world was to see the remarkable rise and then the debilitating decline of political democracy. At first it seemed that in the West of the early 1920s democracy was indeed advancing as much of the monarchical and aristocratic leadership of societies was discredited by the enormous carnage. Then came the right-wing totalitarian states, starting with Italy in 1922 and rising to their zenith in the 1930s, celebrating once again armed conflict. At first, the new states nearly everywhere were adopting universal male suffrage. In some nations, women also began to vote, and the initiative, referendum, and recall — instruments of direct popular control — gathered some support. Labor unions became stronger, and major social legislation in some nations established an eight-hour day for workers and guaranteed government-sponsored insurance programs. Only in Italy did democracy suffer an early setback after the war with the rise of the Fascists.

THE POSTWAR WORLD

In central and east central Europe, new nations were coming into being after the demise of the old orders and old elites. These states, however, were born because of the disruptions of the war and not as a result of long periods of orderly incubation and political ferment. Ethnic groups suddenly aspired to become new autonomous nations under Woodrow Wilson's gospel of self-determination pronounced at Versailles. Most of these regions were agricultural, and the rural aristocracy with its nearly feudal lords had been the social and political backbone of the old regimes, especially in the Austro-Hungarian Empire and in East Prussia.

These new states sought to modernize themselves quickly by adopting the constitutional and democratic reforms of the West. And they focused their energies on the redistribution of land which ended up being divided, often creating sometimes less productive farms. Political parties based on the peasantry and smaller landowners in turn became the chief source of support for democratic institutions in the western states that bordered on Russia.[1]

In Germany there was in R. R. Palmer's words, "a revolution without revolutionaries," which resulted in the abdication of the kaiser and the military high command. In their place came the Social Democrats — old leftists who were often moderate trade union officials and party managers, and not the fiery Bolshevik followers of Lenin. Essential to the stability of German politics, though, was the Catholic Center Party. Although the Socialists were numerous, the Catholic party had strong appeal that cut across economic classes. During the Weimar years, three chancellors were Catholic, half of the cabinet members were Catholic, and the officials in the Reichskanzlei were Catholic, as were most of the Prussian judiciary. Palmer has said of the new Weimar Republic, "Never has there been a revolution so mild, so reasonable, so tolerant."[2]

To add to the optimistic tone of the times, some foreign policy changes occurred as well. In 1922, Germany and Bolshevik Russia signed the Treaty of Rapallo, and peace seemed assured on the continent. By 1925, the European nations concluded a series of treaties at Locarno and pledged to each other their mutual goodwill, military guarantees, and general peace. In 1928, the United States took the initiative in the Kellogg-Briand Pact to outlaw war as an instrument of foreign policy. Peace and utopian aspirations were in the air.

As a part of the war settlement, however, Germany was forced to pay reparations — which it called a "dikat," a dictated peace. It also was required to admit war guilt and to relinquish some of its border regions. When in 1923, the reparations were not forthcoming, the French army moved into the industrial Ruhr Valley of Germany, and even Pius XI criticized the precipitous action. Still it was not the political conflicts, but the economic depression that ripped some of these democratic governments apart at their very seams in the 1930s. As the European nations and the United States tried to refinance the German debt and change its methods of payment, the very stability of the economies changed.

Even earlier the fragility of the young democracies began to become apparent. As Eric Hobsbawm has noted, "By 1914, even the last two autocracies of Europe, Russia and Turkey, had made concessions in the direction of constitutional government, and Iran had even borrowed a constitution from Belgium." But in the period of 1918 to 1920, "legislative assemblies were dissolved or became ineffective in two European states, in the 1920s in six, the 1930s in nine, while German occupation destroyed constitutional power in another five during World War II." In this period the threat to liberal political institutions came from the right rather than from the left. Outside of Latin America, those rightist regimes shared some common characteristics: all were against social revolution, all were authoritarian and hostile to liberal political institutions, all favored the military and the police, and all were nationalistic.

The Fascist right differed from the more traditional right, however, in its ability to effectively mobilize the masses, as it used political theater such as rallies, symbols, and rituals more powerfully. As Hobsbawm has concluded, "The Fascists were the revolutionaries of counterrevolution." They did not seek a return to traditional values, to the old order of king and church, and they were not afraid to embrace savage rhetoric and do savage deeds. Often but not always, the backbone of Fascism was the middle and lower middle-classes; indeed in Italy, 13 percent of the movement was students. Some Fascists, however, such as the Romanian Iron Guard, drew their support from the poor peasantry; the Hungarian Arrow Cross, on the other hand, was mainly working-class. In Germany, Adolf Hitler came to power through the complicity of the traditional right and respectable business interests, as did Mussolini in Italy. In Spain, General Francisco Franco simply incorporated his Spanish Falange into a larger union of the right. And in neighboring Portugal, a right-wing authoritarian regime under a former economics professor, António de Oliveira Salazar, was established in 1932 and lasted until 1973.

The conservatives feared generally social revolution and the power of the working class and looked for some security against the changing tides. Thus in Italy and in Germany the ultraright took control of the government not in a coup, but with the approval of the old regimes. Both movements spawned a supreme leader who soon fostered a dictatorship. It seemed in those days that liberalism, after its first bloom, had few friends or persistent advocates. In Latin America, the Fascists' influence was eventually felt as well. The ascendancy of Jorge Eliécer Gaitán in Colombia and Getúlio Vargas in Brazil underscored how right-wing states were being planted in the New World throughout the 1930s and early 1940s.[3]

In Hungary the Bolsheviks were successful for a time in establishing a Communist reign of terror under Béla Kun, who in turn was toppled after a civil war with pro-Hapsburg forces. In Germany, the populace had to accept the abrupt end of the kaiser's regime and the beginning of a weak republic — an experiment that would give way to the triumph in 1933 of another new man of violence. In neighboring Austria, the empire was split asunder, and economic troubles overcame that nation. But there two skillful Catholic politicians — Monsignor Ignaz Seipel and Dr. Engelbert Dollfuss — dominated that nation's politics. In 1934, Dollfuss was assassinated by the Austrian Nazis, but the Catholic-led coalitions held together until 1938, when Adolf Hitler seized his homeland under the banner of Anschluss.

Elsewhere, the new Czechoslovak state, which was created by the Versailles Treaty, was in sentiment pro-French, and it incorporated some of the anticlerical attitudes of that nation. President Thomas Masaryk was quoted as having said in 1918, "We have got rid of Vienna [the Hapsburg monarchy]. Now we will get rid of Rome!" He pushed through a Separation Law based on the French model and reestablished in 1915 the Czech National Church, founded in the fifteenth century by John Hus, a heretic burned by the Catholic Church. But as so often happens in politics, especially coalition politics, Masaryk and his ally, Eduard Beneš, needed new allies and eventually turned to the Catholic or Christian Socialist Party.

Responding to six years of attacks, the Vatican on March 6, 1926, had its episcopate issue a pastoral letter in Bratislava that banned the sacraments of baptism and marriage and the last burial rites to Communists, Socialists, Freemasons, and assorted liberals.

Needing Catholic support, Beneš traveled to the Vatican and initiated talks about the need for a concordat. The Vatican's response, however, was measured and very restrained. But in February 1928, some three years after the commemorative celebrations for John Hus, the agreement was signed, and the Czech ambassador now expressed his government's deep regard for the pope. Relations between the Holy See and the government remained peaceful until Hitler's attempt to take over the Sudetenland to incorporate more German-speaking peoples into the Third Reich. The Church leaders, more than many political figures of the time, vigorously opposed that annexation. But the Western democracies did not rise to the challenge.[4]

In 1920, local "soviets" seized several factories in Italy and inadvertently laid the groundwork for their antithesis — Mussolini's Fascists. The new men of violence of the right and of the left were moving toward their common historic destiny and their bloody struggles. In Russia, the Bolshevik cadres both experienced and exploited the misery of their own people while seeking to deal with the famine and also exporting revolution to the West. Sometimes it seemed as if Pope Benedict and the United States food administrator, Herbert Hoover, were more concerned about the starving masses there than their own new government. The south of Russia was hit by one of the worst famines in modern history, with hundreds of thousands starving to death. On August 5, 1921, a concerned Benedict wrote to his secretary of state that from the "Volga Basin to the Black Sea, tens of thousands of human beings destined to the cruelest death cry out for help."[5]

As has been noted, in Poland the Bolsheviks began their major thrust into the West, and it was there that the Vatican had established a new listening post headed by a former librarian and an unlikely candidate for danger and diplomacy, Monsignor Achille Ratti. His task was initially, though, to help sort out the conditions of the Polish Church that had become confused after years of German, Russian, and Austrian interference. The boundaries of apostolic sees, the relationship between religious orders and the secular clergy, and the conflicts between Polish and bordering Catholic hierarchies added to the sensitive nature of his mission. But most immediate and stark were famine, economic decay, and the threat of cholera and typhus emanating from Russia and elsewhere.[6]

Added to the Vatican's concerns was the precipitous decline in the stability of foreign Catholic missions — especially in German and French colonies. Benedict's first postwar encyclical, *Maximum Illud*, issued on November 30, 1919, dealt with the need to recruit and train a native clergy as soon as possible for those lands. The end of Muslim rule in Palestine and Syria created other problems for the Roman Catholic Church as it sought to protect both the faithful there and the holy places of Jerusalem.

Thus the Vatican recognized — in many cases even before the great powers — the brave new world that was being created. In 1920, Ratti was called back to Rome to report on conditions in Poland. The Polish government, now under the leadership of authoritarian Marshall Józef Pilsudski, had asked that Ratti be named papal nuncio to Warsaw. The pope agreed. But back on the eastern front, Pilsudski began a major offensive and seized Vilna, which in turn led to a fierce Bolshevik counterattack that advanced within striking distance of Warsaw, some twelve miles away. Only Ratti and the American ambassador remained at their posts. As a French military contingent under General Maxime Weygand assumed responsibility for Warsaw's defenses, the Russians fled, with the Polish armies following them and seizing land in the Ukraine and the White Russian regions. The Poles had saved the West.[7]

In Italy, Benedict watched as his fellow countrymen insisted on taking control of the border city of Fiume under the quixotic leadership of romantic poet Gabriele D'Annunzio. The Italian government did nothing to stop the dramatic march, and thus lost control of its own foreign policy. The march on Fiume would be imitated by another march in late October 1922 — that of Mussolini's call to the Fascists to parade through Rome after he was offered the premiership by a cowed King Victor Emmanuel III. First farce and then tragedy occur in history's cycle of repetitions.

The war resulted conservatively in an estimated 8.5 million killed, 21 million wounded, and 7.5 million prisoners and missing. And then, the aftermath of the war and the Bolshevik Revolution led to 1.5 million refugees fleeing their homeland in Russia. In the Baltic states, Poland, Germany, the Balkans, Greece, Turkey, and China, refugees streamed in carrying too often cholera, typhoid, and other communicable diseases. Overall, in the period from 1914 to 1922, it has been estimated that 4 or 5 million people became refugees. In Russia, land seizures by the Communists further disrupted the farms and worsened famine, thus causing millions more deaths. In Turkey, over 1.5 million Armenians were systematically destroyed in the first modern holocaust — a precursor of what the Nazis would bring.[8]

Witnessing these occurrences, Benedict XV pleaded for charity, relief efforts, and dedicated volunteers to save human lives, but often to no avail. The Holy See under Benedict and later, under Pius XI would refuse to consider joining the League of Nations, in part because of the view that it was enforcing the controversial Treaty of Versailles. That view apparently altered sometime after the Locarno Conference, and the Vatican began to see the League of Nations as a forum for international reconciliation. Later though, in the 1930s the Vatican viewed the League as full of Freemasons and also as having usurped the papal prerogative as mediator in international disputes.

In Milan, the headquarters of the Fascist movement and a major industrial center of Italy, the archbishop, Andrea Cardinal Ferrari, died in 1921. Faced with the importance of that see and recognizing Ratti's increasingly difficult position in Poland, Benedict transferred him back to Italy, and, consequently, helped to create his successor. In June, Ratti was made a cardinal after he arrived home, and he saw a new Italy being created, one that he would both seek to make peace with and yet end up in fierce conflict.

In that nation, appealing to the frightened middle class, Fascist leader Benito Mussolini, former schoolteacher, former Socialist newspaper editor, and genuine war hero, portrayed himself as the only viable and vigorous alternative to Communism and aggressive socialism. Many members of the Italian clergy had a deep distrust of his Black Shirts, but those collections of thugs and brigands were in some parts of the Italian state the only "law and order" present. When a bomb exploded in Milan, the new Cardinal Ratti allowed the Black Shirts to guard the cathedral during a requiem Mass.[9]

On January 22, the fragile Benedict died. His papacy had led to a marked increase in diplomatic relationships with some important nations, including Britain, Holland, Germany, the new Austria, Czechoslovakia, Hungary, Yugoslavia, and Poland. Portugal and France were also back in the fold, as were a variety of Latin American states. Benedict was a fitting heir to the Leo XIII–Rampolla style of diplomacy.

THE ECLIPSE OF A SCHOLAR

The biography of Achille Ratti, who was to take the name of Pius XI, is an inspiration to all those who love the academic life and a warning to those who would abandon it for the world of action. He was born on May 31, 1857, in a semi-industrial village called Desio, ten miles to the north of Milan near the foothills of the Alps. His father was the manager of a small silk mill and the brother of a well-known priest, who furthered Achille's vocation. The young man proved to be a rather serious student, a dedicated seminarian, and a devoted adherent to the established authoritarian traditions of the Church of the late nineteenth century. He received a doctorate in canon law at the Gregorian University and a doctorate in theology at the Sapiential University. Then at the Academy of St. Thomas he received acclaim, getting twenty-five marks out of twenty-five in examinations for the doctorate of philosophy. He consequently was presented to Leo XIII, who laid his hand for a long time on Ratti's head, thus blessing unknowingly his distant successor.[10]

Appropriately, Ratti was assigned at first to teach courses in what was called then "sacred eloquence" and in dogmatic theology at the Senior Seminary in Milan. On the basis of his scholarly interests and successes, he was named one of the doctors of the famed Ambrosian Library in 1888. That fine facility was founded by Frederico Cardinal Borromeo, the cousin and successor of St. Charles to the see of Milan. For twenty-two years Ratti excelled in the rarefied and dignified atmosphere of a great research library, a place that he charmingly called, "the silent meeting-place of the learned Milanese... and a second native land to all seekers after truth." In 1907, Ratti became the prefect of the library, and then in 1912 he was called to Rome to be vice-prefect of the enormous Vatican Library. In 1914, he succeeded to become the prefect of that treasure house.[11]

In that period he was to become a well-known figure in the international scholarly world — visiting some of the other great European libraries and research centers. Ratti, a vigorous and determined athlete, established a reputation as a fine Alpine mountain climber and was well-known for his ascent up the treacherous Monte Rosa. He was to say once that such activity was a healthy recreation that required hard work and constancy and helped to move the mind "upward to think of God Himself, Nature, Nature's Creator and lord."[12] At times, it seemed he led a Walter Mitty existence — a quiet bookish person who scaled mountains and even volunteered for an excursion to the North Pole being planned by the Duke of Abruzzi. It was as if he lived in a mundane world but dreamed of distant adventures — and those adventures would indeed find him.[13]

During his time at the Vatican Library, there was a passageway from its collections and treasures to the papal apartments, and he formed an attachment with the beleaguered Benedict. A cultivated and learned man himself, Benedict reached out for some companionship during the war, and also for historical background on the very difficult questions posed by the combatants' claims that were arising as a result of that conflict. In addition, Ratti had done research on diocesan administration which would prove to be essential in his first diplomatic post.[14]

To the surprise and consternation of some, Benedict accepted the recommendation of his secretary of state that Ratti be sent to Poland to give the bishops there some advice on how to restore their Church's operations after the end of czarist dictation. After some quick and learned study, the new apostolic visitor, as he was called, traveled to Poland. He immediately increased the number of bishoprics by ten, encouraged the revival of clerical studies, assisted in the formation of the Catholic University of Lublin, and dealt with the powerful controversies revolving around ethnic disputes and new national boundaries. He also established a reputation as a man of intense devotion, officiating at the festival of Corpus Christi in 1918, visiting the sanctuary of Our Lady of Czestochowa, and kneeling for two hours in the snow at the site of the Black Madonna of Vilno.[15]

To add to his responsibilities, Benedict had given him jurisdiction over the countries that escaped recently from czarist domination: Finland, Estonia, Latvia, Lithuania, and Georgia. Several months later, his span of responsibility included Russia itself, and he wrote to Benedict asking for permission to actually go into the Bolshevik state, concluding, "I think that more than programs are needed to save this immense country. Catholic blood is necessary and that of Catholic priests." The pope's blunt response was, "Prepare yourself." Later, while Ratti was waiting for a visa to go into the Soviet Union, the Vatican named him the papal nuncio to Poland. On July 3, 1919, Benedict gave him the titular archbishopric of Lepanto, and in the same year Ratti was named the Pontifical High Commissioner to the International Commissions on Upper Salesia, which, as was noted, was to prove to be a major source of controversy. He soon found himself involved in disputes between Polish and German officials and clerics on the future of that region, and eventually three representatives of the Polish episcopate were sent to Rome to request his removal.[16]

With the support of the Vatican, he had encouraged charitable efforts to alleviate the harsh conditions in Poland and also in Hungary, and was preoccupied with the Church's immense problems arising in Latvia, Finland, and Lithuania and with internal disputes among the Uniate Ruthenians. Ratti was ultimately successful in putting together a concordat with the Polish state, and he established a reputation for courage when he stayed in Warsaw in the summer of 1920 as the Russians advanced, and then were forced to retreat. In February 1921, Cardinal Ferrari, archbishop of Milan, died of throat cancer; Ratti was named his successor in that important see in June and then appointed a cardinal. After the installation ceremony, Benedict called three of the new cardinals together, including Ratti, and observed almost matter-of-factly, "Today I have given you the purple [vestments], but one of you will soon be white."[17] Five months later it was so.

At the conclave following Benedict's death, the College of Cardinals divided at first into two blocs or factions — those favoring Merry del Val and also Giorgio Cardinal La Fontaine of Venice, and those favoring Cardinal Gasparri and others allied with Cardinal Maffi. Neither side could get the two-thirds majority, or thirty-six votes, necessary to name the next pope. After a third day and then a fourth day of voting, Cardinal Ratti's total began to climb, until on the fourteenth ballot he received forty-two votes. Apparently Gasparri had quietly orchestrated a coalition for Ratti, whom many did not realize was a protégé of sorts of his. It was Gasparri who had encouraged Benedict to name him to the Polish post and then to the see at Milan. Later Gasparri was renamed secretary of state when Pius XI was installed.

One of Pius's first major acts was to give his blessing from the outer balcony of St. Peter's to the city of Rome and to the world. Not since Pio Nono and his self-inflicted exile had a pontiff made such a statement. Standing in the crowd in St. Peter's, an observer remarked, "Look at this multitude of every nation; how is it that the politicians who govern the nations do not realize the immense value of this international force, this universal spiritual power?" The comments were made by Benito Mussolini.[18]

Observers of the time described the new pope as a sixty-five-year-old man, portly, of medium height who carried himself well. He had a broad chest, a bullet-shaped head, and round shoulders, and projected a sense of vigor and power. The British chargé d'affaires at the Vatican, Ogilvy-Forbes, observed that he gave the impression of being a schoolmaster featured in Victorian stories. He was kindly and considerate, but still he was the headmaster who ruled over his charges. The American cardinals concluded that he was "wonderfully balanced," although he appeared at times a little cold and distant to some. He was a northern Italian, it was said — one whose emotions were restrained, controlled, and disciplined, a person who emphasized the importance of reason.

The new pope spoke slowly, precisely, and with thought, as befitting his origins as a well-known scholar. Although he appeared to some as mild-mannered and diplomatic in his bearing, he was to show himself as being made of tougher fiber than one would expect considering his background and training. His critics were to say that he was given to unaccountable rages when crossed, and that he was stubborn, or as one of his biographers observed, Ratti was a man of "holy obstinacy."[19] The day after Pius's elevation, Antonio Cardinal Vico remarked, "Do you see that.... That's a pope to make men tremble." Later Nazi leader Hermann Goering confessed on meeting the pope, "For the first time in my life I believe I was afraid."

Initially, Ratti was willing to make the difficult choices necessary to further the Church's interests and placed the prestige of the papacy behind major diplomatic settlements with the most frightening states of that era. He was, however, immediately unsuccessful in dealing with the Bolshevik regime. Then very quickly he found failure in negotiating with the Nazis, and in the long run he was mistaken in his confidence that he could continue to have amicable relationships with Mussolini and the Fascists.

THE NEW BARBARIANS

The papacy and its popes had grown up believing that they could have dealt with any modern regime just as their predecessors had for nearly two thousand years dealt with so many others. But the totalitarian states that were coming into view were different in many ways from even the harshest realities with which the earlier popes had had to deal. These new men of violence were to create a world of mass destruction and unheard of brutality. Probably it is not that they were any more barbaric than the worst of their kind in Western history; it was that they now had the tools of modern technology by which to perfect genocide and mass destruction. It was in such a world that the scholarly and diplomatic Achille Ratti moved. At first he tried all of the subtle and charmed arts that so characterized the best of Vatican and papal diplomacy. In the end he and his Church were reduced to angry expressions of betrayal and to concerted efforts to stop the totalitarian regimes from reaching into the families and the Church life of traditional Roman Catholic people. In the final furnace of experience, the violence of the new barbarian states would be stopped, not by the reasoned entreaties of Popes Pius XI and XII, but by the courage and military might of the Western allies.

It was said of the new pope that he stayed all his life true to his origins — a Lombard from the lower bourgeoisie class who combined shrewdness, tenacity, and complete freedom from sentimentality and impulsiveness. Unlike his aristocratic predecessors, Leo XIII and Benedict XV, he had little sympathy for the Catholic democratic movement, and he seemed to exhibit himself as a strong authoritarian personality. Pius XI had a highly developed critical faculty, but he lacked both the political insight of those predecessors and also their skepticism in dealing with world leaders to whom truth is useful only when falsehood is no longer an ally. When Pius XI realized he was being deceived or duped, his reaction was highly critical, emotional, and personal, as with Mussolini. He could be tough, courageous, obstinate, and irritable when contradicted.[20]

With all of his problems, Pius XI would gratefully write near the end of his life to the Hungarian faithful that he was still happy to be living in such stirring times. In periods of stress, he became calm and almost serene in his responses, and his encyclicals and speeches could be remarkably blunt, to the chagrin of some of the more measured members of the Curia, including at times his last secretary of state, Eugenio Cardinal Pacelli. Once in response to a speech by Mussolini, the pope simply observed, "When it is a question of saving souls or avoiding greater evils, We would find the courage to treat [*trattore*] with the devil in person." His views were best summarized in his observation that "the Church belongs to all nations and is superior to all nations."

In 1929, he signed concordats with both Fascist Italy and with the Socialist government of Prussia. He maintained friendly relations with the secular governments of France and explained to his critics that he would indeed engage in politics in order to save souls and proclaim the glory of God. Still he opposed the Catholic Action movement being involved in party politics, a policy which hurt the Church in the long run as it tried to deal with the Nazis and the Italian Fascists. Yet, as will be seen, within two weeks time in 1937, he ended up condemning in his encyclicals both atheistic Communism in *Divini Redemptoris* and also Nazi Germany in *Mit Brennender Sorge.*[21]

On one public occasion, Mussolini praised the pope saying, "We had the good fortune to be dealing with a truly Italian Pope" — at least that is what he proclaimed during the honeymoon period with the Vatican after the signing of the Lateran Treaty. It was said often that the pope and the Fascist dictator were somewhat alike: they were men of courage, action, and determination, men who exhibited a willingness to take chances, and who were intolerant of opposition, but they were very different in important ways that grew with their estrangement.

IL DUCE AND THE LATERAN TREATY

It is difficult in this day and age to understand the popular hold that Benito Mussolini had — not just over the Italian people, but over the minds or at least in public statements of many Western leaders. Franklin Delano Roosevelt, a shrewd and cynical judge of the strengths and weaknesses of men, publicly at least showed him deference for a time. British foreign secretary Austen Chamberlain and even Winston Churchill praised him as well. Privately, however, Churchill ventured the view that Mussolini was a cruel swine, but still he was thankful for his powerful opposition to the Bolsheviks.

The American ambassador to Italy from 1921 to 1924, Richard Washburn Child, encouraged Il Duce to write his autobiography and even provided a foreword to it. The ambassador compared Mussolini to Theodore Roosevelt, and concluded that the Fascist leader was working on a program of "applied spirituality!" Lord Curzon, who had taken the measure of many men across the world, summarized it more accurately: he called Mussolini "that absurd man." And Pope Benedict, who knew the young Mussolini, once characterized him as a blasphemer.[22]

Since his fate and that of Pius XI were so intertwined, it is best to know a bit more about the Italian dictator. Benito Mussolini was born soon after the death of Garibaldi in 1883 in the Romagna region to a blacksmith and a school mistress. His father was a bitter and almost savage man, Benito confided. He spawned in turn a son who acquired a reputation for bad-temperedness and brutality of his own. Benito quickly proved to be a bright but misanthropic fellow who taught school and then went to Switzerland, where he barely squeaked out an existence; by 1903, he was expelled by the government from that gentle country.

At first he was a Socialist journalist, but departed from that party's views when he became an advocate of war both to purify the Italian soul and to lead it to more colonial exploits. He read Marxist analyses of class conflict, learned from Vilfredo Pareto about the power and limitation of elites, and inculcated in himself Friedrich Nietzsche's gospel of the will to power and the imminent emergence of a new superman in history. Mussolini was an anticleric all his life, although he hid it well in his later years and was praised even by Pius XI on February 13, 1929, as a man sent by Providence to deliver Italy from its woes. It was a terrible misjudgment on the pope's part.

Although Mussolini was not at first a nationalist, he became more of a patriot during World War I and more concerned both with Italy's "civilizing mission" in Africa and its need to turn the Mediterranean into an Italian sea, "mare nostrum," as in the days of Imperial Rome. He reached back into that past and sought to restore the old salute and the dreams of a once powerful people united through belief, work, and discipline.

After the war, this new Fascist leader emphasized the importance of Italy obtaining more of those disputed lands on its northeast borders, and he watched enviously Gabriele D'Annunzio's romantic march on Fiume. By 1919, Mussolini called his new movement "Fascist" after the expression for the bundling of twigs in Roman iconography, a sign of strength through unity. The early Fascists were violent, anticlerical, and antimonarchical. Mussolini, however, blithely explained, "We are libertarians above all."[23]

At first, even he did not have total control over the Fascist groups. In some regions, those collections of former soldiers, thugs, and hoodlums were run by semi-independent chieftains, or "ras," who were involved in protection rackets, impromptu beatings of Socialists, and some genuine social reform. Fascist historians said that Mussolini and his colleagues saved Italy from the left-wing extremists who had encouraged strikes, work stoppages, and then violence in the Italian cities and towns. In 1921 alone, there were 1,134 strikes, with 723,862 strikers involved in the loss of 8,110,063 work days.[24] The police and local magistrates, both in urban and rural areas, often looked the other way as the Fascists restored law and order in their own manner.

In 1921, Mussolini's Fascists received only 7 percent of the total parliamentary seats. But in a short period in 1921–22, Mussolini adopted two strategies: he posed as protector of the parliamentary system from the assaults of the left, and he also threatened a coup d'état against the government if it did not meet his demands.[25] As the situation grew more tense in Italy, especially in Milan, the king in an about-face decided to reject his government's advice and refused to call out the military to restore discipline. He then turned to Mussolini and named him prime minister of Italy at the young age of thirty-nine. It was only after that decision that the famed march on Rome began as thirty thousand jubilant Fascists poured into the city. Later the king, the prime minister, and his cabinet attended a Solemn High Mass in the Basilica of St. Mary Queen of Angels to celebrate the change of power.[26] Thus, as with Adolf Hitler in 1933, these new men of violence came to power peacefully — not in a democratic election, but with the connivance of the old elites. Soon the Fascists would control the legislative branch, and Benito Mussolini would become the dictator of what was supposed to be a new and invigorated state.

It has been alleged that Pius XI was a willing dupe of the Fascist government — one whose sympathies were clearly in that right-wing direction, and that only later in his reign did he realize the error of his ways. There is an element of truth in that criticism, but it is somewhat unbalanced historically. There is no question that Achille Ratti was an Italian nationalist, proud of the great history and culture of his people and wedded to many of the attitudes of nineteenth-century clerical authoritarianism. Still though, he was a more subtle and sophisticated man than would seem to be implied by many of his critics. Because his heart belonged to Italy and because he surely leaned in its favor in the previous war does not mean that he suspended his enormously honed critical faculties in Italy's cause.

It appears that early in his papacy and in the few months that he spent in Milan before it, Ratti exuded some of the genuine pride many Italians felt as they listened to Mussolini preach the secular gospel of Italian glory and reconstruction. As will be seen, Pius XI insisted not just on a treaty to create a tiny nation-state, but also on a far-reaching concordat to protect the Church and guarantee its sway over important areas of Italian life. Any treaty requires some level of trust, and Pius seemed to have a guarded sense that Mussolini could be counted upon to honor those documents. This was a man we can work with, he concluded early on. However, the Duce reneged on the concordat, and almost immediately after the pope was critical of that backsliding.

The Roman Curia breeds a unique sort of diplomat, one raised in the traditions of European court etiquette, standard protocol, and generally codes of reciprocity.[27] Mussolini, however, was a man of the street — some said a man of the gutter — and he wished to establish a form of corporativism that totally embraced all aspects of communal life, which united society and the state, and depreciated intermediary institutions between the individual and the government. We now call that approach totalitarianism and understand its full and terrifying implications. The key to its success, though, is the ability to mold the education of the young, an area the Church has historically protected from outside influence because it too understands what is at stake. The difficulty with striking a deal with Mussolini was that his regime was not simply a government, but an aggressive, incoherent philosophy: a mixture of pagan violence, ethnic chauvinism, and blurry-eyed Nietzschisms.

The Church does better in dealing with politicians than with ideologues. And as the pope felt more betrayed, his remarks became more pointed. Anti-Vatican critics simply said at the time that it was two stubborn Italian males arguing with each other. Later though, Mussolini would be seen as the precursor, the inspirer, and finally the junior partner of Adolf Hitler.

But in the 1920s, both the pope and Mussolini decided to make common cause to reach an agreement over the Roman Question.

The Duce is recorded as having observed, "It is incredible that our Liberal Governments could have failed to see that the universality of the papacy, heir of the universality of the Roman Empire, represents the greatest glory of Italian history and tradition."[28] This was the same man who in 1908 referred to priests as "black microbes who are as fatal to mankind as tuberculosis germs." This was the same man who in 1921 attacked "the rival Vaticans of Rome and Moscow with their charlatans who market miraculous drugs to give happiness to mankind. We do not believe in schemes, in saints, in apostles; we do not, above all, believe in happiness and salvation."[29] A year later, he argued in a different mood that "the Latin and Imperial tradition of Rome is today represented by Catholicism.... The sole universal idea which exists today in Rome is that which radiates from the Vatican."[30]

Mussolini, however, appreciated that an agreement with the Vatican would add to his prestige, both at home and abroad, especially after the success of the International Eucharistic Congress held in Chicago in June 1926, which underscored the hold that Catholicism still had on elements of the democratic West.[31] The Duce was willing to extend major concessions to reach such an understanding, an understanding which he promptly violated. Only then could he proceed to build his new Italian state — in order to *credere, ubbedire, combattere,* "believe, obey, and fight."

Initially the Fascist government made some conciliatory moves. It gave to the Vatican Library the splendid Chigi collection of books, dispatches, and manuscripts — surely a gift the former head librarian appreciated. Fabio Chigi was a papal diplomat who played a major role in the conferences at Westphalia that ended the Thirty Years War, and later he became Pope Alexander VII (1655–67). On its part, the Vatican allowed a member of the House of Savoy to be married with religious pomp and ritual in a historic chapel.

The government in turn restored the cross to the Roman Coliseum and ordered that the crucifix be returned to the walls of schools, universities, tribunals, hospitals, and other institutions where it had been banned after 1870. In addition, when a vocal group of anti-Catholic American Methodists tried to set up a university, a chapel, and a school near the Vatican, the Italian government stopped them after the Holy See protested. The Methodists were told they could either sell the land back or it would be appropriated for the erection of a memorial to Dante! To further his allegiances, the Duce also banned indecent films and bad plays and curtailed houses of prostitution.[32]

In addition, the Italian government took part in the celebrations at Assisi to commemorate the seven hundredth anniversary of St. Francis's death. Ironically, Mussolini was to call the gentle friar "the most saintly of Italians and the most Italian of saints." And at that ceremony, the papal representative, Cardinal Merry del Val, characterized Mussolini as "the man who has raised Italy's reputation in the world, and is visibly protected by God." The last remark was a reference to the recent attempt by an unbalanced English spinster to assassinate the Duce. In 1925, the Fascists also moved to suppress the Freemasonry order — to the delight of churchmen. Leo XIII would have clearly approved. And the regime was rather successful in crushing the activities of the Mafia in Sicily, a group that was revived partially by the American government as a third column against the Fascists in World War II.[33]

Essential to Mussolini's early strategy was the need to destroy the Popular Party of Don Luigi Sturzo. Soon that reform expression of Catholic democracy would become a casualty in the pope's willingness to end the anticlericalism of the Italian government and to cooperate with the Duce. On June 9, 1923, under heavy Vatican pressure, Don Sturzo resigned his position as general secretary of the party and later went into exile. The pope insisted that the Church was not getting involved in partisan politics in Italy, but he clearly gave the back of his hand to the Partito Popolare.[34]

By 1926, Mussolini apparently decided to move on the Roman Question. After considerable negotiations, the two sides reached an agreement in early 1929 on the treaty, a financial note, and a concordat. Pius was reported to have hesitated before signing the document, and his secretary of state, Gasparri, is supposed to have watched several men fighting in the streets of Rome and sarcastically wondered what happened to their concordat. It was also claimed that the worried pope became almost hysterical with his reservations and decided it might be better to leave the signing of the treaty to his successor. But Gasparri insisted, "No, no, Your Holiness! Now or never." And so, on February 11, 1929, Mussolini and Gasparri signed the treaty in the Council Hall near where Charlemagne had been received by Leo III. The Vatican had insisted that the agreement had to be ratified by the king and Parliament and not just the Fascist regime in order to underscore its permanence. Privately, Gasparri predicted quite accurately that Fascism would last only twenty years.[35]

The treaty of 1929 established "lo Stato della Città del Vaticano" — a tiny city-state of 109 acres. Initially Pius XI wanted not only the old Leonine City, but a modest collection of Vatican buildings together with the Villa Doria Pamphili behind the Janiculum Hill. Mussolini countered that the government would lease the Villa to the Holy See for a nominal fee, an offer the pope rejected. Pius XI ended up accepting the Basilica and adjacent Vatican buildings as well as St. Peter's Square. Also, specific buildings were regarded as papal properties: the Basilicas of the Lateran, St. Maria Maggiore, and St. Paul's Beyond the Walls, and the buildings attached to each of them; the Palace of San Callisto in Trastevere; the former convent buildings attached to the churches of the Twelve Apostles,

Sant' Andrea della Valle, San Carlo ai Catinari, and the palace at Castel Gandolfo, together with the Villa Barberini. Several other buildings were given diplomatic immunities, and others were exempted from taxation or expropriation by the state.[36]

The final treaty consisted of a preamble and twenty-seven articles that among other provisions recognized the independence and sovereignty of the Holy See, even in international relations; affirmed Catholicism as the sole religion of Italy; created Vatican City as an independent state and defined its territory; and gave that city the right to issue coins and stamps and establish transportation and telecommunication links to the outside world. Other provisions provided for unhampered diplomatic relations with other nations; protected the person of the pope against attacks and vituperation; recognized the desire of the Holy See to stay out of temporal disputes; and prohibited air flights over the city-state. The House of Savoy was recognized as the sovereign in the kingdom of Italy.

Financially, the Holy See accepted 750 million lire in cash and one billion lire in 5 percent negotiable government bonds. The concordat had a preamble and forty-five articles which regulated the status of religion and the Church in Italy. It granted the right of the Church to free public exercise of religion; assured the sacred character of Rome; and guaranteed the right of the Vatican to communicate with Catholics across the world. The Holy See would select its own hierarchy after presenting names to the government for its review. Newly appointed bishops were to take a loyalty oath to the state, and Church authorities were to be accorded benefices, but Italian benefices had to go only to Italian citizens. The government gave up the right of *placet* and *exequatur.** Priests and religious were exempt from military service and jury duty. Among other provisions, the state respected the importance of the sacrament of matrimony and supported religious instruction in public elementary and secondary schools by Church-appointed teachers. Clergy were not allowed, however, to engage in the activities of political parties.

The sovereign pontiff was vested with "the plenitude of legislative, executive, and judicial power," and the ordinary administration of the city-state was left to a governor, nominated by and responsible to the pope alone. The pope on legislative matters was to be advised by a councillor of state, who served at the will and pleasure of the pontiff. Thus, unlike the Law of Guarantees, the treaty and the resulting concordat were documents jointly agreed to by the state and the Church and not imposed by the authority of government, such as the Law of Guarantees was after the Risorgimento.

When the pope was told that his new papal city-state was tiny, he eloquently remarked, "When the territory includes Bernini's colonnade and

---

Placet refers to the collection of controls exercised by a state over ecclesiastical authorities; *exequatur* refers to only one particular control which is claimed by a government.

Michelangelo's dome, as well as the treasures of science and art that are contained in the Vatican archives, libraries, and galleries; above all, when a territory houses and guards the tomb of the Prince of the Apostles, then surely it is fair to claim that in the whole world there exists no territory greater or more glorious." Mussolini said it more mundanely, "The Vatican is great on account of what it represents, and not on account of a square kilometer, more or less."[37]

And so on July 25, 1929, Pius XI left the Vatican and went beyond St. Peter's Square into the kingdom of Italy. The exile of Pio Nono was over. He also sent his first official message as sovereign of the Vatican State to the king of Italy, Victor Emmanuel III, graciously conveying "a great and fatherly Apostolic Benediction," on him, the royal family, Italy, and the world. Even in the remote areas of Sicily and in the northern frontier regions word was carried of the ratification of the Lateran Treaty, and some of the faithful prayed for the pope who had, in his own phrase, "given back God to Italy and Italy to God."[38]

As for Pius XI, there were some rumors of discontent in the Sacred College of Cardinals with the treaty. But finally all were persuaded to sign the congratulatory address to the pontiff. The pope said he had consulted each cardinal, and all were favorable, but then he added that even if all had been opposed he would have acted as he did. Some Curial officials, most notably Monsignor Montini (later Pope Paul VI), expressed serious reservations about the viability of the agreement. On the other side, liberal anticlerical critics in Parliament were also critical, and Mussolini had to defend his concessions as well. He argued in the debates that the Vatican was as far away from Italy as any other foreign state. As noted, he paid tribute to Pius XI saying, "We had the good fortune to be dealing with a truly Italian pope." After some cheering, he added, "I do not think that he will be displeased that the Fascist Chamber should have given him this sincere tribute of applause."[39]

Mussolini's position finally prevailed in Parliament, but he still was accused of having abandoned the Risorgimento and its anticlerical traditions by giving too much to the Vatican. He responded that the Church was not sovereign, but was subordinate to the laws of the state. Then in one of those strange references to his own unique interpretation of history, the Duce commented in passing that Christianity would probably have perished like other obscure Eastern sects if it had not become Catholic at Rome where it found a favorable environment in the "swarming ant-heap of Levantine humanity which savaged the subsoil of Rome and for which a discourse like the Sermon on the Mount opened up new horizons of revolt and emancipation." Having made that observation, he then went on to observe, "We have not resurrected the Temporal Power of the popes. We have buried it."[40]

He also argued that while the concordat recognized "the sacred character of Rome," there was no provision for a return to a rite of sanctuary for those disobeying the laws of the state. Also, while Catholic religious instruction had been extended through secondary schools under this agreement, that requirement was rejected at the university level. Then in a rather eventful aside, Mussolini insisted, "Education belongs to us: these children must, of course, be educated in our religious faith, but they need to integrate this education. We need to give the youth the sense of virility, of power, of conquest." Amid all of those observations, though, the Duce remained quite complimentary toward the pope. Pius XI, however, was later to respond, "The state is not there in order to absorb, swallow up or annihilate the individual and the family: that would be contrary to reason and nature alike." Thus, the background of a major point of contention was being set in place.[41]

Mussolini thought of himself as a philosopher, historian, novelist, and man of letters, as well as a person of vitality and power. In seeking to explain Fascism, one observer has said that it was a movement of action, not words with no real official doctrine. Actually it did have strands of thought and often bizarre ideology that its adherents referred to. Mussolini, though, while not maintaining a coherent doctrine, had a lively appreciation for ideas. He identified with the work of the neo-Hegelian Active Idealist philosopher Giovanni Gentile, who was named the first Fascist minister of education.

Among other tenets, Gentile's philosophy held that the Kingdom of God is created by the human spirit in its own thought. Truth is the process of thought that is immanent in the human spirit, not preexisting or objective. Thus organized religion is founded on myths, but contains elements of truth. Fortunately, some can kick away the prop and attain the contemplation of Actual Idealism. By 1932, the Holy Office placed his confusing works on its Index of Forbidden Books.*

Gentile sought to introduce a complicated system of religious inculcation in the primary schools, but insisted no such instruction take place even at the secondary level. He observed in the *Italian Encyclopedia*, "Fascism respects the God of ascetics, saints, and heroes, and also God as he is perceived and worshiped by the ingenuous and primitive heart of the people." As almost to echo him, Mussolini explained, "The state, as conceived and realized by Fascism, is a spiritual and ethical unit for the organization of the nation, an organization which in its origins and growth is a manifestation of the spirit. . . . transcending the individual's brief spell of life, the state stands for the immanent conscience of the nation."[42]

Later Mussolini, emulating his once pupil Hitler, would try to introduce elements of ethnic purity into a land refreshingly free of such nonsense —

---

*Gentile's term as minister lasted for about a year and a half. In 1944, he was assassinated by a group of four Communist partisans.

into a people who prized themselves on their toleration and cosmopolitanism rather than on exclusivity and bigotry. Later, in 1937, in his encyclical *Mit Brennender Sorge*, Pius XI challenged the Nazi ideology and embraced a sentiment that surely applied to both Fascists and Bolsheviks: "Whoever detaches the race or the nation, or the State, or the form of the State, or the Government from the temporal scale and rises them to be the supreme model, deifying them with idolatrous worship, falsifies the divinely instituted order of things."[43]

THE FASCIST ONSLAUGHT

It was on that issue that the Catholic Church with its universal constituency and its long history would come into quick conflict with the new paganism. In addition, with the terrible experience of the last war, it was the papacy that pleaded for peace and reconciliation at the time. The Fascists refused to accept that prescription; as Mussolini wrote, "War alone keeps up all human energies to their maximum tension and sets the seal of nobility on those peoples who have the courage to face it." Peace destroys the fundamental virtues of man; education for war is the objective of Fascist control of the schools. Opposing that train of thought, the pope spoke repeatedly of the homicidal and suicidal aspects of war, and he warned in August 1938 of the consequences of exaggerated nationalism — the true curse of that time.[44]

The Church had long recognized the critical importance of educating children. And now so did the advocates of Fascism. To some extent the battle between Mussolini and Pius XI revolved around two issues: who would control the education of the young, and how independent would Catholic social action movements continue to be. In terms of the first, the Fascists acknowledged the importance of training the young in "the religion of their fathers," as they put it — a nod to Catholicism. The Church was invited to be a collaborator in building the new Fascist "school of heroes." To further its objectives, though, the government took particular aim at destroying the Catholic Boy Scouts. Going back to 1868, the Church had fostered the Gioventù Catholica Italiani — a collection of guilds and organizations for children of all ages. In 1915, the Church, imitating Lord Baden-Powell's movement in Britain, began its own Catholic Boy Scouts. The Fascists, years later and by then in power, insisted that the youth group was affiliated with the opposition Catholic Popular Party.[45]

In its place, the Fascists created their own youth movement complete with para-military drills, marches, and hierarchy. In 1926, a bill was introduced into the Italian Parliament recognizing "the Institute of National Balilla for the assistance and physical and moral education of youth." These young warriors ended up threatening the more pacific Catholic groups and youngsters, just as their elders had unleashed intimidation and violence against the Socialists years before. The movement adopted symbols and rituals of the Church for its new political religion, and in 1925 the Holy Office felt compelled to condemn the Fascist catechism "as a blasphemous parody of the Catholic catechism." The Balilla Creed ended with the statement, "I believe in the genius of Mussolini, in our Holy Father Fascism, in the Communion of its martyrs, in the conversion of Italians, and in the resurrection of the Empire" — a crude imitation of the revered Nicene Creed. It was shades of the French Revolution and its cultic religions all over again.

The pope protested the violence unleashed against the Italian youth groups and encouraged the spread of the news of those assaults outside of Europe since the press was censored within the Italian state. Finally Pius XI was forced to compromise, and on January 22, 1927, he formally ended all branches of the scouts that were to be dissolved by government decree anyhow. He did not wish to make difficulties for the Italian government, he noted. Candidly the pope reflected, "When the fate of Our dear Catholic scouts was being decided, We had to make sacrifices in order to avoid still greater evils, but We have placed on record all the grief We felt at being compelled to do so."[46]

The second target of attack was Catholic Action — a cause dear to the heart of Pius XI, who meant it to be an apostolate of the laity focusing on social activities that recognized the principles of Catholic thinking of the period. This pope did not see it as affiliated at all with the Popular Party, about which he had real reservations. Catholic Action then was supposed to be "outside and above politics" in the language of the Vatican. For the Fascists, such a group, however, violated the corporate unity of the state-society and thus posed a threat.

When the Fascists objected to the organization as a national body, the Vatican agreed to decentralize it on a diocesan basis. When the Fascists objected to its partial autonomy, the Church put it under the strict control of the local bishops. Still, there was some overlap in membership between Catholic Action and Don Luigi Sturzo's party — as one would expect in a land that was becoming increasingly devoid of Catholic oriented public activities. Even after the dissolution of the People's Party, Fascist attacks continued on the Catholic Action movement since they could tolerate no alternatives to themselves.[47]

In 1931, two years after the concordat was ratified, the Fascists lodged a major attack on Catholic Action. The pope claimed that the real objective was to solidify the Fascists' control over the youth of the Italian nation. Quietly, Mussolini masterminded the challenges, but publicly he stayed away from the issue. The Duce was supposed to be full of rage at the pontiff, but still he decided to remain above the fray, leaving others to do his dirty work for him. Pius XI came under increasing condemnation by party functionaries, and he bluntly observed, "Fascism declared itself to be Catholic. Well, there is one way, and only one way to be Catholics, Catholics in fact and not merely a name, true Catholics and not sham Catholics . . . and that is to obey the Church and its head." But that could not be in the new totalitarian Italy.[48]

Violence against Catholic Action groups continued, and at one rally Fascists shouted, "Death to the traitor Ratti," and on another occasion they set fire to the bishop's palace in Verona. Attacks on the clergy and on the pontiff escalated, but this time Pius XI proved tough and uncompromising. Mussolini's response was to call upon Fascists to defend his revolution against any person and at any cost.[49]

The disputes continued, and on June 29, 1931, the pope issued an encyclical called *Non Abbiamo Bisogno,* "We do not need this," which was sent to the outside world through Monsignor Francis Spellman of New York, who flew to Paris with the papal letter. This was a different sort of encyclical from a very different pope. Pius XI enumerated in detail the Fascists' attacks on Catholic Action and on the Vatican. The aggression was seen as an attempt to turn the people to a pagan worship of the state and to a "species of religion which rebels against the character of the highest religious authorities." Then the letter announced, "We do not fear, for the fear of God casts out the fear of man." The statement concluded with a call to prayer and a reference to the Vicar of the Redeemer.[50]

The Fascist press in response attacked the Vatican, Don Sturzo then in exile, and the Jesuits, of course, for having a hand in the writing of the encyclical. Then quietly the rhetoric on both sides cooled down publicly as a result of some understandings. The final settlement made Catholic Action a diocesan affair under the bishops who alone chose leaders who would not be involved in political parties inimical to the regime; the professional associations of Catholic Action would engage in only spiritual and religious functions; and the youth associations would refrain from athletics and sporting events. Thus, by 1931, Catholic Action was finally neutralized and rendered impotent. But still it was an outpost away from the embrace of the totalitarian state.

During and even after his reign, the pope was also criticized for having been too supportive of the Fascist government's imperialistic conquests. He was accused of not protesting against the maltreatment of Catholic minorities under Italian rule. In 1928, he responded to one allegation of supposed inactivity toward the Austrians by having the archbishop of Vienna declare the Vatican's sympathy for the German population of South Tyrol. "Tell your Catholic flock," he said to Gustav Cardinal Piffl, "the pope has done what he could, but that he is not free."[51]

The Italian clergy too often proved to be camp followers for the government's actions abroad, and the Vatican said little. Also when Italy seized Ethiopia (Abyssinia), — the pope's sympathies clearly were with Italy to such an extent that those leanings hurt the Church's image and missionary efforts in African nations. Pius actually lent credence to the Fascist claim that its aggression was "defensive." Yet, the pope himself had misgivings about the war and feared that if Italy lost in Ethiopia then the Coptic Christians might be able to curtail the Church's efforts at proselytizing.[52]

It has not been the usual policy of the Vatican to support or condemn one side or the other during war. And it is difficult to sustain the objection that the Fascists were encouraged by such papal neutrality. They could not have cared less. Actually, the Vatican issued no statement on the hostilities, and when the Italians celebrated their victory by lighting up Rome, the Vatican remained tellingly dark. Still the French press attacked the pope for behaving as Pontius Pilate on the issue, and *L'Humanité* insisted that the Vatican was secretly lending the Italian state money for arms in the war. It was also charged by some that the Lateran Treaty was agreed upon by the government in exchange for future Vatican support of the invasion.[53]

On December 16, 1935, the pope specifically indicated that he would say nothing on the invasion. Quietly, though, he did encourage a peaceful settlement and may have asked Latin American nations to vote for a lifting of League of Nations' economic sanctions against Italy for its invasion of Ethiopia. Still it was clear that some members of the Italian hierarchy such as Ildefonso Cardinal Schuster of Milan had directly encouraged the Fascist cause. The prelate insisted that religious establishments should hand over silver and gold objects to be melted down in support of the war effort.[54]

It was not unusual for members of Catholic hierarchy to support their nation's interest, as was obvious in World War I. The difficulty was that the pope is the primate of Italy, and thus has a special role in the Italian Church. Lastly, the completion of the Lateran Treaty gave credence to the view that the pope and Fascism were close allies. As for the Duce, Mussolini was to observe smugly to the Germans, "Why they [the Church hierarchy] even declared the Abyssinian war a Holy War!"[55]

On May 12, 1936, in his address to the promoters of the World Exhibition of the Catholic Press, Pius XI indeed seemed to support the Italian government's policy in Ethiopia with his reference to "the triumphant joy of the great and good people." Although his remarks were immediately followed by a reference to the need for peace, the Fascist press played up the former statement, and there was a report that Mussolini even wanted the pope to crown Victor Emmanuel emperor of Abyssinia.[56]

On his part Mussolini did not heed the words of the Risorgimento figure Francesco Crispi that "Rome cannot have two kings." For a while Rome indeed had two kings and a dictator too. But by 1945, the last king of the House of Savoy, Umberto II, would be deposed when a republic was established. However, the Duce along with his last mistress ended up hung dead by their heels and spat upon in a gas station in Milan. Only the pope, then Pius XII, remained. Italy became a republic, but the Lateran Treaty continued.

Because of the concordat, there was some talk of the possibility of a later Italian government having a veto over future papal elections, as had happened in the past with some of the older Catholic states. But Pius XII, Eugenio Pacelli, was in fact not seen as a pro-Italian candidate, but as pro-French, and his successor popes were not dictated by anyone. By 1978, a non-Italian was elected for the first time in nearly five hundred years, thus ending the popular view that the pope had to be from Italy in order to have close relations with that state.

The treaty had specifically mandated that the Vatican state would remain outside of international congresses, except those devoted to peace; thus the pope did not seek international recognition for any agreements, as some had suggested. The Vatican would be neutral, above secular disputes, although it was still available for international arbitration and would continue to concern itself with matters that impinged on religious and moral questions. Pius, however, chose to continue to stay out of the League of Nations, even though some had proposed entering at the time.

The Fascist regime also agreed to a financial settlement to pay for the lands and structures seized by the first Italian government. The Law of Guarantees had originally granted 3,325,000 lire to the Holy See, which Pio Nono promptly rejected. His secretary of state said that the pope did not "accept alms from such hands" and would rather "beg his bread from door to door." The Holy See thus became very dependent on the gifts of the faithful especially, to the chagrin of some Italian Curia officials, on the largess of the Americans.[57] It has been estimated that the U.S. at that time provided more money for the upkeep of the Holy See and for Peter's Pence than all the other nations put together, and about half of the funds for the foreign missions. As has been seen, Benedict nearly bankrupted the Vatican with his vast humanitarian efforts during the war.

The new treaty gave the Vatican a cash payment of 750 million lire and consolidated stock worth nominally one billion lire. The Vatican could only withdraw the cash in graduated amounts from the Bank of Italy, and it agreed to limitations on stock sales as well in order to guard the financial markets. The Vatican subsequently put the 750 million lire in Italian government stock and in French and Hungarian railroads.[58] Thus the payments for the confiscations by the Risorgimento leaders and its heirs were finally completed.

Pius XI, the librarian turned diplomat, had done what Pius X could never have done, what Leo was too timid to do, and what Benedict laid the tentative groundwork for, as he achieved a final settlement with the Italian state. And the pope did so, not with the sons of the Revolution or the liberals, but with a right-wing regime, the dictatorship of the Fascist party. Perhaps only Mussolini could have given so much, as he recognized the claims for territorial and diplomatic independence, for a fiscal settlement, and for a guarantee that Catholicism would be the official religion of the nation. In so doing, Pius XI had to make common cause with the man whose destiny was ultimately linked with violence, racism, and war.

Mussolini started out being the role model for Hitler — if one can use that expression as it relates to dictators creating totalitarian states rather than children occupied by innocent play and growing up to be healthy adults. Hitler was also a man of bluster and of extremes, and Mussolini had already been established for over a decade when Hitler came to power. But the Führer had more military and economic might in Germany than Mussolini had in Italy, and thus became more of an international threat. At first the West cheered when Mussolini stopped the Germans from imposing their rule on Austria in 1935, but he was to become soon the Third Reich's ally after Hitler supported his march into Ethiopia, and the democracies vainly protested.

In the Spanish Civil War, Mussolini aided General Francisco Franco's forces, and he supported the Munich settlement and attempted to establish a friendly regime in Albania. Then in 1939, the year Pius XI died, the Italian Duce and his people became allies in the war against the West. By then the ailing pope and the world saw a different Mussolini, and it was the latter-day dictator that is most remembered today. Some Italians, even Italian-Americans, recalled that the Duce gave them moments of pride and confidence; others see his early years as a sham prelude to the real play. In life, it is the third act that so often counts.

Pius XI was not preoccupied totally with Italy; he addressed other diplomatic challenges as well. As noted, earlier in his diplomatic career, he became the Vatican's outpost to ascertain some understanding of the Bolshevik regime in the new Soviet Union. At his coronation, only Italy and the Soviet Union were not represented. Pius tried to enter into some negotiations with the latter government to help alleviate the persecutions of some of the Christian people there and to assist, as his predecessor had, with famine relief.[59] Despite some tentative overtures on the part of the Vatican, both sides understood the nature of each other's belief system.

Various popes, including Pius XI, have expressed disdain for Marxism. On May 15, 1931, the pontiff marked the fortieth anniversary of Leo's encyclical *Rerum Novarum* with his own *Quadragesimo Anno,* which outlined nonsocialist alternatives to achieving social and economic justice under capitalism. In more contemporary words than Leo's, Pius observed that "in our days, not only is wealth concentrated, but immense power and economic domination are concentrated in the hands of the few, and those few are frequently not owners, but only the trustees and directors of invested funds, who administer them at their own pleasure. This power becomes particularly irresistible when administered by those who, because they hold and control money, are able to govern credit and determine its allotment, for that reason supplying, so to speak, the life-blood to the economic body, and grasping, as it were, in their hands the very soul of production, so that no one dare breathe against their will."[60]

This pope was to condemn Marxism for reasons that had been frequently repeated: its materialism leads to attempts to end religion; its insistence on class warfare destroys social harmony; and its denial of private property infringes on human rights. The Communist ideologues were more than equal in their denunciations, especially in the *ABC of Communism,* written by Nikolai Bukharin and Eugeni A. Preobrazhensky, which became a Russian classic and primer for the Soviet movement.

In it, the authors observed that "the Soviet power must exert the most fervent propaganda against religion.... All religions are the same poison, intoxicating and deadening the mind, the conscience; a fight to the death must be declared against them.... Our task is not to reform, but to destroy all kinds of religion, all kinds of morality." The commissar of public education in Moscow, Anatoly Lunacharsky, in a similar vein, concluded, "We hate Christianity and Christians. Even the best of them must be looked upon as our worst enemies. They preach the love of our neighbours and mercy, which is contrary to our principles. Christian love is an obstacle to the development of the Revolution. Down with the love of our neighbours; what we want is hatred. We must learn how to hate, and it is only then we shall conquer the world."

On April 8, 1928, the official Soviet newspaper, *Pravda,* declared that the great task of the day was to fight against religion, and in 1929 a constitutional amendment passed which forbade "religious propaganda." The first Christian church to feel the wrath of the Soviets was the Russian Orthodox. As early as 1920, six bishops and 6,775 priests in that Church were put to death, some being buried alive and thrown into quicklime. Others ended up in concentration camps, the beginning of the gulag system. Lenin personally insisted on checking daily the death lists of Orthodox clergy. The Communists went after the wealth and religious treasures of the Orthodox Church to appeal to the poorer classes and attacked personally the prelates. Cardinal Gasparri, on behalf of the Vatican, offered to pay cash for the religious vessels, but the Communist attacks were simply ploys to destroy the Russian Orthodox Church and not meant to aid the poor or to assist in famine relief.

At first the Roman Catholic Church was left alone. In 1923, the attacks began. In a juvenile gesture, a figure of Pius XI was set up in a park in Moscow so people could toss objects at it. More seriously, on March 2, 1923, all Catholic clergy of Petrograd were forced to appear in Moscow and were tried because they taught catechism to children. By March 30, Dr. Edmund Aloysius Walsh, who had headed up the Vatican relief efforts in that nation, claimed that 50 percent of the Catholic clergy of Russia had disappeared since the Revolution. In 1927 Pacelli had some serious discussions with the Soviet commissar for foreign affairs, Georgi Vasilyevich

Chicherin, in Berlin about normalizing relations; but when Stalin took control of the Soviet state, any progress was reversed. Ominously, a five-year plan written by a committee headed by Stalin declared that in 1934–35, "Atheistic cells must work with greater energy" to destroy all ministers of religion.[61]

By March 1937, Pius XI in his encyclical *Divini Redemptoris* directly criticized Communism and recommended instead a society founded on social justice, Christian love, and a respect for the proper contributions of hierarchical order. Unfortunately, he also used the expression "corporative system," which looked as if he were favoring Fascism over the Communist alternative. From the beginning, this pope entertained no real illusions about Bolshevism and the feelings of the Marxist cadres toward religion.[62] In that spirit, his successors would follow until finally the Communist system collapsed of its own weight, and also because of the accumulated grievances of ethnicity and long-lasting religious impulses. When the Marxist kingdom passed from the earth, even the once moribund Russian Orthodox Church experienced a resurgence in that troubled land.

THE NAZI ONSLAUGHT

Pius had dallied with the Fascists and condemned the Communists; he also had to deal with the Nazis, who came to power in early 1933. By then, Eugenio Pacelli was his secretary of state, having been appointed when Pius retired his aging friend Gasparri in 1930. Pacelli had been the papal nuncio in Bavaria and then Berlin, and the author of various concordats with several individual states there, although he could never reach an agreement with the whole Reich. Tensions though were increasing on a series of fronts. For a variety of reasons, some Catholic bishops refused Christian burial to Nazis killed in fighting and brawls; to the Nazis, this was another verification that the Catholic Church was committed to one party, the Center political organization, which was even headed by a priest.

Meanwhile, in Germany, the adherents of a variety of Catholic youth, women's, and labor groups grew enormously, becoming especially strong in Düsseldorf, Cologne, and Berlin. Some Catholic bishops resented such movements and said little at first when the Nazis challenged those groups. When Hitler came to power, however, he quickly recognized the benefits to be gained by reaching some agreement with the Roman Catholic Church, just as Mussolini had. Although both dictators were baptized in that religious faith, it was obvious that neither retained any allegiances to it or was in the least influenced by its controlling morality. Both were more advocates of Nietzsche and his superman mentality than they were fond admirers of the faith of Augustine, Aquinas, or Francis of Assisi.[63]

Hitler quickly made the first move by encouraging a concordat and sending Franz von Papen to Rome. Both Pacelli and Pius XI had serious reservations about any formal compact with the Third Reich, but they ended up reaching such an agreement, probably because Hitler threatened to close the Catholic schools and harass the Church's youth movements unless an understanding was finalized.[64]

Even before Hitler's ascendancy as chancellor on January 30, 1933, Catholic bishops in Germany had warned about the dangers of Nazism. In February 1931, for example, the Bavarian bishops maintained that "National Socialist Christianity is not the Christianity of Christ." Later, bishops in Trier and Ermland openly supported the Center Party in order to stop the Nazis at the electoral polls. By February, though, the Nazi party had won 322 seats and parliamentary government was being overtaken as it had been in Italy. The new chancellor, Adolf Hitler, reached out to the Church hierarchy by calling the religious creeds "the most important factors in the preservation of our national welfare." And then he went on to praise the Holy See and advocate closer ties.

Privately, Hitler pledged that he would not make Bismarck's mistake and challenge the Catholic Church directly. Instead, he would move to curtail the Center Party and show Catholics that they were in better hands with the Nazis. Although he was born and nominally raised a Catholic, Hitler claimed that the Catholic Church was initially a Jewish affair that was smuggled into Europe, and succeeded only because its organization was Aryan. Jesus of Nazareth, in his view, was also an Aryan! Although Hitler respected the power of the Church, he despised the priests, whom he saw as hypocrites interested only in power, and lamented that he had to support the pro-Catholic Franco army in Spain because of the dangers of Bolshevism. He actually enjoyed the Republic's assault on the Catholic clergy before the Civil War began.[65]

Hitler, who like Mussolini saw himself as a philosopher and a man of letters, publicly claimed that he regarded Christianity as a national asset and as a bulwark for national regeneration. The concordat, completed after only eight days of negotiations, was signed on July 20, 1933. It protected on paper freedom of action and association for Catholic organizations, freedom of religious teaching in schools, and freedom of access of bishops to their faithful and to the pope.

The concordat also left the nomination of bishops entirely in the hands of the pope. The Vatican in turn agreed to forbid all clergy from actively supporting or being members of any political party. Cardinal Pacelli let the Nazis know that the Vatican viewed with indifference the demise of the Catholic parties in the Reich.[66] By that time, the Center Party and the Bayrische Volkspartei, which was a complementary organization in Bavaria, had been dissolved, and the German Reich took another step on the road toward totalitarianism. Later, Papen was to suggest that the signing of the concordat implied the approval of the Holy See for the National Socialist form of government and its peculiar doctrines. The

Vatican newspaper, *l'Osservatore Romano,* quickly contradicted Papen's conclusions.

Hitler was said to have boasted, "I shall be one of the few men in history to have deceived the Vatican." Apparently, the Church and the Reich had secretly agreed that they would join together to oppose the Soviet Union and also outlined the duties of conscripted priests. This was at a time when the Treaty of Versailles prohibited conscription in Germany. Also, the Vatican attempted to protect baptized Jews from the German government, but the Nazis refused to put that pledge into the treaty, giving only their verbal promise on the issue.[67]

The wary Vatican tried for genuine normalization of relations with the Reich; the Nazis on the other hand saw their own efforts only as another propaganda tool to bind the Catholics to the regime and to undercut the powerful forces of Catholic dissent in its land. Eugenio Pacelli, later Pius XII, defensively argued in 1945 that the agreement was "the attempt to save the concordats with certain German states by means of territorial and substantive enlargements as Germany moved into a quite uncertain future."[68]

Almost immediately, the Nazi Reich violated the provisions, and between 1933 and 1936, some thirty-six notes of protest were directed by Pope Pius XI to the government. Many were simply not answered. As early as September 1934, the pope was clearly fed up with the long list of complaints from Catholics about violations of the concordat after only three months. He was prepared to criticize openly the Reich, but Cardinal Pacelli urged a more moderate approach. The Nazis, however, attacked priests in 1934, calling them "black moles" and charging that the pope's grandmother was a Dutch Jewess — the ultimate insult in their vocabulary.

By 1936, the pope insisted that he no longer regarded the Nazis as a shield against Bolshevism and bluntly told one German diplomat, "If you want a *Kulturkampf* again, you can have it." Pacelli apparently tried to mollify the pope, but Pius was firm in his animosities. When the cardinal primate of Austria, Theodor Innitzer, supported the Anschluss, or forcible union of Austria and Germany, and even saluted Hitler, the Vatican disassociated itself from him. The cardinal was summoned to Rome, where the pope himself called him "very simple-minded."[69]

Late at night on March 20, 1937, priests across Germany received an encyclical directly from the pope, which was to be read at Mass the next morning. The letter, which was inspired by a group of German bishops, condemned the violations of law and the un-Christian teachings of the Nazi Reich. Privately, one of the chief critics of the Reich, Michael Cardinal von Faulhaber, had already irritated the Nazis by his criticisms of the government from the pulpit and had received support from the Vatican, which obliquely reminded Catholics of St. Ambrose who had stood up to the civil authorities of his time.[70]

By 1937, then, the pope was ready to outline the suffering condition of the Church and moved on to denounce its Nazi ideology point by point. Directly, the pope observed, "Only superficial minds can...make the mad attempt to confine within the boundaries of a single people, within the narrow bloodstream of a single race, God the Creator of the world, the King, and the Lawgiver of all peoples before whose greatness all people are as a drop in a bucket."[71]

The pope then went on to insist, "Every attempt to dislodge moral teaching and moral conduct from the rock of faith, and to build them on the shifting sands of human regulations, sooner or later leads the individual and the community to moral destruction." Bluntly Pius insisted, "The number of such fools, who today attempt to separate morality and religion, is legion." Concluding, the pope prayed for the persecutors and the oppressors of the Church. The Nazis responded with a series of "immorality" trials against Catholic clergy, as Hitler promised a propaganda campaign that would leave the Church reeling.[72]

It is easy to say in Pius's defense that a realistic pope saw the Nazi regime coming to power and hoped to protect his Church by virtue of a treaty or concordat. Indeed that is so, but it has also been said that Pius XI actively turned the German clergy, and by implication the German Catholic community, away from opposition to Hitler's party. The Germany hierarchy, as has been noted, opposed the Nazis in the early elections and supported the Center Party. Yet several weeks later, the hierarchy and the party dropped its opposition — probably due to the direct intercession of Pius XI. Cardinal Faulhaber recorded on March 24, 1933, that there was a greater "toleration" of the Nazi government in the Vatican, and that the Holy Father saw Hitler as a voice against Bolshevism. Two years later, on August 20, 1935, the German bishops wrote Hitler, "In the face of this proclamation of the pope's influence, millions of men abroad, both Catholics and non-Catholics, have overcome their initial mistrust and accorded credit to your government."[73] The Vatican probably concluded that it was futile to let the Catholic Church in Germany be left standing alone in opposition to Nazism.

Thus, the pope had come to recognize very quickly the limits of Vatican diplomacy and the perils of concordat policy. By seeking to reach some settlements with these new states, some have argued that he often placed the Church in greater peril and seemed to give his concurrence to having Catholics let down their guard. The Church had dealt with barbarians before, but these totalitarian states were a new breed.

VATICAN DIPLOMACY ELSEWHERE

In another instance, in dealing with Spain the pope was at least more publicly circumspect. After the end of World War I, the usual isolation of Spain began to break down, and there was increasing criticism of government corruption and military misadventures. A Captain General Miguel Primo de Rivera y Orbaneja of Catalonia put his province under martial law and demanded that the Spanish king dismiss the ministers responsible for the military disasters in Morocco. Instead, the monarch, Alfonso XIII, asked the general to form a government; he did, but insisted that he rule by military decree.

Respecting the power of the Roman Catholic Church, he set up an audience for the royal family with Pius XI. The king and queen genuflected thrice before the pope and kissed his foot and hand in obedience. Alfonso read a speech with historical references that spoke of Spain's support of the faith against Islam and the heretics. He then offered to lead another crusade if Pius would be another Urban II.

Primo de Rivera governed for six years until 1930 and proved to be a mild ruler. Given to a life of pleasure, he is reported to have observed, "Had I known in my youth that I would one day have to govern this country, I would have spent more time studying and less time fornicating." Finally, he resigned, left for Paris, and died in a nightclub there. Under pressure from socialists and liberals, the king abdicated, and Spain on April 14, 1931, had a republic.

The new government began attacks on the Church, the clergy, and traditional ways of Church life. The Vatican tried at first to temper its reactions to those abuses. In May 1933, Pius issued an encyclical, *Dilectissima Nobis,* which condemned the vandalism against the Church, but avoided attacking the Republic.

Soon a Catholic party, headed by a young lawyer, José María Gil Robles, was formed and became rather successful. Finally, Gil Robles was named prime minister. But by 1936, the peculiarities of the electoral system led the legislative branch, called the Cortes, to end up in the hands of the left wing instead of in the right, which had received more votes. The setting for a civil war was being laid. A popular front government of Socialists, Republicans, Communists, and anarcho-syndicalists took over. The prisons were opened, enabling so-called political prisoners to leave, and rumors and tales of murder, arson, and destruction of church property and clergy were rampant.

After a series of political murders, a number of Spanish regiments in Morocco mutinied on July 17, 1936; a career military officer, General Francisco Franco, mastered the situation, and by July 19 military garrisons all over Spain supported him and the Falangists. Despite the usual view that the Church was supportive of the neo-Fascist Franco, the Vatican had previously reached an accommodation with the Republican government. Three times during the civil war, Franco tried unsuccessfully to get the Vatican's recognition. Still as the left stepped up its attacks on the Church, the Vatican ultimately turned to the right for protection. Church buildings, especially in Barcelona, were burned, and an estimated 7,937 clergy were killed as the brutality on each side continued.

Franco's forces handed back their own retribution as an estimated forty thousand people were executed in the struggle. After Franco's forces won, the Church faced another Fascist regime with skepticism and with some hostility. As in Italy, the government sought to absorb all educational, social, and religious organizations into its now state-run apparatus.[74]

The Vatican was not, as some critics charged, led by men who regardless of fact empathized with authoritarian regimes. In fact, while Pius XI did not have a great regard for democracy, he actually was quite willing to make common cause with the left-wing Republic of France, thus continuing to pursue Leo's policy of *ralliement*. In the process, Pius also had to discipline strongly some of his own hierarchy as he tried to reach a compromise with the government, and on one occasion in 1925, he actually forced the bishops to retreat from a statement attacking that government. Many of the episcopate had been appointed by Pius X, and their views reflected his extremism.

Pius XI even took on the antirepublican and intregalist Action Française headed up by Charles Maurras. That name was used to describe a political association and also a journal which sought to reestablish the monarchy in France. Although its main directors were actually atheists, its intellectual influence was great among conservative Catholics, especially some of the clergy in France and later the youth in Belgium. The Curia had pushed for a condemnation, but Pius X (who once said of Maurras, "I bless his work") suspended publication of the decree, as did Benedict, who was preoccupied with the war. Pius XI, after receiving new complaints, informally condemned the Action Française through Pierre Cardinal Andrieu of Bordeaux. When some of the Curia staff members claimed that they could not find the initial decree, the pope indicated that he would fire those responsible for its loss. Miraculously it reappeared in time for his signature.[75]

The Action Française responded with a vicious series of attacks on the pope and resurrected the old anticlerical themes, so familiar to European journalists. The Vatican had previously forbidden priests to give the sacraments to the Action's adherents, and it required that those of them at death's door had to recant before they received the last rites and forgiveness. When Louis Cardinal Abillot was indiscreet enough to write a letter of regret to the Action Française, the pope summoned him to Rome, removed him from the Sacred College of Cardinals, and he ended his days in a Jesuit order house.*

---

*Eleven out of the seventeen French cardinals and bishops probably supported Maurras. Pius XI acknowledged Maurras had one of the finest minds alive, but that in life reason is not enough.

Later, the Action Française's directors sought to make amends with the new Pope Pius XII and recanted what the Church regarded as their erroneous teachings. As for Maurras, after his long history of belligerent polemics and later support for the Nazis, he requested to be reconciled with the Church on his deathbed. The importance of Pius XI's action, though, was that he showed very clearly that the Vatican was willing to negotiate with Republican, left-wing, or Socialist governments in order to protect the Church and the faithful. And like Leo XIII, he in fact would take positive steps to remove the Catholic Church once and for all from the ranks of those who romantically or obstinately clung to the remnants of the Ancién Regime in France.

Actually the Church had made some major strides in that nation. Throughout the war, the French clergy received renown for their courage and faithfulness to French troops and to the laity. Some 32,700 clergy were mobilized for active service, and 4,618 were killed; 9,378 received the Croix de Guerre, 1,533 the Medaille Militaire, and 895 the Legion of Honor. In 1921, the French government resumed diplomatic relations with the Vatican, and by 1937, the French ambassador to the Holy See, M. Françoise Carles-Roux, matter-of-factly indicated that relations were excellent and that "the Church in France has the respect of the nation and the public authorities."[76]

Across the channel in neighboring England, the Holy See allowed some discussions to continue between Désiré Joseph Cardinal Mercier and important Anglicans, including Lord Halifax, on the possible reunion between that Church and Rome — a perennial topic of interest over the years. The Anglican archbishop of Canterbury, however, was rather apprehensive, probably reflecting the true feelings of the majority of his fellow churchmen. After Cardinal Mercier died, some of the impetus for such discussions was lost. The pope, though courteous to the idea and to the principals involved, was himself increasingly leery, and he ended up criticizing the World Conference on Faith and Order, a Protestant group at Lausanne, which met in August 1927. He emphasized that the Church must insist on the primacy of the Roman pontiff and the unerring deposit of faith that it had. After that message, delivered in his encyclical *Mortalium Animos,* talks with the Anglicans were broken off. In 1930 with the close of the Anglican Conference at Lambeth, the pope departed again from that other church's prescriptions and reaffirmed Catholic dogma in his encyclical *Casti Connubii,* which condemned birth control and sexual relations outside of regularized marriage. By then, Vatican support for Mussolini's incursion into Ethiopia also alienated some English as well, as did Franco's cause in the civil war in Spain.[77]

In the western hemisphere, the pope's main problem was Mexico. In that nation, the attacks on the Church went far beyond the usual anticlericalism. As late as 1870, the Church had owned about a quarter of the land of Mexico, and its clergy even charged for dispensing the sacrament of marriage. By 1917, a democratic-based party pushed through a Law of Separation similar to France's, and the Jesuits and Spanish priests were expelled. Churches were confiscated by the state, and other religious institutions were sequestered. Religious activities and processions outside the churches were prohibited. But until 1926, the law was generally disregarded. Then Plutarco Elias Calles came to power. What his ethnic or religious origins were remain unclear, but Calles was at one time a schoolteacher and then a bartender. In 1910, he became a police inspector and later a colonel in the army. In 1926, the Mexican government under Calles systematically attacked Catholic schools and orphanages and even drove the Sisters of Charity out of a hospital in Durango. In response, the Church in Mexico began a three-day period of "mourning for the death of liberty in Mexico."

The Vatican's response was that the Church would comply with the law by refusing to officiate at liturgical ceremonies and thus imposing an "interdict" on the nation. That harsh decision was reminiscent of the medieval Church and its battles with recalcitrant monarchs. Now it was being applied in a very different situation. The churches were in the words of one observer "open, but priestless." Catholics were also urged to undertake what amounted to an economic boycott similar to Gandhi's techniques in India.

In 1926, the pope in his encyclical *Iniquis Afflictisque* denounced the continued attacks on the Church in Mexico. He bluntly declared, "The Mexican Government has reduced ministers of religion to the level of outlaws and criminals, and made the preaching of religion a crime." Later, even George Bernard Shaw urged the American press to publicize the pope's concerns, but there was little exposure of the stories. In some Latin American nations there was some support for the pope's letter, but the European states stayed out of the dispute, in part to protect their nationals' interest in Mexico.

However, in the United States, the administration had serious reservations about Calles's regime in general. President Herbert Hoover sent his ambassador, Dwight Morrow, to encourage a moderation of that regime's attacks on the Church or face economic sanctions. The United States was somewhat successful: church property was supposed to be protected, bishops were to be restored, and the churches opened up once again. Still, though, the Church suffered great losses, in part due to the poor caliber of its clergy and the lack of recognition on the part of the Vatican of exactly what was happening.[78]

In picking up Benedict's concerns, Pius also became a pope of the foreign missions. He too pushed for a native clergy and in 1925 sponsored a well-received "Missions Exhibition" at the Vatican. Overcoming considerable opposition, he consecrated the first six Chinese bishops at St. Peter's in

1926 and the first Japanese bishop in 1927. He supported other episcopal consecrations in India, Southeast Asia, and China in 1933, and pushed for closer ties to the Eastern churches. In very many ways, he was indeed a fitting heir to the legacy of Benedict XV.[79]

OPPOSING THE TYRANTS

As he aged, the once fine athlete began to feel the ravages of time, especially from arteriosclerosis and heart disease. He reached a point where life became painful, and in stoic reserve he offered up those pains to the world's suffering people. Pius XI had called back to Rome another Benedict protégé, Eugenio Pacelli, and named him a cardinal in December 1929, and then secretary of state in February 1930. Almost as if seeking to choose his successor, Pius XI encouraged Pacelli to visit the Eucharistic Congresses in Buenos Aires and later in Budapest, and conduct religious pilgrimages across the world.

In the autumn of 1936, Pacelli traveled to the United States at Pius's encouragement and met President Franklin Delano Roosevelt. Pius XI was to say of the Americans, "All my life I have entertained the greatest admiration for this young and vigorous people." The Curia, however, had opposed at one time the Catholic bishops' desire to create a National Catholic Welfare Conference and actually told Pius that his predecessor was ready to sign a decree dissolving it. That claim was false, but Pius respectfully followed what he thought was his predecessor's wishes. Later, after American prelates protested, the pope looked at the issue more carefully and in a rare occurrence countermanded his own order.

After Pius died, the *New York Times* reported that he had personally approved of Bishop Michael Gallagher's rebuke of the radio priest Father Charles Coughlin of Detroit. In his broadcasts, Coughlin had excoriated President Roosevelt as a liar and a person who betrayed America to Jews and foreigners. The pope was also reported to have agreed with George Cardinal Mundelein of Chicago's vigorous attacks on Nazism.[80]

In his last years, Pius XI began to be seen as a major critic of totalitarian governments, of racist politics, and of those who celebrate war and military might. Just before the beginning of a second and more terrible world war, he died on February 10, 1939, and was buried under St. Peter's.

The leadership style of Achille Ratti became even more of an enigma as the years of his reign receded. He was by nature an unostentatious, simple, sober man, who seemed to treasure the world of libraries and the pleasures of scholarship, and yet also secretly yearned for some adventure in life. Unlike some of his fellow popes, he was not by training or temperament a diplomat, and yet it was diplomacy that marked his reign.

He had a penchant for the neat treaty and the ironclad concordat as instruments to make secular governments obey, but it was his unfortunate destiny to live in an era when some of the states that he confronted were a new breed of polity, one of authoritarianism, of totalitarian reach, and of incredible addiction to violence and mass destruction. Diplomacy was new to him, and so it seemed to fascinate him, even though Pius was tough enough to realize that treaties are only observed when it is in all parties' interest to do so. In the secular world, diplomacy and military force are not opposite approaches to power politics; they are part of a continuum of persuasion and force. For the Vatican, such a continuum is, of course, truncated. As Stalin once observed, the pope has no military divisions. So there is an excessive reliance on suasion, world appeals, and written encyclicals to the world — which is often deaf, as it was deaf in the 1930s to its own self-interests and later to its own sense of decency.

The Curia style of politics is subtle, patient, and convoluted — as befits the historic past in which it was founded and flowered. But in the twentieth century, the pope was to try more pointed pronouncements and blunt speaking. Some of his own Curia colleagues were surprised and often dismayed as he openly confronted the totalitarian regimes when they attacked the Church and the larger cause of humankind.

In his dealings with the Curia and the national hierarchies, he brooked little opposition; once when a cardinal said that he thought it was his duty to offer advice, the pope snapped, "Yes, when you're asked for it." He led by the force of his stoic personality and by his personal integrity. Church historian and an ambassador to the Vatican Ludwig von Pastor observed once of Pius XI, "He almost always went against the advice given him."[81] Gone was the whimsy of Leo, the devotion of Pius X, or the broad humanitarian reach of Benedict. Achille Ratti had all his life a firm sense of himself, an unending view of his time and place, and an interior reserve that was little understood.

He clearly overestimated the fruits of diplomacy, especially in dealing with Mussolini. Once in despair he faulted himself for having signed agreements with "people without faith and without God." Yet, with all the criticisms of those overtures, Pius XI still gave the Church a treaty that outlived its architects. The Duce did fool him a bit, as he did others; they miscalculated his energy for achievement, his personality for true character. Mussolini was a Potemkin village sort of leader — a false front hiding the rotten timbers of his life.

In his reign then, the pope explored the farthest reaches of diplomacy — giving him a record of solid achievements and a series of lessons in failure. His successor would know even more intensely the problems of playing international politics in a world where force was the only answer to these new men of violence.

Most fittingly Pius's last words were, "Let there be peace." As for Mussolini, his observation on learning of the pope's death was simply, "Thank God the stubborn old man has gone."[82]

CHAPTER SIX

PIUS XII
AND THE SPIRITUAL
TWILIGHT OF THE WEST

That stubborn old man in the Vatican accomplished one other feat denied to most human beings: he reached beyond the grave and named his own successor. The week before his painful death, he confided that he had sent his secretary of state, Eugenio Cardinal Pacelli, abroad so often to prepare him for the papacy. "He will make a fine pope," he concluded. Pius XI had even said once that if he were sure that Pacelli would be elected, he would resign the papacy, a rare sort of praise.[1]

THE BLACK NOBILITY

Indeed, for generations, the Pacelli family had been associated with the papacy. Eugenio's great-grandfather had been minister of finance under Gregory XVI. His grandfather, Marcantonio, was undersecretary in the Ministry of the Interior under Pius IX and followed him into exile in Gaeta in 1848. Later he was also instrumental in the founding of the Vatican newspaper *l'Osservatore Romano*. Eugenio's father was the dean of the Consistorial College of lawyers, which prepared cases for beatification, among other matters, and was president of a Catholic Action group that promoted the teaching of Christian doctrine. His brother, Francesco, had helped to negotiate the concordat of 1929. Both of his sisters had married Vatican officials — one the director of the Catholic hospital Bambino Gesù in Rome, and the other an administrator of the Holy See and a papal gentleman-in-waiting.[2]

At the early age of six, Eugenio, like so many Catholic boys across the globe, created an altar in his bedroom and practiced being a priest. He was a serious, somewhat detached person who exuded a sense of piety.

130

Later one observer claimed he gave off "the odor of sanctity." And another, Henri Bordeaux, said he "has the sublime greatness of a mortified almost translucent body, which seems destined to serve only as a cover for a soul." Although in later years and in official photographs he seemed ascetic, regal, and aloof, in fact, he impressed his contemporaries as a steadfast, friendly, and charming person. Kaiser Wilhelm wrote, "Pacelli is a likeable, distinguished man, of high intelligence, and exquisite manners, the perfect pattern of an eminent prelate of the Catholic Church."

As a young man, he wanted to be a simple parish priest, but he was sent, on February 14, 1901, to the Congregation for Extraordinary Ecclesiastical Affairs — the Vatican foreign office — and matured under the eagle eye of the shrewd Monsignor Gasparri. He was offered in 1908 a faculty position in canon law at Catholic University in Washington, D.C., an appointment he turned down in obedience to Pius X's wishes.[3]

In 1911, the youthful Pacelli was named by Pius X undersecretary of the Congregation for Extraordinary Ecclesiastical Affairs, and in 1914 he became the secretary under then Cardinal Gasparri. More importantly, he was later transferred to Germany, where he presented Benedict's unsuccessful peace plan. He was papal nuncio to Bavaria from 1917 to 1920, and then nuncio to Germany through 1929. During some of that time, he worked with Achille Ratti, who had been sent by the Holy See to Poland. In one of the most dramatic episodes of his diplomatic career, his residence in Munich was invaded in 1919 by Communists during the "Spartacist" uprisings. Facing a determined and unyielding cleric, they withdrew, and Pacelli established a reputation for personal courage and sangfroid. That experience, however, left on him an indelible imprint about the brutal nature of Communist thuggery.[4]

A POPE IN TRAINING

By 1930, Ratti, then Pius XI, had decided to retire Gasparri, and he summoned Pacelli to Rome to become eventually secretary of state. There is evidence that on some occasions Pacelli was much more prone to quiet diplomacy and to accommodation with the totalitarian states than was Pius XI. As has been noted, as he grew older, Ratti became more vocal as his concordats were abrogated by the Fascists and the Nazis, and he expressed his "deepest regret" that he signed compacts with "people without faith and without God." As for the Bolsheviks, he never misjudged their intentions, unlike many leaders in the West. It was clear overall that he and he alone set the tone of his own reign, and that he was deep down a courageous and principled man.

Ratti's critics said that his denunciations of the totalitarian states were based on their challenges to the institutional Catholic Church and that he never clearly defended individual rights and civil liberties. There is some truth in that observation; he was in fact above all else the pope of the Roman Church and not the defender of liberal or even humanitarian traditions. Still, in the last years of his reign, he was clearly a foe of the Nazi regime, as well as of Mussolini.

Facing serious health problems, Pius XI encouraged his secretary of state to go to the International Eucharistic Conference in Buenos Aires in 1934, to Uruguay, and to Brazil. In 1936, Pacelli traveled across the United States, visiting twelve of the sixteen Church provinces, and later met President Franklin Delano Roosevelt at his ancestral estate in Hyde Park. It was said of the meeting that ironically "Roosevelt spoke as a pope, Pacelli as a politician and diplomat." It would prove to be an acquaintanceship of immense importance during the next war.

In that country, Pacelli even appeared before the National Press Club in Washington, D.C., explaining the Vatican's policies. He also represented the pope at the coronation of George VI in 1937, gave a major address at the International Eucharistic Congress in Budapest in 1938, and socialized easily with French liberal politicians of the Third Republic. Blessed with a photographic memory and possessing a real gift for speaking foreign languages, he was frequently called upon as an orator to address a variety of audiences.

Trained primarily as a diplomat, Pacelli retained confidence in the techniques of discussion, nuance, subtlety, and written agreements of understanding. It was the way of Curia international politics since the Renaissance, and he was clearly formed by those traditions and experiences. During his time as papal nuncio in Germany, he had devoted much of his intensive effort to the signing of several concordats with various German states, since the political climate would not permit a national agreement until Hitler's centralized regime emerged.

Some of his contemporaries were critical of his performance, however. In 1937, the Spanish ambassador said he was "no real counterweight to Pius XI, because he was completely devoid of will and character. He hasn't even got a particularly good mind." The British chargé d'affaires, Hugh Montgomery, said he was "a good man, a pious man, not devoid of intelligence, but essentially there to obey." Pacelli's close associate, Domenico Tardini, put it more guardedly, "By nature gentle and almost shy, he was not born with the temperament of a fighter. That is what distinguished him from his great predecessor."[5]

Pacelli was later to be called pro-Nazi because of his refusal to name Hitler's regime directly in his criticisms after he became pope. Pacelli did indeed respect Germany and German culture, but he was clearly aware of the hostile nature of the Nazi government. In 1945, he defended the concordat he signed with Hitler when he was secretary of state, but he once admitted that no signature of the German government was worth the paper it was written on. And when the Germans remilitarized the Rhineland in

1936, Pacelli remarked to the French ambassador, "If you had entered with 200,000 troops, you would have done an immense service to the world."[6]

After Pius XI's death, Pacelli, his secretary of state and by then also his papal chamberlain, pronounced him "truly dead." He apparently did not tap his predecessor's forehead with the traditional silver hammer. Experience has it that conclaves do not turn to the secretary of state to be the successor to the dead incumbent.* In addition, Pacelli faced strong opposition in some quarters. The Italian government let it be known through one of its Fascist news organs that the world needed "a new man" as pope and not one associated with any "political factor." Generally though, the Italian press was favorable to the Roman-born prelate.

The Germans, as usual, less subtle than the Italians, actually issued a warning against the election of Pacelli. The Nazi press criticized the idea of "a political pope," angrily predicting that the policy of Cardinal Pacelli would lead to "a crusade against the totalitarian States." The Western democracies and their media were overall more complimentary of the cardinal secretary of state, although the former Weimar chancellor, Dr. Heinrich Brüning, reportedly concluded that "there was much naivety in Pacelli's makeup, particularly in that he believes in temporizing with the present regimes in Germany and in Italy." And others concluded, "Cardinal Pacelli is a *man of peace,* and the world needs a *pope of war.*"[7]

When the College of Cardinals convened, the members seemed to have reached a very clear consensus on Pacelli, whose strength was especially pronounced among the non-Italian members. On the first ballot, Cardinal Pacelli received thirty-five of the sixty-two ballots — seven short of election; the second ballot gave him forty votes, and then on the first afternoon ballot he received every vote except his own. Jean Cardinal Verdier summarized the deliberations simply: "The Sacred College could not fail to choose Pacelli for the Papacy."[8] Pacelli was elected on his sixty-third birthday. He was the first papal secretary of state to be chosen pope since 1667 and the first pope of Roman birth since 1721.

Before his coronation, Pius XII, as he called himself, appointed as secretary of state Luigi Maglione, the papal nuncio in Paris. When he died in 1944, Pacelli became in fact his own secretary of state, assisted by Monsignor Tardini, who was head of the Congregation for Extraordinary Ecclesiastical Affairs, and more eventfully Monsignor Giovanni Battista Montini, head of the Congregation for Ordinary Affairs. Years later Montini, ambushed in a Vatican power play, would be exiled and sent to the archbishopric of Milan, then resurrected politically by his friend John XXIII, and finally elected himself as Paul VI. It would be shades of Benedict XV all over again.[9]

---

*Some notable exceptions are Hildebrand, who became Gregory VII in 1073; Fabio Chigi, who became Alexander VII in 1655; and Giulio Rospigliosi, who became Clement IX in 1667.

REACHING FOR PEACE

Immediately after his coronation, Pius XII moved on the diplomatic offensive to settle some of the tensions with the Nazi regime. Citing as precedent Leo XIII's early overtures to Bismarck to end the *Kulturkampf,* he proposed to write a personal letter to Hitler on the occasion of Pius's ascendancy to the throne of St. Peter. Then the pope on April 21, 1939, sent an emissary to Mussolini asking for a five-power conference which would include Great Britain, France, Germany, Italy, and Poland, and which was meant to prevent the outbreak of another war. Bolshevik Russia was not included in the Vatican's proposal.

Mussolini seemed positive at first, but Britain and France, remembering the Munich betrayal, were very wary; and the Germans were firmly negative. Pius sent his nuncio to Berlin to see German Foreign Minister Joachim von Ribbentrop, who was warned that a conflict would likely bring the United States in on the side of the democracies. The Nazis, though, made it clear that they were ready for war. So was Mussolini; when he was advised that Russia might join the British and French, the Duce responded, "What Russia does makes no difference." He was proven to be very, very wrong.

Then the Germans and the Russians signed a nonaggression pact in late August 1939. The way to war was clear. The French ambassador to the Vatican urged the pope to condemn the Germans as they continued their aggressive designs. Instead Pius made a general but still eloquent appeal. "Nothing is lost by peace; everything may be lost by war," he argued in vain. Quietly, the pope though urged the Poles to appease the Nazis on the Danzig and corridor issues, hoping to avert the imminent conflict.[10]

On September 1, 1939, the Reich armies invaded Poland; soon its Russian Bolshevik ally attacked from its west, and free Poland was dismantled. Immediately the French and the British governments moved to Poland's ill-fated defense. Mussolini succinctly commented that Poland had been "liquidated." World War II had begun. The pope's initial response was to emulate the behavior of his predecessor, Benedict XV, as he pledged to maintain absolute neutrality. But this war was more stark, more mad, more obviously a battle of good and evil.

Still, the pope could not avoid the obvious, and on October 27, 1939, he issued his encyclical *Summi Pontificates,* which praised the Polish people and their dedication to the Catholic faith. It was clearly an anti-Nazi letter, and the Vatican Radio followed up by broadcasting a personal testimony of one victim that outlined the horrors of that invasion to the world, thus angering even further the Reich leaders. The Nazis then moved to seize the Catholic Church's property in various areas in Poland in violation of the concordat that Pacelli had struck.[11]

Unknown at the time and rather remarkable considering his diplomatic inclinations, Pius was involved in conversations concerning a possible coup against Hitler. In January 1940, the pope received a representative from some German generals who indicated they were going to topple the Führer. They wanted to inform the Western allies so as to prevent military action in the West before their coup took place. Pius dutifully informed the British ambassador to the Vatican, Francis D'Arcy Osborne, but the British government was skeptical.

In April 1940, President Roosevelt sent his personal representative, former U.S. Steel executive Myron Taylor, who like FDR was a nominal Episcopalian, to the Vatican with a special message. Such a step was a personal victory for Pacelli and for his close friend, American prelate Francis Spellman. The wealthy Taylor owned a villa in Florence and was close to Pacelli, who had stayed at his New York home in 1936. The charming FDR referred to the pope, whom he had met only once, as his "good old friend" and had Taylor use the pope as a conduit to Mussolini to try to discourage the latter's participation in the conflict. Taylor even asked the pope to threaten the Duce with excommunication if he went to war on the side of Hitler!

In May 1940, Hitler overran the Low Countries. The pope sent his personal blessings to the people of Belgium, Holland, and Luxembourg, but the French government demanded that he directly condemn the Nazis and not simply send an expression of sympathy for the victims. Privately the pope responded, "We would like to utter words of fire against such actions; and the only thing restraining Us from speaking is the fear of making the plight of the victims worse."

Even then, the Italian government threatened the pope because of those telegrams of sympathy. Mussolini called the papacy a cancer, and he wanted to blow up the pope and the monarchy as well. Pius pointedly responded, "We were not intimidated by pistols pointed at Us once; we will be even less frightened next time" — a reference to the Communists' Spartacist incident in 1919. Then he concluded, "The pope cannot on certain occasions remain silent."[12]

Still, while he denounced the heinous acts of aggression, Pius did not use the undiplomatic word "invasion" in characterizing the violations of the Low Countries. Looking at the military situation, the pope surely must have resigned himself to the eventuality that he would be facing a Nazi-controlled world, one that would hold vast areas of Catholic Europe in its grip. The anti-Nazi tone of *l'Osservatore Romano* quieted down, although the Vatican Radio, run by the more aggressive Jesuits, continued its attacks on the German government. Again and again the pope appealed to Mussolini to remain neutral, but the Duce refused now to even read Pius's letters. On June 10, 1940, Mussolini led a very reluctant Italy into war against France and Great Britain. Roosevelt condemned the action, saying of the Duce that the hand that held the dagger stuck it in the back of its neighbor, France. It was a masterful use of ethnic stereotyping by a master orator.[13]

While many of the Italian clergy patriotically rallied around the Italian armies, the Vatican stayed quiet. Thirty Italian bishops sent a telegram to the Duce praising his actions, but the pope was still urging Britain and Germany to enter into peace negotiations. The French Cardinal Eugene Tisserant sadly observed, "I fear that history will tomorrow have to reproach the Holy See with having pursued a policy of convenience to its own exclusive benefit — and little more. And this is a terribly sad thing, especially for one who has lived under Pius XI." Even Pacelli's close friend, Archbishop Spellman of New York, wrote to Secretary of State Cardinal Maglione that the prestige of the pope had sharply declined due to his unclear pronouncements and the pro-Axis sentiments of many Italian bishops. Spellman claimed that American Catholics no longer had confidence in the pope's impartiality because he seemed to have sympathy for Mussolini's imperial designs. Fortunately for Spellman, Maglione did not show the offensive letter to Pius.[14]

Having been unable to stop the war, Pius XII emulated not his immediate predecessor, but Benedict XV, and sought to work to alleviate the problems of the suffering, the prisoners of war, and incarcerated civilians. By then, the Nazi assault was moving toward its high-water point, and the Western democracies seemed impotent and close to collapse. To add to the pope's problems, the Germans had a new ally — the atheistic Marxist regime in Russia, which the papacy had historically feared even more than the lunacies of the right.

Then on June 22, 1941, Hitler, in one of the most consequential miscalculations in the history of warfare, turned his armies east and attacked the Soviet Union. Stalin had been warned before the attack, but refused to believe it. As the Nazi armies crossed the borders, he vanished from public view. It was as if he had a nervous breakdown and could not function. Soon though, he regained his composure and the Red armies faced the Nazi onslaught. Churchill publicly supported his old Bolshevik enemies, saying he would ally Britain with the devil to stop the Nazis. He did, and so eventually did the Americans. It was the valor of the Red armies more than any other single factor which destroyed Hitler's war machine forever.[15]

THE AMERICAN CONNECTION

With the United States still not in the war, FDR made a controversial decision — to extend Lend-Lease aid to the Soviets — and he asked the Catholic Church to support his decisions and thus limit the political fallout at home. Roosevelt wrote directly to Pius, "I believe, however, that this Russian dictatorship is less dangerous to the safety of other nations than is the German form of dictatorship. The only weapon which the Russian dictatorship uses outside of its own borders is communist propaganda, which I, of course, recognize has in the past been utilized for the purpose of breaking down the form of government in other countries, religious beliefs, et cetera. . . . I believe that the survival of Russia is less dangerous to religion, to the Church as such, and to humanity in general than would be the survival of the German form of dictatorship."[16]

To pacify the pontiff, the American administration indicated that it would use its new association with the Russian leaders to assist in guaranteeing freedom of religion in the Soviet Union. The Vatican knew, as did the United States, that the Bolsheviks had already invaded eastern Poland, Finland, Bessarabia, and Bukovina and had also absorbed the states of Latvia, Estonia, and Lithuania, so FDR's sanguine observations may have lacked some persuasiveness. Pius had few illusions that freedom of religion or an end to obnoxious antireligious propaganda would come about through American intervention. Still he was willing to acknowledge a distinction between the Soviet regime which the Vatican condemned and the Russian people, for whom he expressed his personal regard. As for Lend-Lease, the Vatican decided that was a military question, and the Holy See stayed away from the issue. Roosevelt got what he needed, and the American hierarchy was notified by the pope's agents that it was not to criticize U.S. efforts to be an arsenal for the new Allied forces.

After the bombing of Pearl Harbor, FDR candidly laid before Pius the American war objectives. The Allies would defeat the Germans first and then turn to the Japanese. The president also insisted that the United States did not seek any territorial aggrandizement. A few months after that attack, the Vatican in March 1942 agreed to a Japanese government request for diplomatic relations, a move that clearly annoyed the president, who criticized the poor timing and the domestic backlash that would eventually result. A very sensitive American hierarchy tried both to support the pope and yet mute the obvious American reaction inflamed right after the attack in Hawaii.

The progress of the war in North Africa in late 1942 made it apparent that the Allies were on the offensive. Meanwhile the heroic defense of Stalingrad from August 19, 1942, to January 30, 1943, spelled out to astute observers that the Soviets would not surrender and retreat from the fields of battle as the czarist forces had in World War I. Even Hitler had to acknowledge what was obvious to others, that his futile campaign for control of that city was a major turning point. With the British under Churchill promising no truce, the United States newly entering the conflict, and the Russians standing firm, the Vatican as well as others could see a new war emerging.[17]

Despite those changes, Pius was concerned with FDR's unexpected announcement made with Churchill at Casablanca that the Allies would accept nothing but "unconditional surrender." To the pope, that statement would embolden the Axis powers and frighten their populace to fight on to the death. To Roosevelt, it was a message that the United Nations, as they were to be called, regarded their opponents as a contagious disease to be permanently eradicated. The war against the Nazis and their collaborators became now a moral crusade, and it was Roosevelt and Churchill more than the pope who gave the war its true moral dimension as a battle of good against evil.

As the Allies moved across North Africa, it soon became apparent that they would begin an assault on Italy. It was also obvious that Rome would become sooner or later a theater of the war. The pope, both as bishop of Rome and as a Roman by birth, was deeply disturbed. He used his considerable influence with Roosevelt to protect the city and pushed the American Catholic hierarchy to employ also their good offices to guarantee that Rome would be treated as an open city. Roosevelt, with a considerable number of Catholics in Congress and in the Democratic party, gave general guarantees to protect Rome, especially the Vatican and its domains.

But he reminded the pope that the Fascists were still operating in a city which had real military importance for a variety of reasons, including being a railroad nexus. Still FDR was clearly sympathetic to Pius's pleas. Churchill and the British, recalling probably the destruction of their own London and its beloved Parliament, were less willing to give guarantees, although the prime minister did promise to exercise all possible restraint. British Ambassador Osborne, however, took the occasion to remind the Vatican that it made no protests when religious buildings at Canterbury, Coventry, and St. Paul's in London were hit by the Germans.[18]

In late November 1942, the pope grew increasingly concerned when Churchill told the House of Commons that the Allies would vigorously attack Italy from bases in North Africa. In December, the Vatican urged the Italian ambassador to have his government remove all military commands from the city. The king had favored that step before, and Mussolini agreed in principle to the proposal, saying that he had no intention of hiding "beneath the umbrella of Catholicism." On December 16, the Duce informed the Vatican that he would agree to removing both German and Italian commands from the city, and that he himself would leave.[19]

But when the British and the Americans disagreed on the conditions of an open city, Mussolini stalled. Then when the Allied invasion in Africa bogged down, the Duce no longer seemed interested. In May 1943, as the Allies centered their advances on North Africa, the pope addressed a personal plea to Roosevelt asking that the "treasured shrines of religion and art" be spared from ruin.[20] As noted, Roosevelt on June 26 promised to refrain from bombing civilian sites, but he warned that the Axis might bomb the Vatican in order to charge the Allies with such outrages.

On July 10, the Allied forces landed at Sicily, and later Rome was bombed for the first time. The war was moving closer. Although the bombing was aimed at the marshaling yards of San Lorenzo and Tiburtine, some of the bombs did fall on civilian areas, including a hospital, religious buildings, and the largest cemetery in Rome. For two hours, a distraught Pius watched as the city of his birth was being attacked. Without any escort, the pope raced to the site of the disaster with Monsignor Montini, carrying two million lire for immediate assistance.

In the stricken area the pontiff walked through the rubble and the dead, hearing the cries of the injured. There he observed the destruction of the sixth-century Basilica of San Lorenzo, one of the most revered of Catholic churches. Its roof had fallen in, damaging the vestibule and destroying the facade. Near it bombs had ripped through a local cemetery, Campo Verano. There the graves of his own family were torn apart, and the tombs of the Pacellis were demolished.

Pius stood alone and wept over the site, and then prayed near the basilica. By then a crowd had come to see the pontiff—the bishop of Rome—and he comforted them while Montini distributed alms. Five years later, the pope was to remark, "Up to the last day of Our life, We will still remember this sorrowful meeting."[21]

After Mussolini was finally removed from power on July 25, 1943, the Vatican quickly asked the new government under Marshall Pietro Badoglio to declare Rome an open city. The British, however, planned more attacks on the city, but General Dwight Eisenhower limited such possible sites to airfields around Rome. Then on August 13, the Allies hit Rome again, seeking to destroy Fascist morale, and bombs fell, this time near the Basilica of St. John Lateran, the great church of the early popes.* Again Pius appeared to comfort the injured, giving the last rites, praying for the dead, and dispensing alms. As he moved through the site and its victims, his pressed white cassock became stained with blood.

As the Allied forces and the new Italian government tried to reach terms of an armistice, the Vatican pushed again for guarantees on the safety of Rome. On September 3 in Palermo, Sicily, an agreement was secretly signed, and General Eisenhower moved to parachute the 82d Airborne into Rome to protect it from the Nazis as the Allies invaded Salerno. The paratroopers, with the help from the Italian troops, would seize the airports and hold off the Nazi forces until the Allied armies advanced into Rome.

DEFENDER OF ROME

Uncertain of exactly what was happening, the Vatican on September 10 ominously sealed the entrance of Porta Santa Anna and closed the huge

---

*From the early years of the fourth century until the late fourteenth, the Lateran Palace, not St. Peter's, was the home of the Papacy. The palace took it name from its one-time owners, the Laterani, a wealthy Roman family.

doors of St. Peter's at noon — in part to protect the Jewish refugees inside the city-state. Meanwhile, the Nazis returned to Rome and took control. Two days later, the doors of St. Peter's were reopened, and the Vatican was now surrounded by Nazis, with the pope becoming a virtual prisoner. By then the pontiff seemed to stand alone, protected by only the token forces of the Swiss, Noble, and Palatine guards, who were, however, now armed with rifles and machine guns. Meanwhile, the Italian underground, unable to count on a quick Allied victory, took to guerilla warfare, sabotage, and even assassination to harass the Nazis and the Fascists.

Faced with the possibilities of considerable attacks on Jews and others, Pius had opened up Rome's churches, religious institutions, and the Vatican itself as asylums. Phony Vatican ration tickets, identity cards, and even papal certificates flooded the city and were oddly respected by the German forces, as the Vatican looked the other way at the numerous forgeries. In addition, the pope refused to acknowledge Mussolini's new "Italian Social Republic" (the Republic of Salò) — a puppet regime in Northern Italy supported only by Hitler's whim and forces. The Duce was at first furious with Pius, but later he quietly sent his mistress, Clare Petacci, to the Vatican to see if the pope would act as an intermediary with the advancing Allied armies. Pius, disgusted with Mussolini, reluctantly forwarded his request for sanctuary to General Eisenhower, who curtly rejected it. Later, on April 28, 1945, Mussolini and his mistress were killed by Italian anti-Fascists. On April 29, 1945, Hitler committed suicide. Pius went to his chapel and prayed for the repose of both of their souls.

With the Nazis in control of the city, they began a major assault on the Jews of Rome. On September 27, 1943, the chief rabbi of the city was informed that he had to deliver one million lire along with one hundred pounds of gold or the Nazis would begin attacks upon the Jewish community. The Jews were unable to raise that ransom, and the chief rabbi appealed directly to the pope. In less than a day, the Vatican treasurer was under orders to come up with the gold; probably the Church officials melted down their religious vessels to deliver the ransom.

Later, the Gestapo attacked the Jews again, and the Fascists ordered that Jews be rounded up in every province and sent to concentration camps. Pius vigorously protested privately to the German ambassador, and eventually, three weeks later, some of those victims were returned. Throughout the city, priests and nuns and members of religious orders smuggled Jews to places of sanctuary in churches, monasteries, and other institutions. It has been estimated that over five thousand Jews were granted asylum. Still of the twelve thousand members of the Jewish community there, less than half would survive.[22]

The Vatican newspaper called the persecutions "unreasonable, unchristian, and inhuman." When the Holy See recognized the Badaglio regime as a legitimate government of Italy, Mussolini was inflamed. Ironically, the Fascists were actually now being restrained by the Nazis from attacking church property and personnel. On November 5, 1943, the Vatican was hit by four fragmentation bombs, reportedly from a German-designed plane under the command of Fascist anticlerics. The Fascists, in violation of the Lateran Treaty, also surrounded a block of pontifical buildings invading the Lombard College, the Russicum, and the Jesuit Oriental Institute. Those buildings had provided asylum to the Italian resistance leaders and to beleaguered Jews.

Later, in February 1944, the Fascists attacked the famed Abbey of St. Paul's, which under the Lateran Treaty was acknowledged to be an extraterritorial property in possession of the Holy See. In February, the Allies hit Castel Gandolfo, the pope's summer residence. Also, on March 1, a German-designed plane bombed several more buildings, including one near the papal apartments. Rumors also circulated that the Nazis were trying to persuade the pope to leave the Vatican and take asylum in some area they controlled, probably Liechtenstein. The pope promptly rejected all such suggestions. However, he did call the cardinals together, and on February 9, 1944, told them that each was free to choose to leave the city. He, however, would never yield. The cardinals all pledged to stay. Later, the Allies launched a devastating and unnecessary attack which destroyed the historic abbey of Monte Cassino, home of the great Benedictine monastic tradition. The pope in sorrow, however, refused to criticize the advancing Allied armies, although he was privately dismissive of Roosevelt and his supposed guarantees.[23]

Throughout March, attacks on Rome continued, but at the end of the month the Nazis declared Rome an open city. As the war in southern Italy continued, Rome still seemed in serious jeopardy. On May 12 Pius publicly prayed to the Mother of God to protect the center of the Catholic world. By June, the Allied armies had reached Tivoli and the Alban Hills, and then on June 4 the Nazis withdrew. The Allies moved quietly into the city. The next day enormous crowds gathered to pay homage to Pius, who diplomatically praised both sides for sparing Rome. As for his own role, he simply said that he too had shared the sufferings and hardships of his fellow Romans. After the war, on June 27, 1948, a plaque was erected at the Basilica of San Lorenzo to the pope, calling him "Defensor Civitatis" — the Defender of the City.[24]

The persistence and activities of Pius XII in saving Rome from greater calamity were genuine acts of heroism. And his leadership in protecting the Jews of the city of Rome was his finest hour. He was the pope he dreamed himself to be and that the world demanded. But that record was to be clouded and compromised by a series of attacks against him and the Church for its alleged silence during the war, especially for his reticence in speaking out against the Nazis by name and his refusal to bear moral witness to the genocide against the Jews and others.

THE SILENCES OF PIUS

Such a discussion on those issues must recognize that foremost Pius XII was by training and by temperament a diplomat. His major role model for being the pope during a terrible war came from watching the activities of his patron, Benedict XV. As has been seen, Benedict emphasized the Holy See's impartiality and focused his efforts on humanitarianism and charitable activities; he strongly tried to stop Italy from entering the war; and he did not denounce the combatants by name. Pius XII was to follow those precedents generally. Benedict was also the target of vociferous energetic criticisms, but nothing compared to Pius — for World War II was more clearly a battle of good and evil, if one can call Stalin an ally of good. And just as Benedict was supposed to be sympathetic to the Central Powers because of their autocratic regimes, Pius was supposed to be an admirer of things German, which it was charged affected his judgment.

In fact, as noted, right after the invasion of Poland, Pius in his encyclical *Summi Pontificatus* did denounce the war and the concept of the totalitarian state. While some may have thought that reference was not pointed enough, the Nazis stopped publication of the letter in Germany, saying its effect on public opinion would be damaging to Germany. When the Poles remained unsatisfied with the encyclical, the pope had Vatican Radio report on the brutalization and terror in that land. In a meeting on January 1, 1940, the German ambassador to the Vatican protested about those criticisms, and Monsignor Montini, representing the pope, at first equivocated, and then countered with a litany of German attacks against the Church in Poland by the occupying Nazis.[25]

Still it is a matter of record that some Vatican officials seemed to welcome the Nazi attack on the Soviet Union, maybe hoping that each of the Church's opponents would exhaust or even annihilate one another. One Curial official, Archbishop Celso Constantini, blessed Italian soldiers about to do battle with the Soviets as forces who "at this decisive hour, defend our ideals of Freedom against the red Barbarism." After the German invasion in June 1941, Stalin indicated that he wished to "collaborate with the pope against the coercion and persecution of the Catholic Church in Germany." He insisted that he was really "a champion of Freedom, of Conscience, and Religion." And in fact, the Soviet government did loosen some of the restrictions on religious communities in its nation. But the Vatican knew better. When the pontiff was reminded of Stalin's sarcastic comment — "How many divisions does the pope have" — Pius responded, "Tell my son Joseph he will meet my divisions in Heaven."[26]*

The pope ended up, though, agreeing with Roosevelt that Hitler's regime was the more dangerous of the two and must be defeated militarily, even

---

*Stalin's remark came in a conversation with French Premier Pierre Laval, who asked him to remove restrictions on Catholics in the Soviet Union in order to conciliate the pope.

if it involved cooperating with the Soviets. Pius was still the realistic diplomat. The Germans in turn speculated that Pius's pro-Allied attitudes were really due to the fact that the Vatican was now financially supported mainly by American Catholics, and they even argued that he was sent special funds from President Roosevelt.[27]

Yet, in January 1942, at the Rio de Janeiro Conference, the Vatican encouraged the South American nations not to break off relations with the Axis powers as the United States had demanded.[28] And the Vatican in the same year was also still sending birthday greetings to Hitler, giving Reich Foreign Minister Joachim von Ribbentrop presents, and receiving high-ranking Nazi dignitaries. But by 1943, unconditional surrender was proclaimed, and it was clear that there would be no negotiated peace for either the Vatican or anyone else to broker.

Facing new realities on the battlefield, the Nazi leadership in late 1942 began to back off from its persecutions of the Church in Germany. Earlier in April, in Ankara, Turkey, German ambassador Papen had approached papal nuncio Archbishop Angelo Roncalli (later Pope John XXIII) about reexploring the pope's five-point peace plan.

In his Christmas address in 1942, the pope referred to the deaths and the "progressive extinction" of hundreds of thousands of people because of their race or nation, a clear allusion to the Jews. The Allies claimed that the pope should have named Germany specifically, while the Germans criticized the pope for his injustice to their people and for becoming "the mouthpiece of the Jewish war criminals." On January 24, 1943, Ribbentrop passed on a warning that if the Vatican renounced its traditional neutrality, the pope was to be reminded that "Germany does not lack physical means of retaliation." Pius's response was calm and to the point: in the struggle between the Church and the state, it was the state that would be defeated. The German ambassador, Diego von Bergen, concluded, "Pacelli is no more sensible to threats than we are."[29]

In July 1943, in his encyclical *Mystici Corporis Christi*, Pius denounced the "legalized murder" of the deformed, the insane, and the incurable as being acts against natural and divine law. Later, when he was told that the Germans could very well win the war and that he ought to trim his policies accordingly, Pius responded, "If the Germans win, it will mean the greatest period of persecution that Christians have ever known."[30]

What exactly the Holy See knew about the war and its brutalities is unclear. The papal nuncio in Berlin transmitted messages between the Vatican and the German episcopate in the regions of the old Reich and in Austria. Communications though in Poland and other occupied regions were not as reliable or frequent, and thus the Holy See was often uninformed about the full horrors of the war. Archbishop Adam Stefan Sapieha of Krakow, however, wrote the pope and described in gruesome detail the extent of Nazi terror in their concentration camps. Sapieha, whose archdiocese included Auschwitz, sent news to the Vatican in February 1942, indicating that those camps denied all human rights to inmates and were run in his words by those "who have no feelings of humanity." He did, though, warn against the publication of that information since it would give rise to further persecutions. Sapieha did not, though, specifically cite the suffering of the Jews in his region, of which he obviously was aware. The Vatican later explained that the documents sent by the Polish bishops were not published because the Holy See feared that the Catholic faithful would "become the victims of even worse persecution."[31]

In the same vein, Monsignor Domenico Tardini had explained previously to concerned individuals that a public condemnation of the German government would increase the persecution of the Catholic Church in Poland, and that it would prevent the Vatican from communicating with the Polish episcopate and thus impeding its charitable work there. Yet, on June 2, 1943, the pope in a speech broadcast in Polish praised the saints and heroes of that Catholic land and lamented the harsh treatment of the people there. The Polish leadership and hierarchy thus received the speech that they had so ardently desired.

Later, some historians were to allege that the German bishops blindly supported their nation's war effort, and that any Catholic who rejected military service during the war could count on little support from the clergy. Undoubtedly, the German hierarchy, like most of the other nations' bishops, supported its country as in World War I. Also there were indeed some Nazi-sympathizing clergy such as Bishop Franz Jósef Rarkowski, who characterized Hitler as "the shining example of a true warrior, the first and most valiant soldier of the Greater German Reich." Yet, as before the war, the majority of the Roman Catholic hierarchy were anti-Nazi, although many applauded the bravery of the soldiers of the Fatherland in its war against its enemies.[32]

In addition, some of the Catholic hierarchy did specifically attack Nazi-sponsored measures, such as euthanasia for the infirm and the mentally defective. Bishop Clemens von Galen, of Münster, a persistent critic of the Third Reich, also vigorously denounced the concentration camps and the Gestapo. Hitler, however, refused to respond to him, fearing that he might antagonize the Catholic population in his Reich and also in his armies. Alfred Rosenberg, the Nazi theorist, though, did write that after the war Bishop von Galen would be shot for his transgressions.

As early as July 6, 1942, the German episcopate had signed and published a pastoral letter which was read throughout the Reich, protesting the Nazi attacks on churches, schools, monasteries, and convents. And it criticized by name Rosenberg's book, *The Myth of the Twentieth Century,* which was labeled anti-Christian. Nazi leader Reinhard Heydrich warned that the bishops' letter was an example of "what a bitter and irresponsible enemy we have in the Catholic Church."

Despite those occurrences, some modern-day historians have continued to argue that the German clergy, like the pope, did not do enough because they were cowards and because they supported Hitler's war against Communist Russia. They were bold enough in protecting the Church's interests, it is claimed, but they said little about the extermination of the Jews. Unlike in France, Belgium, Holland, Italy, and elsewhere, the German clergy made little effort to hide Jews in church buildings and to give them overall critical aid and comfort.[33]

What is not emphasized, though, is that the strength of the Nazi war machine and the extension of its killing apparatus was not as firmly entrenched in the occupied regions of the democratic West as in Poland, the captured eastern states, and, of course, Germany itself. And some of these Eastern European regions had no historic experience with the liberating forces of the Renaissance, the Enlightenment, and the Napoleonic emancipation of the Jews; instead they had exhibited persistent and popular manifestations of anti-Semitism over the years.[34]

As has been seen, the Church and the Nazi regime reached some accommodation in some places. The Führer, remembering Bismarck's problems, chose not to unleash a full-scale attack on the Catholic Church, either inside or outside of Germany, fearing the allegiances of its faithful. The Church did oppose the Reich and many of its measures nearly everywhere, but its leaders often did not directly attack the Nazis by name for fear of making matters worse. Perhaps they should have. Still, accommodation is not collaboration, especially in a world of incredible brutality and terror.

The charges leveled against Pius XII for his silence are varied and have been given extensive publicity, not just by historians but in the popular media. The playwright Rolf Hochhuth, in his drama *The Representative* (or *The Deputy*), has dramatized those criticisms and argued that Pius was not only silent when he should have borne witness, but also that he was a coward and a man driven by the base motive of protecting primarily the Church's economic interests.[35]

Those who knew Pius took immediate umbrage when that play was presented, for that figure was not the man they recognized. Defenders of the dead pontiff, including prominent Jewish leaders, rejected out of hand the dramatic caricature. And those familiar with the historical record have a difficult time sustaining the notion that Pacelli the man was ever cowardly, even under the most frightening of circumstances. He was especially at that time a mild, easy-tempered, sensitive person, more given to diplomacy than events often warranted, and clearly not as confrontational as his predecessor. But in defense of the Church and tenets of basic decency, he was unwavering in his personal integrity.

However, the indictment against Pius is more complex than the simplistic critiques. The charges are these: (1) Pius XII never issued a direct condemnation of the unspeakable acts of war and violence carried out by the Germans and their accomplices; (2) his silences cannot be attributed to a lack of knowledge about the facts of what was going on; and (3) he chose to continue to remain silent even when he himself knew that he should take a stand and after victims and governments pleaded with him to speak out. By virtue of his very office and because of the moral role he assumed, the pope was required to bear witness to the truth, to give heart to the opponents of the Nazis, and to expose, regardless of the cost to his Church and to others, the gruesome record of genocide and countless other brutalities that the Nazis were implicated in.[36]

In reviewing those assertions, one can admit that, concerning the pope's alleged silence, it appears that initially he did emulate Benedict XV's impartiality during the First World War, which was the historic policy of the modern papacy during armed conflicts. But also, from the beginning, Pius departed from that policy, tone, and inaction. He immediately sympathized with the Polish nation after the invasion, and there was even an earlier rumor in August that the pope was flying to Berlin to face down Hitler and insist that he avert going to war.

Pius then became associated with those opposing the Nazi invasion of the Low Countries, even while he was silent about the Reich's aggression against Denmark and Norway, and said nothing about the Russian seizure of the Baltic States, Bessarabia, and Bukovina. The Vatican was also silent after Italian attacks on Greece in October 1940* and after the Axis invasion of Yugoslavia in April 1941.

As has been seen, the pope did lend his support to the German generals' plot to depose Hitler — not exactly a neutral or weak-kneed action. As the war progressed, there is no question that the pope focused his energies on protecting Rome, probably in part because of his enormous influence and leverage there. That effort does not mean that Pius neglected the conditions of the war elsewhere. It has also been alleged that the pope did not delineate for individuals the right or the duty to condemn unlawful wars and thus gave no solace to men wishing to avoid the draft. The implication seems to be that the Nazis and Fascists would have respected conscientious objectors, as in the democratic West. His nonresponse is seen as being in contrast to Pius XI, who during the Spanish Civil War instructed the faithful that any oath required by the Republican government which violated the interests and teachings of the Church was null and void. At Christmastime 1944, Pius XII proclaimed that there was indeed a duty to oppose aggressive war as a solution to international disagreements, but then it was charged that his concern was too late to have any effect. Also in 1944, the pope specifically referred to the horrors of the Dachau camp, but as they related to atrocities against Catholic clergy.[37]

---

*Some have countered concerning the aggressions of Fascism that the Lateran Treaty mandated that the Holy See would not intrude in Italian affairs.

Pius is also taken to task for not denouncing the disruption of Jewish communities that were reported as early as 1941, or the religious slaughter of Orthodox Christian Serbs in Croatia. It is also further charged that only later in 1945 did he speak out, and then it was to justify his own silence. One defense of Pius is that he did not know until after the war the full extent of the Nazi crimes. Surely that is true — the world and even well-briefed leaders did not fully comprehend the incredible horrors of what has become known as the Holocaust and related genocidal campaigns.

As early as May 12, 1942, however, Pius was informed about a system of *mass* extermination of Jews from Germany, Poland, and the Ukraine. One observer said that the pope "wept like a child at the news." When, however, the Vatican informed Archbishop Sapieha in Krakow of those findings, Sapieha tossed the message into a stove saying, "If I give publicity to this and it is found in my house, the head of every Pole would not be enough for the reprisals *Gauleiter* Hans Frank would order.... It is not just the Jews.... They are killing us all." It was probably this gruesome information that led to Pius XII's serious admonitions at Christmas 1942.

The absence of Vatican representatives in German-occupied countries and the forced isolation of the papal nuncio in Berlin did curtail somewhat the communications from those areas to the Holy See. Only by the end of the war did the world know of the total estimate of six million Jews and countless others who perished in these campaigns of genocide. Initially, when some of this information was relayed to the Vatican from Polish and German clergy, the Holy See and other governments argued it was extremely difficult to verify those atrocities.[38]

While the pope did not know the specific details of the Holocaust, he surely was aware, however, that a Nazi-organized system of concentration camps where Jews and others were being systematically slaughtered was being established. President Roosevelt, in a letter to the pope on October 22, 1941, specifically referred to the massacre of the Jews behind the German front in Russia as "surpassing everything known since the most brutal and historic epochs in mankind."

In fact, in 1942, the Vatican formally intervened in Slovakia to protect Jews destined for deportation and death in Poland. Thus, the generalizations that the Vatican was unaware of the workings of Nazi genocide and also that the pope was uncaring are both proven to be incorrect in this case and also in Romania.[39]

In the latter nation, the Holy See and its nuncio in Bucharest insisted that the government of Marshall Alexander Averescu curtail its harassment of Jews. In January 1942, Jewish groups in Cernuti (in the Ukraine) sent a direct appeal in Latin to the pope for help in their efforts not to be deported across the Dniester and Bug Rivers. In October, the Jewish leaders in Switzerland asked for the pope's intervention on behalf of Romanian Jews, and a similar request came from Jews of the Banat region. In February 1944, Archbishop Roncalli recorded that the grand rabbi of Jerusalem, Isaac Herzog, profusely thanked the Holy Father and the Vatican for their charity, but the rabbi also expressed his own concern for another fifty-five thousand Jews beyond the Dniester River in the dismal Transnistria region, then under Romanian occupation. The rabbi insisted to Roncalli, "The people of Israel will never forget the help brought to its unfortunate brothers and sisters by the Holy See and its highest representatives at this the saddest moment of our history."

Some historians have criticized not only Pius's alleged silence, but the general refusal of many Western leaders to care for Jewish refugees, to protest genocide, and to bomb the concentration camps. For them, there were few heroes in the circles of the influential. It is clear that the pope as well as other leaders in the West were knowledgeable about unspeakable acts and mass atrocities that were being perpetrated.[40]

As for Pius XII, the question continues to be why he did not specifically denounce the Nazis by name. Pius's defenders have noted, almost with relief, that some victims of the Nazi terror asked him not to speak out since it would only make matters worse. There is limited but clear verification for that observation. The archbishop of Krakow, the German bishops at Fulda in 1943, and several Jewish groups all urged silence. One historian, Carlo Falconi, has observed, however, that the decision on whether the pope should speak out "should not have been left to the weak and the most timorous."[41] That is a rather easy position to take twenty years after the war and sitting comfortably in one's study.

Still Falconi is correct in at least one regard: the pope was overwhelmed with appeals from the Allied powers, Jewish groups, and national emigres to break his supposed silence. In addition, some members of the Sacred College of Cardinals urged Pius to address the question of individual conscience and the war. As has been seen, Eugene Cardinal Tisserant also insisted that Pius XI would have been more aggressive and not so accommodating. Actually that characterization is incorrect. Even when Pius XI criticized the Nazi philosophy, he did so from the perspective of the harassments being directed at the Catholic faithful and did not directly address the early German assaults on law and in society aimed at the Jews. After non-Aryans were banned from public office and the legal profession in 1933, after the Nuremberg laws were passed in 1935, and after more attacks on the Jews in 1938, Pius XI was silent in each instance.

As for the Vatican's monumental efforts to alleviate suffering, the arguments of his critics are that Pius XII was expected to do more than perform humanitarian works and seek to ameliorate the problems of the persecuted behind the scenes. Falconi dissents again: "The challenge was not only one of speaking out so as to fulfill a duty toward his office, but of speaking out as a duty to Christianity and mankind. His refusal to speak out played into the hands of evil as this grew bolder and fiercer and became more provocative. Silence amounted to complicity with iniquity." As for Pius's far-reaching humanitarian efforts, they are also dismissed. "The Church is not the International Red Cross." The Church is meant to testify to the message of the Gospels and to guide the consciences of the faithful.

Throughout the war and after, the Vatican engaged in extensive humanitarian campaigns. The Holy See operated a far-flung information bureau that helped find the location of thousands of prisoners of war. And especially in the postwar years from 1945 to 1948, the Vatican supplied hundreds of convoys that sent food, medicine, and clothing into war-ravished Europe. The Pontifical Relief Commission spent billions of lire in its efforts.[42]

Years later, Pius's close aide and then cardinal, Giovanni Battista Montini, soon to be elected pope himself, revealed that Pius felt that a direct condemnation of the Nazis would have been both useless and harmful. Indeed, the pope made the same argument citing his experience in 1943, when the Vatican's publication of various documents led to difficulties with the Nazis. Later he observed to the cardinals that every statement he made had to be seriously weighed so as not to make the situation of the victims more grievous and insupportable.

Still it has been maintained that the pope seemed to confine his concerns to Catholic victims and did not extend them enough to Protestants, Orthodox Christians, or Jews. It is a matter of record that Catholic bishops, on their own and probably with Vatican approval, often openly criticized the Nazis and Nazi collaborators and did speak out against the deportation of Jewish communities, but many times they too were referring to Jewish Catholics.

As for the Nazi leaders themselves, they generally avoided attacking the Catholic hierarchy publicly, although there was apparently some discussion of actually kidnaping the recalcitrant pope. After Hitler suggested imprisoning him in the Wartberg in Upper Saxony, calmer minds prevailed. Pius must have contemplated that he might be deported to a concentration camp or denied his liberty. There was a rumor that he had given to the patriarch and archbishop of Lisbon, Gonçalves Cardinal Cerejeria, precise directions and authority in case he had to assume control of the Church if the pope were seized by the Reich's forces.

The exiled primate of Gniezno and Poznan, August Cardinal Hlond, also reminded the pontiff of religious prophecies from the saintly Don Bosco (1815–88) and others which had predicted another papal exile. Perhaps this was to be the time, he seemed to imply. Legend has it that when someone mentioned that he might indeed be arrested, Pius replied, "They will not take the pope, only Cardinal Eugenio Pacelli." Another story is that once when he was to hold an audience with numerous German armed forces in attendance, the pope decided to express publicly and unequivocally his strong condemnations of the violations of human liberties under Nazism. Then the diplomat came out, and he tossed the speech aside saying, "My duty is to simplify things, not to complicate them."[43]

BEARING WITNESS TO THE HOLOCAUST

It is clear that Pius himself agonized over his own silence. During the war, the thin pope reduced his food intake, his weight dropping to a dangerous 125 pounds, and he refused to heat his private apartment in the winter almost as penance and mortification. At times, the pope pushed *l'Osservatore Romano* and the more aggressive Vatican Radio to criticize the Germans — to say what he wanted to say but felt he could not. Oddly, when Pius did speak out and called Catholics "the spiritual heirs of the Jews," his address was not even reported by *l'Osservatore Romano*.

Thus, Pius the diplomat failed Pius the pastor, his critics charged. The Church and the world needed a clear voice, a steady moral compass, and the pope was not it. Even the non-Catholic clergy — led by the Anglicans — asked him early in the war to head up a religious league to condemn the conflict. He refused, lamely citing the Vatican's prohibitions against interfaith activity.

Was it that the pope was too diffident, too given to diplomatic gestures, too much of a Germanophile? Was it that the Church was and remains too anti-Semitic to appreciate the true horrors of the Jewish people? Perhaps, but still there are other views. Pinchas E. Lapide, the Israeli consul in Italy, concluded authoritatively, "The Catholic Church saved more Jewish lives during the war than all the other churches, religious institutions, and rescue organizations put together. Its record stands in startling contrast to the achievements of the International Red Cross and the Western democracies. . . . The Holy See, the Nuncios, and the entire Catholic Church saved some 400,000 Jews from certain death."

As noted, some fifty-five thousand Jews were finally permitted to leave Romania, in part due to the Vatican's pressure after it received an appeal from Grand Rabbi Herzog. When Pope John XXIII was profusely praised for his services in rescuing the Jews when he was apostolic delegate in Turkey, he went out of his way to say that he acted on "precise orders of Pius XII." Lapide reported how Pius in fact directly intervened with the Italian government in one instance he knew of to halt the transport of five hundred Jewish refugees from Czechoslovakia into Poland and Germany, and sure Nazi extermination. The pope fed them, clothed them, and even set up a school for their children. The Jews later wrote a letter of thanks for "your lively and fatherly interest in our physical, spiritual, and moral well-being."

In other instances, the pope intervened to give some Polish Jews Vatican credentials before they were shipped to the United States. In addition, Church officials ran a virtual "underground railroad" from Assisi through

Florence to the port city of Genoa for Jews disguised as Catholic pilgrims. It appears that also at least fifteen thousand Jews were housed at one time or another at Castel Gandolfo, the pope's summer residence.

In addition, throughout Italy, the Italian army virtually ignored Mussolini's order to participate in the genocidal campaigns instigated by the Third Reich. The Italians not only protected the Jews of their own nation, but foreign Jews as well, and 85 percent of that nation's Jewish population survived the war. Hannah Arendt has explained their protective reaction: it was "in Italy the outcome of the almost automatic general humanity of an old and civilized people." At a Jewish concentration camp in Ferramonti, Calabria, for example, the barracks were even divided into kosher and non-kosher areas, male prisoners were addressed as *signors,* and Jewish doctors were allowed to provide care for needy villagers surrounding the camp. The commandant in 1943 sought permission to release his prisoners before the Germans could move in and destroy them. Still some eight thousand Jews did perish, and some Italian police helped to send Jews to camps at Fossoli di Carpi (near Modena) and Bolzano, among others, where prisoners were transported to Auschwitz and Birkenau. In 1944, the American Jewish Welfare Board cited Pius and the Church's "Christian love" in incurring risks to save the Italian Jews.

In his private messages, the pope did indeed speak out against the atrocities. In April 1943, he bluntly told the Slovak government that the Holy See assumed that it would never forcibly remove the Jewish race from its nation, and that if it did, the Vatican would deplore publicly those moves. In June 1944, the pope directly called upon Admiral Miklós Horthy de Nagybánya to prevent attacks on the Hungarian Jews, which he did.[44]*

Pius did consider excommunicating those involved in genocide, but he concluded it would not only fail to help the Jews, but might even worsen their situation. No doubt he realized, he said, such a step would gain him the respect and praise of the civilized world, but what of the consequences for what he called "the poor Jews." Thus, the silence of Pius XII was really the moral dilemma of one man acting morally in an immoral world.

And yet, it must have still bothered him very deeply. A few weeks before his death in 1958, Pius gave a speech on Benedict XIV, Prospero Lorenzo Lambertini, the scholarly diplomat who many Church historians believe was the finest pope of the eighteenth century. Examining his record, Pius argued that his predecessor was "too conciliatory and docile...in the face of the vehement and excessive claims of the secular courts." He concluded, if "his compliance toward the King of Prussia can be explained by the higher aim of not wishing to worsen the situation of the Catholics in

---

*In neighboring Bulgaria, the regime refused after March 1943 to surrender its Jews in "old Bulgaria," but those in Bulgarian zones of occupation in Thrace and Macedonia were given up to the SS.

that state," the concessions accepted in his concordats with the courts of Sardinia-Piedmont, Naples, and Spain "seem really extraordinary and outside all tradition."[45] Perhaps he had decided to turn to history for some interesting precedents, or perhaps his own record still troubled him so. At times, diplomacy is really not the highest moral ground from which to look out on.

The final estimates are that over sixty million people lost their lives because of World War II — twenty-five million in the U.S.S.R. and fifteen million in China alone. The end of the war did not spell just the triumph of the democratic West; it brought forth as the Vatican feared a resurgence of the world stature and might of the Soviet Union. Decimated economically by the Nazi onslaught and by its own counterattacks, the Russians became nonetheless a military superpower. The price of their participation in the war was control of the Eastern European bloc, meant by the Soviets as a buffer and as a collection of forced allies for the Bolshevik state. Some angry Europeans and Americans later claimed that Roosevelt in particular had "sold out" Poland and Eastern Europe to Stalin. In fact, it was the Russian armies that won and kept control of those regions.

WAGING THE COLD WAR

For Pius, it was what he feared all along. Now the pope would join with the West in an anti-Soviet alliance, throwing his guarded support to the United States and also interjecting himself into partisan politics, especially to stave off Communist election victories in Italy. Pius was to become a Cold Warrior. Amid all those difficulties, he also had to deal with the accusations of close ties between the resurgent Mafia and the Catholic Church in Sicily. To his horror, he found evidence of friendships between the archbishop of Palermo, Ernesto Cardinal Ruffini, and Mafia dons, and also of the corruption by some elements of the Franciscan order on the island.

After the war, the pontiff became more of a dedicated teacher who spoke, wrote, and encouraged study on a variety of subjects, many of them involving contemporary ethical questions. He did not give vague homilies, but delivered carefully researched papers and crafted speeches on an incredible range of topics. It was almost as if he transformed himself from the sensitive novice pontiff of the terrible war into a more hardened and jaded leader, and in the process fought that transformation by returning to theology, Mariology, and moral pronouncements.

After the war and as the years passed, Pacelli became more isolated, more regal; in the process his government became highly personalized, traditional, and centralized. It was said that he and five hand-picked Italian cardinals — the so-called Vatican Pentagon* — ran the Roman Catholic

---

*They included Nicola Canali, Giuseppi Pizzardo, Clemente Micara, Alfredo Ottaviani, and

Church in those postwar years. Even his devoted housekeeper, Sister Pasqualina, worried that Pius "just didn't seem to care as much as he should about his holy image in the eyes of his subordinates." When critics complained of Pius's haughty ways, a powerful Curial official, Alfredo Cardinal Ottaviani, counseled patience: "We are old soldiers.... We must serve the Church blindly." And then he would smile and remark, "Popes pass, but the Curia lives on."

To counteract those impressions of aloofness and disregard, his staff and associates pictured him as really a religious mystic, a saintly presence given to apparitions and visions. And as they did, Pius became still more remote, rigid, and increasingly divorced from the currents of change around him. By the time his successors reacted, those currents became a tidal wave which the popes following him have tried with only limited success to navigate.

First though, one must view the papacy in the context of the Cold War era. It is a hackneyed observation that Catholicism and Communism share some attributes, especially in their pervasive ideologies, their appeal to true believers, and the tendency to see things in extreme rather than in moderating hues. The Church also had sufficient evidence after World War II of the persecutions that Christians were facing in Communist countries.

Since Pius IX in 1846, the Church had indeed historically opposed the materialistic atheism of Communism, its disdain for religion in general, and its advocacy of abolishing private property, including ecclesiastical possessions. In 1947, the early Cold War period, Pius XII wondered almost wistfully why the Communist propagandists hated him so. He should have known the answer. He directly intervened in the Italian elections in 1948 to prevent a Communist victory, resurrected Catholic Action, gave his blessing to Catholic or Christian democratic parties, and directly excommunicated Communists.[46]

He proved to be a most formidable foe of the Marxist states, and the United States tried to exploit those feelings. In 1947, President Harry S Truman advocated unsuccessfully a united Christian front to affirm "those religious and moral principles on which we all agree." Behind the Iron Curtain, Communists on the defensive linked the Church with capitalist imperialists and with the semifeudal social and political structures still prevalent in parts of Eastern Europe. It was also charged that the Catholic Church had hidden or helped former Nazis and Nazi sympathizers.[47]

The Vatican was not paranoid in its judgments of what was going on in those unstable regions. In small Albania, the Catholic Church's organization was destroyed and the clergy virtually wiped out. By 1944, three priests and one elderly bishop were alive and free. In Yugoslavia, the Com-

---

Marcello Mimmi. Some commentators mention Domenico Tardini and Ernesto Ruffini as well.

munist regime of Marshall Josip Tito struck with a vengeance citing both the Vatican's alleged indifference to Fascism there and the Church's ties to Germanic upper classes. By 1949, the Vatican estimated that four hundred Yugoslav clerics had been killed; three hundred imprisoned; one-quarter of the churches closed; and most parochial schools and other Catholic activities suspended. Tito had Archbishop Alojzije Stepinac of Zagreb, the Catholic prelate in that nation, put on trial. He was charged with collaborating with the Ustashia regime there, and with the Germans and the Italians, during the war. Stepinac had in fact rather belatedly criticized the government in 1943 for the slaughter of Orthodox Christian Serbs who had refused to convert to Catholicism. Finally he was sentenced to sixteen years in prison, and then released in 1951. Pius made him a cardinal in 1952. Gradually though, Yugoslavia needed the West's support for its heretical political split from Russia, and Tito eased up on the persecutions.

In Romania, the government turned to a more legalistic basis for persecution as it outlawed Church services and hounded the clergy. In neighboring Bulgaria the Church was, however, generally left alone. In Hungary, churchman József Mindszenty was tried in 1948, as was his successor, Archbishop Josef Grosz. Mindszenty was charged with treason, black market activity, and supporting the restoration of the Hapsburg monarchy. After his incarceration, the physically weakened prelate "confessed" and was sentenced to life imprisonment for treason. During the Hungarian uprising in 1956, he sought asylum in the U.S. Embassy.* Still the regime did not close parochial schools or churches, and in 1950 an independent group of Hungarian bishops negotiated an agreement with the state on their own. Later, though, the government continued its anticlerical campaign and suspended four religious orders.[48]

In Czechoslovakia, the government faced extensive Catholic peasant resistance when it began its campaign of attacks. In Poland, the Church proved to be too strong for even the most determined Communist regime, and in divided Eastern Germany, the complicated military situation led to a muting of any extensive anticlerical campaign. The Vatican was to call the Church behind the Iron Curtain "The Church of Silence," and its designation added to the tensions of the Cold War.

Now with the war over, Pius XII began to reach out and more closely associate the Church with liberal democracy and representative institutions. Also, the pope had formed warm ties with FDR and his representatives; later President Truman sought to continue that association on a more formal basis, although he faced problems with the U.S. Congress on the issue. After intense opposition from Protestant leaders, the president withdrew

*After Vatican relations with the Communist regime improved, Mindszenty's presence in Hungary was an embarrassment to the Vatican, and in 1971 the Holy See had him moved to Rome. The next year he gave up the title of primate of Hungary.

the nomination of General Mark Clark to be permanent ambassador to the Vatican.[49]

As noted, in his Christmas message of 1947, the pope had warned against a Communist victory in the upcoming election in Italy and denounced those parties that denied God and the importance of liberty. Even with his enormous efforts, eight million Catholics still voted for the Communist-led coalition. Those denunciations probably did not affect Italian elections at all levels as much as hoped; in the municipal and regional elections in 1951, for example, the Communists actually improved a bit their electoral count from 1948.

Pius though was undeterred. Six times in five years the pope expressly ordered that Catholics who supported the Communists be excommunicated. He excommunicated those involved in the trials of Stepinac, Mindszenty, and Groesz. He excommunicated those involved in the banishment from Prague of Archbishop Josef Beran and those who organized a separate Czech Catholic Action group, thus confusing the faithful. He also excommunicated those Catholics anywhere who were willfully active in the Communist ranks. The pope was called by assorted critics un-Christian, a tool of imperialism, an ardent enemy of the U.S.S.R., a provocateur, and a peddler of hate.[50]

As noted, Pius had been the first person ever to assume the papacy who had visited the United States. He appeared at press conferences, transversed the continent, and spoke directly to the president of the United States right after the latter's landslide reelection in 1936. When Church prelate Francis Spellman attacked the president's wife, Eleanor, Pacelli (then pope) directed that the attacks cease. In general, the Church in America was headed at that time by obedient men who were more builders than intellectuals, and by 1950 the Church had grown to twenty-seven million members, with thousands of churches and schools. The old immigrant Church had become stable, wealthier, and more self-confident. Observers noted that Pius seemed to relax more with American pilgrims than other groups at the Vatican, and he seemed to understand the importance of this new boisterous world power.[51]

In 1946, Pius called a rare consistory and named thirty-two new cardinals, four of whom were from the United States, including John Glennon of St. Louis (who died in Ireland on the way home), Samuel Strich of Chicago, Edward Mooney of Detroit, and most importantly Francis Spellman of New York. Spellman, who was a close associate of Pacelli's and who helped finance the Vatican during the war and in the immediate postwar years, had been offered even the secretary of state position by Pius, although Spellman seemed to express no real enthusiasm. The pope also named Americans to important diplomatic positions in the Curia and encouraged Americans to head Catholic orders, including the Capuchins, the Vincentians, the Marianists, the Sisters of Notre Dame, the Congregation of the Resurrection of Our Lord Jesus Christ, and two branches of the Franciscans and the Carmelite Fathers.[52]

Like most Europeans, the Curia and the pope had real reservations about the sudden assumption to great power status of those political parvenus, the Americans. The war ended with that nation and its president, Harry S Truman, unleashing a wave of incredible destruction, opening up the atomic age. Catholic theologians traditionally had made a distinction between justifiable and unjustifiable wars based on several criteria, including the important requirement that the belligerents differentiate between combatants and noncombatants. The use of nuclear weapons did not permit that, as it rained terror on adults and children, women and men alike, first in Hiroshima and then in Nagasaki. But certainly that age-old distinction between combatants and noncombatants had been badly breached before, in the terrible fire bombings stretching from London to Dresden to Tokyo. The constraints of rational theology and its practitioners such as Pius XII could not keep up with the new brutalities of mechanized and aerial warfare.

After the war, the anti-Nazi alliance quickly disintegrated as the Cold War pitted the Soviet Union and its allies against the democratic West led by the United States of America, thus changing the geopolitical realities. And the Vatican became for the Communists a fifth column behind the Iron Curtain and a staunch foe outside of those regions. Protestant America thus ended up becoming the new Austro-Hungarian Empire — a shield behind which the Holy See and its causes could seek protection. In the United States, the Catholic hierarchy led by Spellman became the most vociferous constituency in the anti-Communist crusade during the Cold War and the McCarthy period. In fact, Senator Joe McCarthy was a Catholic and had been inspired in his first reckless anti-Communist charges by a priest who saw that as a popular and viable issue.[53]

Truman's major initiatives — NATO, the Marshall Plan, Point Four, aid to Greece — were all aimed at curtailing the Soviet Union's reach in Europe. As noted, the pope, the Italian clergy, and Italian-American relatives all worked to prevent Italy from going Communist in the free elections in the late 1940s. Pius had not struggled to preserve Rome and to ameliorate the war conditions in his own land to see it fall now to the new barbarians, the cousins of the Bolsheviks. Gone was the compromising Pius XI, who undercut the Christian-oriented Popular Party, gone was the subtle diplomacy of Benedict XV on matters political, gone were the smug equivocations of Leo XIII about democratic institutions. Pius XII saw the new political and social realities, and he responded very decisively and fairly quickly.

The Holy See continued to be an American ally in the Cold War throughout Pius's reign. Spellman, though, fell somewhat out of favor after he misappropriated a gift from the Eisenhower administration when he was attempting to curtail the activities of the charismatic television preacher Monsignor Fulton Sheen. Sheen in New York was the chief fundraiser for the missionaries and found that his superior Spellman had billed the organization for powdered milk that was being given by the United States government at no cost. Pius was forced into the conflict and found that his old friend Spellman had lied to him about the nature of the transaction, and for a long time his influence was diminished. Thus reputations are made and broken in the closed world of Vatican politics.[54]

THE REGAL ASCENDANCY

In that period of the late 1940s and 1950s, Pius XII also reasserted his own lifetime reverence for the Blessed Virgin Mary by proclaiming the doctrine of Mary's Assumption into heaven body and soul. His proclamation was based on the foundations of papal infallibility — the first time such a claim had been made since Vatican I.

Thus Pius, freed from the constraints imposed during the war, moved to extend his teaching sway over a huge number of areas. And rather than simply resort to short statements of religious blessings for this group or that, he spent hours and days actually researching professional, scientific, occupational, and athletic sources so that he could talk to people in ways that reflected their own special interests.

One of his associates, Cardinal Tardini, observed that he once visited the pope in 1958 to find him sitting behind a collection of books dealing with the natural gas industry. Pius noted that he was to address a group from that area and that he was researching the subject! That observation could be seen as humorous, but in fact the story testifies to a rare public and religious leader who resorted not to the usual banalities, but who chose to speak with some authority on the interrelationships of industry and ethics in particular economic areas. Pius did the same when talking with athletes, citing the benefits and salutary aspects of exercise on the spiritual life. He conversed with newly married couples with ease, celebrated patron saint days with well-grounded biographical data, and reached out to present the Church to the world in rather informed directions.

In some ways the very traditional pontificate of Pius XII helped lay the groundwork for the more open approach characterized and popularized by John XXIII. Some of his other encyclicals and speeches pointed the way for new directions that eventually found their culmination in the Ecumenical Council, Vatican II. Using some of the older theological formulations, Pius began to make some tentative steps toward new definitions of the role of the Church, the liturgy, and the importance of biblical studies.[55]

In 1943, in the midst of the painful calamities of war, he issued a letter called *Mystici Corporis Christi* — the Mystical Body of Christ. That long encyclical argued that the Church is the embodiment of the Mystical Body of Christ, with Our Lord as founder, head, support, and Savior. Christ rules his Church through his vicar, the pope. This union is vastly superior to any physical or mortal body, as we are joined to God by faith, hope, and charity. The pope then concluded by condemning false mysticism, quietism, and the downgrading of Christ. While it surely did not help lay the groundwork for ecumenical ties to other churches, it did reaffirm the faith during the worst years of the war. In a more contemporary view, Pius in another letter, *Mediator Dei,* issued a plea for more active participation in the sacred liturgy of the Church. The pope even called for the use of vernacular languages instead of Latin on some occasions and pushed aside reverence for things simply because they had "the aroma of antiquity."[56]

Again, in the midst of war on September 30, 1943, Pius issued an important new charter called *Divino Afflante Spiritu.* With a sense of confidence, he urged Catholic scholars to use the findings of recent archaeological excavations to understand the contexts in which the Sacred Scriptures were written and first interpreted. Pius encouraged scholars to return to the original texts, informed by a knowledge of biblical and other Oriental languages and by textual criticism. He concluded that the real meaning of a biblical passage cannot always to be determined by the rules of grammar and theology and that it can be legitimately enriched by understanding history, archaeology, and other sciences.

Pius also had a great interest in the Eastern churches, and he encouraged its different liturgies, even in the Vatican. On March 12, 1946, in a ceremony marking the anniversary of his coronation, he called on the Armenian cardinal, Pietro Agagianian, to celebrate a pontifical Mass in the Armenian rite in the Sistine Chapel.[57]

Several times Pius also reached out to the Chinese Catholic Church, praising its ancestral customs and also beatifying in 1946 twenty-nine Chinese martyrs. In the same year, he named Thomas Tien-Ken-Sin a cardinal. Able to communicate by radio, the pope conveyed his greetings to fourteen Eucharistic Congresses, two national conventions, and six Marian Congresses in the period from May 1939 to September 1947. He also proclaimed 1950 a Holy Year and granted indulgences to Catholic pilgrims who came to Rome, a splendid boon to the economy of his native city as well as a sign of substantial religious piety.

During those years, Pius continued his interest in history and archaeology and declared to the École Française in 1948 that he enjoyed scientific discoveries in those fields. He concluded confidently that the Church had nothing to gain by spreading false legends and nothing to lose by finding out what really happened in the past. Back in 1935, Pius XI had named Pacelli the chancellor of the Pontifical Institute of Christian Archaeology and his fascination remained unabated.

In his pronouncements, Pius seemed to be especially drawn to those two important lay professions: law and medicine. As for the former field, he had been trained in both canon and civil law, had been offered a position on the faculty at Catholic University of America in canon law, and was previously a professor of public law at the Accademia dei Nobili Ecclesiastici. Both he and his family had a special regard for the legal profession.

His most interesting public statements, though, are in the very complex areas of biomedical ethics. He reminded physicians both of the importance of life and the need to recognize that beyond that life is immortality. But he was also rather sophisticated and sensitive in dealing with issues such as euthanasia, the technological aspects of prolonging life, and the very difficult issue of when life ends, or should end. For anyone who has faced that last issue, Pius offered both guidance and solace on the questions of what are the proper limits of treatment.

His teaching emphasis was best expressed in October 1947 when he told the International Radio Conference, celebrating the fiftieth anniversary of Marconi's discoveries, "How great is man that he is able to conquer and dominate the forces of nature. But that same human mind should understand that man himself did not make what he discovered."[58]

But science had its limits. On February 21, 1943, the pope talked knowledgeably about the possibilities of the new discovery of atomic energy. But two years later, the United States dropped bombs on Hiroshima and Nagasaki. The pope then had to express his grave concern that that source of energy should be used only for peaceful purposes.

After the war, Pius also became directly involved in international affairs and political affairs. In 1948 he supported the idea of uniting Europe into a federation — probably seeing it as a restraint on nationalism and war — and he urged that new Europe should be based once again on the Christian religion and the values of Christian civilization. As noted, the pope in 1945 had urged a resurrection of Catholic Action in Italy, and then several years later he insisted that citizens had a duty to vote, that those who did not sinned grievously, and that while one should vote one's conscience, a person should not support those who did not respect the rights of God and of souls and the welfare of all.[59]

The postwar world brought with it increasing wealth and luxury in the West, and consequently income flooded the Vatican investment portfolio. Back in 1942, Pius XII had founded a bank called the Institute for the Works of Religion. Staffed by a small group of trained men, the bank moved Vatican assets quietly and quickly across national boundaries, looking for the highest rate of return and the most secure investment opportunities, including U.S. war plants. The rapid increase in land prices and speculation in construction hit Rome, and the Vatican took its liquid cash and invested in both Italy and abroad. Soon the Vatican would find itself having to deal with financial speculation schemes, mismanagement of its resources, and allegations of corruption. When Tardini and some members of the Sacred College of Cardinals, including Tisserant, asked for a complete financial statement, their request was refused by the pope.[60]

The Vatican and the Curia proved to be less adventuresome in nontemporal areas. As has been seen, the pontiff tried to emphasize a positive view of the Church, especially in *Mystici Corporis Christi* and in his biblical studies charter, *Divino Afflante Spiritu*, which seemed to welcome the new scholarship. He also revised age-old regulations on fasting to encourage easier reception of the Eucharist, permitted evening Masses, and inaugurated a new Holy Week liturgy. But in 1950, Pius seemed to draw back, and in the encyclical *Humani Generis* he retreated from such innovations. And more consequentially, the Curia focused its attentive criticisms on theologians and scholars who were asking for a return to scriptural, patristic, and traditional sources instead of following the rigidities of contemporary Thomism and pat formula scholarship. Only with Vatican II would many of these scholars reemerge as respected figures in their own Church.

The pope followed up his restrictive encyclical with a proclamation of the dogma of the Assumption on November 1, 1950, issuing in the eyes of some a backhanded rebuke to those who emphasized the importance of having a historical base for dogmatic expressions. That was followed by the Marian Year in 1954, an occurrence meant to underscore the importance of the Blessed Virgin in the life of the Church.

As the years passed by, the pope became more rigid and personal in his governing of the Church. He disliked, for some reason, having to make appointments and promotions, and thus held only two consistories for the creation of new cardinals in seventeen years — in 1946 and in 1953. Tardini said that Pius simply avoided meeting with high-ranking ecclesiastical dignitaries because he was afraid to say no to their ill-conceived requests. Pius, though, did increase the international representation in the Sacred College so as to emphasize the Church's universality. But as befitting a man born and bred in the Curial world, he made no real attempt to either promote collegiality or to challenge the restrictive behavior of that small group.

In 1954, the pope became seriously ill, suffered a bout of uncontrollable hiccups, and experienced serious malnutrition, but eventually rallied and recovered. After his recovery, Pius concentrated power more in the Secretariat of State, creating a titular theologian and a jurist who reported to him. He controlled the powers of the bishops, and thus allowed the rise of stronger Curial departments at their expense. As he once said in 1944, he wanted not collaborators but executors to do his will. At the same time he showed less and less interest in what the departments were doing. The consequence of those decisions and neglect was to increase frustrations among the bishops and the lower clergy — ingredients that probably led to some of the divisiveness of Vatican II. He required senior Vatican officials to address him on their knees, including reporters of *l'Osservatore Romano,* and insisted that prelates walk backward when they were leaving his presence. Except for his nephews, Pius saw his family now only once a year on Christmas afternoon.[61]

To promote his views of a powerful papacy, Pius moved to aggrandize, if not sanctify, the leadership post that he held. He led the way to renew efforts to discover St. Peter's tomb beneath the Vatican Basilica, and he was the first pontiff to invoke infallibility, a doctrine proclaimed at the Vatican Council in 1870. Pius pushed incessantly for canonizing his predecessors: in 1952, he beatified Pius X and canonized him in 1956; he beatified Innocent I in 1956; resurrected the cause of Blessed Innocent V in 1943 and of Gregory X in 1944; and lastly, initiated the cause of Pius IX in 1954. The papacy took on a new and indelibly vigorous impression in order to upgrade the office, and in the process Pius XII himself.

During his illness in 1954, his housekeeper and guardian, Sister Pasqualina, contacted Cardinal Spellman to come to Rome immediately and prevent Pius from publicizing his alleged vision of Christ during his illness.* They feared that he would embarrass himself, but Pius had already celebrated his good fortune publicly. Vatican friends and even the Vatican Radio talked openly of his apparitions and signs. Pius thus became more of a mystic and less of an administrator of his Church. Around him was a plethora of advisors who created a comforting household. Central was a Bavarian nun, Sister Pasqualina Lenhart, who first met Pacelli when he was nuncio in Munich at the age of forty-two, and she was twenty-four. For the next forty years, he was her whole world. On household matters, Pius was obedient to the quiet younger woman who in turn dedicated her life to his comfort and ease. She became known to her foes as "Virgo Potens" — the powerful virgin, an important advisor to the leader of the Church.[62]

As his last years passed, Pius continued his speeches and discussions in a variety of languages and on a variety of topics — politics, medicine, sports, marriage, footwear, communications, mineral extraction, surgery, cinema, animal slaughter, tourism, and a host of other areas. Sometimes, even the Curia was startled at his observations, as when in 1951 he talked on the limitations of births, periodic continence, sterilization, and artificial insemination.[63]

Frail, but committed to his duties, the pope had received injections of "living cell" therapy from a Swiss gerontologist, Dr. Paul Niehans, who made it from finely ground tissue from freshly slaughtered lambs. Those treatments were supposed to have contributed to his ability to carry on, although some did raise questions about the ethical implications of such treatments. On October 3, 1958, however, the Vatican reported that the pope had a serious illness, and eight days later he died, to the surprise of

---

*Pius had considered resigning if he became too infirm to carry on his duties.

many informed observers. The newspapers had previously started printing stories of Vatican scandals, some involving Pius's own nephews, and they were soon declared personae non gratae by Curia figures. Sister Pasqualina, who had been so rude to even powerful cardinals, was given twenty-four hours to vacate her apartment. The shadow government — the pope's last court — was coming to an abrupt end.

The media would intrude even in death, with its television cameras entering into his sick room, and with his personal physician (really an eye doctor), Riccardo Galeazzi-Lisì, speculating about the details of his patient's demise. One cardinal, the patriarch of Venice, noted in his diary in a matter-of-fact way and without recourse to emotion the final reputed hours of Pius XII. He also related that there had been a new method of embalming employed by the papal physician that left the pope's body in such a sorry state that bystanders could hear loud popping sounds from inside the casket as the remains of Pius decomposed before his final interment and turned the pontiff's skin green.[64]

For generations the Pacelli family had dedicated itself to the papacy — the papacy in triumph and in exile and distress. Their gentle, sensitive son assumed that high position in the most terrible of circumstances, and he moved from one leadership style to another — the consummate diplomat, the careful pontiff, the preaching theologian. In each, he served the Church in ways that were oftentimes innovative and dedicated.

But he sought to place around him, as he admitted, not colleagues but people to execute his will. The Church he loved seemed to be regal, settled, and serene, but underneath his throne there were currents of criticism and dissent that were seeking expression. That phenomenon is not new in the history of the papacy. What was new though was that the agent of change, the water carrier of reform, would be a successor pope — another diplomat not favored by the Curia, an old man meant to be a transitional figure between the rigidities of Pius XII and another generation of safe men waiting for their place in the Vatican sun. But Pius's successor would change the very landscape in a relatively short period of time, and in the process the world of Eugenio Pacelli suddenly became very dated and very remote.

CHAPTER SEVEN

JOHN XXIII
AND THE PROMISE
OF AGGIORNAMENTO

After Pius died, it was said that his influence would last for over a century. In fact, it ran its course in two years. The austere, intellectual, regal Pacelli would be replaced by a homely, overweight seventy-six-year-old nondescript cardinal who caught the international public imagination and left his positive impression on the Church in a very short period of time. No pope in this century has proven to be so popular so quickly. The other popes in this study, including even at times the crafty Leo XIII, have been dedicated and committed men who were insistent on keeping society somewhat at arm's length from the Catholic Church. They were in one sense traitors to the world — to its values, its élan, its sense of secular progress. That distance is the strength of the Roman Catholic Church, and that is its profound weakness. Pope John was an exception to that approach, for he embraced with love and vitality the world and its diverse peoples. With that receptivity, he created enormous enthusiasm and goodwill and also unwittingly undercut in some ways the traditions and authority of the Church for which he lived his life.

THE APOSTLE OF GOODWILL

As the cardinals arrived for the conclave, they were faced with an embarrassing spectacle. As noted, the new embalming techniques of the pontifical physician, Dr. Riccardo Galeazzi-Lisì, on Pius's body were deficient. The odor of his remains and the eerie popping sounds from his casket conveyed a sense of immediate decomposition and decay that nauseated the papal guards near it. Some bitter critics said it was a fitting metaphor for the last years of a declining pontificate.[1]

The very organization of the Roman Curia had been neglected in many ways. There was no cardinal chamberlain, and there had been no secretary of state since 1944; the number of cardinals was at a low point of fifty-five, and nearly half of the cardinals (nineteen) were seventy-eight years of age or over.* Pius was both an authoritarian and a mystic, a centralizer and a person who cut himself off from the congregational chieftains in Rome who populated the Curia.[2]

Because of the advanced age of the College of Cardinals, the conclave faced a real problem with succession. There was, however, a strong minority movement that advocated reforming the Church; some of those changes in liturgy and biblical scholarship had been initiated by Pius himself. In fact, it was speculated that Pacelli avoided dealing with the Curia because even he found it too conservative! The hero of some of the progressives was Giovanni Battista Montini, the archbishop of Milan, but he was deliberately not made a cardinal by Pius, and the tradition of choosing from those ranks was too powerful to be ignored by the conclave.[3]

The Pacelli wing of the College of Cardinals controlled through various appointments and interlocking relationships the major departments, congregations, and agencies of the Roman Curia. They had no intention of losing those positions of privilege and power, which they identified with the traditions of Catholicism that had hardened since the Council of Trent which ended four centuries before. They too wished reform, but the reform they desired was more power to curtail the experiments, the dissenting views, and the unorthodox opinions of the national episcopates and their theologians, especially in the non-Latin countries of continental Europe. Their major candidate at first was Giuseppe Siri, the cardinal from Genoa, who at fifty-two, however, was deemed by some much too young for the papacy.

Thus there was a generational problem — the younger candidates did not have large followings or much experience — and so behind closed doors the conclave turned to a man some viewed as a transitional figure, Angelo Giuseppe Roncalli, the patriarch cardinal of Venice. Roncalli was an amiable, seemingly simple, pious churchman, one who had performed well in diplomatic positions and who conveyed a sincere impression of good humor and general toleration. He reminded people of a benevolent uncle, an easygoing duffer, the classic European country priest. Smarter than he seemed, Roncalli confidentially told one French colleague that he would be chosen pope if the conclave were looking for a man with "common sense."[4]

---

*Only sixteen of the current cardinals had been in attendance at the previous conclave in 1939; for the 1958 election, Cardinal Mindszenty of Hungary and Stepinac of Yugoslavia were not permitted by their governments to attend, and Cardinals Constantine and Mooney of Detroit, Michigan, died just before the balloting.

When his diary, *The Journal of a Soul,* was published after his pontificate, it was criticized for its lack of critical introspection, its seemingly naive expressions of faith, and its remarkable confidence in the strange ways of God. All his life Roncalli placed his career and his good fortune in the hands of the Almighty. He said he wished to be above all a good and obedient priest. He wrote in his diary, "I intend to use joviality, pleasantness and happiness with all persons, but to act in seriousness and modesty, especially with those who have mistreated me." It seems difficult in the latter part of the twentieth century to understand such a man, but it was such people who had built and maintained the Catholic Church through heresies, revolutions, plagues, and its own insolence.[5]

Angelo Roncalli was born on November 25, 1881, in a small village near Bergamo, to a humble and religious family. After his election to the Chair of St. Peter, it seemed remarkable to reporters that his relatives were still tilling the fields as they had done for generations.[6] What else should they do? That was their living. There were thirteen children from the Roncalli marriage, and they lived the life of simple sharecroppers with half of their produce going to pay their landlords. Angelo once quipped, "There are three ways of ruining yourself — women, gambling, and agriculture. My father chose the dullest."[7]

His was really an extended family that at times expanded to thirty people. The family was poor, hardworking, and undemonstrative emotionally, and Roncalli was to say that his elders were "a bit surly but truly good and worthy folk."[8] Later as pope, he would somewhat defensively explain to his family why he did not grant them titles, saying he did not wish to lift them out of their "respected and contented poverty." On another occasion, he observed that he owed his priestly vocation to his family "which was not as poor as some like to make out, but was above all rich in heavenly gifts." In his youth, Angelo was especially close to his pious great uncle, Zaverio, and at the age of ten he entered the neighboring junior seminary. It seemed that he never desired to be anything but a priest.[9]

Six months after his ordination in 1904, Roncalli became the secretary to Monsignor Giacomo Radini-Tedeschi, the canon of St. Peter's and an ally of Mariano Cardinal Rampolla, the secretary of state of Leo XIII. Years later, Roncalli as pope recalled that his patron was "my spiritual father,...the Pole Star of my priesthood." Radini-Tedeschi, who became bishop of Bergamo, called then "the most Catholic of cities," proved to be a powerful church reformer in that small ecclesiastical universe and a strong supporter of laboring people and unions.[10] In 1905 Roncalli also became acquainted with Carlo Andrea Cardinal Ferrari, the powerful archbishop of Milan who was deeply distrusted by Pius X. Soon Roncalli developed an interest in one of Ferrari's predecessors, the Council of Trent reformer St. Charles Borromeo, who had also been a cardinal of Milan in the sixteenth century.[11]

Historian Hannah Arendt has argued that many of his contemporaries thought Roncalli a bit "stupid, not simple, but simple-minded." But in fact he wedded his own commitment to obedience with the pride of a self-made man and the self-confidence of a person who is content to do God's will here on earth.[12] Like many leaders, he had a clear sense of himself, a good sense of timing, and an almost innate feel for the right gesture or the inspiring phrase.

Despite the fact that Roncalli was a cautious and pious priest, he nearly got caught up in the web of Modernist denunciations so approved by Pius X. Such accusations could have ruined a career of much promise, and Roncalli quickly scurried away from powerful forces that dealt in guilt by association. Some have concluded in retrospect that Roncalli was easily cowed by that near mishap, but such is the problem of living in a closed ecclesiastical society. It is probably for this reason that John XXIII was remarkably permissive in dealing with unorthodox and dissident theologians during his term as pope. Years later as pope, he asked to see the Curia file on himself, and to his chagrin he saw a reference to his alleged Modernist associations. In the file, he angrily penned, "I, John XXIII, Pope, declare that I was never a Modernist."[13]

On the surface he would seem to have had much in common with Pius X — being poor, humble, devout, and later fascinated by the appeal of Venice. But Roncalli retained a critical eye toward his sainted predecessor even during his own papacy. He judged Pius X, "certainly holy, but not fully perfect in that he let himself be overwhelmed by anxiety and showed himself so anguished." Probably that is as close as one pontiff comes to criticizing another one in modern times. His friend Cardinal Ferrari was even more blunt concerning Pius's excesses: "He will have to give an account before God of the way he let his bishops down when they were attacked." As has been seen, Benedict XV, himself under scrutiny earlier during the Modernist hysteria, ended the attacks by simply observing, "There is no need to add epithets to the profession of Catholicism. It is enough to say, 'Christian is my name, and Catholic is my family name.' "[14]

In 1911, Roncalli quietly became a member of the diocesan congregation of the Priests of the Sacred Heart, making him a diocesan religious committed to perpetual vows of obedience and promising to live in deep commitment to the ways of the Spirit. When the war came to Italy in 1915, Don Roncalli was called up for active military service and became a hospital orderly stationed in Bergamo, and later a chaplain. In 1918 he was employed as a warden of a student hostel. In all these jobs he performed credibly, but they were not exactly stepping-stones to higher glory.

Then in 1920 he was called to Rome to be the national director for the Propagation of the Faith as part of Benedict's continuing preoccupation over the fate of the missions. How a little-known provincial priest was chosen for the position is unclear. Some say it was due to Benedict's friendship with Radini-Tedeschi; others say it was Roncalli's organizing efforts at the Italian Eucharistic Congress in Bergamo.

When he met with the pope, Benedict simply told him, "You will be God's traveler." From that position he came to know both Italy and also the intricacies of the imposing Roman Curia better. His viewpoints broadened, and in 1921 he was named a monsignor; the revenues of his agency more than doubled in two years, and Roncalli became a recognized figure in ecclesiastical circles. He met for the first time another accomplished Curialist bureaucrat — Giovanni Battista Montini, whom he later raised to the cardinalate and who became his successor, Paul VI.

AMBASSADOR TO THE EAST

On February 17, 1925, Roncalli was summoned to see the secretary of state, Pietro Cardinal Gasparri, who informed him that he was the new apostolic visitor to Bulgaria, the first one in over five hundred years. After his term in "purgatory," as the reassignment was called, he was promised a post in more hospitable Argentina, which then had a large Italian Catholic population. Roncalli protested that he knew nothing about Bulgaria, but Pius XI had already for some reason concluded that Roncalli had been chosen by Providence for the position.[15] Remembering his own years in Poland, the pope insisted that Roncalli needed a more prestigious title than he had had when he was apostolic visitor, and so Pius XI made him an archbishop in the bargain. The pope also gave Roncalli a copy of *Scintillae Ignatianae* — a collection of maxims of St. Ignatius Loyola, meant to tide him over like the good soldier that both Roncalli and the author were in the service of the papacy.[16]

Bulgaria was a confusing country for the Vatican. It had over sixty thousand Catholics of various rites, who survived in a hostile Orthodox religious environment. In 1924, Bulgaria experienced some two hundred political assassinations, and the government of King Boris III responded with many arrests and widespread executions.[17] It was in such a world that the mild-mannered diplomat found himself. Roncalli's new flock embraced about forty-eight thousand Latin rite Catholics living mainly in urban areas and fourteen thousand in the Uniate Slavic rite mainly in the rural areas. By cart, horseback, and mule, the new apostolic visitor with his interpreter crisscrossed Bulgaria. Soon the stranger was being called "Diadu," or "the good father." He modestly assumed that their praise was due to their love for the pope rather than the esteem they felt for him. More importantly during this time, he came to understand the practical importance of getting along with other religious denominations — an early lesson in what would be called later ecumenism. And he encouraged that prayers be said in Bulgarian rather than in the French taught by French missionaries.[18]

Roncalli's stay was supposed to be a short one, he was told. Instead, he was assigned for ten years to the diplomatic backwaters of Bulgaria. At times he worried about his lackluster dead-end career, but once again he trusted in God's ways. He noted in his diary that many of his trials were not caused by the Bulgarians, but by the Roman Curia to whom he reported. He lamented over the petty meanness of the Vatican, saying "everybody is busy talking and maneuvering for a career." Part of his problem was that he had to deal with three different Vatican departments, often having three diverse views of how matters should be handled — the Secretariat of State, Propaganda Fide, and the Oriental Congregation.[19]

Even the pope who appointed him was quick to criticize. He was markedly unhappy when his representative allowed the Bulgarian Orthodox patriarch, Stefan Gheorghiev, to send his secretary to reciprocate a visit from Roncalli. The pope found that demeaning to the prestige of the Holy See; Roncalli blandly responded that it was not so intended, that the patriarch was a very busy man. Pius XI simply stared at his delegate and inscrutably pronounced, "One sows and the other reaps." Later when Roncalli wrote a critical letter to the Curia, the pontiff read it and characterized it, "Behold the wrath of the lamb."[20]

Unfortunately for Roncalli, King Boris III of Bulgaria, originally from the House of Bourbon-Parma, was raised a Catholic, but had to convert to Orthodox Christianity in order to assume the throne of that nation. When he decided to marry, he chose to ask for the hand of King Victor Emmanuel III's daughter, Princess Giovanna. A dispensation was granted by the Vatican, and the marriage was performed according to the Catholic rite at Assisi on October 25, 1930. The royal couple had agreed that their children would be raised as Roman Catholic. Then a week later, on October 31, the couple was married again, this time according to the Orthodox rite in the Cathedral of St. Alexander Nevsky in Sofia. Pius XI was furious and publicly denounced the royal couple on Christmas Eve, and Roncalli consequently took some of the blame both from the pope and from the king for the dispute.

The archbishop was subsequently banned for a year from the Bulgarian court. And when he visited Rome right after the Orthodox baptism of the couple's son, Prince Simeon, the pope acted in a rather boorish manner. He kept Roncalli kneeling before him for forty-five minutes as a penance. Years later, he extended his regrets to Roncalli — saying he apologized as Achille Ratti, but not as Pius XI, calmly adding, "I give you my hand in friendship." Roncalli later said only his pride was hurt, and he graciously dedicated one of his volumes on Borromeo to that pontiff. The usual view in the Curia at that time was that Roncalli was in general a naive diplomat, one given to such foolish hoodwinkings by smarter men, but Roncalli was rather clear as to what the limitations were that he faced. In an Orthodox country where the Catholic Church was simply tolerated, he felt it was better to exhibit what he called "unbroken and nonjudgmental silence."[21]

At times, however, even the ebullient Roncalli grew weary and depressed. In 1929, on the twenty-fifth anniversary of his ordination, he had an intense sense of being forgotten and frustrated over the lack of progress in his career.[22] The years passed by — ten in all — and then in late 1934, the Vatican informed Roncalli that he had been transferred to be apostolic delegate to Turkey and Greece. Istanbul was, of course, the major city in Turkey, and it was the descendant of the great capital called until 1930 Constantinople — the famed center of eastern Christianity. Roncalli arrived and soon visited the Cathedral of the Holy Spirit; there in its courtyard was a statue dedicated to Benedict XV, the Pope of Peace who was called "the protector of the East."[23]

The dictator of Turkey, Mustafa Kemal, or Ataturk, as he preferred, was waging a vigorous and often aggressive campaign to modernize his state, ruthlessly suppressing national customs and traditional Islam. He went on to ban the old Arabic alphabet and non-Western dress, including clerical garb. So Nuncio Roncalli wore a business suit and a bowler hat, looking like a hefty Italian banker, it was said! Philosophically he was to observe, "It will become apparent that clothes do not make the monk."[24]

On the ecclesiastical front, Roncalli as early as 1936 had tried to introduce some words of Turkish into the liturgy, a step that won the praise even of Ataturk. He was, however, soon denounced to Rome; in frustration, Roncalli called some of the reactions of his superiors "my only real cross." On top of his immediate difficulties was the Italian invasion of Ethiopia, which added to tensions with the Turkish regime due in part to the fact that Roncalli was still an Italian citizen. He had also been given the responsibility by the Vatican for its relations with Greece, since the government there wanted no special Vatican representative named. He proceeded very cautiously there too, and in a surprising and warm gesture he visited some of the thousand-year-old Greek Orthodox monasteries at Mount Athos that were still operating in that peninsula. Then in 1939 Pius XI died, and the next war soon came. With Italy in the conflict, Roncalli's position became even more difficult, especially in Greece, which had strong ties with Britain.[25]

The German ambassador to Turkey during this period was Franz von Papen, who originally had been a supporter of Hitler, arguing that he could be controlled by the right sort of conservative influences. Now as the war began, Papen insisted to Roncalli that the conflict would be over by November 1940, and that Catholicism could end up being "the formative principle" of the new German social order. Roncalli was unimpressed and sharply demanded on one occasion, "And what shall I tell the Holy Father about the thousands of Jews who had died in Germany and Poland at the hands of your countrymen?"[26]

Roncalli however dutifully reported Papen's offer to the Vatican without any endorsement on his part, but Monsignor Tardini at the Secretariat of State's office bluntly concluded of the archbishop, "This fellow has understood nothing." He among others felt Roncalli was simply naive and gullible, and two decades later even as Pope John's secretary of state, he exhibited at times the same disdain for Roncalli's capabilities.[27]

Caught up in the vortex of war, occupying a diplomatic post in a sensitive city with fairly open borders, Angelo Roncalli became a source of invaluable information for the Vatican and also a strong ally in the underground to save the Jews on the run. As has been noted, Pius XII was buffeted by immense forces on the question of how far to go in attacking the Nazi and Fascist tyrannies. Roncalli was a witness and a participant in a small but meaningful way in that struggle. Later when he became John XXIII and quickly an international folk hero, there was much praise for his work in Turkey in helping an estimated twenty-four thousand Jews. Some even contrasted his caring attitude with the alleged silence and indifference of Pius XII, but as Roncalli himself acknowledged freely, he acted under specific instructions of the pope.

Still, through his activities and the assistance of King Boris, thousands of Jews from Slovakia who had been sent to Hungary and then Bulgaria, and who were destined for concentration camps, received transit visas for Palestine. Roncalli signed the visas and Papen, representing a very different and more humane strain of German life than Hitler, was credited with overlooking the archbishop's activities. Later Roncalli would testify in writing to Papen's complicity — a letter that probably saved him from the death penalty at the Nuremberg trials.[28]

Roncalli listened to the Grand Rabbi of Jerusalem plead for 55,000 Jews in the Transnistrian region, but by June 1944 he was reporting the arrival of only 730 passengers from that area. Legend has it that Roncalli issued thousands of fraudulent Catholic baptismal certificates to Jews. In fact, the true story is that he forwarded to Vatican diplomats in Hungary and Romania "Immigration Certificates" issued by the Palestine Jewish agency. At times though, both the Vatican and Roncalli insensitively expressed concern that the Holy Land was being flooded with Jewish immigrants, as if they had so many other offers of asylum from which to choose.[29]*

Then on December 6, 1944, Roncalli was shocked to receive a telegram from Monsignor Tardini informing him that he had been appointed papal nuncio to France. French General Charles de Gaulle had insisted to the pope that the current nuncio, Monsignor Valerio Valeri, had been pro-Vichy and had to go. Pius refused at first, but he recognized that Valeri's position was untenable under the new regime after the liberation of France. Some critics of Roncalli claimed that Pius sent him to Paris as a calcu-

---

*In the first year of his papacy, Roncalli asked that the expression in a Good Friday prayer that referred to "perfidious Jews and infidels" be eliminated. When one cardinal insisted on using that slander, the pope cut him short and demanded "say it over — the new way."

lated rebuke to the haughty general — the implication being that Roncalli was a naive bumpkin. In fact, Pius clearly wanted Roncalli in that position, overruled Tardini's objections, and informed his nuncio that he was the pope's choice for that position. "It was I, Monsignor, who thought of you myself, and I made the decision — no one else." Now, at sixty-three, Angelo Roncalli held the Vatican's most prestigious diplomatic position. He humbly responded that "where horses are lacking, the donkeys trod along," a supposed reference to himself as a second-level diplomat.[30]

While in Paris, he sensitively dealt with the government's demands that thirty allegedly pro-Vichy bishops be dismissed, getting that number reduced to three; dealt gingerly with the left-wing priest-worker movement, which put clergy into the factories mainly in suburban Paris to continue their pastoral work; and advised the Vatican on nominations for bishops and three cardinal positions. Roncalli was criticized then and later for not having the sparkling wit and conversational veneer that is so appreciated in French intellectual life. Jesuit Robert Rouquette judged that Roncalli made a poor impression in Paris and was written off by many as a "clown," But Jacques Dumaine reported that Roncalli "is more artful than subtle, he has had much experience and radiates a lively bonhomie." And the anticleric and former premier of France Édouard Herriot remarked, "If all the priests were like Roncalli, we would have no trouble with the Church."[31]

When confronted with Vatican charges against the Jesuit Pierre Teilhard de Chardin for his philosophy mixing Christology, anthropology, and evolutionary biology, Roncalli pushed them aside. He simply asked, "This Teilhard fellow ... why can't he be content with the catechism and the social doctrine of the Church, instead of bringing up all these problems?" Roncalli was never a great admirer of theological distinctions and complicated theories, which may explain in part his toleration for avant-garde theologians during his brief term in office as pope. He was to conclude, "In France ideas are born with wings. Without a touch of holy madness, the Church cannot grow."[32]

Roncalli was by temperament a man interested in faith rather than theological constructs. The purpose of the Church was to help men and women reach salvation, he believed. Roncalli, the diplomat, still respected the pastoral life, the simple habits of clergy who minister to the souls and sensitivities of real people living in a world still in the after-shock of the last terrible war. Later, Maurice Cardinal Feltin offered a character sketch of him at that time. He found the nuncio always friendly, understanding, and adept at smoothing out problems; but he was decisive, firm, and strong in his actions. He thought Roncalli to be "subtle, perspicuous, and far-sighted," a person who could slip through "the grasp of those who sought to exploit him."[33]

While the Curia moved on implementing the conservative strictures in Pius's encyclical *Humani Generis,* some French theologians as well as others were put under the new microscope and denied teaching faculties. Roncalli basically stayed away from the controversy, and later he was to resurrect some of these discredited scholars, who would play major roles in Vatican II.

In 1951, he was appointed by Pius XII the official Vatican observer to UNESCO, a very different approach than the pope's predecessors had used in recognizing or usually ignoring international organizations. Then on November 14, 1952, Roncalli was asked if he would consider taking the prestigious see in Venice. He was seventy-one years of age. This would be his last post, he concluded philosophically. He had lived by the admonition of St. Martin, who said that he "neither feared to die, nor refused to live." Finally, Angelo Roncalli would return to the pastoral life and would be able to undertake diocesan reforms similar to what his patron, Radini-Tedeschi, had done in Bergamo a generation ago, and those the great saint Charles Borromeo had concluded four centuries before in Milan.

Venice is not just a city; it is a dream, a fantasy of art and architecture. And it was on such a decorative stage that the aging diplomat arrived from Paris. Roncalli was in many ways a traditionalist, and he loved ritual and ceremony. He came to Venice on March 15, 1953, in a procession of colorful gondolas, saying that he wished to humbly introduce himself. He recalled his family, quoted Petrarch, and praised Marco Polo, the great explorer of the Far East. And in characteristic rhetoric, Roncalli went on, "I commend to your kindness someone who simply wants to be your brother."[34]

He had been previously named a cardinal, in January 1953, at Pius XII's second and last consistory. Twenty-four new men were selected in all, fourteen of them non-Italian. The internationalization of the College of Cardinals was truly beginning. The pope also named Alojzije Stepinac of Yugoslavia, Stefan Wyszyński of Gniezno-Warsaw, Poland, and also a brilliant young prelate, Giuseppe Siri, the archbishop of Genoa since 1946. Some said that Pius saw the last as the heir apparent, although the pope never seemed to concur publicly.

In March 1954, the pope nearly died, and Roncalli wrote that while he owed much to Pius, he hoped that he would not die at that time since it would interrupt his plan to visit his parishes and the proposed diocesan synod. Also, rather surprisingly, he opposed adding another feast, Regalitas Mariae, the Queenship of Mary, to the Church calendar. He saw it as counterproductive to ecumenical efforts — a rare objection from a high-ranking clergyman in those days.[35]

Pius miraculously recovered, and later, after a crude power play, he either personally instigated or simply allowed his Curia inner circle to transfer Monsignor Montini to Milan. He was not to be given a cardinal's hat either. Roncalli was dumbfounded at the harsh treatment of his friend. It has been argued that Montini was too liberal, too powerful, too close to the papal throne. Seeing their opportunity, the conservatives finally eliminated his influence and stopped him from being Pius's successor by denying him the red hat. Ironically, the conservative "Pentagon" leaders laid the groundwork for a greater revolutionary — the amiable and aging patriarch of Venice. It has been maintained, however, by several close associates of Pius that he himself made the decision to transfer Montini to Milan without a red hat. The pope had lost confidence in his closest associate because of his involvement with leftist-leaning youth movements, and because Montini regarded Fascism, not Communism, as the greater threat to the Church. Also, Pius felt that his successor had to be a more decisive leader than Montini would be, realizing that the latter could be elected later — which is what happened.

In his diocese Roncalli focused on what he called spiritual renewal and the "perennial youthfulness of Christian and religious life." On the one hand, he was impressed by the liturgical reforms of the archbishop of Bologna, the Franciscan Giacomo Cardinal Lercaro. And at the other end of the spectrum, he invited conservative Cardinal Siri to talk to a Catholic Action group. In 1956, the Supreme Congregation of the Holy Office (the old "Inquisition") demanded that he respond to complaints concerning the pronouncements in the local Christian Democrat newspaper which advocated an "opening to the left" politically. Roncalli disliked engaging in condemnations, but he felt compelled by the Vatican to criticize what he called an opening at "any price," which was "a very grave doctrinal error and a flagrant violation of Catholic discipline." Several years later he himself would be criticized for just such a gesture toward the U.S.S.R.[36]

At the time, Roncalli also expressed some interest in creating a commission to focus on the ecumenical movement — a precursor of what would become during his term as pope the powerful Secretariat for Christian Unity to be headed up by Pius's former confessor, the Jesuit Augustin Bea. Back in Venice, Roncalli was preparing for a diocesan synod in November 1957. It was at this synod that he first used the term *aggiornamento,* meaning an updating or reform of the ways of the Church to fit in with modern society. At that session he denounced authoritarianism and paternalism — criticisms which were seen then as veiled references to Pius's style of administration.[37]

The easygoing Roncalli had some problems with the laity of Venice — a rather conservative group, even noticeably so in conservative Italy. His modest proposal to remove the iconostasis in St. Mark's Cathedral, the marble Gothic screen, and wheel it away at Mass time so the faithful would see better, produced a firestorm of opposition, and he backed down. Roncalli was to remark on one occasion that "We are not honored as museum keepers, but to cultivate a flourishing garden of life and to prepare a glorious future." Later he recorded in his diary the major event of the day — Pius XII had died.

THE TRANSITIONAL POPE...

As has been noted before, Roncalli's reactions were rather restrained on learning of Pius's death, especially for a pontiff that both rescued him from the backwaters of Vatican diplomacy and treated him with surely more respect than Pius XI. When the College of Cardinals met, it would contain only fifty-one voting members, and the average age was older than Roncalli, who was a month shy of seventy-seven. There was some speculation of reaching outside the ranks of the cardinals, especially to Archbishop Montini, but that was not possible in the eyes of most, although he may have received several votes on the first balloting. Thus, the conclave would be left with a very divided convention of those conservatives wishing to continue the theological policies of Pius XII; those wishing some modest changes, especially in administrative organization; those advocating major reforms; those craving some spiritual regeneration; and those who really were not sure what they wanted.

In a universe of fifty-one people, such divisions make for a highly fractionalized group process in which consensus is difficult to reach. Of the fifty-one cardinals seventeen were Italian, six French, three Spanish, and three Brazilians, among others. Of the seventeen Italians, eleven worked in the Vatican Curia, and six governed dioceses. Roncalli was one of the few patriarchs of the western Church and a mildly progressive figure who had extensive diplomatic experience. He had had his run-ins with the Pacelli bureaucracy, but his placid personality was such that he had not alienated many people over the years.[38]

There was surely a feeling that the Church needed a change in style and tone — a Good Shepherd, who would also support the prerogatives of the bishops and cardinals. As noted, the conservatives at first supported the young Cardinal Siri; the progressives, Lercaro of Bologna, who was called by an acquaintance Luigi Santucci, "an after-school cardinal, a holiday-excursion cardinal" — that is, a not so serious fellow. There was much support for the cultured Armenian, Pietro Cardinal Agagianian, a Curialist "more Roman than the Romans," it was said. One critic remarked that he was "more doctrinaire at sixty-three than Pius had been at eighty." There was also some support for the seventy-nine-year-old aristocratic Benedetto Aloisi Cardinal Masella, the moderate prefect of the Congregation for the Sacraments and an experienced diplomat himself. The successful candidate would need two-thirds, or thirty-five votes.[39]

Before the conclave, Roncalli was a frequent visitor to influential clergy in Rome, especially cardinals and prominent individuals who were well connected in Church politics. He was seen initially as a dark horse, one likely to emerge only in a long, drawn-out conclave. But actually he entered with a strong core of supporters, mainly former French colleagues and non-Curial Italians who were loyal throughout the balloting. After four days of inconclusive voting, Roncalli finally prevailed, in part because of the concurrence of the leader of traditional Curia Cardinals, Alfredo Ottaviani. Although the proceedings are secret, Roncalli himself said that he and Agagianian bobbed up and down in the balloting like peas in a boiling pot. He must have understood what was happening earlier than most of his colleagues. When he was elected, he pulled out a written statement for the secret conclave members and boldly announced, "Vocabor Johannes," "I will be called John" to the surprise of the cardinals and later the Vatican experts.

Roncalli said that he took the name John because it was the name of his father, the name of the church he was baptized in, and the name of a variety of cathedrals throughout the world, most especially the Lateran Basilica, the pope's own cathedral in Rome. The last legitimate pope to use the name was John XXII, who reigned from 1317 to 1334. There had been a later John XXIII, Baldassarre Cossa, who was an antipope elected in 1410 and who was alleged to have been a pirate who killed, cheated, and tried to perjure his way to the papacy.[40]

Before that election, Roncalli was visited in his cell by Ottaviani and his conservative ally, Ernesto Cardinal Ruffini of Sicily, who talked of what "a beautiful thing" it would be to call a Church council soon. They had in mind another Vatican I or Council of Trent to correct the errors of Church members and the sins of the world. Roncalli was to observe that "everybody was convinced that I would be a provisional and transitional pope," *papa de passagio.* Mainly what was expected was that he would restore the papacy to a more normal state of affairs and end the neglect and decay of the later Pacelli years.

Before the conclave, he had been asked by concerned conservatives if his friend Montini would be returned to Rome as secretary of state if he became pope. Roncalli shrewdly responded that since he was not going to be pope, the question was moot. He met several times with Monsignor Tardini, still the pro-secretary of state and the man who had been over the years so critical of Roncalli for his alleged naivete as a diplomat. To the surprise of many and the comfort of the conservatives, he later prevailed on a reluctant Tardini to take the secretary of state's position, even though the latter protested that they had frequently disagreed in the past, that he was tired from previous years of service, and that he wished to focus on his orphanage project. John insisted, and Tardini knelt down in obedience, later remarking on the strange turn of events, "Such is life." The pope was not a man of the Curia, and what he knew he generally did not like. However, he made major overtures to the bureaucracy, and in the process he may have forfeited the chance to bring about the very changes he was later to embrace.[41]

Almost immediately, he called a consistory to name twenty-three new cardinals, thus exceeding the rule of Sixtus V (1585–90), who set the limit at seventy. John named Montini and Tardini and also new cardinals from places like the Philippines, Japan, Mexico, and Africa that had never had cardinals before. Still a man of tradition in so many ways, he restored the fur bonnet used by the Renaissance popes in place of the white skull cap that kept slipping off his head. He even sat down and created a new coat of arms, but protested that the lion (meant to represent Venice) was too fierce, too Germanic-looking.[42]

At his coronation, he insisted on preaching a homily in a language that many of his listeners could understand, Italian, and he told the Vatican newspaper to drop the august titles when they referred to the pope. When the mayor of Bergamo decided to name Roncalli's brothers "Knights of the Italian Republic" (Cavalieri della Republica Italiana), John demurred. After his coronation, they went back home to till the fields.

He met easily with the press, simply calling himself a shepherd, and never sought to emulate the ways or the intellectual sway of his predecessor. One priest, Antonio Samoré, said that while meeting Pius was like taking a stiff oral exam, meeting John was like talking to one's grandfather. After that coronation, he received visits from various chiefs of state. To one, Prime Minister John Diefenbaker of Canada, the pontiff remarked, "Well, here I am at the end of the road and the top of the heap."[43]

Very quickly he also assumed the duties of bishop of Rome, visiting its churches, the children's hospital, Gesù Bambino, and even the Regina Coeli prison by the Tiber River. The children at the hospital, many of them suffering from polio, called out "Viene qui, viene qui, Papa" ("Come here, come here, Pope"). And he waddled along, replying, "Quiet now, I'm coming. I'm coming to see you." In the midst of the worst elements of the city at the prison, John simply remarked that he was "Joseph, your brother." As he reached the sealed off section of the prison, he asked that the gate be opened, "Do not bar me from them — they are the children of the Lord." Inside he embraced a convicted murderer, among other felons. Later, on the Feast of the Epiphany, the pope sent the entire prison population a complete chicken dinner with wine. The press loved this new pope as it followed him around. But John had a more carefree sense of himself. Once he looked at his figure in a full length mirror and laughed, "O Lord, this man is going to be a disaster on television." One of his more favorable biographers observed, "When Angelo Roncalli became John XXIII, a new man seemed born in him; it was as if mediocrity had given birth to genius."[44]

John is supposed to have said that he had "flung open the windows of the Vatican" to let in the air. Perhaps he never said that, but he surely acted as if he had. Roncalli was made pope in part because important elements of the conservative Curia thought he was reliable. They hoped they could use him to regenerate the institutional Church by reasserting their authority and the Vatican's magisterium. That is why they wanted the Council. At first they were correct in their assessment.

THE NEW PENTECOST

In January 1959, John XXIII claimed that he had been inspired by the Holy Spirit to call a Church council. Actually, it had been suggested to him by various people, although he probably forgot the authors and just incorporated the suggestions into his own. He had hesitantly proposed it to Secretary of State Tardini and was delighted when the conservative Curialist agreed. Five days later, on January 25, 1959, John announced the idea to the eighteen Curial cardinals at the Basilica of St. Paul Beyond the Walls in Rome. They sat quietly, almost stunned. Later Tardini asked John to go more slowly, and the Vatican newspaper even buried the dramatic story inside the pages of its daily edition. Finally, John XXIII allowed the Curial apparatus to set the Council agenda by having the traditional commissions and agencies serve the needs of the Council. Progressive critics would conclude that the results were highly predictable. The initial drafts on the basic questions before the Council would contain the same defensive, traditional, triumphalist expressions of criticism of the world and stale reaffirmations of the righteousness of the Church. There were no surprises.

Actually both Pius XI and Pius XII had considered the idea of calling a council together. Pius XI wished to emphasize the unity of the Church after the horrors of the First World War, but he became preoccupied with resolving the "Roman Question." As for his successor, Pius XII received from Ruffini and Ottaviani a memo in February 1948 advocating a council which would focus on traditional concerns: clarification of Church doctrine, the threat of Communism, the moral constraints on war, reform of canon law, ecclesiastical discipline, and a definition of the doctrine of Mary's Assumption. Pius XII hesitated, however, in having the bishops leave their dioceses for so long a period of time, but he did set up five secret commissions to prepare for such a council if he decided to call it after all. John had the benefit of that material.

Pius decided that whatever a council could do, he could do better and faster, and so it never came about. He defined the doctrine of the Assumption of Mary himself and issued his encyclical *Humani Generis,* which condemned various errors, heresies, and unorthodoxies. When John explored the idea of calling a council, Cardinal Spellman in New York concluded that the pope had "been pushed into it by people who misconstrued what he said." Cardinal Lercaro of Bologna, supposedly a progressive, judged that the pope was either "rash and impulsive," due to his inexperience and lack of culture, or that he was a man of "calculated audacity." Even Cardinal Montini in Milan privately said that calling a council was a mistake, that at least three more years of preparation were needed, and that "this holy old boy doesn't seem to realize what a hornet's nest he is stirring up." But Montini's friend, Oratorian priest Giulio Bevilacqua, responded, "Let it be, the Holy Spirit is still awake in the Church."[45]

Thus it seems that neither the progressives nor the conservatives welcomed the idea of a Church council, especially of the sort that John called together. Later Sister Pasqualina, in a rare visit back to the Vatican, also warned the new pope that people looked to the Holy See for leadership and that it could not and should not repudiate its authoritarian heritage. It would lead to "an ecclesiastical tragedy," she judged. John good-naturedly blessed her, complimented her beauty, and remarked "let change take care of the future."

They said it would take four years of preparation; the elderly pontiff gave the bureaucracy only two. While John was talking of opening up the windows of the Church, the Curia was continuing its policies of blacklisting theologians and authors. Such discontinuities led to the quip in Rome, "Tardini reigns, Ottaviani governs, John blesses." The pope at times seemed remarkably reticent, almost as if he expected the Council to just happen. At one point he remarked, "I am only the pope around here." And when he was asked how many people worked in the Vatican, he concluded — "about half!"[46]

The appointment of Domenico Tardini as secretary of state and then president of the Ante-Preparatory Commission was meant to calm the Curia and also to place some real management skill in charge. Tardini in turn wished to use the reliable experts (*periti*) from the Roman universities rather than import nonnative talent and alien ideas. Thus another safeguard for the Curia was in place, and John seemed either unaware or in agreement. Still, Tardini would make it clear that it was the pontiff who was insisting on changes, not he. Privately he referred to John as "the one up there," until the pope remarked to his surprise, " 'The one up there' is the Lord God of all. I am only the one on the fourth floor."[47] When he was cardinal, Roncalli was supposed to have said to Pius XII, "Holy Father, you will leave a difficult heritage for any successor who tries to emulate you in your role as teacher and master of the Word." Later, however, he remarked to Georges Cardinal Grente that one should simply do the opposite of one's predecessors to make one's mark. John was clearly aware of the Roman gossip, criticizing him as a man of limited abilities, especially in comparison to Pius. Again, Cardinal Spellman in New York was supposed to have said that John had the intelligence of "a simple banana man peddling his fruit." But John was a wily old cleric who lived by the maxim that one should notice everything, turn a blind eye to much, and correct a few things. Earlier in his career, he had observed, "Well, priests have to give up so much, marriage, children — so many pleasures forbidden. They must be allowed the greatest clerical sport: criticism of superiors."[48]

He decided early that the cardinals should relinquish the plurality of positions that some held which had created a sort of interlocking directorship of power and influence among Curia officials. When some cardinals disagreed, a distraught Pope John reportedly said, "They have refused the

Pope." After that refusal, he ordered the changes made, and then wrote a public letter accepting their resignations with gratitude.[49]

When he made his announcement concerning the Council, he also pledged to call a synod for the diocese of Rome and to order a thorough review of canon law. He called a synod for his own new diocese because he recognized, as did Pius in his last year, that the city of Rome and its environs had undergone enormous social and economic changes since the war. There were now over two million people with 190 parishes, and while Rome had over three thousand priests, most of them were not involved in pastoral work, but were employed by the Curia or were religious assigned to Roman universities.[50]

John the bishop actually in 1959 devoted more time to the synod than to preparing for the Council. But the results were predictable and disappointing. The synod ended up insisting that Roman priests had to wear the cassock or black soutane at all times; be marked by tonsure or shaven crowns; avoid the opera and races; not use cars unless absolutely necessary; never be alone with a woman; deal only in the most careful ways with Communists, Freemasons, and heretics; and beware of faith healers and psychoanalysts. The synod was a bad dress rehearsal for a wide-open ecumenical Council that the pope would advocate.

John magnanimously praised the synod's decrees for their "beauty and inner coherence, with occasional delicate touches that result in an unexpected psalmody, bringing clarity to the mind and savour to the heart." Privately however, he observed that "nothing is perfect in this world," and that his successor could call a second synod. Still he observed, "It will always be the humble Pope John who celebrated the first."[51]

CHANGING FOREIGN POLICIES

While the pope was reviewing the work of the synod and also preparing for his Council, John was beginning to effect a major change in the Vatican's policies toward Communism and the Holy See's basic foreign policy assumptions as well. For the first two years of his pontificate he seemed, however, to adhere to the policies of Pius XI and Pius XII toward Communism. Then he began to make a clear and calculated attempt to disengage the Vatican from Italian domestic politics and from its historic pro-West Cold War allegiances. When the leader of the Christian Democrats, Aldo Moro, tried to create a coalition government by forming an alliance with the Socialists (PSI), John proved sympathetic. This was the so-called opening to the left (*apertura a sinistro*) that the Curia had condemned under Pius and that Cardinal Roncalli was forced to censor while in Venice.

John did not directly align himself with Moro at first, but on April 11, 1961, he received Prime Minister Amintore Fanfani and celebrated the hundredth anniversary of Italian unification. He was sending the message that he and the Vatican would abstain from interfering in political issues. Then on April 2, 1962, the pope met with Moro and called him "an excellent Catholic, a statesman, a man of great social concern."[52]

The pope aroused suspicions in other ways. In his early attempts to reach out to the Orthodox churches, he came into contact rather quickly with the Russian leadership. His overtures to the Orthodox Christian community and their hierarchies, asking them to come to the Council, were complicated both because of their age-old animosities toward Rome and of the influence of the U.S.S.R. John the diplomat was aware of the ancient jealousies between Athens and Constantinople, and between them and the patriarchate of Moscow which was a department of the Soviet government. He issued a general invitation to his upcoming Council and left it to the Orthodox churches to decide how they would be represented, but he received no response. At first, Athens had balked at the idea; then Patriarch Athenagoras of Constantinople (Istanbul) informed Cardinal Bea that he could not attend the Council. Later the patriarch of Moscow would not agree to come either, probably because the initial invitation came through Constantinople.

The pope then changed course, and on September 27, 1962, sent Monsignor Johannes Willebrands to Moscow with an invitation; later the Kremlin agreed that two official Orthodox Church observers could go to the Council. Then the other two Orthodox prelates protested about breaches of protocol and a divide and conquer approach being used by the Vatican. Years later Athenagoras finally met with Pope Paul VI in Jerusalem — the first such visit since the schism in 1054.[53]

During this period the Soviet government and Premier Nikita Khrushchev had apparently decided to work with Pope John, whom they saw as likely to abandon the staunch anti-Communist policies of Pius XII. As for John he stopped referring to "the Church of Silence" behind the Iron Curtain and also ceased characterizing many long-suffering mainland Catholic Church leaders in China as schismatics, when he realized the difficult options they had faced over the years.

In their overtures, Vatican diplomats quietly assured Communist leaders that the Council would not be attacking Communism or embarrassing any observers from Eastern Europe or the Soviet Union. John was personally delighted when Stefan Cardinal Wyszyński and sixteen other bishops from Poland, four from each Germany, three from Hungary, three from Czechoslovakia, and all of the Yugoslav bishops arrived to attend the Council. However the bishops of Romania and Albania were absent, and most of the Catholic bishops of Communist China remained imprisoned.[54]

Also the pope began secret negotiations to free Church prelate Jósef Slipyi, the archbishop of Lvov, from jail, using among others the services of American magazine editor Norman Cousins. Later Franz Cardinal König of Vienna would be allowed to visit Cardinal Mindszenty, who had been granted asylum and was still living in the U.S. embassy in Budapest. Eventually he would be allowed to emigrate to Rome. Pope John also took up the case of Archbishop Josef Beran of Prague, who had been under restrictions from 1947 to 1964, seeking to better his plight.

The pontiff's positive relations with the Russians began when they responded to his statement during the Berlin crisis of August–September 1961. The dangerous confrontation between the United States and the U.S.S.R. over the latter's harassment of that divided city eventually led to the threat of military action by the nuclear powers and the building of the Berlin Wall. John appealed to all involved for a peaceful settlement, including those who did not believe in God, or in His Christ as he put it. For some reason, Khrushchev was pleased with the tone of the message and praised the pope. The Soviets saw quite correctly a break in the policies of Pius XII. Later during the much more dangerous Cuban missile crisis, the pope with the prior approval of both sides appealed to the Americans and the Soviets to choose negotiation over war. His dramatic appeal was praised throughout the world, including by the Kremlin.

Khrushchev's son-in-law, Aleksei Adzhubei, the editor of *Izvestia*, visited the pope on March 7, 1963. The interview lasted only eighteen minutes and was a rather simple expression of hospitality on the part of the pope, but it was a major step in normalizing relations between Russia and the Holy See. The pontiff asked Adzhubei and his wife about their children and expressed delight that one was called Ivan, or John. At one point, he poignantly observed, "You say you are atheists. But surely you will receive the blessing of an old man for your children." They fell quiet and left deeply moved.[55] John even began to study the Russian language in order, he said, to "show how much he loved that great people."[56]

But John's overtures brought increasing criticism in Italy, where the pope had announced that he wished the clergy to stay out of partisan politics. When some of the hierarchy, including Cardinal Ottaviani, disagreed publicly, John uncharacteristically rebuked the dissidents and reminded them of their duty of obedience to the pope. The cardinal had openly criticized the left leanings of what he called "sacristy pinks." When John near the end of his life issued his universal call for peace and brotherhood in his encyclical, *Pacem in Terris,* the last remnants of Pius's foreign policy came tumbling down. President Kennedy, who was himself seemingly seeking to abandon some of the clichés of the Cold War, remarked, "This encyclical of Pope John makes me proud to be a Catholic."

Issued on April 11, 1963, the encyclical is addressed to "all men of good will," and begins with a ratification of the traditional Catholic view that by the use of natural reason all can understand the need for peace, liberty, and a moral order. John started off with a long history of the duty to respect the inalienable rights of people. Those rights include not just speech, religion, property, and association, but also the right to social services, medical care, employment, culture, education, and vocational training. He also emphasized the right to freedom of movement and expressed concern for the plight of displaced persons.

John then talked of the match of duties and responsibilities with rights and liberties. Men have a right to expect a political order characterized by truth, justice, charity, and enlightened cooperation, he argued. John reminded politicians that they must adapt the laws to the conditions of modern life. He noted three great changes that have marked the era: the progressive improvement of the economic and social conditions of workers; the increasing awareness by women of their natural dignity; and the political independence of nations once subject to foreign domination.

He further expressed his disapproval of imperialism and foreign economic domination, asked for respect for minority rights, and strongly condemned the arms race. In a positive sense John urged assistance for underdeveloped nations, praised the United Nations and its agencies, and urged Catholics to cooperate with Christians "separated from the Apostolic See." Laying aside some of the old prohibitions on such joint endeavors, John simply observed, "a man who has fallen into error does not cease to be a man."[57]

Also in the same month, April 1963, the Christian Democrats lost strength in the elections in Italy, and the pope was attacked for having made it fashionable to support socialism, to look the other way at Communism, and even to allow a visit of Khrushchev's son-in-law inside the Vatican gates. The Christian Democrats were probably hurt more by the downturn of the Italian economy, but to some it did not seem to matter.[58] John had weakened the Church's historic resolve against the left.

Pope John's image as a fair and compassionate world statesman was enhanced in other quarters, especially after his appeals for mutual restraint during the explosive Cuban missile crisis in October 1962. He had stressed over the years what he called *convivienza* — living together — and as a recognition of his efforts he was awarded the Balzan Peace Prize on May 1, 1963, and on May 10 he visited the Quirinale, the palace of the Italian president, to view the giving of that award to other people as well. "Peace is a house, a house for everyone," he explained.[59]

MOTHER AND TEACHER

On domestic social concerns, Pope John had earlier issued his controversial *Mater et Magistra* on July 15, 1961. That encyclical marked the seventieth anniversary of Leo XIII's *Rerum Novarum* and the thirtieth anniversary of Pius XI's *Quadragesimo Anno*. One of the longest papal letters, some twenty-five thousand words in length, John's encyclical affirmed the recent papal tradition of support for private enterprise and private property and presented a critique of Communism and socialism. But the state must act in a positive way to promote a healthy economy and widespread prosperity. In such activities, the principle of subsidiarity should be honored, that is, those activities undertaken by the state should be restricted to efforts which private groups or individuals cannot accomplish themselves.

The letter introduced the concept of "socialization," defined as the "growing interdependence of men in society giving rise to various patterns of group life and activity and in many instances to social institutions established on a juridical basis." There are advantages in such an interdependence which promotes higher standards of living and the welfare state. There are disadvantages in that it makes it harder for individuals to exercise their freedoms, to work and think individually, and to enrich their personalities. The letter moved on to emphasize a need for a true living wage for workers and their families, a fairer redistribution of wealth, a more disinterested assistance to poorer nations, and a sense of the brotherhood of man. And as befits a true son of the soil, the pope spent some time talking about the problems of farmers.

John criticized economic imperialism and strongly urged the laity to participate in an apostolate to the world for social justice. And lastly, he gingerly acknowledged some aspects of the population explosion, but denied it was a serious difficulty and put his faith in scientific and technological discoveries to find solutions. Some feared that his letter was another opening to the left, especially with its concept of "socialization," which seemed too close to "socialism." In the United States, many conservative American Catholics agreed with commentator William Buckley when he said, "mater si, magistra no."

By the end of 1961, John would be celebrating his eightieth birthday. He had observed earlier that when he was chosen in 1958, the prediction was that he would be a provisional and transitional pope. "Yet here I am, already in the eve of the fourth year of my pontificate, with an immense program of work ahead of me to be carried out before the eyes of the whole world, which is watching and waiting." To those who compared him unfavorably to Pius, he responded that everyday language was the language that Jesus used, and that "simplicity contains nothing that is contrary to prudence." When he was approached by Cardinal Spellman about the possible canonization of Pius XII, he sidestepped the request.[60] Still he took comfort from reading the lives of two of his powerful and rather unsimple predecessors: Leo the Great and Innocent III — men more attuned to Pius XII's style of leadership than John's![61]

The conservative Cardinal Siri, holding dearly on to Pius's legacy, called Pope John's pontificate "the greatest disaster in ecclesiastical history" — that is, the last five hundred years in his litany. Later at the beatification process of Pope John, he indicated, however, that he had been wrong.[62] Not all of Pacelli's circle was as critical of John XXIII. The pope began to form a very close collaboration with the Jesuit Augustin Bea, a former confessor of Pius's, the person who helped Pius write his liberal charter for advancing biblical studies, *Divino Afflante Spiritu* (1943), and a man who would help provide strong direction for a very unclear Council.

BEGINNING VATICAN II

As a preparation for the Council, the Vatican had sent out questionnaires requesting topics for discussion, and over 76 percent of the prelates and Catholic institution leaders responded. Basically they revolved around minor reforms and a modest desire for more autonomy. The "voti," as they would later be called, were extensive and would be published in fifteen huge volumes.[63]

Peter Hebblethwaite reports that John decided in the beginning that "the president of each subcommittee would be the prefect of the corresponding Roman Congregation, or the dicastery." Thus the conservative Curia with John's approval would provide tight direction for the Council. Excluded were some of the major theologians of the time, men who would be important figures in Vatican II and much later. Those included Jesuits John Courtney Murray and John L. McKenzie from the United States; Karl Rahner and Hugo Rahner from Bavaria; Frenchmen Henri de Lubac and Jean Daniélou; and French Dominicans Yves-Marie Congar and Marie-Dominique Chenu.[64]

On June 5, 1960, Pope John noted in passing that the decision to use the Curia did not exclude the enlightened wisdom of churchmen from elsewhere, but his statement had little impact. He went on though and insisted that the Council had its own structures and organizations that would be different from the Roman Curia, but the meaning of that observation was unclear. What was apparent was that the excitement over the Council was eliciting a great deal of public discussion, media coverage, and scholarly attention. One prominent liberal theologian, Hans Küng, openly insisted that the purpose of this Council was "reform" in its broadest sense. His book, *The Council, Reform, and Reunion,* stirred a great deal of attention on both sides of the Atlantic with its positive discussion of the Protestant Reformation, the role of the Bible in worship, the development of a people's liturgy, the use of the vernacular, the reform of the Curia, the divorce of the papacy from politics, and the end of the Index of Forbidden Books. Surprisingly, Küng portrayed the Council of Trent as a reforming Council that ended the abuses of the Renaissance Church and not as a defensive reaction to the Reformation. Roncalli had found some of the same evidence in his work on St. Charles Borromeo, the great churchman of that Council.[65]

In the midst of all this, the pope turned to his new friend, Cardinal Bea, to head up a special secretariat — one dedicated to Christian unity that would be the agency responsible for communicating in a positive way to non-Catholic Christians. Now with the appointment of Bea, John had reached into the closest circle of Pius's admirers and found an old man who represented, however, a very new way of looking at the world and thus at the agenda of the Council. Still some conservative Curia members recalled to each other that Bea had been the author of Pius's liberal letter on biblical studies, and that he seemed back in 1949 to ignore the Holy Office warning against extensive ecumenical contacts. They never forgot an infraction — real or even just reported.

Then on December 2, 1960, the pope met Dr. Geoffrey Fisher, the Anglican archbishop of Canterbury. This was the first time that a pope and an archbishop from that see had spoken since the Reformation. Fisher was somewhat cool at first and sought to lecture John that the world would perhaps never see a "return to Rome," or a reunion of Protestant and Catholic churches, especially on Catholic terms. John, though, was hospitable as usual, saying later that they talked of St. Gregory the Great and St. Augustine's mission to Canterbury. No photographs were taken and the public announcements were low key. Fisher, though, left charmed by the pope, and later the archbishops of York and Canterbury appointed Canon Bernard Pawley as their personal representative to the Holy See.[66]

Throughout all of this Pope John was becoming an increasingly popular personality internationally. Then in the summer of 1961, Secretary of State Tardini died, and the pontiff quickly named Amleto Cicognani, the former nuncio to the United States and a more moderate person, to take Tardini's place. Some historians of the papacy have seen this change as the beginning of Pope John's liberation as a reformer and as a leader in the ecclesiastical changes that came out of the Council that he himself had called.

There is no question that Vatican II (1962–65) had a profound impact on the Roman Catholic Church, far beyond what its Church Fathers originally imagined. What exactly John XXIII's intentions were and what his view was of the first session, the only one that he lived through, is somewhat clouded historically.

As for the Council, the preparatory work had been moved to the Central Commission after Tardini's death headed by Alfredo Cardinal Ottaviani — a charming, shrewd, and conservative figure at the apex of the Curia bureaucracy. The Central Commission became not just a coordinating agency, but actually a watchdog that thought it could veto the work of the other commissions. In November 1961, Ottaviani proclaimed that the Council should author a new Profession of Faith, which would repeat the anti-Modernist oath of Pius X and also condemn again the errors listed in *Humani Generis,* reaffirm the doctrine of Mary's virginity, reassert the primacy of the priesthood, and attack those who emphasized the sinfulness and guilt of the Catholic Church over the years. It was the same old conservative agenda, and immediately enormous resistance ensued. It appeared that the power of the Curia, even without John's intervention, was beginning to wane.

Still, the pope praised the Central Commission several times for its work, and on February 22, 1962, he issued a letter, *Veterum Sapientia* ("the wisdom of the ancients"). It was a rigid defense of the importance of Latin in the life of the Church. It was more conservative than even Pius's pronouncements on the topic. One possible consequence that some feared was that a council held in Latin would favor the Curia which dealt with that language every day in its work. That prediction did not hold true.

When the Curia, however, began a systematic attack on Bea and his Biblicum Institute, the detached pope responded sharply, expressed support for the orthodoxy of the Institute, and ordered Cardinal Pizzardo, who led the assault, to send a letter of apology to Bea. The conservative dean of the cardinals, Eugene Tisserant of the Biblical Commission, was also involved, and the pope wrote to Secretary of State Cicognani, "The time has come to put a stop to this nonsense." Either that commission would prove useful to the papacy or it would be abolished, he warned. Quite correctly, he began to conclude "reforms have to begin from above."[67]

Then the pope ordered that the schemas be circulated to all the members of the Council early to invite debate and discussion. Cardinal Montini, speaking for the pope, opposed the constant negative tone of the conservatives. A distraught John had already looked at some of the drafts of the schemas and is supposed to have held up a ruler and said, "Seven inches of condemnation and one of praise: is that the way to talk to the modern world?" The conservatives, however, had their own reservations. Ottaviani, observing the general drift of events, glumly remarked, "I pray to God that I am to die before the end of the Council and that way I can die a Catholic."[68]

Pope John talked of his contribution to the Council as being his "personal suffering" and seemed to have a premonition of his own death as he pushed for an earlier session than most thought possible. He rewrote his last will and testament and calmly said that he awaited "the arrival of Sister Death." He also drafted an edict concerning the period that the Chair of St. Peter was vacant, restricting photos of the pontiff on his death bed, and prohibiting people from living in the papal apartments during that period. It was clear that the experiences of the previous pope were what he had in mind. He also rejected the request of Josef Cardinal Frings of Cologne and his colleague Julius Cardinal Döpfner of Munich that the Council be postponed. Time was of the essence.[69]

On September 11, 1962, John gave a speech in which he heralded the advent of the Council a month away to help it gain some focus. He accepted the distinction between addressing the Church internally (*ad intra*), and the Church addressing the world (*ad extra*) — a view popularized by Léon-Josef Cardinal Suenens of Belgium. Still, of the seventeen schemas being prepared, only two dealt with the outside world. John admonished that "we expect a contribution based on intelligence and experience that help to heal the *scars* of the two world wars that have so profoundly changed the face of all of our countries." Like all mothers, he observed, Holy Mother Church detests war. The thoughts of Cardinal Suenens were obvious in John's very different declaration. Two weeks later, on September 23, he received confirmation that he had stomach cancer, the cause of death of two of his sisters.

In the first two years of his papacy, before the passing of Secretary Tardini, Pope John's views on major church reform seemed contradictory. Partly it was the complexity of this allegedly simple man. It must be remembered that there were several sides to the aged cleric who assumed the papacy in 1958. First was the young, pastorally oriented priest who had been accused of Modernism and who later in fact embraced the need to relate the methods of presentation (but not, he said, the articles of faith) to the contemporary world. There was the easygoing diplomat who understood the non-Catholic world, especially that of the explosive Balkans and the Middle East, more than most. Then there was the nonjudgmental archbishop and later cardinal who seemed less worried about theological controversies and incipient heresies than losing the souls of simple people.

Yet Roncalli was really not in his heart as progressive or as liberal as Montini, for example. Montini was in fact very sympathetic to the more speculative theologians of the time such as Yves Congar, Henri de Lubac, Pierre Teilhard de Chardin, and Hans Küng; to the worker-priest experiment in France; and to the pro-left wing of the Christian Democrats in Italy. Montini was a man of ideas more than his friend Roncalli, and as such he was more influenced by the unorthodox winds of change. In some ways even Pius XII at times was more receptive to those movements than his own archbishop-diplomat successor.

He actively introduced fewer reforms than Pius XII or even Pius X. On a personal level, he avoided using telephones and dismissed television, seeing it as promoting worldly values and saturated with effeminate programs. Overall, unlike Pucelli, he had little interest in technology or advanced scholarship. And he issued one of the strongest reaffirmations of priestly celibacy of that time.[70]

Oddly, John praised the early drafts from the Curia, while he called for a positive aggiornamento — a true opening to the world. As noted, he is supposed to have said that he thought it was important that he open the windows in order to let fresh air into the Church. Whether he said that or not, he exhibited a confusing behavior at times. Was he supporting the Curia, or was he supporting those who were asking for substantial changes?

In addition, he originally placed great emphasis on the ecumenical nature of the Council, one that would boldly aim at the reunification of Christianity. But quickly it evolved into a Catholic Council with non-Catholic observers, not non-Catholic participants.[71] Some saw his behavior as a series of skillful Machiavellian responses: he kept the Curia on his side, but supported those who wished to undercut its very powers. The bishops, nearly all appointed by Pius XII and through the Curia process, were seen especially in the first session as docile and rather conservative. They were no more willing to recommend radical changes than the priests in the Roman synod years before. The bishops were, however, displeased at times with the ways they had been treated by the Vatican bureaucracy and by Pius over the years, but they surely were not great reformers.

There is a myth that Vatican II tapped into tremendous popular discontent among the laity, who saw their Church as hopelessly out of date. There may have been some of that feeling among segments of the native populations or clergy in Third World countries, but actually there is little evidence that the Council rested on such broad popular unhappiness. For example, it has been estimated that in 1956, only ten out of six hundred bishops in Latin America exhibited any strong social consciousness in an area of the world where one would have expected such a sense.[72]

The discontent in the Church was expressed mostly by members of the hierarchy who were weary of the tight controls of the Curia, by those in the religious orders uneasy with the restrictions of their superiors, and by speculative theologians, especially in the non-Latin European faculties and seminaries, who were under continuous scrutiny. The Council was not a popular revolution, as much as a revolt *at first* of the "out" clergy against the insiders, mainly those in the Vatican hierarchy. Roncalli as pope was now the ultimate insider with recollections still of how he had been treated in the past. He was definitely not a man of vengeance or a person preoccupied with paying back slights; but he had an old man's memory. His successor would be even more sensitive to those slights by the Curia that he had once so skillfully navigated and later been humbled by. Roncalli, however, left the Curia alone; Montini as Paul VI would begin in a limited way to reform it.

A second problem that the Catholic Church faced is typical of large and/or multicultural empires or realms. That is the relationship between the central city or capital and the provinces. That concern is especially important in a Church that continues to characterize itself as the "one, holy, catholic, and apostolic Church." Here the word "catholic" means universal — that is, an institution that transcends boundaries, tribes, and cultures. The Curia feared that changes in theological metaphors in the liturgy and in patterns of authority would accentuate the powerful centripetal or decentralizing tendencies prevalent in the postwar world. Already political colonization was dying, and even Conservative British Prime Minister Harold Macmillan would later talk of those irreversible "winds of change" begun between the world wars.[73]

The previous pope had written a long lyrical encyclical on the Church as the Mystical Body of Christ, with Jesus and his vicar on earth at the head. Now the Church would in Vatican II change the metaphor and speak of the nonhierarchical "People of God." It is by our language that we define ourselves. In a world of decentralization and complexity, the "People of God" could quickly become a thousand peoples, and with the introduction of the vernacular in even the sacred canon of the Mass, the Catholic Church would speak in a thousand tongues. Later at the Council, and often under John Paul II, the meaning of that metaphor "People of God" would be deliberately downplayed.

The progressives saw those changes as being responsive to the needs of the faithful. The conservatives saw the changes as a new Tower of Babel. As for John, he issued a papal encyclical reaffirming the centrality of Latin in the life of the Church, although some said he did not mean to deny the use of the vernacular in Mass; still his successor would deal Latin the greatest blow imaginable by rendering it essentially obsolete in the sacred liturgy of the Church.

Which was the real Pope John? When John spoke of his agenda for updating the Church, he enumerated three great projects: a synod for the Roman diocese, the Council, and a reform of canon law. The synod was to be a sort of dress rehearsal for the larger and more complex Council. As noted, the conservative clergy showed little desire or inclination to engage in major changes in that diocese, even at the instigation of the bishop of Rome himself. Institutions without danger hanging over them rarely reform themselves democratically. Even John's pastoral intention to minister in a sensitive way to priests who had left the Church was generally ignored by the clergy. Although he was an admirer of reforming bishops, past and present, his experiences in the synods in Venice and in Rome should have taught him a lesson about the limits of rejuvenation from the bottom up. And as for the reform of canon law, that was only completed by John Paul II on January 25, 1983 — twenty-two years to the day after John XXIII's original announcement.

On October 11, 1962, John XXIII called the twenty-first General or Ecumenical Council together, an occurrence that some would later say was the most significant religious event since the Protestant Reformation. There in St. Peter's Basilica, above the remains of the first pope and surrounded by Bernini's magnificent baldacchino, the Council began. Over 2,600 bishops attended, a marked increase in the number of participants from Vatican I, where only 737 were in attendance. The pope entered the Basilica of St. Peter's, abandoning the *sedia gestatoria* (the portable elevated chair), which he disliked, saying it made him seasick, and walked up the main aisle, looking to the right at the impressive statute of his first predecessor, Peter the Apostle. He had decided to use a less pretentious throne to sit on, and in his opening address John emphasized the pastoral role of the Council. After the beautiful tones of the traditional hymn "Veni Creator Spiritus," the Mass was said in Latin with some parts in Greek.

The pope's sermon, which lasted for thirty-seven eventful minutes, struck a strong and reforming note. He called history "the great teacher of life," and criticized the "prophets of doom" [misfortune] who "are always forecasting disaster, as though the end of the world were at hand." John then went on to say that the Church "brings herself up to date where required," so as to spread her message to "all men throughout the world." While the Church never departs from the patrimony of truth, she has to look to "new conditions and new forces of life introduced into the modern world, which have opened up new avenues to the Catholic apostolate."[74]

He also pushed aside the notion that Vatican II should continue the judgmental and defensive tone of Vatican I. John argued that the fundamental doctrines of the Church were well known and that focusing on that approach was not necessary. He calmly observed "the substance of the ancient doctrine of the *depositum fidei* is one thing; the way in which it is expressed is another." Pope John observed that the world expected a leap forward in doctrinal insight and the education of conscience and concluded that "errors often vanish as swiftly as they arise, like mist before the sun." He also observed "nowadays, the spouse of Christ [the Church] prefers to use the medicine of mercy rather than severity. She considers that she meets the needs of the present day by demonstrating the validity of her teaching rather than by condemnation." The Church is thus the "loving Mother of all." He then spoke of Christian unity rather than of the need for outsiders to "turn to Rome."

After the Mass, the Sistine Choir sang Palestrina's *Missa Papae Marcelli*, and the cardinals then paid their homage or obeisance to the pope. Canon law required that Pope John read out the oath of Pius IV from 1564 with its declaration that "I confess and hold the Catholic faith" and that "outside of which no one can be saved." In 1887, Pius IX added a reference to "the primacy and infallible magisterium of the Roman Pontiff" — sentiments that did not exactly support the tone that Pope John had presented that day.

Appropriately the Council opened with the question: "Ecclesia, quid dicis de te ipsa" — "Church, what dost thou say for thyself?" On October 11, 1962, after the first day of the Council was over, John appeared before a huge crowd of people, mainly Catholic youth who were carrying torches that evening. There he called out from his window, "Dear children, dear children I hear your voices.... My voice is an isolated one but it echoes the voice of the whole world.... Now go home and give your little children a kiss — tell them it is from Pope John."[75]

In the days following, the pope then met with the diplomatic corps, with the press, and with observer-delegates on the general themes of his Council. His aides referred to "the brethren in Christ" or non-Catholic Christians. To the amazement of the Council and others, the two delegates who had arrived from Moscow expressed their "unaffected friendship" for the pope.

Then the Council began. Despite the offer from Richard Cardinal Cushing of Boston to pay for a simultaneous translation system, the Vatican refused, and so the proceedings of the entire Council were conducted in Latin. In preparation for the Council's deliberations, a survey had been taken of the Church's leaders to ascertain the topics to be covered. Over 9,300 proposals had resulted and then were submitted to preparatory commissions appointed by the pope. In June 1960, over seventy documents, or schemas, were produced. In the months that followed, the Council's major deliberations revolved around the liturgy, the sources of revelation, the importance and role of mass communications, Christian unity, and the nature of the Church itself.

THE CURIAL OPPOSITION

One of the most dramatic events of the Council came at the very beginning during the first organizational meeting. Powerful members of the Curia, led by Cardinal Ottaviani, called for the election of sixteen members to each of the ten conciliar commissions, with the pope appointing eight more members to each group. Then in a startling departure, Achille Cardinal Liénart of Lille proposed instead a delay and argued that the Church Fathers should meet in national and regional caucuses and agree on slates for each of those openings. Cardinal Frings of Cologne immediately seconded the resolution on behalf of other German-speaking cardinals. The applause was overwhelming, and after only fifteen minutes the first business session was adjourned by the president of the Council, Cardinal Tisserant.

When, however, the Italian hierarchy felt slighted by the results of the voting, John helped to redress the balance of it, mainly by including members of the Curia from corresponding congregations on those commissions. Generally the pope, though, stayed out of the Council's business. The first major debate was on the question of liturgy, and once again the overwhelming majority of the Council participants rejected the Curia-prepared draft. Underlining that discussion, though, was the more contentious issue of the powers of the bishops to run their own dioceses and to be seen in a collegial way as the successors of the Apostles.[76]

Conservative Cardinal Ruffini argued that the draft, or schema, had to be judged by the precepts of the encyclical *Media Tordei,* which affirmed the supremacy of the papacy. The implication was to denigrate the national congresses or groups of bishops. Then there was a long discussion on the importance of Latin vis-à-vis the vernacular languages for use in the liturgy. Addressing the Council, the Melkite patriarch of Antioch, Maximos IV Saigh, ignored the Latin tongue and spoke in French to the Council members. He admonished them that in the Eastern Church every language is liturgical if one glorifies God.

Cardinal Tisserant recalled for the Council that Hebrew and Greek had been used by the original Christians, and that Slavic languages and Chinese had already been recognized by the Congregation of Rites as permissible. But for many in the Western Church, Latin was still a powerful sign of unity. Cardinal Siri of Genoa reminded listeners of Pope John's own encyclical, *Veterum Sapientia,* celebrating the use and study of Latin, which had been recently issued. Some native bishops cited the problems of dealing with endless tribal dialects, although in the end the African bishops overwhelmingly supported the use of the vernacular.[77]

In the debates Cardinal Spellman spoke out against the giving of communion under both species, bread and wine, and against concelebration. And Cardinal Ruffini raised questions of hygiene for those drinking from the same cup or chalice. Even Pius XII, though, had approved concelebration, and the practices of receiving communion under both species were already used in the Oriental rites, said Paul-Emile Cardinal Léger of Montreal. Ottaviani warned, however, "Are these Fathers planning a revolution?" Too many changes would scandalize the faithful. Then he was cut off from going way over the fifteen-minute time limit. Infuriated, he boycotted the Council for the next two weeks.

On November 1, the Feast of All Saints, Pope John preached in Latin and then moved into Italian to praise the Church and some of its traditional reformers. He said that there was "only one art, but a thousand forms." With that upbeat observation, the Council resumed its debates. The pope again generally stayed out of the discussions, but when the elderly Bishop Peter Čule of Yugoslavia pleaded for including St. Joseph in the canon of the Mass, he was rudely cut off by Cardinal Ruffini. Then the pope unilaterally added such an insertion of St. Joseph's name three days later, showing that the canon, which had not changed since 610 in the reign of St. Gregory the Great, was also alterable.[78]

The Council moved on to a controversial debate the sources of revelation, which began with a discussion of a schema prepared by Ottaviani's preparatory theological commission. The issues were fundamentally dogmatic and went to the heart of the alleged historic differences between conservatives and progressives and even between traditional Catholics and what they considered were the influences of the Protestant Reformation.

On November 14, the debate on the revelation draft began. It came down to a simple question: How is the word of God delivered to humankind? Individuals may come to know that there is a God, that God has certain characteristics or attributes, and that by the use of right reason we can arrive at those natural truths. But the dogma is that God has intervened in human affairs and given us greater knowledge to obtain a deeper, richer faith. The question is simple; the answer is complex and a source of great contention.

Since the Council of Trent, the Catholic Church has taught that revelation comes from two sources: the Sacred Scriptures and the traditional testimony of the early Church. The Protestant Reformation was partly fought over the insistence of its leaders that the Bible and the Bible alone is the source of God's revelation. Thus, it reduced the importance of the Church, the patristic Fathers, the medieval theologians, and the magisterium of the pope and the bishops. Cardinal Ottaviani warned against any radical departures and asked for the protection of "safe doctrine." It is best to accept the schema prepared by his commission, he argued. But Cardinal Liénart insisted that there were not two sources of revelation, but only one, the word of God. Cardinal Siri brought forth the specter of a new expression of the Modernist heresy if one did support the schema, but opposition to that document mounted. The Cardinal from Vienna, Franz König, observed that the schema had nothing to do with the pope's program at all. Cardinals Suenens, Bea, and Ritter of St. Louis added their agreement to that view.[79]

After hours of confusing debate and a controversial parliamentary move by the conservatives, the pope personally intervened. He withdrew the schema from discussion and appointed a special balanced commission to be composed of members from the theological commission and the Secretariat for Christian Unity. Cardinals Bea and Ottaviani were to be copresidents. In effect, he had thrown his support against the Curia and its drafts.[80]

At times, the question was raised of who was actually running the Council. Pope John's answer was a nonreassuring, "no one." Candidly the pope explained to a group of Pakistani bishops, "Nobody around here knows how to run an ecumenical Council. After all none of us have ever been to one." Actually the Council was supposed to be managed by a council of presidents made up of eight cardinals, but in reality that group rarely met, and the Secretariat for Extraordinary Affairs had the responsibility for oversight, with Secretary of State Cicognani as president. More influential, though, were Cardinal Montini and Cardinal Suenens, who provided some of the intellectual focus for the Council.

On October 11, 1962, Montini proved to be remarkably prescient in his prediction of how the Council would proceed. He laid out a plan that would eventually be followed: the Council should focus on the nature of the Church itself; it should, though, place great emphasis on the Church's relationship to the outside world; the Council should acknowledge papal infallibility and primacy, but go on to discuss collegiality and the important role of the bishops; it should also acknowledge the legitimate roles of the hierarchy, the clergy, and the people. Its attention should be directed in the second session to the mission of the Church. The third session should emphasize the relationship between the Church and the outside world: non-Catholic Christians, civil society, culture and the arts, the world of work, and relationships with the Church's traditional enemies.

Throughout it all, Pope John remained somewhat detached. On November 19, he told the French bishops that he was like the biblical patriarch

Jacob, who was simply watching his sons quarreling. "Yes, there is an argument going on. That's all right. It must happen. But it should be done in a brotherly spirit. It will all work out. I, I am optimistic." To the conservatives who complained about the actions of the progressives, John philosophically recalled that the disputes were even worse at the Council of Trent. His view of the acrimony was simply, "We are not friars singing in a choir." When the controversies about the Roman rite and Latin ensued, the pope not too subtly expressed his admiration for the different Ambrosian rite used in Milan.[81]

The Council then moved on to a discussion of the nature of the Church itself. On the fourth day of debate, December 4, Cardinal Suenens again argued for redrafting the schema by asking for a reconceptualization of the entire work of the Council. He argued that seventy plus documents needed to be pulled together, apparently speaking with the encouragement of the pope. By the end of November, John was reportedly dying, and he was promoting a speed-up in the work of those drafting the schemas between the sessions. The second session was scheduled on September 8, 1963, and a new coordinating commission was instructed to reduce the drafts to under twenty.

The Council also dealt with a statement on the role of the communications media and the question of unity with the Eastern Orthodox churches. The first issue was one on which it was comparatively easy to reach consensus. There was much criticism, however, that the tone in the draft schema on the latter issue was once again that the Orthodox churches should simply "return to the true fold" of Christ, that is, the Roman Catholic church. The patriarch of Antioch argued that the text before the Council would insult the Orthodox churches, and also that one had to realize the unique history and differences of the Oriental Catholic churches vis-à-vis the Latin church.

The patriarch vicar from Egypt, Monsignor Elias Zoghvy, speaking in French, explained the differences between Eastern and Western Catholics. He noted not only differences in liturgy and emphases, but also differences in theology, but not necessarily dogma. He also cited the long history of autonomy and decentralization that characterized that branch of Catholicism. Archbishop Asrate Mariam Yemmeru of Abbas Abba, Ethiopia, reminded his listeners that their rite, said in Gagez, or classical Ethiopian, dated back to the fourth century and included a continuing dialogue between the celebrant and the faithful. The schema was eventually combined with another decree on ecumenism prepared by Bea's commission. In effect, the initial draft was defeated.

Cardinal Ruffini had defended the schema in its entirety, but Cardinal König noted that there was no mention of freedom of conscience. Cardinal Ritter also emphasized the need for a clear statement on the relations of church and state and freedom of conscience as well. The most remarkable speech however was made by Bishop Emile-Joseph de Smedt of Bruges, who to rising applause denounced the Catholic Church's proclivities toward triumphalism, clericalism, and juridicism. He argued that the schema on the Church conveyed too much the impression of an institution arrayed in battle garb, one that was a pyramid with the people on the bottom, and characterized by an excessive legalistic attitude.[82]

Meanwhile, *l'Osservatore Romano* noted increasing anticonciliar activities, especially among right-wing groups in Italy and France. There were attacks on the so-called Modernist tendencies that Roncalli allegedly exhibited when he was a young priest, the supposed pro-Communist tilt of the Vatican's foreign policy, and the constant assaults on the Curia government.

At the Council, the influential Cardinal Montini urged the Fathers to state the mind and will of Christ by defending collegiality and by being more ecumenical. He also became increasingly critical of the Curia, whence he himself came, and of the delay in the Council's work. Observers thought that he was speaking on behalf of the pontiff. Soon it would be Montini who would be setting the agenda and controlling the tempo of the Council.

GOOD POPE JOHN

As noted, since late September 1962, Pope John was aware of his precarious physical condition. Resigned and trusting in God as always, the pontiff concluded, "At least I have launched the big ship — others will have to bring it to port." Finally on December 8, a recuperating Pope John seemed well enough as he ended the first session. When he was asked what he wished to do after the Council ended, he wistfully replied, "Spend a day tilling the fields with my brothers." Then for the next six months, he focused on foreign policy questions, especially the Vatican's relations with the Communist bloc and his call for world peace, enumerated best in his encyclical *Pacem in Terris*. He realized that his life was ending, and he seemed to plead with himself that he wished to die as a priest and as a pope, setting once again an example of the redemptive value of suffering. The Vatican observer Malachi Martin stated that at the end of his life Pope John realized what a terrible mistake the Council was and he regretted it. If that is so, that record has never been clearly established.[83]

Stomach cancer can be a painful end, and Pope John simply remarked, "The first duty of a pope is to pray and suffer." He observed the irony of it all though: "Out there the world exalts me, while here the Lord rivets me to this bed." Gustavo Cardinal Testa, an old friend of Roncalli's, was consoled by the pope, "Dear Don Gustavo, we have to face things as they are. I have had a long life and served the Church and left some sort of mark on history. By God's grace, I haven't behaved badly."[84] On June 3, he died surrounded by his family and Vatican officials. And, yes, at this death, they tapped his brow to certify the end.

There is no question that Pope John XXIII was the most popular pope in this century, one respected and loved both outside as well as inside his Church. He was to them good Pope John, the symbol of decency and good humor. As he once said, "All the world is my family." In his life, he was generally nonjudgmental, but not the simple fool of God that some people thought. His personal assistant, Monsignor Loris Capovilla, once observed, "Pope John was a father to everyone, but a friend to no one."[85]

But John was also not the great manipulative leader or the shrewd peasant visionary that some of his admirers seemed to herald after his death. As a good Catholic and as a good priest, he believed in the Church and in the moving directions of the Holy Spirit. The Council of the bishops was the successor to the Council of the Apostles, and he did not feel that he had to intervene daily in its deliberations. In some ways, he seemed to believe that the very idea of a council, its introduction and its opening, was his contribution. He was never a great theologian preoccupied by dogma. He knew what he believed in and was comfortable with it. Pope John thought however the Catholic Church had to become modernized in the ways it expressed its message. He said to one ambassador, "We must shake off the imperial dust that has accumulated on the throne of Peter since Constantine," and he kept on referring to the need for a "new Pentecost."[86]

He was like most revolutionaries a traditionalist at heart. It was this pope also who so celebrated Latin, just before his successor nearly eviscerated it. It was this pope who was comfortable with the various early drafts, until his Council ripped them to pieces. Still he set the tone of openness, of aggiornamento, that emboldened the bishops who, for reasons of pastoral concern and also probably plain old-fashioned revenge, tried to humble the once arrogant Roman Curia.

As noted, Cardinal Siri of Genoa once called John's papacy the most disastrous since the corrupt Renaissance popes five hundred years ago, although he later recanted. The post–Vatican II Church with its modern bishops and priests has come to accept the assumptions and the practices of the Council. It is over, and one must live with its consequences, they seemed to be saying. The majority opinion, however, is positive toward the Council, its legacy, and its patron, John XXIII.

The fussy, arrogant Curia was routed. Good for the Vatican Fathers, the historians and newspaper reporters of the time seemed to say! But on reflection, one can see that some of what the traditionalists warned against came about. The Roman Catholic Church has been an authoritarian institution with a sense of unity, a well-recognized ritual, and clear boundaries. Its orthodoxy, especially since the Council of Trent, had been rigid, but effectively passed on to each generation, socializing people in the ways of Holy Mother Church.[87] Vatican II and the more radical forces that it unleashed caused considerable damage to that unity and continuity. Reforms of ongoing institutions are extremely difficult, and reformers inevitably have problems with providing balanced leadership that does not open the floodgates of extreme behavior. People usually do not revolt against conservative or even authoritarian governments as much as they do under the easy mantle of change. Thus reform is so dangerous to institutions and to leaders who believe that they can manage it.

But John would not know of those problems. He lived and died an optimist and never had to bear the consequences of the revolution that he began. Thus he will be forever "Good Pope John."

CHAPTER EIGHT

PAUL VI:
THE PERILS OF
AGGIORNAMENTO

Even before the death of Pope John, the name of Giovanni Battista Montini was raised as a possible successor. The ailing pontiff philosophically said to his friends, "I am here to prepare the place for Montini." At the end of his life, he observed, "Providence has most worthy priests all ready to take my place. The first of them is Montini." The person he was so deferential toward became the first cardinal he created — the archbishop of the important industrial city of Milan, an experienced Curial bureaucrat, and a major figure in the Vatican for over three decades. As with any public figure, reservations had been raised over the years about Montini's performance. Even John XXIII jokingly once referred to his longtime friend as the Hamlet-like bishop ("Amletico"), while Curia conservatives, it was said, had so feared him that they conspired to get his patron, Pius XII, to ship him off to Milan without the traditional recognition of a cardinal's hat.[1]

As for Montini himself, he enjoyed the company of Pope John, but he deeply revered the regal and dignified Pius XII. As has been seen, Montini had serious concerns about calling a Church council in the first place, but he soon became an articulate defender of it, although Pope John may have told him to be more reserved in his comments so as to protect his future candidacy as pope. It was to fall to Montini to finish up the Council, to direct it, to contain its consequences, and finally to celebrate its confusing legacy.[2]

THE SUPREME CURIALIST

He was called "the but pope" — a man of hesitations, of waverings, of ambiguity. Indeed his personality was rather different from that of his immediate predecessor. Their attitudes toward life and people are summarized in two striking anecdotes. Like the saints and hermits of old, Montini at times wore a hair shirt with metal points to mortify his flesh. Pope John on the other hand would phone the Vatican grocer telling him where to get the best Parmesan cheese in Reggio Emilia or the finest cornmeal for polenta. The rather old-fashioned Roncalli was immediately celebrated as a reformer. The quiet, gentle, and slightly built Montini was in many ways a liberal intellectual who ended up satisfying neither the archconservatives nor the progressives, in part because he had components of both in his complex spiritual character.[3]

Giovanni Battista Montini was born on September 26, 1897, in the family villa at Concesio, a small suburb of Brescia in northern Italy. His father, Giorgio, was the managing editor of a militant Catholic daily, *Il Cittadino di Brescia,* and had interests in land, banking, and publishing enterprises. Giorgio was committed to spreading the tenets of Pope Leo XIII's social encyclical *Rerum Novarum* and was involved in organizing Catholic congresses to deal with questions of justice and fairness. With Don Luigi Sturzo, he founded the Partito Populari Italiano (the Italian Popular Party), and he was named the president of the Catholic Electoral Union by Pope Benedict XV. Later Giorgio became one of the first Catholics allowed by the Holy See to run for public office when that pontiff loosened up the Church's restrictions on Catholic participation in the political life of Italy.

Giorgio was elected to Parliament three times, in 1919, 1922, and 1924, and became an articulate opponent of the new Fascist enthusiasms. As a member of the Aventine faction, he boycotted the Mussolini-controlled Chamber of Deputies after the murder of Fascist opponent Giacomo Matteotti. Giorgio Montini's wife, Giudetta, also came from a wealthy family and during their marriage was involved in charitable causes and religious activities.

Their second son, Giovanni, was educated at first by the Jesuits and later by the Fathers of the Oratory. In poor health, he was unable to join the military and for a while was not even permitted to enter the seminary. But in 1920 he was ordained a priest and went to Rome to study at the Gregorian University, the state University of Rome, and the famed Accademia dei Nobili Ecclesiastici.

Montini spent several months in 1923 in Poland, but was severely affected by the cold weather and was reassigned to Rome. He was soon transferred to the Federation of Italian Catholic Students and appointed their ecclesiastical assistant, or a sort of chaplain. Soon he was coming into contact with men who would be a part of his life on into his papacy: most especially Giuseppe Pizzardo and Amleto Cicognani. Montini was quickly put on the firing line in the battle being waged against Catholic youth groups by the brutal Fascist organizations; in their cause he proved himself to be both discrete and courageous.[4]

He was also increasingly involved with the Vatican's Secretariat of State, and in 1937 he was named the substitute secretary of state for Ordinary Affairs. His counterpart was the blunt-talking Monsignor Dominico Tardini, who was the equivalent for Extraordinary Affairs and who, as has been noted, became Pope John XXIII's secretary of state. In 1944, Cardinal Maglione died and Pius refused to appoint a new secretary, thus running the powerful office himself with increasing responsibilities for both Montini and Tardini. As noted, the pontiff candidly remarked that he wanted not collaborators, but agents to carry out his policies.

Montini was not only a personal assistant to the aloof pontiff, but he was also involved in high-level diplomacy and heroic efforts to assist prisoners of war, refugees, and missing persons. He supervised many of the Vatican's far-flung relief efforts, was close to the emerging Christian Democrat party, and struck up a friendship with the genial Archbishop Angelo Roncalli. In 1951 he visited the United States, met General Dwight D. Eisenhower and Dr. Tom Dooley at a commencement ceremony at Notre Dame University, and became well known among some segments of the hierarchy in that emerging superpower.[5]

Then in 1954, while the pope was recovering from a nearly fatal illness, conservative Vatican mandarins engineered Montini's transfer to Milan. Just as the conservatives had a generation before forced Della Chiesa out of the Vatican to the see of Genoa, it was speculated that now other conservatives conspired to transfer Montini to Milan. And once again, the exiled victim was denied the cardinal's hat. As has been noted previously, exactly why Montini was forced out remains unclear. Some said however that Pius himself had reservations about his political attitudes. One lame excuse was that he had not notified the pope of a resignation as promptly as he should have. More likely, the conservatives or the pope himself were unhappy with Montini's support of the Christian Democrat prime minister Alcide de Gasperi and of Don Luigi Sturzo, who both wished to curtail the Vatican's influence in Italian politics at that time.[6]

In any case, a shocked and deeply depressed Montini packed to leave the city, saying that he felt now like an orphan. Before he departed, he asked Pius what he should do in Milan. The pontiff's reply was simple, "Preserve the deposit [of the faith]." Later Pius, recovering from a serious illness, finally decided to deliver by radio a lavish tribute praising Montini to the people of his new see. Still that appointment marked the first time in six hundred years that the archbishop of Milan had not been named a cardinal. It has even been speculated that Pacelli's relations had Montini denied a red hat because of his knowledge of certain unpleasant facts about their activities. In any case, Montini left hurt and depressed and later observed, "Milan appeared to me like an immense hostile forest." Roncalli, then a cardinal himself in Venice, tried to console his friend by observing that one could fall out of favor with the Curia and still see one's career survive.[7]

For seven years Montini worked feverishly to reassert the Church's influence in that industrial and largely Marxist city, saying Masses in factories and industrial plants, visiting as many as thirty churches a day, and holding throughout the region conferences which addressed the relationships of the Catholic Church and the world's problems. Pius XI once said that being archbishop of Milan was a tougher job than being pope, and Montini surely was as active as Ratti had been in that same see. There was some talk of Montini as a possible successor to Pius XII, and he was called by some at the conclave in 1958 "the great absent one." But the custom of choosing from the College of Cardinals was too strong, as Roncalli himself quickly surmised; indeed the last person elected pope who was not a cardinal was Urban VI in 1378. The new Pope John, refusing to see himself as a transitional figure, took control easily, and then quickly named more cardinals than expected. On the top of his list was Montini, and so too were some of the conservatives who had so distrusted him in the past.

At the first session of the Council, Montini spoke only twice, but he published a series of newspaper columns for the Milanese faithful that strongly criticized the conservatives in the Curia. As has been seen, he and Belgian Cardinal Suenens provided some of the overall conceptual framework that turned a vague idea into an operational imperative. There is no question that Montini now seemed to accept John's vision, and the ailing pontiff's initial reservations about him vanished.[8]

Before his death, Pope John candidly observed, "I don't have very long to live. I must therefore be very careful in everything I do to stop the next conclave being a conclave 'against me', because then it might destroy the things that I have not been able to achieve." When that conclave met to choose his successor, some eighty-one members were eligible to vote, with a much larger non-Curial and non-Italian group of cardinals than ever before.[9]

INHERITING THE PROGRESSIVE LEGACY

Montini was the favorite of most of the progressives and stayed in Milan until forty-eight hours before the conclave began. While he was discrete, major liberal cardinals led by Liénart, Frings, Suenens, König, Léger, and Alfrink had met and decided to support Montini, although other names were raised. The choice before the College of Cardinals was clear: would it choose to continue the Council in the spirit of Pope John, or move to end it as quickly as possible?

Before the cardinals were sequestered, the introductory homily was given by Monsignor Amleto Tondini, who rather inappropriately attacked the recently deceased Pope John. He criticized his simple optimism and the enthusiastic applause of the masses, and ripped into the Church's traditional foes: scientism, materialism, and moral relativism. It would be better, he argued, if the Council let questions "mature" for some time — the traditional Curia prescription for inaction.[10]

It was a clear challenge not only to the memory of Pope John, but also to the candidacy of Montini and his allies. The cardinal from Milan stayed stoically quiet, his eyes closed, and his lips pursed. It was the haunting voice of the worst sentiments of the Curia that he and others were hearing. The conservatives led by Siri and Ottaviani had decided on Ildebrando Cardinal Antoniutti, prefect of the Congregation of Religion, as their candidate. The only way they could prevail and prevent Montini from getting the two-thirds majority necessary to be pope was to drag out the balloting and force a compromise candidate on a deadlocked conclave.

Under the rules of the Church then in force there were three ways a pope could be chosen. He could be elected by the College of Cardinals; he could be selected by a small committee of cardinals chosen for that purpose; or a candidate could be proclaimed by acclamation or "inspiration." It was rumored that Cardinal Cushing was inspired to make such a motion, but to no avail, and the voting proceeded. The last pope elected by acclamation was Gregory XV in 1621, and it seemed to many to be an unlikely precedent for more democratic times. On February 24, 1996, Pope John Paul II ended the election of the pope by any other method except election by the College.[11]

At first, the conservatives' strategy proved successful as Montini received only about thirty votes and Antoniutti around twenty. Lercaro, the real favorite of some of the progressives, also received around twenty votes. Another compromise candidate from the Curial ranks, Francesco Roberti, head of the Apostolic Segnatura, was waiting in the wings and was mentioned as an alternative.

Lercaro was more of a radical on liturgical reform and on the need to address the plight of the poor. To the conservative Curia, he was thus more to be feared than Montini, the Vatican bureaucrat that they knew and had worked with over the years. The second and third ballots were also inconclusive, and then in open violation of the conclave's rules Gustavo Cardinal Testa, an old friend of Pope John, blurted out loud for all to hear, that the politicking and maneuvering should stop for the good of the Church and that the frontrunner should be chosen. Although he himself had doubts about Montini's fortitude, Testa probably helped to break the deadlock, and on the sixth ballot Montini was elected.

Rumors soon circulated that he had promised to keep Amleto Cicognani as secretary of state so as to garner the votes of conservatives. That explicit deal probably never happened. Indeed it was the progressive leader Cardinal Suenens who, by persuading some Lercaro supporters to come around to Montini, had provided the support necessary to conclude the balloting. Testa was later to observe that "hair-raising things" happened in the conclave, but said that he was not at liberty to disclose them without the approval of the pope.[12]

Montini, who had over the years more experience as a staff person than as a line administrator, had some serious reservations about his own candidacy. Years later after the election, he was to say that he was chosen to be pope not because of his aptitude for the position or because he could best govern the Church during a time of turmoil, but rather because he could suffer and thus make it clear that it is the Lord and no one else who guides and saves the Church.

He once defensively remarked to Lercaro that the latter should have been elected pope, and as noted he meekly deferred to the conservatives by keeping Cicognani on as secretary of state, passing over Suenens at their insistence. To the surprise of all, however, he took the name Paul to symbolize that he was to be an apostle to the modern world. Ironically, or perhaps appropriately, an English newspaper, *The Tablet,* printed at this time his article, written while he was still a cardinal, defending Pius XII of charges that he had been silent during the Holocaust. Montini was to be ever loyal to that memory, even repeating his defense in the heart of Jerusalem in front of Jewish audiences.

Unlike his predecessors in this century, Paul VI was highly conscious of the limits of papal authority and of the need to build a consensus for what turned out to be fairly radical changes recommended in a very short period of time by a council that was given to windy discourses, poorly written statements, and periodic bouts of disorganization. Pope John had wanted, for his own purposes, the Council to be called quickly, but his agenda was often unclear. He seemed content at times just to have had the distinction of calling a Church council together, and he initially accepted the conservative Curial drafts. In fact, of the thirty-six cardinals who could be classified as conservative in the Council, twenty-one had been raised to that rank by Pope John. When it was suggested that the Church buy new audio equipment for the Council, the pope insisted that it could be rented for the short duration that he expected it would take. Still his openness to the world and his generally nonjudgmental character led a very traditional pope into the ranks of the reformers. Indeed in many ways he created those very ranks. He became, in the words of the Italian journalist Carlo Falconi, the first "antipope."[13]

As has been seen, the first session ended with some confusion and disappointment for conservatives and progressives alike. Later at the papal conclave some twenty-two to twenty-five cardinals declined to vote for Montini, even when the outcome was clear. Mostly Italian and mainly in the service of the Curia, they were the permanent civil service that was in virtual opposition to the very Council that Montini swore he would uphold. The second session would thus be even more difficult than the first.

Paul immediately cleared the air and boldly announced his commitment to the agenda of Pope John's Council. He was aware of his reputation for indecisiveness, but he forthrightly remarked in private that he was more liberal than John was, which was true, that he knew exactly what he was doing, and that he was going to do it at his own pace.

To the consternation of the progressives, though, Paul bent over backward to accommodate the Curia and the conservatives, allowing them to recite over and over again their catalog of horrors at these new initiatives. In part he was patient in order to build a consensus and prevent a wholesale schism, as had happened after many other Church councils. But in part, he also shared later some of their reservations, especially toward the *periti* (experts or theologians), who were embracing more radical proposals than Pope John or even the Fathers in the first session had imagined.[14]

Some innovations struck at the very core of the Church's authority, while others challenged even the established dogmas of the Catholic Church. Paul was an apostle to the modern world, and he was a true progressive reformer, but he was also the guardian of the magisterium and the "deposit of the faith." His most authoritative biographer, Peter Hebblethwaite, has called Paul "the first modern pope," characterizing him as a discerning person who sought to understand the signs of his times. He was knowledgeable not only about traditional theology and Thomism, but also about Fascism, Nazism, Communism, the Third World, feminism, ecology, and the disarmament and peace movements. It is hard to imagine, but in his spare time he enjoyed listening to the rock musical *Jesus Christ Superstar.*

Paul insisted on encouraging dialogue — even with those inside and outside the Church who were his bitterest critics. When he went to India, millions turned out to see this symbol of an alien faith, not because they wished to learn about Catholicism — the religion of European missionaries — but because they revere in their own tradition what are called holy men, of which he surely was one.

When one dissident theologian, Karl Rahner, remarked sardonically that he had once been forbidden by the Holy Office to write about concelebration and now Paul himself was concelebrating the Mass, the pope simply smiled and enigmatically responded, "Yes there is a time for laughter and a time for weeping."* During his tenure in office, he stubbornly protected priestly celibacy and yet opened up the Church more than ever to talented women in other ministries. His successor, Karol Wojtyla, or John Paul II, whose career he helped to advance, reacted against both Popes John and Paul's legacies in 1985. The Extraordinary Synod in that year abandoned the language of "the People of God," and resurrected the older pessimism of the times so familiar in the pre-Johnniane era.[15] That was not to be Paul's way.

---

*There had been concelebration in the Latin rite routinely for priestly ordination.

THE SECOND SESSION

To the surprise of nearly every observer, the pontiff set September 29, 1963, as the date for the opening of the second session of the Ecumenical Council. In a sign of respect and collegiality toward the bishops, the pope allowed them to wear the *mozzetta,* or the elbow-length cape symbolic of their episcopal jurisdiction that is not worn outside the bishop's own diocese. The bishop of Rome thus reached out to the other successors of the Apostles.

Paul, though usually a diffident man, was not above crowd-pleasing gestures. Before the session began he gave the Roman Curia a half day off after his long address to them and noted that he would grant them a pay raise because of the increased cost of living in that city. He praised the Curia, but acknowledged that since it had not been reorganized since 1908, it may "have grown ponderous with a venerable old age, shown by the disparity between its practices and the needs and usages of modern times." He added that the Curia needed "to be simplified and decentralized, and to adapt itself to new functions," and then he concluded his address with charming praise for "this old and ever new Roman Curia."[16]

At the opening ceremony on September 29, the pope also abandoned the *sedia gestatoria* at the doors of the basilica and walked up the aisle. There, dressed in a bishop's miter and not the elegant triple tiara, he greeted the crowds by waving rather than giving a formal blessing. In his address, Paul associated his reign with the Council of his predecessor and called John's original summons a product of "divine inspiration."

Paul portrayed the Council as the logical complement to Vatican I in the nineteenth century with its excessive attention paid to the primacy of the papacy. He identified four challenges that needed to be addressed in the coming session: the Church must formulate a new awareness of her own nature; the Fathers should stress renewal and reform necessary to stripping away the defective aspect; there must be an emphasis on the unity of all Christians; and there should be a dialogue between the Church and the modern world. In a dramatic gesture at the opening meeting he turned to the observers from the other Christian communities and offered an apology for anything the Catholic Church had done over the centuries to lead to separation. It was an extraordinary overture from the leader of a denomination that had once argued that it contained a monopoly of religious truth and that those outside of its fold could not achieve salvation. Then Paul concluded with a theme that would become increasingly important for the Church in the later part of this century — he insisted that Catholics must aid "the poor, the oppressed, the suffering."[17]

The pontiff had challenged the Council Fathers to return to the most difficult task before them — one of self-definition, of reformulating the mission of the oldest institution in the Western world. Although the bishops believed as an article of faith that the Council was directed by the Holy Spirit, they had to do its business through committee work. And many times the opaque fuzziness of committee drafts and the ad hominem debates seemed to tax even the legendary inspiration of the Spirit of the Trinity. Added to that normal human failing — committees — was the deliberate strategy of the conservatives to obstruct the workings of the Council because of their minority status.

It was clear by the second session that the conservative strength was weakening and that the progressives had overwhelming support, adding over three hundred of the nearly twenty-five hundred bishops to their ranks since the first session. The conservatives thus attempted to maintain control over the agenda of the Council and its committees by appealing to the pontiff for fair play and judicious reconsideration of Council proposals. The assumption behind their strategy was that the Curia would outlive the Council, indeed outlive another pope, and it would restore sanity to the Church if it did what it did best — delay.

Most critical then were the deliberations on the nature of the Church, the schema titled *De Ecclesia*. Debate began to focus on two key issues: the collegiality of the bishops and the revival of the deaconate. On behalf of the Theological Commission, its president, the conservative Cardinal Ottaviani, warned the Council that the deposit of faith must not only be guarded, it must also be presented to all. But the methods of presentation were the issue. An initial show of support for the schema was overwhelmingly positive, with 2,231 favorable votes of 2,301 votes possible. But that balloting was misleading. For what emerged was a long, tedious, and inconclusive debate that lasted for the first five weeks and did not seem headed to closure. In disgust, one American cardinal, Richard Cushing of Boston, simply went home.[18]

Half of the session was over, and there still was not a full agreement on what the Church was in the eyes of its own Fathers. In addition, the session, unlike the previous one, was totally open to the press. The world could see the disagreements within the Catholic Church. The world could also see that the stereotype of a monolithic hierarchy and docile clergy was false. The bishops were united in their faith, but they knew the Church and its mission through different perceptions of their own cultures and their own life experiences.

The Armenian patriarch, Ignace Pierre XVI Batanian, for example, wanted more of a discussion of the universal priesthood of the faithful, the authority of the hierarchy over the laity, and the need for greater spirituality. Archbishop Ermenegildo Florit of Florence criticized the excessive theological aspects of the document; African Cardinal Laurean Rugambwa wanted a longer discussion of evangelization and the importance of missions; the exarch for the Ukrainians in Canada, Archbishop Maxim Hermaniuk, asked for a greater explanation of the collegiality of bishops. And on it went. The lay auditors, invited by the pope, added a note of gratitude, however, when they expressed their thanks for the invitation to be observers.

Before and as the second session was progressing, Paul had begun a series of modulated speeches aimed at building specific support for his way of doing things. Earlier on September 12, he had addressed a formal letter to Cardinal Tisserant, dean of the College of Cardinals, emphasizing the papal role as the apex of the Vatican hierarchy; on September 14, he addressed a letter and an exhortation to the bishops of the world which underscored his position as the head of the Universal Church; on September 21, he addressed the members of the Roman Curia, focusing on their dedication to the papacy and its policies; on September 22, he spoke to journalists, laying out a public relations offensive and also stressing as the son of a journalist his affinity to them; on September 26, the pope spoke to an assembly of pilgrims, highlighting himself as the pastor of his flock; and on September 29, he addressed the Church Fathers as St. Peter's successor, speaking to the successors of the other Apostles.[19]

Even though he emphasized that he wished to stay out of the day-to-day deliberations of the Council, Paul would interject himself at times, often using others to carry his messages or concerns. Probably with the pope's encouragement, Cardinal Lercaro in the debate on the nature of the Church issued some guidelines on the definition of the Mystical Body of Christ, the importance of baptism in defining the membership of the Church, and the insistence that the Eucharist was not just a sign of unity but "a dynamic entity." He then emphasized that the Church was "a new people, a new creation." Lercaro urged that more views should be included in the draft dealing with the aspirations of "the men of our time."[20]

Metaphors define reality, and the Fathers debated whether the Church could best be described as the Kingdom of God, or the Family of God, or the People of God. At stake too was the definition of collegiality. Did the bishops inherit that "right" by the nature of the apostolic succession from the twelve disciples of Jesus or were they granted those powers by the grace and pleasure of the pope? Was the debate on collegiality to be cast as a matter of divine origin or as an organizational reorientation? The conservatives in the Curia clearly favored the latter view. But that position, as Paul knew, would virtually prohibit serious dialogue with the Eastern Orthodox prelates — a serious matter for a pope who was fascinated, as was John, with the notion of Christian reconciliation.

The Fathers debated if the pope was infallible by himself, even if it meant being in opposition to the Church. Could the Church be infallible as a whole if it were in opposition to the pope's exercise of infallibility? Archbishop Lawrence Shehan of Baltimore tried to clarify the issue saying, "Such definition is never to be understood as against the consent of the Church. For since we believe the pope to be infallible through Divine assistance, by that very fact we believe that the assent of the Church will never be lacking to his definition, because it cannot happen that the body of the bishops will be separated from its head, and because the universal Church cannot fail." However, progressive theologian Hans Küng, already under scrutiny from the Holy Office, went on to argue that there were historical instances of popes preaching heretical doctrines who were successfully opposed by the Church councils of their time.[21]

The Council also engaged in a lively debate on the question of restoring the permanent deaconate and opening it up to married men. Francis Cardinal Spellman of New York criticized such a restoration as an unnecessary step, saying of its past history, "Let us not indulge in archaeology." He was joined by Corrado Cardinal Bacci, who warned that the proposal was dangerous and would lead to a decline in vocations to the priesthood. But the progressives, led again by Cardinals Suenens and Döpfner, defended the proposal as necessary in some parts of the world, and Döpfner added probably ironically that the Council of Trent provided some support for a separate deaconate.

As expected, such a discussion of a married deaconate led to the obvious question of relaxing the mandatory celibacy requirement for clergy in the Latin Church. The Vatican quickly issued a statement reaffirming the obligation of celibacy in the West and noting that it was based on the Gospel and represented the total gift of the priest to Christ and to his Church. Some have made the assertion, however, that Pope Paul himself may have recognized the need for married priests in certain missionary areas, but if so he suppressed those sentiments at the time. His own mentor, Pius XII, had in fact proven to be more flexible than many previous pontiffs when he admitted former married Anglican priests into the priesthood of the Latin rite. There was some disjointed discussion of the role of the laity in the Church as well in the Council's long deliberations. In the past, it was sarcastically said that the functions of laymen were *credere, orare, obedire, solvere* (to believe, to pray, to obey, and to pay).

In the deliberations, Cardinal Ottaviani rose to attack the *periti,* or theological experts, who had led the bishops, in his opinion, astray on the issue of a married deaconate. But progressive leader Cardinal Suenens went on to speak of the varied missions of the Church and its diverse charisma, and then urged that the number of lay auditors be increased, and that even women be invited into that group. "Unless I am mistaken, women make up one-half of the world's population," he blithely observed.[22]

Some right-wing papers immediately attacked the mere mention of women in the hierarchy of the Church. The crude Italian newspaper *Il Borghese* spoke of the resurrection of the apocryphal "Popess Joan" and of furtive Boccaccio-esque encounters. The English paper *The Tablet* spoke of the approach of "the paladin of ecclesiastical neofeminism." As the years passed, the Church hierarchy, especially in the Vatican, felt increasingly threatened by the demands of women for positions of high authority in the Church, especially ordination as priests. In November 1995, the Vatican claimed that the ban on women as priests reached the threshold of being an "infallible" statement.[23]

To resolve the impasse on the *De Ecclesia* schema, four questions were to be posed on October 16 to the Council: the sacramentality of the episcopal order; its incorporation by rite in the college of bishops; the supreme power of the college in union with the pope; and the restoration of the deaconate for married men. Then the Church Fathers were abruptly informed that a vote on the issues had been delayed. Apparently the pope had intervened and even ordered printed statements containing those questions destroyed. Finally, though, on October 30, the propositions were put to the Church Fathers and were overwhelmingly approved. The pope publicly at least stayed out of the controversy. Bishop John J. Wright of Pittsburgh, a noted intellectual and progressive, called the votes "a turning point" in the history of Vatican II. However, the Theological Commission, under Cardinal Ottaviani, continued to delay implementing those understandings, and apparently Paul intervened to get more cooperation.

The pope, though, was facing two immediate problems of his own, the first being the increasing pressure he felt from those who claimed that Pope John's foreign policy initiatives were hurting the Christian Democrat party and anti-Communist forces in Italy, a matter of deep interest considering both Paul's own sympathies and also the deteriorating political situation in that nation. Thus the pope suddenly seemed to be more receptive to the conservative concerns enumerated by Cardinal Siri, the head of the Italian Bishops Conference.

The second problem was increasing dismay over the Council's delays on the drafts on ecumenism and on the Jews. Under Popes John and Paul, Cardinal Bea, as well as other high-ranking Church leaders, had promised greater overtures to non-Catholics, and a strong statement against anti-Semitism, which many argued had sometimes been nurtured by the Church over the centuries.

The schema on ecumenism (*De Oecumenismo*) had three chapters dealing with the principles of Catholic ecumenism, the practice of ecumenism, and relations with Christians separated from the Catholic Church, which included both the Eastern churches and those separated from the sixteenth century on. To those chapters were added chapters 4 and 5 on religious liberty and on the role of the Jews in salvation-history. The Americans were especially supportive of those chapters and had received commitments from the Council leadership that the full draft would definitely be voted on before the recess. However, the leaders then informed the major sponsors, through Cardinal Bea, that the draft would not be voted on due to the press of time. Once again, it appeared that the progressive majority was being thwarted by the conservatives, and now with the tacit consent of the pope.

Pope Paul, however, was secretly planning a trip to the Middle East and was unwilling to push then and there for the draft on the Jews. He did not wish to alienate some of his Arab hosts, a consideration which the Council members did not know about at the time. The Vatican was also under strenuous pressure from some Arab states, especially Nasser's Egypt, and from Catholic prelates who had to return home to Arab states to avoid issuing any statement that could be seen as favorable to Israeli's political interests. The postponement of chapters 4 and 5 caused great dismay among many Church Fathers and a bitter sense of letdown, which focused on the pope and especially his advisors. Actually the pontiff in late November increased the membership on the various commissions of the Council and named mostly progressives to those openings. But those developments seemed to go unnoticed.[24]

On November 22, the world was shocked by the assassination of President John F. Kennedy. The pope expressed his deep condolences, and the Vatican diplomats shortly began to reassess the implications for American foreign policy and the Holy See's interests in aligning itself so closely with the United States in its definition of the Cold War.

In its deliberations the Council proposed what became a much criticized draft on the communications media and then returned to issues dealing with Christian unity. Finally, though, on December 4, the session's time had run out. The pope appeared to close the session and received very little enthusiastic applause from the bishops. He tried to recite the achievements of the Council so far and mentioned the ongoing reforms of canon law, another favorite project of his predecessor. The pope praised the laborious debates as true exercises in freedom of expression and approved the new liturgical constitution. He did not mention the question of what constituted collegiality and the role of the bishops. Clearly there was a genuine sense of disappointment that marked the end of the session.

APOSTLE TO THE HOLY LAND

And then the pope, with a sense of drama of which he was supposed to be devoid, electrified his fellow bishops with the announcement that he was visiting the Holy Land in January. Thus instead of talking about Christian unity and Jewish reconciliation, the Holy Father was to come with outstretched arms as a pilgrim, as St. Paul, to the believers and nonbelievers alike. He would meet with Orthodox and other Eastern religious leaders, especially Patriarch Athenagoras of Constantinople, and he was to walk in Jesus' footsteps through the sacred city of Jerusalem and its biblical environs, there talking to Jewish and Arab peoples. The sullen bishops perked up and began cheering, and then rhythmic clapping started to burst out of St. Peter's Basilica, as they marked their approval of the pope's startling announcement.

Earlier, in July 1963, the then-Cardinal Montini had submitted a report on the religious and social situation in Palestine, underscoring in the process his early interest in that region. As pope he had also read with great attention a book called *Jesus, the Church and the Poor* by Père Joseph Gauthier, a priest who ran a housing project in Nazareth, Israel, which outlined the abuses visited on the unfortunate in that area, and who urged the pontiff to retrace the footsteps of Jesus on the Way of the Cross.[25]

When Paul VI left Rome to great cheers, he began an exciting itinerary, one that indeed followed in the path of Christ and his Apostles. On that trip, he stood at the banks of the River Jordan, where John the Baptist preached and had baptized the younger Jesus of Nazareth. He traveled the road from Jericho and walked to the Damascus Gate, where he was greeted by enormous pressing crowds and where a banner overhead read "Welcome to the Apostle of Peace." At one point, Paul actually picked up a little handicapped boy to shield him from being trampled.

He stopped at various Stations of the Cross on the Via Dolorosa and later entered the Mount of Olives, prayed in the Garden of Gethsemane, and on Sunday went past Bethany to Israel, visiting Bethlehem, the summit where the Sermon on the Mount was delivered, Mount Tabor (the site of Christ's Transfiguration), and Jesus' favorite town, Capernaum. Always reaching for a meaningful historical gesture, Paul wore the Cross of St. Gregory given by Queen Theodolinda to Pope Gregory in the year 603.

Everywhere he went, the pontiff was greeted by enormous crowds. Security at times seriously broke down, especially at the Damascus Gate, but Paul emerged from the pressing masses, smiling and deeply impressive to Catholics and the largely non-Catholic observers. The heir of Peter walked as the Apostles had walked, in the footsteps of Jesus of Nazareth.

Paul saved some of his most important gestures for the meeting with Athenagoras, the patriarch of Constantinople. For the first time since the schism of 1054, a patriarch and a pope met, and did so at the Church of the Holy Sepulcher in Jerusalem. They embraced, and Athenagoras remarked, "We should understand each other, we should make peace, we should show the world that we are once more brothers." The pope offered him a chalice, but they did not concelebrate the Mass together, for they were still apart in many ways. However Paul observed optimistically, "A day will come when all Christians of the world will drink from the same chalice."

The next day the pope celebrated a Mass on the Feast of the Epiphany at the Altar of the Magi in Bethlehem. He spoke of the need for religious unity, and then traveled back to Jerusalem to meet with Athenagoras again. He accepted a pectoral chain from the patriarch, symbolizing the apostolic succession, and asked that they read the Gospel of St. John, chapter 17, together. Later the pope met the Anglican archbishop of Jerusalem and several Lutheran representatives as well. But still, he candidly acknowledged that for some Christians the greatest obstacle to reunion was the papacy itself. At one point, Athenagoras asked Paul, "What do we do now?" And the pope noncommittally responded, "I don't know. When I get back, I will consult the cardinals and see."

The pope in a sermon recognized Abraham, the common patriarch of the three major monotheistic religions: Judaism, Christianity, and Islam. He met with Jewish leaders and took time out to once again defend Pius XII's record, remaining always more loyal to him than Pius had been to his one-time aide. He gave King Hussein of Jordan a valuable eighteenth-century clock and an electrocardiogram machine meant for a hospital in that nation, a nice mixture of heritage and technology, the old and the new. The monarch in return presented the pontiff with a plaque made from the wood of olive trees in the Garden of Gethsemane.

Then he returned from Amman to Rome's Ciampino Airport. The pope's entourage went up the historic Appian Way, where according to legend the fleeing St. Peter was supposed to have seen Jesus and stopped and asked him, "Quo vadis?" (Where are you going?) Jesus responded, "I am going to Rome to die in your place." Peter returned back to the city and to his fate as a martyr of the faith. Like the emperors of old, Paul VI knew the sounds of the elusive triumph as he approached the heart of the city. Now he, not John XXIII, was truly the pope of his Church in his own right. And at the same time as Paul was traveling through the shrines of Jerusalem and the triumphs in the Holy Land, his aides were laying the groundwork for another milestone visit — this one to the United Nations in New York City.

THE THIRD SESSION

But back in Rome, the intrigue and discontent among the Council forces continued. Albert Cardinal Meyer of Chicago forcefully pleaded with the pope for the religious liberty draft, claiming it was "the number one and most important question in the whole schema on ecumenism." Paul was noncommittal. Then he decided to name a committee headed by the progressive Cardinal Lercaro to supervise implementing liturgical reforms. But that announcement was followed by a statement that limited the right of the episcopal conferences to oversee their own liturgical translations; however, after protests mounted to that step, an amended version followed. Also Paul invited controversial Redemptorist priest Bernhard Häring to give the Lenten retreat, and the pope urged him to help the Curia open itself up to the spirit of the Council. Häring had been silenced by that very group in the 1950s.[26]

On May 17, 1964, the pope announced a new secretariat to deal with "non-Christian religions," but seesawed again by naming conservative Paolo Cardinal Marella as its president. At times he seemed consumed by the need to balance his gestures and nuances. In another development, Paul appeared to back away from Pope John's more tolerant foreign policy, and he reiterated criticisms about atheist Communism and its oppressive ideological system. Whether he was concerned about the Italian political situation or was just trying to appease the Curia conservatives, the cautionary note is what prevailed.

Then as the third session of Vatican II was about to begin, Paul received a letter signed by a group of conservative cardinals, bishops, and religious superiors maintaining that the Council's discussions on collegiality were full of "novel" opinions and doctrines, that they were scripturally invalid and not grounded in the wisdom of previous councils, and that such views were coming from unreliable people with nondoctrinal biases. The Church was losing its hierarchical focus, the model that had been so secure and successful up to now. The pope, clearly upset, pondered their charges, while trying to remain true to the spirit of aggiornamento. At one point though, Paul remarked, "History is moving too quickly for us: the institutions don't give enough time for theological reflection to mature: collegiality is an example."[27]

On September 14, partly as a response to those warnings, he reasserted his support for a definition of Church power that involved the bishops, saying, "We are in duty bound to recognize the apostles as teachers, rulers and sanctifiers of the Christian people, 'stewards of the mysteries of God' (I Cor. 3, 1), witnesses to the Gospel, ministers of the New Testament, and in some sense, the very reflection of the 'glory of the Lord' (2 Cor. 3, 6–18)." Still in the lonely hours of the night, he studied the historical treatments on the subject of collegiality from past Church authorities.

Thus Paul seemed to accept the Council and yet insist that it had to be reined in. He warned against the wish to "hide, weaken, change, deny if need be those teachings of the Catholic Church which are not acceptable today by the separated brethren."[28] Meanwhile, the Curia in its day-to-day operations continued to restrict the application of the Council's decisions and the new spirit it embodied. It sought to curtail mixed marriages, delay any reform of the liturgy, slow up the establishment of an episcopal synod, tighten up on seminary training, and reaffirm the central philosophical importance of Thomism. Conservatives also intended to thwart any statement on religious liberty, curtail changes in the administration of the missions and religious orders, restrict overtures to the Eastern churches, and contain expressions of ecumenism.

On September 14, 1964, the pope, dressed in red vestments, opened the Council and concelebrated Mass with twenty other prelates similarly dressed — a sure sign of a collegial mood on his part. He emphasized the papacy as a form of service, not domination, praised the prerogatives of bishops, and greeted warmly the Catholic lay auditors and non-Catholic observer delegates. The Council then went back to the hotly debated and contentious topics that had marked the end of the second session: religious liberty, Judaism, ecumenism, and the nature of collegiality.

The debate on the draft on religious liberty began on September 23 with a new and improved schema that stressed the dignity of man as the basis of toleration. But soon Cardinal Ruffini warned that the declaration should be titled "On Religious Toleration" not "Liberty," for those in error had no rights. The Spanish cardinal, Quiroga y Palacios, added that the document seemed to favor liberalism and was more appropriate for Protestant countries than Catholic ones.

The progressive spokesmen, including American Cardinals Cushing, Meyer, and Ritter, supported the statement, and Cushing paraphrased Thomas Jefferson by asking for "a decent respect for the opinions of mankind." The Americans had been ably assisted by the Jesuit John Courtney Murray, another theologian once under suspicion in Rome, who provided some of the framework for both the Council's departure on religious liberty and also earlier for the American Catholic position celebrating the separation of church and state during John F. Kennedy's difficult campaign for the White House in 1960.[29]

Some of the Eastern European bloc prelates, suffering from the restraints imposed by the Marxist states they lived in, supported religious liberty for their own reasons. The Council overwhelmingly approved the draft on religious liberty and turned quickly to hear Cardinal Bea, who was due to leave in order to return a sacred relic, the head of St. Andrew, to the Greek Orthodox Church. Five hundred years before the relic had been given for safekeeping to Pope Pius II by the last Byzantine prince who was fleeing the onslaughts of the Turks. At the Council, Bea spoke eloquently on the declaration on the Jews; he emphasized that the document should have no implications for Arab-Vatican relations and was meant to bring once and for all an end to the charge of deicide against the Jewish people.

When the draft was postponed in the second session, Cardinal Bea had philosophically observed, "What is put off is not put away." Now patiently and rationally he tried to counter the attempts to amend the text even further by not including the deicide exclaimer, and also by emphasizing the idea of encouraging the conversion of the Jews to the true faith, Catholicism. That was obviously not what Bea and his ecumenical secretariat members had in mind. In the debates Cardinal Ruffini rose again, this time to note that one cannot kill God, so the deicide charge was simply incorrect. He also observed that the Church had saved many Jews from the Nazi onslaught and that the Jews should rid the Talmud of anti-Christian remarks. He went on to argue that the Jews had in the past inspired the Masons in Europe to attack Catholic clergy.

The draft went back to committee, and the Council took up the schema on divine revelation that had been such a problem in the first session. The Council also continued its difficult debate on the question of collegiality. The conservatives launched a major offensive to bottle up both the religious liberty schema and the statement on the Jews. Somewhat disconcerted, seventeen leaders of the progressives directly wrote the pope, denouncing the violation of the rules of the Council. Paul immediately insisted that the two documents would be placed under Bea's secretariat, but he then appointed a balanced commission to seek improvements in the religious liberty draft. The declaration on the Jews would be gingerly voted on as an appendix to the *De Ecclesia* document. Also, when there was some talk in the Council on the issue of birth control, the Church Fathers were reminded that the issue was not up for discussion and that a special papal commission was looking at the controversial subject.

The world had changed so much since the last Vatican Council under Pius IX. The forces of totalitarianism, technological progress, atomic war and nuclear energy, rampant tribalism and brutal nationalism, a pervasive and at times irresponsible mass media, and the incredible rapidity of change had boggled the modern mind. The Church Fathers sought somehow to deal with all of those phenomena and yet retain what they liked to call the traditional deposit of faith. Here in the draft on the modern world all of those forces were somehow supposed to come together. The Church must recognize "the signs of the times" as it was phrased, but did that mean embracing those secular trends or accepting the assumptions of those times? The draft called for a dialogue with all people of goodwill, but what would such an exercise lead to — confusion, comity, enlightenment, heresy, unity? Through it all, Bishop La Ravoire Morrow of India insisted, "Religion is not fear, but love."[30]

Its critics called the Church too hierarchical, too Western, too juridical, too repressive of free expression, too medieval, too wealthy, too clerical, too domineering. Before there was a dialogue with the world, there needed to be a dialogue within the Church itself. One of the changing signs, for example, was the role of women — what of the Church's prohibitions? On another controversial topic, Cardinal Suenens pleaded for broader understanding of the issues involved in birth control, exclaiming: Let us avoid a new Galileo affair. One is enough for the Church, he proclaimed. Later he toned down his remarks.

The Catholic Church also had to confront directly the increasing masses of the poor — especially in the so-called Third World nations. One religious superior, Father G. Mahon, observed, "We cannot remain silent about social justice. The Church is not a mere spectator of the world's miseries, it is not called upon to save disembodied souls, but men." The Council also discussed the nature of modern war and the problems of adapting the traditional "just war" theology to atomic warfare, which made no distinction between combatants and civilians.[31]

Pope Paul decided to embrace another historic gesture when he appeared at one of the Council's working sessions and sat at the head of the Council Presidents' table. This was the first time that a pope had appeared at a Church council since the Council of Trent. Cardinal Agagianian had informed Paul earlier that the draft on the missionaries was rather non-controversial, and that he should lead that discussion if he wished to come. The pope dutifully praised the document, and then was embarrassed when it was subjected to withering criticism. The Vatican had earlier announced that the pontiff was going to make another extraordinary pilgrimage, this time to India, and those plans were fulsomely praised by Agagianian at that meeting. But the pope finally left the gathering, a bit angered at the cardinal's bad advice.

Then on November 16, 1964, the Doctrinal Commission received an addendum or a note to chapter 3 of *Lumen Gentium*. This "Nota Explicativa Praevia" apparently came from the pope himself and was meant to explain that papal authority must be more specifically acknowledged in the draft. Some said that the note was still another concession to the conservatives, but it is probable that Paul himself had some reservations or second thoughts about the language that had been voted. The note concluded that the term "episcopal college" was not meant to be viewed as a body of equals, but "a stable body" of individuals; that bishops can exercise their powers only in authority with the hierarchical Church; that the use of the word "college" here means with the pope and never without him; and that an episcopal college acts only sometimes in a collegial way. With those caveats Paul actually won over a substantial portion of the conservative minority, who voted for the final draft, but in the process he alienated some important progressives with what some said was his ill-timed intervention.

To add to his problems, the pope also decided to insist on amendments at the very end of the session on the document on ecumenism. Eight out of the nineteen amendments that the pope submitted were similar to those reservations that originally came from the conservative minority and had already been rejected by the secretariat. The progressives were dismayed at the last-minute delays, but many of the changes actually were minor linguistic equivocations. Then the Council was informed by Cardinal Tisserant that the draft on religious liberty, which so many had expected would be voted on in the third session, would be carried over into the fourth. The American delegation was especially distraught, for it was their issue in the eyes of the media and many others. Their leaders appealed directly to the pope for a vote, but their appeal was in vain.

The Council again ended in a mood of sad resignation. Paul was portrayed by some as having betrayed the spirit of his predecessor and having given way to a small, recalcitrant minority. The pontiff added to the criticism by designating Mary the "Mother of the Church," a title that was considered to be unappreciated by many Protestants seeking greater ecumenical ties.

The attacks on the pope continued after the Council. Paul privately tried to explain, "I am perhaps slow. But I know what I want. . . . The declaration of religious liberties has been held over out of respect for the rights of the minority. That is the only motive: respect for them. I could not simply ignore them. But in substance, nothing has changed. Religious freedom remains intact." Later in speaking to an Anglican observer, Canon Bernard Pawley, the pope elaborated, " 'I think Anglicans often understand what is going on among us better than anyone else. They have a hierarchy. They believe in the Church. I have clear principles on which I act in times of difficulty. I must act in faith. I must show that I understand the aspirations of the two sides when they disagree, that I love them personally, that I respect their institutions and ways of thinking. As captain of the ship, I have to keep her on a steady course...so you bring all along with you. I am not going to act in a hurry. We have made great strides, but we have made them together.' (Meaning that the new documents, though not being rushed, had had an almost unanimous vote.) 'It is better for me to go ahead slowly and carry everyone with me, then to hurry along and cause dissension. Especially when I speak in public, I must show that I love all my sheep, like a good shepherd.' "[32]

The pope was indeed sensitive about the pace of the Council. The session that had shown such real progress was pictured in a darkened way by both Church progressives and their sympathetic allies in the media. And once again, Paul left the dissensions of the institutional Church for the exotic pilgrim fields. He had been criticized as a Hamlet, an indecisive, frightened, confused purveyor of consensus politics, an unworthy successor to the daring good Pope John. But when he arrived in India, he was greeted by millions of non-Catholics, nonbelievers in his creed. When some Indians were asked why they traveled to see Paul, they responded that they had heard that a holy man ("Bura Guru") had come, and that their faiths revered such men. Thus it seemed that Hindus and Buddhists had a better understanding at times of the pope than some reforming and conservative Catholics halfway across the globe.

The site for Pope Paul's second great pilgrimage was the subcontinent of India, which at that time embraced over a half a billion people, of whom only 1.2 million were Catholic. Back in June 1963, the archbishop of Bombay, Valerian Cardinal Gracias, invited this pope as he had his predecessor to visit that nation. Later Paul accepted, but insisted that it be a spiritual pilgrimage, set in Gandhian simplicity and open to people of all creeds and classes. There would be no Roman pomp and no Indian castes on this visit.

On December 2, the pope arrived in Bombay and in the Indian tradition greeted his audience with closed palms, uttering "Namaste!" (used for greetings and farewell). He thoughtfully knelt to give communion to orphans, one of whom told the gentle pontiff that he had no parents or any relatives at all. Paul saluted the great religious traditions of India and quoted the Upanishads, the sacred scriptures of Hinduism. "Truth alone triumphs, not falsehood. The divine path to liberation has been laid with truth." To stress the very old Christian tradition in that nation, the pope said Mass in the Syro-Malankara rite, as the sick and the lame surrounded the altar to receive Paul's blessings.

Later he spoke eloquently of the problems of poverty. The British newspaper *The Guardian* observed that Paul had received a greater reception than any previous visitor to India because he was a holy man in a nation that loved holy men. With his dignity, charm, and sense of propriety, he added to the initial positive impression that he made on his arrival. Paul's remarks in Bombay on the need to further disarmament and the use of those savings for social betterment were also well received. Later, on January 20, 1965, he was formally invited to address the United Nations, where he would stress those same concerns.[33]

THE FOURTH SESSION

During the interregnum between the third and fourth sessions, Pope Paul was heavily criticized for having allegedly abandoned the draft on religious liberty. As noted, Paul began to educate himself more extensively in the literature on that subject and even called in the American Jesuit John Courtney Murray. Consequently, the pope gave his consent to the same general document that the conservatives had opposed voting on in December. Paul knew that he needed a final statement on religious liberty *before* he made his appearance at the United Nations. Also, he instructed his associates that when difficult matters arose in the upcoming Council session, he wanted to be informed early and not at the last moment.

Then the liberal pope met again the conservative pope. This time it came when he greeted the Jesuits who were getting ready to elect a new superior general of their order. In his talk Paul emphasized the vow of obedience to the pope and the need for the order to take the lead and aggressively challenge atheism. He had also created a Secretariat of Nonbelievers to study atheism and nonbelief, headed by Franz Cardinal König of Vienna, who insisted on not having to come to Rome full-time to lead the committee.

Before the session began, the Council was being attacked from the right again. Some 430 Council Fathers had signed a petition to the pope asking for a strong condemnation of Communism, and Curia officials continued to insist that John XXIII's embrace of the Russian leaders had cost the Italian Christian Democratic Party a million votes in the 1963 elections.

On June 6, 1965, Archbishop Marcel Lefebvre also criticized the Trojan horses of heresy that had invaded the citadel of the Church, but he praised the pope's last-minute note meant to restrict the concept of collegiality. Meanwhile the Vatican quietly sent Cardinal König to visit Cardinal Mindszenty at the American embassy in Budapest. In 1964 the Holy See had reached an agreement with the Hungarian Ministry of Cults, which allowed the pope with government approval to name bishops and to permit the Church to teach catechism to children under the age of eleven. Mindszenty was not a part of those negotiations. Clearly both the pope and the American government hoped that the cardinal would soon leave the embassy and end his exile, so that relations with the Hungarian government could become normalized again.[34]

The pope prepared for the new session, desiring as he put it that it would end as it began — spontaneously. It had to be a session short on speeches and long on good committee work to finish up its business. The session began on September 14, 1965, when Pope Paul walked into St. Peter's Basilica with a simple cope, a miter, and a crozier. He came once again as the bishop of Rome, devoid of the more regal trappings of the historic papacy.

Paul remained a complicated figure to comprehend for those seeking easy answers. In January 1965, he had named twenty-seven new cardinals. They included Lawrence Shehan of Baltimore, John Heenan of Westminster, the Swiss theologian Charles Journet, and his elder friend and long-time mentor Giulio Bevilacqua. The pope had also convinced a reluctant Patriarch Maximos IV Saigh of Antioch to accept the honor. He celebrated Mass himself in the Italian language in various Roman parishes during Lent, striking a blow for the use of the vernacular in the liturgy. And on June 10, 1965, the pope went out of his way to praise Galileo Galilei, the astronomer persecuted by the Catholic Church.

But he also issued an encyclical, *Mysterium Fidei,* which took to task esoteric errors in Eucharist theology, apparently a swipe at certain Dutch, Belgian, and French theologians who were changing the definition of transubstantiation, codified at the Council of Trent, by abandoning some of the philosophical categories of Aristotle. The pope had also previously criticized those who pushed for changes in mandatory celibacy and who intended to make the Church more like the world, rather than vice versa. In addition, Paul dragged his heels on reforming the Curia, as he had indicated he would do in order to facilitate the implementation of reforms in the postconcilar period.

These were the uncertain beginnings of the Council's fourth session. The pope did make known, however, his intention to call a synod in the near future, and then to everyone's surprise he did it the very next day. His promulgation established a synod of bishops on a permanent basis, with most of the members elected by national or regional conferences of bishops and with 15 percent of the members to be appointed by the pope. Paul thus had partially stolen the thunder of the progressives on one of the most sensitive issues before the Council — collegiality.

As the pope pressed on, the first item on the agenda was once again the text on religious liberty. The same issues of theological error, the privileged status of Catholicism in certain nations, and the dignity of those in error were rehashed again and again. Conservative Archbishop Lefebvre attacked the draft as rooted in the objectionable secular philosophies of Hobbes, Locke, and Rousseau.

On September 20, the Council leadership had actually rejected a proposal that the schema be presented to the full Council for a preliminary vote. Apparently, though, the pope this time intervened and the Council Fathers were asked to indicate their disposition on the draft. By a vote of 1,997 to 224 they approved the document. Paul probably had grown weary of the debate; he also knew that on October 4 he was due to address the United Nations, and he needed a strong statement on religious liberty. The issue had to be settled, and so he moved in the direction of a resolution.[35]

For one day, October 4, the Feast of St. Francis of Assisi, Paul would engage in a marathon performance in New York City and in the United Nations. It would be one of the high points of his tenure and one of the most extraordinary moments in the history of the modern papacy. Pope Paul, the first pope to travel by airplane, also became the first sitting pope to visit the United States. Paul arrived in New York City, and his caravan went through Harlem and Central Park to St. Patrick's Cathedral. Outside the cathedral, the massive crowds pushed forward to greet the pontiff — a tiny, faraway figure to most of us at that event. Inside, a star-studded crowd, headed by the Kennedy family and most visibly the late president's widow, Jacqueline, joined with a frail Cardinal Spellman to welcome the pontiff.

Later at the Waldorf Towers Hotel, Paul met with President Lyndon Johnson, who was tormented by his own devils in his difficult war in Vietnam. For nearly an hour, they praised each other's deeds and ended with a public expression of respect as Johnson walked the pontiff to his limousine on Park Avenue. The pope was the leader of a traditional Church in the process of reform; the president was a genuine domestic progressive caught up in a web of war, violence, and deep discontent at home.

At the United Nations, Paul the modern pope ended once and for all the tradition of isolation begun so ignominiously by Pius IX a century before. Paul the diplomat embraced the type of international organization about which Benedict XV, Pius XI, and even Pius XII had reservations. The pope's speech given in French startled the usually cynical and self-centered world of international diplomacy. He immediately identified himself with the young who sought a better world and with "the poor, the disinherited, the suffering," "those who hunger and thirst for justice, for human dignity, for freedom, for progress." He digressed into a discussion of the nature of the United Nations and nation-states, and also indicated that he supported peaceful negotiations of disputes, disarmament, aid to poorer nations, and religious liberty. Paul slipped by the birth control controversy by supporting improving food production. But the pope's most remembered remark was his plaintive, "Never again war! Never again war!" No phrase was to win him more applause; no phrase was to identify better the United Nations' aspiration of how it would like to see itself.[36]

He insisted on saying Mass in Yankee Stadium, where he was greeted by enormous cheering and cries of "Viva Papa!" Then he visited the Vatican exhibit at the World's Fair, seeing again Michelangelo's *Pietà*, the Christ figure dying in the arms of his mother Mary.

Meanwhile, the Council had begun to take up Schema 13, "The Church in the Modern World," but this time the pope let it be known that he regarded the document as "the crown of the Council's work." Thus it was clear to all that it could not be withdrawn, as some conservatives had advocated. In the debates some discussion of atheism ensued. The learned archbishop of Krakow, Karol Wojtyla, insisted that atheism was a very complex philosophical question and could not be taken up in the Council without great difficulty. In a different tone, the new superior general of the Jesuits, Father Pedro Arrupe, maintained that the Church had not aggressively spread the Gospel. He counseled that a more forceful plan of action be presented to the pope, one which involved the penetration of institutions and structures across the world. The heavy hand of Jesuit tradition was not in the mood of the Council.[37]

On September 29, the Council discussed marriage, and obviously the question of conjugal love came up. The discussions of reproductive obligations versus love and companionship as the objects of such a union were revisited. What was at stake in this discussion was the beginning of the divisive contraception debate. The schema did condemn abortion and infanticide, but did not address divorce or what some churchmen like to call "onanism," or sex acts not open to the possibility of conception.

The Council would move along, approving by overwhelming majorities documents dealing with divine revelation, the apostolate of the laity, and the pastoral office of the bishops. By October 7, the Fathers took up the schema on missionary activity. Cardinal Suenens observed that the problem was not just that "the world does not seem prepared to listen to us, but the fact is we are not prepared to talk to it." The Western nature of Christianity was again commented on. Bishop Donal Lamont of Rhodesia argued, "No land is so primitive as to be unfit for the Gospel, nor is any so civilized as not to need it." But on October 12, the schema was accepted as the basis of a final text by a vote of 2,070 to 15.[38]

On October 11, the pope, in response to encouragement from several prelates from Latin America, directly asked that the celibacy question be withdrawn. While not seeking to infringe on the right of the Fathers to debate what they wanted, he insisted that "it was not opportune to have a public discussion of this topic." However, Paul went on to insist that he would uphold this "ancient, holy, and providential law" to the best of his ability.

Apparently some of the bishops wished to explore the creation of a married clergy to exist alongside a celibate clergy in areas such as Latin America, where a shortage of priests was so apparent. Actually, there had been some discussion of this dual clergy since the times of Pius X, with the idea of adopting the historic practice of the Eastern churches aligned to Rome that had both celibate and married priests. But Vatican authorities were alleged to be concerned that such a step would lead to a discussion of the status of thousands of clergy living in concubinage in Italy and elsewhere.[39] The debate on the clergy then shifted to their role in the modern world, the treatment of priests who had left the ministry, the possibility of reviving the priest-worker movement, the need for priestly obedience, and the plight of assistant pastors. That schema too was passed overwhelmingly.

The Council had already approved a restored version of the draft on the Jews in the previous session. Now in this session, the Fathers ended up deploring and condemning hatred of the Jews and displays of anti-Semitism. In April 1965, the pope unfortunately had casually remarked on Passion Sunday that the Jewish people had not only not recognized Jesus, but had opposed, slandered, and killed him — a remark that was embarrassingly counter to the new views of the Council and the Church.[40]

During its deliberations, the Council was deluged with a stream of quasi-religious anti-Semitic literature as the discussion on the draft continued. One anonymous letter even threatened to blow up St. Peter's if the draft were passed, and another pamphlet had called Cardinal Suenens an agent of B'nai B'rith. Finally the schema was approved, 1,763 to 250 — not by as large a majority as some other schemas had been approved, but it was still an impressive consensus against the age-old traditions of religious prejudice and bigotry.

In the Declaration on the Relations of the Church to Non-Christian Religions (*Nostra Aetate*), the Council affirmed that the Jews were not to be portrayed as a people rejected or accursed by God, for He "holds the Jews most dear for the sake of their fathers: God does not repent of gifts made or calls issued." Later Pope John Paul II, who as a boy grew up not too far from the death camp of Auschwitz, reaffirmed that the Jews are "the people of God of the Old Covenant never revoked by God."[41]

As the Council began its conclusion, the Fathers passed the major drafts that had been debated and that in some cases had been postponed from one session to another. One area that did not command attention was the increasing dissatisfaction of women religious with their lives, especially those in convents. Paul would hear about how rebellious those nuns had become, but there would be no real effort to deal with their concerns. A better fate awaited decrees on seminaries and on Church education.

The pope decided to get broader consensus on the important and disputed document on divine revelation. Language once again went back and forth as Paul genuinely sought to broker a compromise acceptable to a larger number of bishops. It was clear that all were looking for an end to the Second Vatican Council. This would not be Trent, which lasted on and off for nearly two decades, from 1545 to 1563.

Paul announced another balancing act: he would further the canonization process for both Pius XII and John XXIII. And he also celebrated the end of Vatican II by pledging to build another church in honor of Mary, proclaiming a special jubilee for six months after the end of the Council, and presenting a statute eventually to reform the Holy Office. The schema on missionary activity and Schema 13 ("The Church in the Modern World") were being given the finishing touches; speaking on the latter document was Archbishop Wojtyla, who remarked that the draft had to be cast as pastoral in its approach.

There was some dismay at last-minute intrusions by the pope to modify a document on marriage by making specific reference to the conservative views of his two predecessors, Pius XI and Pius XII. For the traditionalists, the idea was to reelevate the importance of procreation above conjugal love as a way of supporting the ban on contraception. After progressive rumblings, some compromise language was added, meeting the scruples introduced into the pope's mind by his more conservative advisors.[42]

There was again some debate on the morality of nuclear armaments and the concept of deterrence and on the long-awaited reform of the controversial Holy Office, which was renamed the "Congregation for the Doctrine of the Faith." Individuals charged with violations of dogmatic orthodoxy were now going to be offered the opportunity to defend themselves. The Index of Forbidden Books would finally be abolished; over the years the list had embraced the titles of some of the most famous works in Western civilization.

By December 7 and 8, the Council was winding down, with the pope celebrating its successes and remarking graciously to the observers, "We would like to have you with us always." Each non-Catholic observer was given a special bronze clock with the emblems of the four evangelists and a monogram of Jesus on the top. Conservative bishops later protested that nonbelievers had been given special treatment — getting in a final swipe at the Council. Paul was dismayed, but his associates had the pontiff deluged with telegrams from other bishops expressing their strong support. Later the pope concluded that the Council had "dislodged us from the torpor of ordinary life."

Paul also took time to praise the *periti,* who had been much criticized by conservatives for their alleged baneful influences over the bishops. And on December 7 the pontiff and Orthodox Patriarch Athenagoras of Constantinople removed the centuries-old mutual excommunication dating back to 1054 that had plagued relations between the two great denominations. In 1967, Pope Paul would travel to Constantinople on another dramatic gesture for Christian unity.

THE POST CONCILAR CHURCH

Now the Second Vatican Council was over, probably to the relief of the pope and most of the bishops. Before him however was a very complex postconcilar period. Would the Council's directions be observed, implemented, or rolled back? Pope Paul, one of the more astute leaders of the Church when it came to organizational behavior, knew well the problems that were ahead. What remained were very basic questions: Was the Church modernized sufficiently to influence the contemporary world? Had it abandoned the deposit of faith to curry popular favor? Had it revised its policies and procedures to encourage dialogue internally, or was it still a closed, privileged monarchical system with just better public relations? Did the Church emerge stronger and more vibrant and thus a better guide to leading men and women to salvation, which is its primary purpose?

Almost immediately, Paul faced problems. Cardinal Siri had said that the proclamations of the Council are "not definitions; they will never bind us." And on November 13, 1965, thirty-eight Polish bishops, led by their primate, Cardinal Wyszyńyski, argued that would be difficult, if not impossible, for the Council's work to be implemented in their nation. Instead the pope must trust completely in their judgment, they argued. Paul responded without hesitation that he expected the work of the Council would be put into effect "emphatically and willingly" in Poland as everywhere.

What the position of the archbishop of Krakow was during this conference is unclear. Later though, in 1972, Wojtyla published a volume, *Sources of Renewal,* that gave publicity to the Council's texts, but stressed its continuities rather than its departures. On another dimension, the Polish hierarchy would also make major overtures for a reconciliation with the German bishops without, however, consulting either its own government or the Vatican. In 1967 Pope Paul raised up the young archbishop, Karol Wojtyla, to cardinal, probably to offset Wyszyński's power. Later the new cardinal would be the major author of Pope Paul's most controversial pronouncement, his reaffirmation opposing artificial contraception.[43]

In this period, immediately after the Council's close, Paul sought to use his good offices to encourage social and economic reform in the Third World, especially Catholic Latin America, to end the long war in Vietnam, and to further contacts with non-Catholic clergymen. On March 23, 1966, the archbishop of Canterbury, Michael Ramsey, came to visit the pope. Paul called the meeting "a sign from God, since the People of God expressed the Spirit of God." Questions of common worship and a joint commission of theologians were discussed, and Paul even offered to open up again the question of the validity of Anglican orders, an issue put to rest by the negative decision of Pope Leo XIII in 1896. Later they were to pray together, exchange gifts, and pronounce the visit a success.[44]

Pope Paul's public image was a varied one then. He was not seen as a warm, open, experimental person as Pope John had been, even though in fact he had been surely more liberal and progressive over the years. On the other hand, he was younger and in better health, and thus able to become the first pope to travel across the globe and increase the visibility of his office and the goodwill of his Church.

THE BIRTH CONTROL CONTROVERSY

However, it was on the difficult issue of contraception that Paul encountered enormous opposition and seriously hurt his papacy, and some argue the Catholic Church as well. The traditional view is fairly clear: the Catholic Church has had a long history of opposition to contraception since the Roman era. Contraception in those days was often linked with infanticide, especially of females and the handicapped, and also with the ascetic anti-Christian sects that were opposed to reproduction.[45]

But in the 1960s, two major changes occurred that forced a reevaluation of the prohibition: the population explosion, especially in poorer nations in the world, and the development of chemical contraceptives — the so-called pill. The pill would make birth control more reliable, free women from many unwanted pregnancies, and promote what some derogatorily called recreational sex. That last consequence was exactly what the conservative hierarchy feared, and it is what happened.

Pope Pius XI in his encyclical *Casti Cannubii* had attacked contraception and a host of other evils; Pius XII in his speech to Italian midwives in 1957 also opposed contraception. But the latter argued that married couples could use the so-called rhythm method of birth control, that is, abstain from sex during the very few days when female ovulation occurs. Since the calculation of those few days was and still is sometimes unreliable, the method was sarcastically referred to as "Vatican roulette."

Pope Paul had insisted that the Council not deal with the controversy, and a commission which included lay people had been reorganized and was charged to review the prohibition in light of new technologies and techniques. The commission had heard testimony that the rhythm method was often emotionally dysfunctional, even for loving couples.[46] The Bible exhorted man and woman to increase and multiply, but in a charming metaphor it also encouraged couples to become "one flesh" in those moments of intimacy and ecstasy that sealed the marital bond and promoted companionship.

The majority of the commission members supported some changes by allowing artificial contraception, and the commission report was sent to the pope and remained for several years confidential. Conservatives, led by Cardinal Ottaviani and Archbishop Pietro Parente at the Holy Office, insisted on the need to continue the prohibition, citing the seamless web of Church tradition on matters of faith and morals. Archbishop Wojtyla, also a member of the commission, dissented from the majority vote and insisted privately to the pope that the prohibition had to stand. The pope was truly divided on the issue. At first he seemed to lean toward the majority's view, but under Ottaviani's powerful influence and Wojtyla's arguments, he ended up changing his mind. Wojtyla actually wrote most of the draft of the encyclical and remains its main advocate. Still for two years the pope put off making any final pronouncement.[47]

The conservatives' argument revolved around an ancient philosophical tradition stressing natural law as one of the moral bases for any society. This view, going back to the Greek Stoics, was accepted by the Roman philosophers and was codified by the early and medieval Church theologians, including the influential St. Augustine and St. Thomas Aquinas. To interfere with nature's possibilities — in this case human reproduction — is immoral, against nature, *contra natura*. Every sex act must be open to the potentiality of procreation; this view is the basis for banning contraception and also for the condemnation of homosexuality. Of course, humankind always interferes with nature in many ways. For the earth, according to the Bible, is there to serve man, and not vice versa. So too in physical relationships or biological developments, the process of nature is obviated, denied, and altered through medicine, human intervention, and public policy.[48]

But sexuality has always been the Church's real obsession, and critics have charged that contraception seems especially threatening to a hierarchy that has been pledged to personal chastity and has only a vague academic knowledge of sexual love and marital tensions. Although Catholicism is a religion with many traditions embraced in its two-thousand-year history, there is no question that there is a long history of antifemale biases among some, but not all, of the Church's theologians. This viewpoint is especially ironic considering the central role of the Blessed Virgin Mary in that faith and also the respect shown to women such as St. Catherine of Siena and St. Teresa of Avila, who have been named doctors of the Church.

The antifemale tradition, however, is longstanding. St. Jerome called women "the devil's gateway...a scorpion's dart...a dangerous species." He insisted that even those married had to refrain from receiving the Eucharist after performing the "bestial" act. St. John Damascene referred to woman as "a sick she-ass, a hideous tapeworm...the advanced host of hell." Tertullian, an influential Church thinker in the third century, called a woman's beauty "dangerous to those who look upon it."

St. Paul, who had in so many ways defined the vocabulary of the very early Church right after the death of Christ, concluded that man would do well not to touch a woman, but if one could not keep the gift of continence, let him marry; better to marry than to burn. His influence was especially apparent in the writings of the most important early Church Father, St. Augustine, a man once given to the intense pleasures of the flesh himself, which he enumerated in his own graphic *Confessions*. He recalled the "bestial movements" and the "violent acting of lust," and insisted that in Eden husband and wife would not be bothered by the "seductive stimulus of passion."

Even the usually moderate and thoughtful St. Thomas Aquinas called woman "misbegotten and defective." Still he admitted, she was valuable as a mother of children. Nonetheless, while St. Augustine and St. Clement of Alexandria wrote against contraception, many of the Church Fathers did not comment on the issue at all, even though contraception has been practiced in a variety of ways in Western Europe over the centuries. The first official condemnation of contraception by the Church came relatively late, from the Holy Office in 1851 and in 1853, although there were earlier expressions of disapproval. Later Pope Leo XIII in his encyclical on marriage did not directly treat the issue either. He insisted, though, that marriage had two purposes: procreation and individual happiness, and he refused to give one priority over the other.

As noted, Pius XI in his *Casti Connubii* forcefully prohibited contraception, attacking anything that deliberately frustrated the fruits of sexual consummation. Conservatives pointed to that encyclical and also to Pius XII's pronouncements to Italian midwives in 1957 for support for their case. But in fact it was Pius XII who for the first time somewhat shifted the teachings of the Church. His approval of the rhythm method showed a thoughtful attempt to provide for some birth control techniques within the rigid formulations that he had inherited. Later however he condemned anovulant steroids as "sterilization," and thus prohibited by Church teachings.

Critics of the ban maintained that the approval of the rhythm method displayed a basic contradiction in Church teachings. Couples were having intercourse when they knew or assumed that nature's bounty was not possible. Is not the intention to avoid conception rather close to using a method that was meant to guarantee contraception? The literature on the controversy is vast, expanding, and long-lasting. But the real outlines of the controversy were these: the commission report was finally leaked out to the press; Paul consequently signed a rather weak encyclical reaffirming the traditional prohibition; the reaction was overwhelmingly negative, especially in the industrialized nations; and in many cases members of the hierarchy and individual pastors and confessors refused to give enthusiastic support to the papal pronouncement. In the United States nearly 90 percent of the Catholic laity disagreed with the encyclical.

THE UNCERTAIN CHURCH

Defensively, Paul insisted that in twenty years he would be seen as a prophet on the issue of contraception. He was wrong. Some time after the reactions set in, Paul addressed a group of pilgrims saying, "Look into my eyes and tell me if I look to you like a reactionary pope. The pope is not a reactionary pope or a progressive pope. He is the pope and that is all."[49]

Furthermore public opinion polls have shown that in America and elsewhere the encyclical helped to undermine papal and Church authority and led to some defections from the ranks of the faithful. Later studies show that Catholic sexual practices and beliefs were similar to other white adults in the United States.[50] Catholics were closer to their fellow Americans than to the Holy Father, and that was especially true of younger Catholics.

In addition, the Catholic Church experienced a massive rupture of clerical resignations and a dearth of new vocations. The Jesuits, especially close to the papacy, were nearly decimated, losing after the Council some 7,000 members, and the number of local priests and, more importantly, parish nuns — the real stalwarts in schools and hospitals — were in marked decline. In the United States alone, about 10,000 priests left the active ministry between 1968 and 1978. From 1964 to 1984 the number of seminarians dropped from 47,500 to 12,000, and 241 seminaries were closed. And from 1966 to 1980, the number of women religious declined from 181,421 to 126,517, after a steady increase in the 1950s and early 1960s. How much of the loosenings of Vatican II contributed to these happenings? How much had the general social upheavals of the late 1960s and early 1970s contributed to the fraying of another institution despite its own strengths? How much of the decline was due to the rigid reaffirmation of clerical celibacy and/or to the birth control controversy and Paul's encyclical?

To the Curia conservatives the answer was obvious: Pope John's gamble was a disaster. Sister Pasqualina, who had told him that the Church was safe only as an authoritarian structure, was a prophet indeed. Others, however, were more disposed to the progressive point of view. The Council came too late to protect fully the Church. The decline and the rot had set in earlier under Pius XII. The Council had in fact mitigated some of the consequences that could have been worse. And every institution — political, social, cultural, educational — had been under severe attack as a vast postwar generation came of age and engaged themselves in great numbers to the corrosive, nihilistic dissent of the period.

To add to the complexities of the Church's troubles, it lost the august beauty of the Latin or Tridentine Mass, for it was Paul and not the Council who approved a totally vernacular Mass. In the process he cast aside the bull of Pope Pius V, *Quo Primum Tempore* (1570), which enjoined that the Roman Missae could not be altered, amended, or dropped. To a friend, the pope admitted the loss of the universal and structured ritual of the Latin Mass, but he insisted that one had in this day and age to bring the sacred liturgy closer to the people and that this could be done only by using their own language. The problem was that in some places the Mass was so popularized that it lost its sense of awe and mystery. Abuses were reported, such as balloon Masses with nuns prancing down the aisles, secular music that distracted from the sacrifice at the altar, priests who seemed more interested in giving catalogs of social work prescriptions without reminding the faithful of the exhortations of Jesus. One Dutch canon read, "Lord, if you exist, come among us." In other churches, the Gospel was replaced with readings from newspapers, novelists, and even Karl Marx!

At the other extreme, the conservative Archbishop Lefebvre in France insisted on retaining the Tridentine Mass, as if it were given by Christ himself at the Last Supper, instead of being only one rite in the long history of the Church. Eventually he would attack the pope, the teaching authority of the Council, and the Church itself. For the longest time Paul manfully sought to avoid a break; his personal nightmare was that the postconcilar period would lead to a massive schism. It did not. In part, Pope Paul was tirelessly patient and skillful, absorbing abuse in ways alien to the instincts of the pontiffs of this century and before. Unlike in the past, though, Catholics who disagreed often did not leave the Church. They simply segmented their lives and beliefs, as in the case of contraception. They continued in the sacraments, or at least nominally in the Church, and picked and chose what beliefs they wished to observe. Some, including Polish prelate Karol Wojtyla, called it "cafeteria Catholicism."[51]

The second problem Paul faced in that period, which has lasted into Pope John Paul II's reign, was the increasing number of theologians, especially those teaching in Catholic universities and seminaries, who reinterpreted, redefined, or even denied what are traditional articles of faith in such areas as the inerrancy of the Bible, the Immaculate Conception, the Resurrection, the Assumption, the Ascension, the infallibility of the pope, and the nature of the Eucharist, among other tenets.

Often they took these articles of faith and, using philosophical or linguistic tools, presented them as mere culturally determined metaphors which did not mean what they traditionally had. Or when they wished to explore the modern worlds of scholarship, as in biblical studies, for example, they simply did so and then said, as an aside almost, that to maintain the Church's position is often a matter beyond reason, that is, it is in the realm of faith.

That differentiation is not a unique view. Even the greatest Church philosophers would probably agree. But what was and is happening is that this explanation is not attributed to a confidence in faith as much as it is a timid cop-out to allow Church biblical scholars both to stay within the formal hierarchy and also participate in scholarly conferences as equals. So the Sacred Scriptures, critics charge, are treated as mere archaeological findings. The difficulty for Pope Paul and other churchmen was that the Church was supporting financially these theologians and scholars who were supposedly abandoning the deposit of faith to which he was so committed.

230 / Vicars of Christ

Since the earliest centuries the Catholic and the Orthodox churches have regarded the Nicene Creed, for example, as truth, not as a string of fourth-century metaphors. Was this modern equivocation another Cardinal Newman–type venture to update only the *methods* of presentation or was it really the treason of the clerics? Still, did not the Council and the popes speak eloquently about religious liberty as a part of the definition of human dignity? Could one insist on such freedom in Communist countries, for example, and deny it in Catholic universities? Paul, a conscientious reader of their works, must have wondered himself what the Council and its celebration of the times had brought forth.[52]

On October 1, 1966, Paul addressed the disputed issue of the relationships between the teaching authority of the Church, called its magisterium, and theologians. He calmly portrayed the theologians as the mediators between the faith of the Church and the magisterium. He called for a communion of understanding, dedicated to preaching the Gospel of Christ. Later a weary pope visited the tomb of St. Celestine V near Agnani. Celestine was the last pope to resign that position. Elected at the age of eighty-five, he was a Benedictine hermit who lasted only five months as pope, and then went into exile in 1294. Was Paul simply indicating how difficult the papacy was, or was he too considering resigning, especially in light of his own decree on the mandatory retirement of bishops?[53]*

As this study has shown, there has been in many ways a real decline in the power and the vitality of popes of the twentieth century after a decade or so of service. But the tradition of life tenure is strong: how can a father resign, it is asked? And how can there be two or more "popes" that the faithful can look to, even if one or more has stepped down or has become a hermit? Apparently, though, both Paul VI and his successor John Paul II have considered that option.

But quickly Paul snapped out of that passive mode. First he began a very critical review of the Jesuit order in late 1966. It was a portent of things to come. Then the pope began to reevaluate the American Catholic Church, finally breaking the power of the ailing Cardinal Spellman over the appointments of bishops. Much later, in 1973, the pope finally appointed Jean Jadot his apostolic delegate to the United States with a mandate to

---

*The hermit, Pietro da Morrone, was a Benedictine monk with links to the radical Franciscans, or "Spirituals." He was known as an ascetic and a major monastic figure whose name was familiar in the Curia and the Court of Naples. He was chosen after the papacy was vacant for twenty-seven months with the twelve cardinals unable to agree on a candidate. He was called "the angel pope" and arrived on a donkey escorted to his consecration by Charles II and his son Charles Martel. Celestine could not speak Latin fluently and soon sought to turn over control of the Church to a group of three cardinals. Finally he abdicated and sought unsurprisingly to return to his retreat. Fearing Celestine would become a rallying point for a schism, his successor, Boniface VIII, kept him under guard, and eventually he was confined to the tower of Castel Fumone. He died in 1296 and was later made a saint in 1313. Dante however placed him at the gates of Hell for his alleged cowardice.

name so-called pastorally oriented bishops to implement the reforms of
Vatican II. Gone would be the builders, the powerful Church prelates, who
had exercised so much clout over the immigrant American Church. Later
his successor John Paul II would move away from the pastorally oriented
approach to a much tougher and sterner set of orthodox bishops and cardinals who were especially attuned to his desire for a restoration of both
papal authority and traditional dogma.[54]

PAUL AND THE SOCIAL GOSPEL

The pope continued in some ways his overtures to the modern world. On
the feast of the Epiphany in 1967 he set up a council dealing with the
laity, which he called "a listening post to the world." He also emphasized
the need for greater social concern in his encyclical *Populorum Progressio,*
which the American *Wall Street Journal* disapprovingly called "souped-
up Marxism." Conservative Catholic critic Michael Novak saw it as an
abstract, unrealistic descent into Third World economics and a departure
from traditional Catholic social philosophy. Others, however, were to hail
it as a gospel of hope and reform.[55]

But Pope Paul in India had seen human misery and the plight of the
Third World nations in a poignant and powerful way. This pope was not
simply talking about the difficulties of the working class in the industrialized West, on which Leo XIII had focused. The great divide now was
between the northern hemisphere and the southern regions. Under the
influence of Vatican II and with Pope Paul's sympathy, the Latin American Church took a marked turn to the left. Attempts at moderate social
reforms, especially in Brazil, Chile, and Peru, had not proven to bring
sufficient relief to the very poor.

At a historic meeting in 1968 in the Colombian city of Medellín, the
Latin American bishops pledged their support to the poor. The pope had
traveled to Bogotá and opened the meeting, giving his imprimatur to the
gathering, although some said he was cautious toward the so-called liberation theologians then coming of age in that region. The bishops ended
up advocating land reform, income redistribution, and greater democracy
for the masses. They castigated the "institutionalized violence" of oli-
garchic rule as a "social sin," and they advocated the establishment of
new movements to further the political and spiritual liberation of the poor.
From that meeting came approval for the creation of "base communities," which supplemented churches in some places, the use of the Bible
for consciousness-raising, and the development of "liberation theology" in
which the Church and its clergy were agents — often radical agents — of
social change. Later in 1969, Paul went to another continent and pledged
in Nigeria to stay until the bloody civil war in Biafra ended. Clearly this
was a very different papacy.

Observing these and other harsh realities around him, the pope strongly attacked both the "euphoria of the age," as he termed it, and the "superfluous wealth of the rich countries." As with Pope John Paul II later, the Catholic Church became a critic of unrestrained capitalism and the harsh values of the marketplace. Armed with a faith that was so old that it viewed capitalism as merely one system of economics among many in history, the modern popes had a perspective that went beyond the calculations of rugged individualism and consumerism so rampant in the late twentieth century.

GUARDING THE FAITH

And again like John Paul II, Paul would be called a social liberal but a conservative in theology. That seemed paradoxical, but in fact anyone who understands the history of the Church can see how that makes predictable sense. The popes view themselves as primarily the guardians of the deposit of the faith; thus they are conservatives in the strictest sense of the word. But in this century, the horrendous tolls of war, the overall brutalizing of society, the maldistribution of wealth, and the exploitation of common people all seem to cry out for the types of humane prescriptions that Christianity in its best times represents. Thus the popes in this century have become voices for peace, social justice, and a more humane community.

In the past they were traitors to the world — that is, they did not accept the advances of philosophical liberalism, progressive democracy, free market economics, and fervent nationalism, especially in Europe. Now as the negative by-products of each of those movements have become apparent and the excesses of those developments have borne fruit, the intransigencies of those modern popes seem to have become more appealing, if not prophetic. The conservative pontiffs in the pre- and the postwar eras suddenly appear to have become rebels in part *against* the signs of their times. That peculiar transformation began with Paul and has accelerated with John Paul II.

Their views on abortion, feminism, priestly celibacy, and contraception are framed as rigid and repressive in the eyes of the critics. Yet the same severity and rigidity seem to give them strength in a world that is bemoaning the lack of values by which to live. Although in our day-to-day lives we equivocate, compromise, and embrace the relativity of right and wrong, we cannot teach our children or protect social fabrics if we constantly confuse good and evil. Like them or not, the last two postwar popes and many more before them seem to comprehend that source of strength. John XXIII generally ignored it. Paul intuitively understood it; John Paul II has expressly reminded all who would listen that this is the way it is to be. The difference is that while Paul had lamented that responsibility, his successor glories in it.

One can see that difference in the treatment of priestly celibacy. There is no doctrinal reason why priests in the West cannot marry. They are married in the Eastern Catholic Church, and that has been the established practice since the Council of Trello in 692. Even in the West, celibacy has been mandated only since the Council of Trent five hundred years ago. But in Paul's statement *Sacerdotalis Caelibatus,* issued on June 24, 1967, he insisted on celibacy, calling it "a dazzling jewel" in the crown of the Church.

Yet Pius XII and later Paul himself in 1969 allowed Anglican married priests to be ordained in the Western Catholic Church. Why can priests who are converts be married, but those who have lived longer in full communion with the Church not be given such an option? And if the notion of celibacy was influenced by the Holy Spirit, as Pope Paul concluded, why has the Spirit taken fifteen centuries in the West and still has not visited the East to provide such guidance on the question? It has been argued by some historians that celibacy is actually a historical development that came out of the policies of the great reforming monk-popes who emerged from a more ascetic tradition than the world of bishops and parish priests.[56]

Pope Paul also insisted that an option on the question of celibacy would not increase the number of vocations. Yet between 1963 and 1983, the Vatican reported that 46,302 dispensations were granted for priests to marry. The argument has been made that for every one dispensation there was another priest who was refused or who did not even choose to go through the process.

Also the Catholic Church, especially in the United States, has been plagued by sexual practices that the Church has found even more problematic than relaxing the ban on celibacy. The Catholic Church has been historically opposed to homosexuality, especially in modern times, regarding it as an unnatural aberration, but it has been estimated that nearly half of its clergy are gay — some of them sexually active, some not active in that orientation at all.

In the 1980s and 1990s the Church was beleaguered with charges of child molestation from so-called celibate clergy, to the extent of nearly bankrupting the dioceses of Santa Fe, New Mexico, and Providence, Rhode Island. The numbers of transgressions were actually very small, but they were highly publicized, along with the instances of sexual liaisons by priests with women both in the United States and elsewhere. It was alleged that the scandal of a bishop in Ireland and a female consort, for example, contributed to the end of the prohibition on divorce in a national plebescite in that conservative Catholic country.[57]

Pope Paul was inundated by a flood of petitions for the laicization of priests, many desiring to enter into the companionship of marriage. While he was genuinely troubled by the requests, he instituted some humane procedures in 1971 to deal with the disposition process for the resignation of priests and their marriages within the Church. His successor has simply slowed down the process to a trickle, believing that once a priest always a priest. But the whole discussion of celibacy underscored to many that Pope Paul was really a conservative and not like Pope John, who once said that he could end the celibacy requirement with a stroke of his pen. Indeed Pope John said that, but it would have been unthinkable for him to do so considering his own background and beliefs. Oddly enough it was Pius XII with his sense of self-assuredness and his willingness to research a question to the very end who probably could have made such a radical change without personal doubts and within familiar theological grounds, but it was not the time nor was the need so apparent then.

Also in 1967 Paul had to deal with the increasing demands for autonomy from the Dutch Church. The issue came to a head with the new catechism, which became a best seller, including its English edition. The text however seemed to equivocate on the virgin birth of Jesus and on the existence of angels and devils. A commission of cardinals examined the catechism and listed ten errors. A supplement, which had to be attached to the catechism, soon appeared to deal with those objections.

At about the same time, Paul also presented his apostolic constitution *Regimini Ecclesiae,* which aimed at reforming the Roman Curia. The pope ended multiple office-holding, barred lifetime tenure and substituted five-year terms renewable twice, guaranteed that all appointees end at the death of a pope, and required all members of the Curia to resign at age seventy-five. In practice the Secretariat of State became the major agency for papal domination of the Curia. Also one could now communicate with the Curia in languages besides Latin. Paul not only was implementing the spirit of the Council, but was effectively asserting the ascendancy of the papacy even further, and now over his true rival — not the bishops — but the permanent bureaucracy.[58]

The ailing pontiff was not up to par in 1967, however, and he decided to appoint Giovanni Benelli, a hard-driving and well-organized cleric, as his chief of staff. Near the end of Paul's tenure, the pope promoted him to cardinal and assigned him to the prestigious see of Florence. His name would be circulated as a possible papal candidate, but he had alienated too many members of the hierarchy over the years and eventually died prematurely on October 24, 1982, at the age of sixty-one.

In the same year, 1967, the pope decided to visit Turkey to meet with Patriarch Athenagoras, the first such visit to that city since Pope Constantine I made the long, arduous journey in the early eighth century. It further underscored Paul's commitment to ecumenical dialogue with the Orthodox churches. During the trip the pope returned to Turkey the military standard captured at the battle of Lepanto and kept in Rome since 1571. Paul went on to call the Orthodox Church "a sister Church," a rare compliment, and he urged that individuals rediscover that unity and diversity and faithfulness can only be the work of the Holy Spirit. Still the recent development of Roman Catholic dogma — especially on the Immaculate Conception, the Assumption, and the infallibility of the pope — greatly hindered reconciliation. Several months later the patriarch came to Rome to visit the pope, as another historic milestone was recorded.

THE NEW COLLEGIALITY

At the same time, Paul had called a synod in Rome — a development arising from the reforms of the Council. Later in the year the pope had an operation for prostate problems, and at the end of the year the recuperating pontiff received President Johnson. It was reported that the usually calm pope shouted at Johnson and slammed his hand down, protesting the American escalation of the war in Vietnam. Whether it is true or not, Paul continued to emphasize tranquility and social justice, and later became an intermediary for peace in that region.[59]

As tensions within the Church increased, the pope was attacked by both the conservatives and progressives. Paul also began to experience the loss of his one time friend and ally Leo Joseph Cardinal Suenens, who had made his election as pope possible but who began turning on the pontiff, arguing that he had betrayed the reforms of the Council. Paul also clumsily forced out Cardinal Lercaro, whom he had supposedly trusted with liturgical reform, and on the same day balanced that dismissal with the firing of the conservative prefect of the Congregation of Rites, Arcadio Larraona. Perhaps he was just getting tired of controversies, realizing that moderates are the most politically vulnerable, even in the Catholic Church.

On March 19, 1968, Cardinal Suenens asked the pope to act more in association with the episcopal conferences. He further urged that the questions of birth control and ordination of married men be taken up at the next synod, supposedly as a way to build some consensus for the pope's positions. But in fairness to the pope, his role did not give him the flexibility to swing with the moods as did his old friend from Belgium.

Suenens started out as one of the Fathers of Vatican II, a close associate of John XXIII and a costrategist with Montini as to the directions the lumbering and floundering Council should go. He pushed for Montini's selection, was denied the secretary of state position because of conservative opposition, and became an opponent of the noncollegial process surrounding the promulgation of *Humanae Vitae*. Suenens was quickly viewed by the media as a very vocal critic of a chastised Paul. Then he discovered the charismatic movement and tried to convince the pope that the Church should move more in the direction of an emotional, experiential, and existential ecclesia. The media loved him, for he was a man of ideas, and the media lives for ideas, if only for one day.[60]

Six months after his *Humanae Vitae*, the pope did call for an Extraordinary Synod to be held on October 11, 1969, in order to explore the relationships between the primacy of the pope and the collegiality of the bishops. At the same time, Paul replaced the elderly Cicognani with Jean Cardinal Villot in the secretary of state position — a person more sympathetic to the notion of collegiality.

In the spring of 1969, the pope also began secret discussions with a Sicilian banker, Michele Sindona, concerning the Vatican's investment policies. That association would come back to haunt the papacy for over a decade, as Sindona and his associate Roberto Calvi were later exposed for illegal dealings across two continents, including in the United States.

In April Paul also named thirty-five new cardinals — raising the numbers of the College of Cardinals to an unprecedented 133 members. The pope announced a new *ordo missae,* a new calendar of the Roman Church, a division of the responsibility of the Congregation of Rites, and the establishment of an International Theological Commission. In addition, Paul finally challenged Suenens in a meeting, criticizing his authoritarian ways in Belgium and apparently at one point asking for his resignation as cardinal. The same prelate who so advocated consultation and collegiality ran his own show by himself it seemed. The cardinal returned the criticism, and the pope cooled down and simply responded, "Yes, pray for me; because of my weakness the Church is badly governed."

Suenens, instead of accepting those rather generous sentiments, went public, attacking the pope again, arguing that he had abandoned the Council's definition of collegiality. To Paul's dismay his accusations were supported by major theologians, including Karl Rahner and Hans Küng. Three French cardinals, including Villot, responded in private letters aimed at becoming public, charging that Suenens's remarks were disrespectful and even slanderous. Later, on June 23, Paul briefly alluded to the fact that he was not insensitive to criticisms that were inaccurate and yet concluded, "It is not easy to hold a post of responsibility in the Church today. It is not easy to rule a diocese, and we well understand the conditions in which our brothers in the episcopate of faith have to exercise their mission."[61]

The pope promised to take legitimate criticisms into account and went on to visit the World Council of Churches in Geneva in June — another startling precedent for a Church that historically had opposed such ecumenical efforts. In July he became the first pope ever to visit Africa, going to Uganda to pay his respects at the shrine of the Twenty-two Martyrs who had been canonized during the third session of the Council. Bishops from all over Africa came and Paul, quoting the words of the Apostle who was his namesake, praised "all the Churches of Christ's reach." To a very sympathetic audience, he observed that it was time for the Africans to become "missionaries to yourselves," for the Church is "well and truly planted in this blessed soil."[62]

He observed that the Catholic Church was by its nature a conservative institution, and that "we are not the inventors of faith, we are its custodians." But then he sensitively observed that the Church favored the adaptation of the Christian life to indigenous conditions, and that "you may, and indeed must, have an African Christianity." Thus away from the burdens of the papacy and the intrigues of the bureaucratic Church, Paul, the modern apostle to the world, liberated if only for a day, did what he knew how to do best: to encourage evangelization of the Third World. The pastor and the diplomat overcame the hesitating theologian — somewhat.

As preparations for the synod began, Suenens publicly insisted that the primacy of the pope was never really an issue. It was the style of papal authority and the balance between the pope and the bishops that he was talking about. The episcopal conferences had not been consulted before the pope's birth control pronouncement. The cardinal also identified himself more with the increasing dissidents in the Church during the difficult 1968–69 period.

Paul in part responded on October 6, 1969, in a talk to the International Theological Commission, in which he stressed the importance of the papacy for the "government, stability, peace, and unity of the Church." Still he emphasized the significant role of the theologians in the magisterium and argued that it was not a question of primacy. In the area of divine truth, the pope observed, "there is only one primacy of revealed truth and faith which people give their assent to in their own way."

The synod stressed its unity with the papacy and urged then some broader reforms, which Paul in part accepted. Some unease seemed to prevail, and as that was happening, Paul was forced to face directly another challenge from the Dutch Church on the question of priestly celibacy. The hierarchy there, closely in touch with the faithful, advocated an end to mandatory priestly celibacy and a restoration of posts to priests who had subsequently married. The bishops were moving to implement their suggestions very quickly. Privately Paul tried to stem the revolt, and Cardinal Villot was sent to reach some compromise. The secretary did propose however one loophole in his draft: where there was an extreme shortage of priests it would be possible to ordain older married men. The pope was not pleased at first, and a diplomatic Villot responded, "Holy Father, act as if this text never existed." Paul, however, then seemed amenable to the exception, although it would not affect the Netherlands, since it was mainly aimed at the Third World. Again, Suenens from Belgium criticized the pope for acting alone on the issue.[63] The pope, though, continued his missionary ways. In November 1970 he visited the Philippines. There he was physically assaulted by a Bolivian painter, Benjamín Mendoza, who came at him with a dagger. Paul seemed not to be injured, but later blood was found on his cassock.

A later synod, which met in the autumn of 1971, would take up the issue of celibacy, and ended up splitting 107 to 87 against the ordination of married men. The pope announced publicly that "the bishops of the entire

Catholic world want to keep integrally this absolute gift by which the priest consecrates himself to God." The archbishop of São Paulo, Brazil, Paulo Evaristo Arns, insisted much later, however, that the pope had confided to him that if the change had passed, he would have carried it out. Apparently, Paul even privately offered an alternative proposal which would have allowed the pontiff to permit the ordination of married men of "mature age and proven life." The pope later did explore other lay ministries and the role of women in some of those ministries as well.

In 1972, Cardinal Suenens was visiting the United States and there met several nuns from the Sisters of Charity, who told him of the powers of the charismatic movement in their prayer house. The prelate suddenly went on to become a full convert to that style of enthusiastic worship, and he began to feel the irrelevancies of his previous causes, including church reform and the ordination of married men.[64]

But such a luxury was not open to Pope Paul. Early in 1968, he had been interviewed by a reporter from *La Stampa,* who said that Russia was the only country in the world where the principle of authority was intact. Paul remarked, "Is that a great strength or a great weakness?" As he approached seventy-five and the tenth year of his pontificate, he began to experience profound depression and a personal sense of sorrow. He worried about the state of the Church and his own leadership of it. At this time, Paul chose to give a sermon in which he observed that "through some crack in the temple of God, the smoke of Satan has entered." He went on to conclude that today any misguided prophet could get media attention, while the authentic voice of the Church was ignored. As expected, elements of the Italian press picked up the sermon and turned it into humorous commentaries on the devil — a topic taboo to the modern mentality.

Paul also had to confront directly the public referendum conducted in Italy on the topic of divorce, which was debated at some length in the early 1970s. In 1970, the Italian Parliament narrowly passed the Fortuna-Baslini Bill permitting divorce in that nation. For four years, the debate continued, and on May 12, 1974, a popular referendum resulted in a strong vote of approval for the law: 59.1 to 40.9 percent. As some of the Vatican officials feared, the acrimony led to a broad-ranging discussion of the role of the Catholic Church in modern Italy. The referendum showed starkly the limits on the ability of the hierarchy to influence the political and social attitudes of the Catholic faithful.

In August 1972, Paul pronounced that the "minor orders" of lector and acolyte were open to the laity and along with the deaconate were no longer simply stepping stones to the priesthood, but were separate and unique. Still these orders were initially reserved in the pope's early decisions to men alone. Then on May 3, 1973, the pope set up a Study Commission on Women and Society, charging it to "gather, verify, interpret, revise, sharpen the ideas that have been expressed on the role of women in modern society." Once again, Paul sought to compromise, to harmonize, to straddle a bit, rather than to command or to ignore. Critics must have wondered, was this another birth control commission with all the perils involved in true dialogue?[65]

He also listened carefully as Suenens, enthralled with his discoveries, spoke of the charismatic movement, and the pontiff affirmed the cardinal's special mission to that venture. Several days later he admitted that the Holy Spirit operates at times outside the institutional Church. While he was reaching out to this new development, the pope also hosted in May 1973 Ambia Shenouda III, pope of Alexandria and patriarch of the Church of St. Mark. The discussion revolved around the elements of unity between the Coptic Church and the Roman Catholic Church. Earlier discussions had concentrated on the common faith articulated in the first three ecumenical councils of the Church. Great Church Fathers such as St. Athanasius, bishop of Alexandria, and St. Cyril, also of Alexandria, as well as the Egyptian hermit St. Anthony, were part of both churches' common patrimony. Still the questions of the primacy of the pope and the fate of the loyal Catholic elements in Egypt presented problems for those advocating joint efforts.[66] But for all of his concerns with things spiritual, the pope's attentions in the remaining years of his tenure were often distracted with the secular, the mundane, and the temporal. He had to come face to face with his decisions on changing investment policies that would lead to various problems and considerable embarrassment for the Holy See.

It starts out as it usually does — with good intentions but bad advice. Concerned about the continuing financial drain on the Vatican, the pope sought to get the so-called Vatican Bank, or Istituto per le Opere di Religione (IOR), to help. But the IOR was independent, with most of its assets coming from religious orders, episcopal conferences, and Catholic organizations, and not the Holy See. Because of the 1929 settlement the main assets of the Vatican were still from the Lateran Treaty made with Mussolini's Fascist regime. Those funds had been invested, and the pope now insisted that they be diversified across a variety of nations to avoid any blame for economic downturns. The man put in charge of that diversification program was Michele Sindona, a Sicilian banker with secret ties to the Mafia and a group called Lodge P-2.

Sindona's good friend was Archbishop Paul Marcinkus, a Chicago-born prelate who was in charge of the Vatican Bank. The bishop had placed millions — if not hundreds of millions — of dollars into Sindona's 140 companies in ten countries. Among those enterprises was Società Generale Immobiliare, Sindona's Italian holding company, which had invested in the Watergate complex in Washington, D.C., the Meurice Hotel in Paris, and an assortment of European luxury hotels. Actually Sindona in 1969 had purchased one-third interest in the SGI from the Vatican Bank. He also bought a controlling interest from the Vatican Bank in the company that provided water for the city of Rome.

Marcinkus and Sindona had interests in a banking and security firm in Geneva, a Bahamian banking operation, and banks in Italy which included partnerships with the Continental Illinois National Bank, among others. Finally in 1981, Marcinkus's major lay assistant was arrested in Rome on charges of complicity in the Sindona swindles and bankruptcies. To many it was clear that the head of the Vatican Bank understood all along what was happening.

But in the fall of 1971, there were only rumors that Sindona and Marcinkus were involved in depositing $100 million in counterfeit American corporate bonds in West German banks. That equity was being used to buy a giant Italian holding company, Bastogi. That deal fell through, but Sindona begin to seize control of Franklin National Bank, the nineteenth largest bank in the United States. Within two years Sindona bankrupted that institution, the first such major bank failure in that nation since the Great Depression in the 1930s. Sindona was charged with fraudulently receiving at least $15 million from the bank, manipulating its foreign currency speculation so that the bank lost $30 million, and transferring $40 million illegally out of Italy. It was alleged, but not proven, that the transfer had been done through the Vatican Bank.

Soon the Sindona empire collapsed. He had illegally removed at least $225 million from his bank in Milan. Five Italian investigators looking into the collapse were murdered, and Sindona was later indicted for those murders. One American prosecutor, John Kenney, said that Sindona was a launderer of funds for prominent Italians and others, and that the Vatican Bank was involved in those operations. Author Richard Hammar has charged that Archbishop Marcinkus plotted to purchase $1 billion in phony securities, and that the respected Eugene Cardinal Tisserant, who died in 1972, was initially involved. Whether those charges are true is not clear, but it has been estimated that the Vatican lost over $200 million.[67] After Sindona, the Vatican then turned to a Roberto Calvi, and Calvi led the Vatican into another scandal with his Banco Ambrosiano of Milan. For years later, three popes would struggle to set right the Holy See's finances and sever ties with the embarrassed banking community, angry investors, and government investigators on both sides of the Atlantic Ocean. The wiles of the high-wired world of twentieth-century finance were too slippery even for the usually adept Vatican operatives.

As has been noted, at about the same time, the pope incurred increasing attacks from conservative elements for his abandonment of the Tridentine Mass established during the reign of St. Pius V in 1570. There was probably very little thought from the Council Fathers that Latin, especially for the Eucharistic Prayer, would be totally abandoned in the Mass, but that was the pope's decision. The chief critic of those changes was Archbishop

Marcel Lefebvre, who was increasingly challenging the pope's authority on that and other issues.

And another right-wing organization, Opus Dei, was growing and seeking permission to become a "secular institute." The Opus Dei movement had been founded by Monsignor Josemaría Escrivá de Balaguer (1902–75) in Spain, who was beatified in 1992. The organization followed a series of ninety-nine spiritual maxims and is characterized by secrecy, theological conservatism, and rigorous spirituality. Its leaders, seeing the difficulties facing the Holy See, volunteered to take over 30 percent of the cost of operating the financially strapped Vatican. But Pope Paul generally was cautious about that group; his successor John Paul II would warmly embrace it and name it a personal prelature in 1982.[68]

In the same year Pope Paul received from the synod an unhappy set of proceedings on the topic of evangelism. The Latin American and the African representatives had been especially displeased with the draft presented by Karol Cardinal Wojtyla. The Polish prelate stressed not the new developments in conversion and liberation theology, but the notion that one should reject the world and much of its values and avoid sin and Satan. The draft was rejected by the synod in 1974. The missionary churches were becoming full-fledged establishments, and the early misunderstandings that Wojtyla embraced would continue when he became pope. Consequently Paul was left with the opportunity to go his own way on the issue.[69] The pope could indeed be forgiven if he smiled at the synod's confusions after the emphasis that the Vatican Council and progressives, especially Cardinal Suenens, placed on its importance. Probably he did not even smirk, but merely carried on his duty and researched the question thoroughly, as his patron Pius XII would have done.

Paul also continued his scrutiny of the Jesuits. The Jesuit general superior, Don Pedro Arrupe, called a general congregation together, which was asked to review his own record in office, among other items. The pope was aware of the marked decline in Jesuit vocations, the opposition from some in their ranks to his birth control encyclical, the Jesuit supposed preoccupation with consultation over authority, the rise among certain chapters of close (but supposedly nonsexual) fellowship with women, and the prominence of Jesuit theologians involved in speculations that the Holy See found troubling. Conservative Jesuits had informed the Vatican of Arrupe's alleged indifference to these pernicious developments. The desire of the members to avoid classes or grades in the order, which had been part of its history, also led to the charge that it was abandoning now its vow of obedience to the pope. The general superior was quickly summoned in the middle of the congregation's proceedings to the Vatican and informed by the pope that there would be no changes in grades.[70]

Thus battered on the left and the right, the pope still tried to exercise consensus leadership, to remain true to his progressive leanings and yet to

preserve the conservative deposit of the faith. Such objectives were somewhat contradictory, at least in the public image he conveyed to the outside
world, and he seemed an equivocating figure. Such is the peril of moderate reformers, as Pius IX had found out very early in his reign. In 1975
at the age of seventy-eight, Paul wrote of himself, "What is my state of
mind? Am I Hamlet? Or Don Quixote? Or on the left? On the right? I
don't feel I have been properly understood. I have two dominant feelings,
superabundo gaudio. I am full of consolation, overcome with joy, throughout every tribulation" (2 Cor. 7:4). In the year before his death, however,
a weary Paul was to conclude a "non-Catholic mentality was increasingly
dominant in the Church."

The Papal Commission on the Status of Women added another controversy with its division on the ordination of women, although it did
recommend that they be admitted to the nonordained lay ministries of lector and acolyte. The deaconate was seen by some as only a short step from
the priesthood, and thus presented real problems for many conservatives.
Later John Paul II would have the Vatican rule that it was an infallible
pronouncement that women were excluded forever from the priesthood.
Under Paul, however, many theologians openly concluded that the New
Testament gave no evidence either way on the issue. Later, in 1975, the
Anglicans indicated that they were moving toward ordination of women,
and that pronouncement ended much of the talk about reunion between
the two congregations, although Pope Paul was remarkably cautious in
reaching that conclusion himself.

And as the years passed, Paul's celebrated patience began to wear thin
as he dealt with Archbishop Lefebvre. At one point the French prelate was
informed that his ordination of priests dedicated to the Tridentine rite was
valid but not licit and that he had to exhibit a public act of submission
for his rebellion toward the Church, the Council, and the magisterium. In
1976 Lefebvre ordained thirteen or fourteen priests and thirteen deacons
and subdeacons. Finally the Congregation for Bishops formally suspended
Lefebvre. Paul called him "the greatest cross of my pontificate." Later the
pope did grant him an audience, but greeted him coolly, saying, "What
have we here, a brother or an enemy?" Lefebvre was intent in continuing
his opposition, expanding his seminary, and ordaining priests opposed to
the work of the Council. But now he was challenging the authority of the
pope as well.

Concerning the controversial changes in the liturgy, Paul insisted that
"not only have we maintained everything of the past, but we have re-
discovered the most ancient and primitive condition, the one closest to
the origins. This tradition has been obscured in the course of centuries,
particularly by the Council of Trent."[71]

Then once again, Paul confounded observers. For reasons of his own,
Paul curtly dismissed the progressive archbishop in charge of liturgical re-

form, Annibale Bugnini, just as he had dismissed Cardinal Lercaro in 1968. Perhaps he was trying to strike a balance after his criticism against the conservative Lefebvre, but it was clear the era of concilar experimentation in the area of liturgy was over. With it some of the decentralization of power to the episcopal conference was abridged as well.[72]

As age took its toll and the pains of arthritis increased, Pope Paul was unable to travel much. In fact since 1970 he had not left Italy after his celebrated pilgrimages across the world as the new apostle to the unbelievers. Confidentially, he had talked with the abbot of Monte Cassino about resigning and ending his days in the Benedictine monastery.

DUTY AND SERVICE

Sensing his own end, the pope in 1977 moved Giovanni Benelli out as his chief of staff, making him the archbishop of Florence and a cardinal. He would be seen as a possible successor in the two conclaves in 1978, but his enemies were legion and he died in 1982. As he observed the pope, Benelli realized that he could never resign: "He cannot come down from the cross." The pontiff himself judged the condition of modern man in increasing critical terms, concluding on one occasion, "He is seized by a frenzy, he is exalted by a fury to overthrow everything (and here we have a worldwide protest) in blind belief that a new order, a kind of rebirth not yet properly perceivable, is inevitably about to dawn."

At eighty, Paul seemed weary of life and ready to end his service. It was his sad fate to have to watch another shocking tragedy — the kidnaping and eventual murder of Aldo Moro, the head of the Christian Democratic party and a friend of the pope. For fifty-five days the drama continued as this high-ranking leader was kept in captivity by the Red Brigades, who charged him with crimes against the people. Moro was a threat to the militant left because he was exploring a coalition government with the Communist Party in Italy. The Red Brigades asked for a release of some comrades, so-called political prisoners in their eyes. Moro appealed to the pope for assistance in the exchange, but Paul was informed that it would be an interference in the affairs of the sovereign state. The pope instead as a private citizen wrote a letter directly to the captors asking for Moro's release and calling him a decent and innocent man. On May 9, 1978, Moro's dead body was found in a parked Renault. At a funeral Mass for the slain leader, Paul lamented, "O Lord, You have not answered our prayers."[73]

On June 29, the fifteenth anniversary of his coronation, he explained that he had kept the faith. "That was my duty, to be faithful. I have done everything, now I've finished." On his deathbed he was asked in passing what he wanted. The pope responded appropriately, "a little patience."[74] Those were his last words, patience, always patience. Those were the skills taught him at his father's knee and enshrined in his mother's faith. Those were the attitudes of the Curia, where he spent his formative years and the sensitivities of his patron, Pius XII.

Montini remained remarkably humble for a long-time ecclesiastical power broker and then prince of the Church. One cannot imagine Pius XI, for example, putting up with the criticisms and disobedience from his own clergy and hierarchy as Paul did. Paul, however, worried that the Council would lead to a major schism as councils had before, and by his patience and fortitude he probably obviated many of those consequences.

Pope Paul was a subtle man, trained in the arts of listening, delaying, and calibrating responses. He was a true Curia politician in the best sense of the term. Paul tried to hold together the progressive impulses of Vatican II for collegiality and decentralization, with his own sense of a conservative stewardship as Peter's successor — a stewardship defined in large measure by his modern predecessors and generally antithetical to the Council's departures. Paul was a highly educated and well-informed person. He somehow embraced the core but not the harsh edges of many new theologies and social movements. In the leadership of institutions such a balancing act is hard to maintain and almost impossible to pass on. His immediate successor was chosen to cast away in part the gloom of the last years of Paul's pontificate, but it would be his protégé, the stronger and more youthful colleague Karol Wojtyla, who would seek to buttress, to restore, and to roll back the Church to its older formulations of dogma, authority, and social concerns.

CHAPTER NINE

JOHN PAUL II: THE UNEASY AGENDA OF RESTORATION

Before he passed away, Pope Paul whispered, "See, so the pope dies like any ordinary man." His last will and testament mandated a "pious and simple" service — as simple as a pope can request in any case. It was in August, the traditional vacation month of Italians, that his reign ended. Almost immediately some of the Curia insisted that the next pope also had to be an Italian in order to deal with that nation's unique brand of politics. That demand was countered by a letter from Third World prelates supporting the election of a pastorally oriented pope who would understand their increasing difficulties in the underdeveloped nations.[1]

CHOOSING JOHN PAUL I

The Curia conservatives moved quickly to derail two major candidates who were being prominently mentioned: Sebastiano Cardinal Baggio, the head of the Congregation for Bishops, and Sergio Cardinal Pignedoli, from the Secretariat for Non-Christians. The former was portrayed as a committed progressive, and the latter had been criticized for being indiscrete in his dealings with the international pariah Colonel Moammar Gadhafi of Libya, who had hosted a conference that attacked Zionism and Israel. The conservatives advocated instead Giuseppe Cardinal Siri — a staunch opponent of Vatican II, Pope John's papacy, and any rapprochement with the left in foreign policy matters. The normally very patient Pope Paul had on one occasion relieved Siri from the presidency of the Italian Conference of Bishops because of his obstinacy.

On the first ballot, Siri led with twenty-five votes; the only other candidate close to him was Albino Luciani, the amiable cardinal patriarch of

Venice. Three times in this century, the College of Cardinals has turned to that ancient fabled city for a pope, and now it was to elect from its citizenry the first pope to be born in the twentieth century. If the cardinals insisted on an Italian and wanted a moderate progressive from outside the Curia, there were really few other candidates of available age and pastoral experience from which to choose. Thus the assets of Albino Luciani seemed to become more obvious as the weeks passed by.

On the third ballot, Luciani received over sixty-five votes, and then he was elected with over ninety votes, while his own went to the liberal Aloisio Cardinal Lorscheider of Brazil. It was truly unanimity for a relatively unknown person. Before the conclave, sociologist Father Andrew Greeley had remarked that the Church needed a "holy man who could smile" — and that is exactly what the cardinals got.

Albino Luciani was born on October 17, 1912, in Forno di Canalo (now Canalo d'Agordo) in the Dolomite Alps of northern Italy. His father was a migrant laborer and a committed socialist, but still he agreed to send his son to a seminary at the tender age of eleven. Later Luciani earned a doctorate in theology at the Gregorian University in Rome and was made vice chancellor of the seminary he had attended in Belluno. In 1958, he was named bishop of Vittorio Veneto, where he was known for his strong pastoral orientation. Luciani generally supported the reforms of Vatican II, although he never played a major role in any of the four sessions of the Council.

In 1969, he was named the patriarch of Venice and insisted that the people there abandon the triumphant procession of colorful gondolas and decorated boats that had so delighted Angelo Roncalli at his own installation. His admirers in Venice said that Luciani dressed in a simple priest's cassock and ate seaweed pizza with students. He soon sold his pectoral cross — a gift from John XXIII which had originally belonged to Pius XII. He did so to raise money, some $14,000, for the causes of the physically handicapped of the diocese.

In a trip to Venice, Pope Paul removed his own stole and placed it on Luciani's shoulders, an act of high approval that embarrassed the humble and unpretentious prelate. In 1973, he was named a cardinal, a normal honor for that ancient see. In his spare time, Luciani also authored a series of fictional letters titled *Illustrissimi,* addressed to famous "historical" figures, ranging from Pinocchio and Figaro to Charles Dickens, Mark Twain, and Empress Maria Teresa of Austria. The letters were designed to present the Catholic faith to common people in understandable formats.[2]

Once elected to the papacy, however, he glumly observed, "I have neither the wisdom of the heart that Pope John had, nor the preparation or learning of Pope Paul." On one occasion he had confided, "I am only a poor man, accustomed to small things and silence." Soon he was repeatedly asking his secretary, "Why did they choose *me?* Why on earth did they choose *me?*"³ For the first time in the long history of the office, an incumbent took a dual name, in honor of the two pontiffs who had so influenced him and advanced his career. Also with that designation, he seemed to refuse to choose between those who respected John's memory and liberal legacy, and those who preferred Paul's more cautious style of reform.

What exactly his views were on the Church and the pressing controversies of postconciliar reform is unclear because of the brevity of his term. Clearly he was pastorally oriented and once even considered, before finally dismissing the idea, that bishops should again be elected as they had been in the distant past. He seemed at ease with ecumenism, advised Paul VI not to issue any definitive statement on birth control, was privately critical of the increasingly controversial Vatican Bank, and, when he was still a cardinal, was charmingly hospitable in welcoming to the world the first "test tube baby," the pretty Louise Brown. Later the Holy Office (renamed by Paul the Sacred Congregation for the Doctrine of the Faith) would formally condemn artificial insemination. Its theologians had never seen the lovely infant.

The new pope showed his lack of experience in diplomacy on several occasions, most apparently when he warmly welcomed General Jorge Videla, the president of Argentina, a symbol of right-wing Latin American regimes.⁴ And despite his reputation as a progressive, he was really rather conservative in many ways. He had denounced "false moralism" during the Italian divorce controversy and had real concerns at first with the Council's decree on religious liberty. Luciani had been a student of Cardinal Ottaviani and had probably been inculcated in some of those rigid Romanist attitudes. In response to popular demand and despite his own inclinations, he restored the *sedia gestatoria* on September 23, and at St. John Lateran Basilica, the bishop of Rome's traditional Church, he criticized those so overcome with creativity that they lead the faithful into "liturgical excesses." What his views were on other pressing questions would never be known. Five days later he was found dead in his bed.

For some reason, Vatican authorities insisted on maintaining that he was discovered dead earlier than he actually was, and that he had been reading that night the world-weary devotional work *Imitation of Christ*, by Thomas à Kempis. Others said that he was absorbed over a distressing report on the abuses of the Vatican Bank or going over a mundane speech for the next day that never came. Rumors spread that "the smiling pope," as he was called, was murdered by various sorts of suspects. A book was even written detailing the alleged conspiracy, and one popular American film, *Godfather III*, had a pope poisoned by the Mafia. It appears, though, that the pontiff had had some serious cardiac problems and was not up to the demanding office he assumed; he probably died of a pulmonary embolism.⁵

Pope John Paul I reigned for thirty-three days — a month in time — and left only two marks on the Church: a remarkable smile that lit up his pictures and appearances and a genuine disdain for the once royal trappings of the office. At his funeral, some spectators sadly commented on how the soles of his new shoes were barely scuffed. Now a very shaken College of Cardinals had to elect a successor — as the faithful waited for their third pope in less than three months.[6]

A MAN FROM A DISTANT COUNTRY

And so in October 1978, the College of Cardinals — some 111 in number — returned to Rome for a second conclave. It was increasingly obvious after the election of Luciani that there would be problems finding another acceptable Italian candidate who could carry the two-thirds plus one vote necessary at that time for election. Part of the reason was the clear split between Giuseppe Siri of Genoa, who at seventy-two was still seen as a protégé of Pius XII and who had been a consistent vocal critic of Vatican II and of Pope John, and Giovanni Benelli of Florence — the fifty-seven-year-old hard-driving administrator who shook up the Vatican bureaucracy when he served Paul VI, and who emerged in this conclave as a candidate and not just a king maker. Three days before the conclave, fifteen Western European and Third World cardinals met to plot a stop-Siri strategy. They put forth the names of Benelli, Ugo Poletti, the vicar of Rome, and Giovanni Columbo, the archbishop of Milan, as candidates.[7]

At first Siri seemed to be very close to being the choice, but strong opposition developed, especially from some Western European and Third World cardinals, and it proved in the long run to be an insurmountable obstacle. In addition, an Italian newspaper, *La Gazzetta del Popolo,* prematurely printed an ill-tempered interview with Cardinal Siri in which he again criticized the Council in harsh terms. The interview was mysteriously delivered to the Roman residence of each member of the Sacred College. Privately the cardinal observed of John Paul I, "You can't govern with smiles or protestations of modesty and simplicity."

Since Pope John, and especially since Paul VI, the percentage of Italians in the College of Cardinals had markedly declined. In addition, in 1963, 55 of the 80 cardinals who elected Paul were Europeans; in 1978 only 56 of the 111 were Europeans. Also Paul VI had prohibited cardinals over the age of eighty from voting, thus eliminating nine cardinals, most of whom were probably conservatives, from having a role.[8] As a group, the cardinals wanted a man who was pastoral in his orientation, was in good health, and could exhibit a personal presence that appealed to the public at large. Some of the favorites of the previous conclave were no longer mentioned; they were in the Italian expression *bruciati* — burnt-out cases.[9]

Before the conclave met, Cardinals Krol and König, both men with Polish roots, had a candidate — the Polish prelate from Krakow, Karol

Wojtyla. Wojtyla was not well known outside of the College and the upper levels of the Vatican bureaucracy. Although he may have received up to ten votes in the previous conclave, his name was not mentioned prominently except in a brief reference in *Time* magazine. Years before, however, it was rumored that the mystic and stigmatic Padre Pio had fallen to his knees when he first met Wojtyla and had predicted that he would be elected pope and that his reign would be marked by an act of violence.[10]

After four ballots on Sunday — the first day of voting — it became more obvious that no Italian cardinal could be elected. Meanwhile, between the rounds of balloting, Wojtyla spent some time reading a quarterly review on Marxism while waiting in the picturesque Sistine Chapel. On Monday afternoon, four foreign candidates emerged: Wojtyla, König (who did not want the position), Eduardo Pironio of Argentina, and Johannes Willebrands of the Netherlands, who soon gave his support to Wojtyla.[11]

Still many of the Italian cardinals declined to support the Polish cardinal until Sebastiano Baggio of the Congregation for Bishops backed Wojtyla. In the end seventeen cardinals persistently refused to concur in his election on the eighth and final ballot. It has been rumored, but not confirmed, that Wojtyla was actually elected on the seventh ballot and refused, accepting the office only after Cardinal Wyszyński, the primate of Poland, insisted that he bow to God's will. After his election, he sat alone at a table beneath Michelangelo's *Last Judgment* in the Sistine Chapel, holding his head in his hands and slumping down in his chair.[12]

Whether the speculation of his initial refusal is true or not, one of the cardinals there, Enrique y Tarancón, simply observed, "God forced us to break with history to elect Karol Wojtyla." Cardinal Benelli generously commented to observers on Wojtyla's close ties to the Vatican Council: "His theological attitude is perfectly correct...what he says comes from his personal convictions. He is the right man at the right time. If there was one man who believed in the Second Vatican Council and had a firm will to carry it out it was Cardinal Wojtyla." Later the new pope would candidly admit that the conclave had taken a gamble in choosing him. There was indeed some concern that at 58 he was too young for the position — making him the most youthful pontiff since Pius IX in 1846. And most startling, he was the first non-Italian elected in 456 years, when the Dutchman Adrian (Hadrian) VI was chosen in 1522.[13]

Wojtyla wished at first to take the name of Stanislaus in honor of the Polish Catholic bishop and saint from Krakow who had been murdered during Mass by the knights of King Boleslaw the Bold nearly nine hundred years before in 1079. But in a more measured gesture, he announced his choice of a name: John Paul II in honor of his predecessors. When he addressed the crowd outside St. Peter's Square in the early evening, he remarked in Italian that the conclave had called him "from a distant country and yet [one] always close because of our communion in faith and Christian tradition." Then he asked their forgiveness if he made a mistake in "your — our Italian language." It was a calculated slip and the crowd loved his gesture. When he playfully continued, "If I make mistakes, please correct me," the crowd responded, "Yes, we will." He was to be the most consummate actor in the history of the modern Church.[14]

The next day he surreptitiously sent his red skull cap to the altar of the Polish Virgin of Ostrabrama in Vilnius in Soviet Lithuania — a special tribute to his people and their tribulations. And in the evening he called home to Krakow to say how lonely he was. "I am sad without my friends," he remarked. Later he was to call the apostolic palace "a cage, a gilded cage." His schoolboy acquaintance, Dr. Karol Poliwka, was to characterize Wojtyla as "a man of loneliness."[15]

He was then, and still remains, a mystery — a public man who commands enormous audiences wherever he goes and yet retreats into private spaces filled with religious fervor, ascetic mysticism, and deep personal loss. He wears heavily his complex and difficult past. We are all formed in so many ways by our childhood and our adolescent years. For Wojtyla those were years of war, of death, and of deepening religious commitment.

THE MAKING OF A POPE

Karol Wojtyla was born on May 18, 1920, in the small, drab city of Wadowice, fifty kilometers southwest of Krakow in the foothills of the Carpathian Mountains, at the end of the tragedy called the Great War. Once he remarked, "During my childhood, I listened to veterans of World War I, talking about endless horrors of battle." He grew to manhood as the Nazis and the Soviet armies ruthlessly divided up Poland. His family roots were in the peasantry, although his father, a strict but loving and religiously devout parent, was a retired military officer in the Polish Army's quartermaster corps and was an admirer of Marshall Józef Pilsudski.

Before he was twenty-one he lost his entire family. His mother, a one-time school teacher, died when he was only eight and an older sister passed away as well early in life; his elder brother, a physician, died of scarlet fever when Karol was eleven; and his father died of complications from a stroke when Karol was twenty. In 1984, Wojtyla recalled the night of his father's death, saying, "I never felt so alone." Sadly he observed years later, "At twenty, I had already lost all the people I loved and even the ones I might have loved." And he wistfully remarked that there comes a time when boys brought up by their fathers (no matter how well and tenderly) make the painful discovery that they have been deprived of a mother.[16]

Unlike most of his modern predecessors in the papacy, he did not seem to be committed at an early age to the priesthood. Wojtyla only chose that vocation a year and a half after his father's death, after he himself had twice been nearly killed twice in freak accidents, and as his world was coming apart in the Nazi-controlled zone of violence. The Church was feeling the full weight of totalitarian oppression, and the cardinal prelate of Krakow, Prince Adam Stefan Sapieha, informed the Vatican that the Poles were being annihilated just as brutally as the Jews. In that horrible environment, Wojtyla wrote poetry, studied philosophy, gained a military exemption by working in a quarry and then a water purification plant, and spent his free time as an actor in the Rhapsodic Theater (Teatr Rapsodyczny, or the "Theatre of the Spoken Word"), founded by Mieczyslaw Kotlarczyk. He was to say that his time as a worker was of greater value to him than his two university doctorates. Those sentiments found expression in a line in his poetry: "How splendid these men, no airs, no graces." Later in 1982 he reflected on how his experience as a worker and his seeing the horrors of Polish deportation "have profoundly marked my existence."[17]

At one point he fell under the spiritual influence of a tailor named Jan Tyranowski, who introduced him to the writings of the Spanish mystic St. John of the Cross as well as to the "Living Rosary" devotions and the Catholic Youth Association. Wojtyla was to characterize him as a saint.[18]

One tale that gained some circulation after he was chosen pope was that Wojtyla was married and that his wife was killed by the Gestapo, a story that has been discredited. One woman, a student contemporary of his, said that Wojtyla "did not avoid feminine company as a colleague, but he did not seek it." In his autobiography he notes how he had female acquaintances but was preoccupied with the theater and literature. Another incorrect story spread after his election is that Wojtyla was imprisoned for a while at the Dachau death camp.[19]

A more dramatic account is that during those dark years, he was involved in the underground in Poland, which sought through the Christian Democratic organization, UNIA, to save Jews from the Holocaust. Consequently he was put on the Gestapo's black list and was labeled an "unwanted person." But he has denied that he helped in such efforts, saying to Polish Jew Marek Halter, "I cannot lay claim to what I did not do." He was anti-Nazi but rather apolitical, seeing liberation as coming through Christian values and prayer. In 1942 he enrolled in the theological department at Jagiellonian University, an action that was illegal and could have led to his arrest and death.[20]

Some time after his father's death, Wojtyla decided to become a seminarian, as the Nazis grew increasingly murderous, putting over six million Poles, or one-fourth the total population, to death in just six years. The Church was also continually attacked, and 1932 priests, 850 monks, and 289 nuns were killed or murdered in concentration camps. The Nazi gauleiter in the Warsaw area, Reinhard Heydrich, ordered that the nobility, priests, and the Jews all had to be liquidated to protect the Reich's interests.[21]

On one occasion Wojtyla himself was arrested, only to be fortuitously let go. Cardinal Sapieha moved several seminarians into his episcopal palace, and there Wojtyla spent the rest of the war, largely unnoticed by the outside world. His absence from factory work was initially reported, but the influential cardinal intervened quietly and his name was never forwarded to the Germans. He had for all intents and purposes disappeared. Wojtyla had wanted to join the austere Discalced Carmelite monastic order, but his confessor insisted that he was made for greater things (*ad maiores res tu es*), and besides Poland desperately needed parish priests after the Nazi genocides. In his autobiography, he affirms that Sapieha himself discouraged him from joining the order.[22]

In September 1946 he was ordained and then sent to the Angelicum, the Dominican house of studies in Rome, to do graduate work in philosophy. Up to then, Wojtyla's education was sketchy because of the disruption of local academic institutions and seminaries in Poland. One can only imagine the excitement of going to Rome for a student who had lived in a Polish city plagued by wartime conditions, food shortages, and the stiff coldness of drafty rooms and endless winters. And above all, he must have endured the loneliness of a young man without any family in a foreign land.[23]

His counterparts found him to be very cheerful, pleasant, forthright, humble, highly intelligent, and generally nonjudgmental toward others. Wojtyla studied under the compelling influence of traditional Thomists, although his own scholarly research examined the mystic St. John of the Cross, the author who charted the *Dark Night of the Soul*. Wojtyla was also attached to the Catholic War Relief Services, in which he assisted Polish refugees outside their homeland, and he came into contact with a Monsignor Giovanni Battista Montini, who would become his patron years later. On one occasion, he also visited Marseilles, France, to meet Father Jacques Loew, one of the founders of the controversial worker-priest movement.[24]

Wojtyla graduated with highest honors; ironically on his doctoral board were two future members of the College of Cardinals that would choose him to be pope. In July 1948, he returned to Krakow and was shipped off for a brief time to a desolate parish at Niegowíci in the Galician countryside thirty miles from Krakow. Then he was soon transferred to Lublin University to become the university chaplain and a faculty member. The Church, having just survived the brutalities of the Nazis, was now under attack from the Communist Party, and about 10 percent of its clergy were imprisoned.[25] The traditional Polish Church was becoming a heroic fortress of martyrs under totalitarian states of the right and the left.

Unlike most Catholic thinkers, Wojtyla gravitated toward the philosophical theories of German Catholic phenomenologist Max Scheler and the Polish thinker Roman Ingarden, as well as the personalist philosophers of the French Catholic existentialist movement such as Gabriel Marcel, Maurice Blondel, and Emmanuel Mounier.[26]

On October 23, 1948, Pius XII named Stefan Wyszyński to be the prelate of Poland, archbishop of Gniezno and Warsaw. A canon lawyer by training, Wyszyński was involved with the Christian worker movement in his nation and had been a vigorous opponent of Nazism and later Communism. Wyszyński immediately moved to reach some rapprochement with the Communists, and he signed an agreement that was criticized in some offices of the Vatican. The basic provisions acknowledged that while the pope had the highest authority on matters of faith, morality, and Church jurisdiction, the episcopate pledged that it would be guided by the national interests of Poland. In the process, the Church's bishops would seek to carve out their own autonomy and identity, but had to do so without threatening the viability of the Marxist state. In exasperation at the Vatican's criticisms, Wyszyński observed, "You talk about the Church of Silence, but here in Rome is the Church of the Deaf."[27]

While Wyszyński was engaged in high-level diplomacy, Cardinal Sapieha assigned, as has been noted, his brilliant protégé just returned from Rome to a poor rural parish in Niegowíci. Wojtyla's admirers were disappointed that he was being confined to such a minor parish, especially after his successes at the Angelicum, but Sapieha was clearly aiming at giving Wojtyla some hands-on pastoral experience.

After a short while, however, he was sent to a parish in Krakow, where he came in increasing contact with intellectuals, students, and artists. In 1947 Wojtyla was awarded a doctorate in sacred theology from the Jagiellonian University, the alma mater of the astronomer Copernicus and the real Doctor Faustus. In 1951, Cardinal Sapieha died, but his successor, Archbishop Eugeniusz Baziak, continued Wojtyla's high-level mentoring, advising him to take a two-year leave of absence to complete yet another doctorate. Responding to diverse needs in his complex personality, Wojtyla also published, under at least four pseudonyms, major works of verse, including dramas revolving around religious themes.[28]

In the early 1950s, Wyszyński came under increasing hostility from the Communists and also from the Vatican. In Rome the Polish prelate insisted that he was not "soft on Communism," but that "I want my priests at the altar, at the pulpit, and in the confessional — not in prison." He and later Wojtyla would consistently insist upon the importance of protecting the flexibility of the Church, but they also usually said that they must avoid partisan politics. As Wyszyński was to find out, state officials insisted on interfering in the choice of bishops, and several members of the hierarchy were arrested during this period. In November 1952, Pius XII named Wyszyński a cardinal in a clear show of support. Later in September 1953 he was arrested by the secret police, the first major Polish prelate to be arrested since the Prussians had imprisoned Archbishop Mieczyslaw Ledóchowski in 1866. Wyszyński was released three years later in October 1956 when a more conciliatory regime came to power.[29]

The authorities also closed down the theological faculty at Jagiellonian University, where Wojtyla had been teaching. At that time he was finishing up his doctoral thesis on Christian ethics and the philosopher Max Scheler, enlarging his circles of friends, and engaging in rigorous recreation, especially hiking and skiing. He would continue that last sport even while pope until at age seventy-four he fractured his hip in a bathroom accident.[30]

In 1956, tensions further increased among the Polish government, nationalist liberals, and the Soviet Union. To calm matters down, Russian armies were withdrawn for a while, and Wladyslaw Gomulka, who himself once had been jailed by Stalinists, came to power promising "the Polish road to socialism." He immediately made overtures to Cardinal Wyszyński, then under house arrest in a monastery for the past three years, and allowed him to resume full episcopal powers.

During those difficult years, Wojtyla was teaching at the Catholic University in Lublin and climbing up the academic ladder, establishing himself as a prolific scholar and a well-regarded teacher.[31] Among other projects he was interested in preparing a study of the *Decretum Gratiani,* the compilation of Church canon law done by the twelfth-century scholar Gratian. Through it all, he continued to express himself as a poet, usually under the pseudonym of Andrzej Jowién. Explaining the appeal of drama and poetry, Wojtyla insisted that art is "a companion to religion and a guide on the road to God." In 1957 and 1958, he was working on an essay on love and responsibility that would become important in understanding his later views on sexuality and contraception.[32]

In his book, Wojtyla argued that "sexual relations outside marriage always cause objective harm to the woman, even if she consents to or positively desires them." As pope, he would even criticize the sinfulness of men who looked upon their wives "with lust" in their hearts. He was widely ridiculed for that remark, but it is in perfect harmony with his view that to treat a person as an object is unethical and immoral. Such a view is a noble signpost in evaluating behavior. But life is so ambiguous at times, and sexual activities such a mixture of the physical and fantasy, that it often does not fit its robust expressions into such hermetically sealed categories. Even love is more complicated than that. The Russian playwright Anton Chekhov noted of love, "Either it is a remnant of something degenerating, something which had once been immense, or it is a particle of what will in the future develop into something immense, but at the present it is unsatisfying, it gives much less than one expects."[33]

CALLED TO THE HIERARCHY

On July 8, 1958, an ailing Pius XII named Karol Wojtyla auxiliary bishop. It was a surprising nomination, for the priest and academic had no extensive pastoral or administrative experiences. The promotion was undoubtedly due to the intercession of Archbishop Baziak, who may in turn have been following some earlier pledges made to the late Cardinal Sapieha. Wojtyla was only thirty-eight years old at the time and probably was not known except by reputation to even Cardinal Wyszyński. Indeed his nomination marked the first time the cardinal had been in effect by-passed in the appointment of a Polish bishop. As for Wojtyla, he never hesitated when asked if he would accept the nomination from Rome. And one of his first acts was to move his mother's and his brother's remains from Wadowice to rest beside his father in a Krakow cemetery.[34]

When Baziak died, Wojtyla was elected capitular vicar of the diocese of Krakow. Traveling to Rome with the Polish delegation to the Vatican Council, he met for the first time the influential Franz Cardinal König, who would years later be an important figure in his election as pope. König remarked that the friendly young bishop before him seemed to lack a sense of self-assurance, spoke German poorly, and was dressed in frayed clothes.[35]

Wojtyla was diligent in working on various commissions, even though at first he said little in the public debates. One Protestant observer to the Council, George H. Williams of Harvard University, however, predicted before the conclave in 1978 that he would be the next pope.[36] The Wojtyla they saw was conservative in theology, but progressive on some social issues. Conversant in several languages, including Latin, he had a distinct advantage during the deliberations in presenting his positions.

One consequence of Vatican II was the increasing emphasis on collegial structures, committees, and commissions. Wojtyla was spotted as a "comer" and ended up on some of those important groups. Thus at a relatively early age, he was becoming known to a wider international audience of clergy and Vatican watchers. Much later in 1977, Basil Cardinal Hume of Westminster met him and concluded, "I was struck by the impression he gave of strength, determination, and durability."[37]

Wojtyla's definitive biographer, Tad Szulc, has disclosed that Wojtyla was one of the major authors of Paul's controversial encyclical *Humanae Vitae,* and in his own papacy he has been its single most consistent supporter in the Roman Catholic Church. It has been speculated that some 60 percent of the encyclical was written by Wojtyla. It is unclear if the progressive cardinals such as König, who supported his candidacy in 1978, were aware of his central role. Wojtyla, a member of the enlarged commission dealing with the birth control issue, did not attend any meetings, but apparently played a major part in shaping the mind of the hesitating Pope Paul.* In his own statements, Wojtyla has never wavered, and as pope

---

*Originally, John XXIII had appointed a commission of only six people; Paul enlarged it in 1964 to fifty-eight, including thirty-four lay people. There were five sessions; Wojtyla had been appointed in 1966 before the last session, but did not come to Rome due to visa problems that Wyszyński had with the Polish government. The final vote was fifty-two to four for reforming the Church's position on contraception.

he has allowed his subordinates to suggest that the ban on contraception approached an infallible declaration, a view that Paul would never have ventured to advance publicly, although he may have contemplated it.[38]

As noted, after Archbishop Baziak's death, Wojtyla was temporarily in charge of the Krakow diocese, but it was left to Cardinal Wyszyński to choose a successor. Under the agreed-upon procedures with the government, the primate was to submit a list of at least three names to the Communist regime, and it could accept or reject any of the nominees. Then the cardinal would forward a name to the Vatican for final approval. It is clear that Wyszyński opposed having Wojtyla named archbishop of Krakow, just as fifteen years later he discounted the idea that his younger colleague could be elected pope. In fact, he put his own name forward if the conclave decided to go "foreign."

After the first session of the Council, the cardinal submitted a series of names to the Communist government, and each was rejected, one at a time, until finally the government received and accepted the name of Wojtyla. Clearly the cardinal did not wish him to become archbishop of Krakow; and just as clearly the Marxist government was responsible for putting in place a man who would become "the Slavic pope," and who helped to end the Communist regime in his homeland. Such is the irony of history. The Polish Communists thought they wanted bishops like Wojtyla, who had a reputation for being apolitical. After he was installed, however, he proved to be in many ways a tougher and more determined foe than they had expected.

And so, on March 3, 1964, Karol Wojtyla at age forty-three was solemnly installed by Pope Paul as the metropolitan archbishop of Krakow. At first he had some difficulties with the local clerical establishment and remarked on one occasion, "Well, what can I do? When Cardinal Adam Sapieha [a predecessor], who was born a prince, looked down on them from his lofty height, they were afraid of him. But I simply can't impress them in the same way — not as a former worker." Indeed, he was the first prelate in the history of that see not to come from the aristocracy.[39]

A SON OF THE COUNCIL

He would speak more often in the later sessions than in the first session of the Vatican Council. Wojtyla addressed the People of God analogy, ecumenism, and religious freedom — all in a positive way. But his views were often traditionally oriented rather than progressive in tone, and he was still a major proponent of a strong papacy, even in discussions about collegiality.

During the Council, Archbishop Wojtyla appeared before some students at the Polish College in Rome to answer questions on Vatican II. In response to criticisms of Pope John XXIII and his rather abrupt call for a council, Wojtyla insisted that the Church had to deal decisively with some immense challenges: the rapid development of technology, a society oriented toward consumption and lacking altruistic values, the population explosion, the wide extent of atheism, and the need for world peace. The Church was becoming less effective under modern conditions, and many contemporary forms of behavior were in conflict with traditional Church ethics.

In four years the Church had undergone, he maintained, an amazing change. An enormous outpouring of valuable opinion had come forth from the upper echelons of the hierarchy and theologians. He acknowledged the important part played by such eminent theologians as Henri de Lubac, Jean Daniélou, Yves Congar, Hans Küng, Riccardo Lombardi, and Karl Rahner. The Church also had come to understand better non-Catholic and non-Christian religions and to recognize that atheism's appeal often came from its claim to liberate man from feelings of alienation. He praised the healthy debates in the Council and the salutary effects of pluralism of opinion shown in its sessions.

Later Wojtyla commented to a friend on the important changes in the relationship between the center and the periphery of the Church — the pope and the bishops, the clergy and the laity. He advocated greater decentralization and an emphasis on collegiality. Also in his view, there had to be an end to "Constantinism," the principle of a close alliance between Church and the political regime which had been so important to Catholicism since the fourth century.[40]

Most dramatically, though, he was in the last session a major mover on the draft on the Jews. Born and raised near the death camp of Auschwitz (Oswiecim), he lived in a town with a large Jewish population and had formed close friendships with Jewish students. Wojtyla was acutely sensitive on the issue of Jewish persecution and called the camp "this Golgotha of the modern world." He went on to be the first pope to visit a synagogue and finally approved the Vatican's recognition of the state of Israel in 1994.

At the Council, he also opposed the attempt of some bishops to condemn Communism. Later he stressed the need for dialogue with atheists and warned, "It is not the Church's role to lecture to unbelievers. . . . We are involved in a quest along with our fellow men. . . . Let us avoid moralizing, or the suggestion that we have a monopoly of the truth. One of the major defects of this draft is that in it the Church appears merely as an authoritarian institution." It was difficult enough to deal with them back home without new provocations.[41]

On May 29, 1967, Paul VI named Wojtyla a cardinal, some said to balance the influence of Wyszyński, who was becoming more intractable in the pope's eyes. As for Wojtyla, he was rather deferential at first to the older man, trying to allay any appearance of differences. At the age of forty-seven, the Polish intellectual and poet was the second youngest

cardinal in the Church and had probably reached the apex of his ecclesiastical career. Celebrating his installation, Wojtyla humorously said to
his clergy in Krakow, "I can't go any higher now." There was no other
position a non-Italian could aspire to in the Catholic Church, or so it
seemed.[42]

Biographer Tad Szulc relates that the Polish secret police had files on
both Wyszyński and Wojtyla. They recorded that the elder prelate was from
a traditional Catholic family, and that he had built his ecclesiastical career
on anti-Communist sentiments. His hard-line position during the Cold War
was very significant in establishing the directions of the Vatican's foreign
policies under Pius XII, but with the advent of John XXIII his influence
diminished as the tenor of that policy changed significantly. The reports
judged that Wyszyński was characterized by a "shallow, emotional, and
devotional Catholicism."

Wojtyla, on the other hand, was presented as an intellectual, one of the
few in the Polish episcopate. He was judged as having roots in the working
class and leftist university circles, and his rise in the hierarchy was seen as
due not so much to his advocacy of anti-Communism, as to the high regard
others had for his intellectual breadth. He was not engaged in "antistate"
political activity, the report stated, and he lacked organizational and leadership qualities. His "secular lifestyle" also brought him closer to young
intelligentsia and students. Recognizing the differences between the two
men, the report advocated that the authorities make additional overtures
to Wojtyla.[43] Later the Communist authorities would regret their sanguine
assessments.

The Vatican Council and its call for greater collegiality spawned more
opportunities for participation, and Wojtyla was appointed to three major
congregations of the Curia — the Congregations for the Clergy, for Sacraments and Worship, and for Catholic Education. He was also a consultant
to the Council for the Laity and was chosen by the pope in 1969 to be a
member of the Synod of Bishops.

A high point of his career was Paul VI's invitation in February 1976 to
give the Lenten retreat sermons to the Roman Curia and the pope. Paul
asked Wojtyla to deliver his lectures in Italian, indicating later to some
that the pope was grooming a foreign successor to be the next bishop of
Rome. In fact, before the conclave that elected him pope in 1963, Montini was supposed to have commented that maybe it was time then for a
non-Italian pope. To an associate, Paul much later remarked that Wojtyla
was "a brave, magnificent man." Between 1973 and 1975 alone, Wojtyla
visited the pontiff privately eleven times, a sign of high regard indeed.

Wojtyla's homilies, published later in 1979 under the title *Sign of Contradiction,* presented a somber picture of the West and its values, although
he was critical of the excesses of both economic imperialism and Marxism.
Still he specifically denounced liberal regimes where "men are sick with af-

fluence and an overdose of freedom." A very frail Paul listened to Wojtyla's spirited defense of his ill-fated encyclical, *Humanae Vitae*. In May 1978, Wojtyla paid his last visit to Paul, and in August he attended his funeral. It was time for another Italian, although as noted there has been some speculation that the Polish cardinal received a few votes in the conclave that named Albino Luciani pope. At the conclave, Luciani related that the Polish prelate was writing furiously — not taking notes it turned out, but working on his next publication![44]

On September 28, Wojtyla was celebrating the twentieth year of his consecration as a bishop in the Catholic Church; in the Vatican apartments Pope John Paul I had just died. Some have recorded that Wojtyla had a premonition that he would be elected pope this time; if so, he was one of the few who predicted that choice, although his godmother had foreseen such an occurrence years ago, and over a century before, the noted Polish poet Juliusz Slowacki insisted that there would be a Slavic pope. His friends recorded that the usually mild-mannered and even-tempered Wojtyla became fretful and preoccupied after news of the pope's death, almost as if he knew the direction the next conclave would take. Except for several years in Rome, he had spent his whole life in Poland. Whatever close human ties he had forged in place of his lost family were in that land.

Although John Paul II took the name of his predecessors, he quickly moved away from both the open style of John XXIII and the caution and hesitations of Paul VI. After making some important gestures of support to the Roman Curia and to the Roman people in his new diocese, the pope quickly established his brand of rule. As noted, although he was a new voice in the Council, he was never seen as a leading progressive force in those sessions. Still he immediately committed himself to its full implementation. His first words seemed to summarize his life, "Be not afraid...."[45]

Rather than characterize Wojtyla as a betrayer of the Council as his critics have, one can view him as having some of the same reservations that Paul VI expressed over the years. Although he was committed to the legacy of the Council, Paul expressed at various times his concern about its diverse directions. On November 23, 1966, he denounced the view that the Council had given the "go-ahead for any kind of arbitrary changes." In October 1968, he pleaded for a return to obedience, and in March of the following year, he attacked the "giddiness" of certain priests. In January 1969, the pope remonstrated, "How many things, how many truths are questioned or doubted? How many liberties are taken with the authentic patrimony of Catholic teaching?"

Commenting on the adverse reaction to *Humanae Vitae*, Paul wondered aloud on September 10, 1969, how the "most poignant pain comes to her [the Church] from the indocility and infidelity of certain of her ministers and some of her consecrated souls, that the most disappointing surprises come to her from circles that have been the most assisted, the most fa-vored, and the most beloved." He spoke frequently of a "crisis of authority and faith," and a year before his death, he concluded that "a non-Catholic mentality was increasingly dominant in the Church."[46]

THE CHURCH OF KAROL WOJTYLA

Still there are major differences between Paul and his successor. Paul was a man who appeared cautious, tentative, and ambivalent. But actually he saw his role as implementing the policies of a council that he himself would never have dared to call in the first place. John Paul II has always praised the movement of the Holy Spirit in the Council, and in his first major address after his election he pledged "our primary duty to be that of pro-moting with prudent but encouraging action, the most exact fulfillment of the norms and directions of the Council."[47] But his actions and especially those in the Congregation for the Doctrine of the Faith have been clearly aimed at rolling back the new order or reaffirming aspects of the old. It is not without reason that the era of John Paul II has been termed the "restoration."

Coming from a nation where the Church knew intense persecution and where the basis of piety was strong and far-reaching, the pope has not been able to understand — or accept — the very complexities of the new Church he heads. The comparatively young pontiff moved quickly, perhaps at times a bit abruptly, to reassert the hierarchical model of the papacy. Occasionally, his role model seemed to be Pius XII, without the aloofness of that Roman cleric. His administration appears often as unyielding as that of Pius XI. And in his search for orthodoxy he has paralleled some-what Pius X's campaign against the assorted errors of Modernism. But this pope is above all a man of ideas, a person who has moved easily with other intellectuals and theologians in a manner similar to the autocratic and well-educated Leo XIII.

The man and the movement came together in another way. The last part of the twentieth century is saturated with the electronic media, and John Paul II is immediately at home in that milieu. The former actor exudes a sense of poise, of timing, of command that adds to the usual aura of the papacy. He is a genuine crowd pleaser, even with those who disagree with his rigid theological views. It has been said in the United States that, while many faithful dislike the message, they love the messenger.

The sources of progressive discontent during this time were manifested in three major focal points, and the pope has moved to exercise greater control over each. The new synods — the symbol of collegiality — have be-come groups that are more often meant to help the pope administer the policies that he initiated and approved. The new episcopal conferences of bishops were also brought to heel and are watched by the Curia as they serve John Paul's bidding. And the Congregation for the Doctrine of the Faith has stepped up its warnings and criticisms of highly visible theologians, some of whom were welcomed a few years ago in the Council and acknowledged by the Church Fathers to be *periti,* or experts.

At the very start of his tenure, the pope would challenge the "liberation theologians" in Latin America, sometimes without fully understanding the complexities facing the Church there. His synods would walk away from the expression "People of God" and its implications, which he himself had once praised, as some in the Church hierarchy were trying to restore the old hierarchical metaphors. As the years have passed, the pope has celebrated the virtues of women, and yet moved almost belligerently to put them in their place, that is, outside the pale of the priesthood, by his exercise of infallible teaching.

He has denounced priests who engage in partisan politics, while he himself stage-managed in major ways Polish domestic affairs and played a significant role in the upending of the Soviet empire. No churchman who has ever assumed the responsibilities of the papacy has ever spoken so graphically of sexual union and pleasure, and yet he seems wedded to characterizing all forms of contraception as part of an "antilife philosophy," associating it with war, abortion, and euthanasia.

This conservative pope has filled stadia with the young and was named by *Time* magazine as its "Man of the Year" in 1995 because of the very surety and self-confidence he exudes in the service of moral values that that very organ of opinion and others so often ridicule. This pontificate of an "outsider" has become one of the most controversial in modern times, accelerating the phenomenon of selective denial of doctrine by a usually docile faithful, especially in the United States and Western Europe. How has this papacy been cast in such complex molds?

One explanation that has been posited is that Karol Wojtyla, despite his incredible intellectual brilliance, is really rather provincial. He has spent nearly all of his life in an Iron Curtain country, a nation without much contemporary intellectual importance or flavor. Poland is a backward land in many ways, blessed with a sense of deep patriotism and intensive piety, but at the fringe in terms of Western culture. Thus Wojtyla for all his exposure to the world of ideas has very limited perspectives.

Perhaps that criticism is somewhat just, but no one is born a cosmopolitan; we all come from somewhere. As one of his friends observed, "He is not a cosmopolitan, but he does have a sense of 'cultural collegiality.'" Some close to Wojtyla would not agree with that sanguine assessment. Three years into his pontificate, the eighty-eight-year-old Carlo Cardinal Confalonieri observed, "We Italians have a universal vision. As for the foreigner at present in the Vatican, he is out of his element, he needs to study the milieu, and he should seek advice through the properly constituted channels." As for the pontiff himself, on one occasion he remarked, "I don't think the eminent cardinals knew what kind of personality I am, and therefore what kind of papacy they were getting."[48]

Another view is that Polish Catholicism is very different from Latin Catholicism. One of the reasons why the Catholic Church has survived over the centuries is because it has been governed by Italians, who tend to be more cynical, more world-weary, and less passionate about ideas, ideology, and religion itself. They regard human nature as somewhat fallen and the Church as a very imperfect institution that helps, as best it can, sinners get a decent stab at salvation. But the path is slippery, life can be sweet, and we all fall victim to various temptations. So when that happens, one looks the other way, uses the sacrament of confession, and covers up if the behavior of the Church and its clergy can lead to scandal.

By contrast, Polish Catholicism is tinged with the celebration of martyrs. Wojtyla's speeches are very much cast in the heroic model, and his own life and tribulations have been witness to its demanding standards. Indeed he himself has observed that "the younger generation grew up in *an atmosphere marked by a new positivism,* whereas in Poland, when I was a boy, *romantic traditions* prevailed."

For such people, compromises are counterfeit and great betrayals. However for popes like Della Chiesa, Ratti, Pacelli, Roncalli, and Montini, who learned their leadership skills in wartime diplomacy, the world is not black and white, but filled with varying hues of grey. One must accommodate, build alliances, work with fools and even evil people. Sometimes the best one can do in life is to minimize suffering by making common cause with very objectionable individuals. Did not Montini imply that in his persistent defense of Pius XII; did not Roncalli live that by working with the Nazi Ambassador Franz von Papen to save Jews in the Balkans? They survived, as Roncalli once bluntly observed, by bending and not breaking. And their moral vision of Catholicism and their role as pontiffs were much more complicated than Wojtyla's.

Then too, the role models of our lives are rarely our contemporaries. They are the heroes of our youth, and the pontiffs that Wojtyla knew were Pius XI and especially Pius XII, neither of whom are good guides to the contemporary world. The first was a stubborn, obstinate, unbending autocrat who dallied with dictators and then exploded in righteousness and self-righteousness against them. And his successor was the epitome of the regal aloof pontiff. Wojtyla never knew Pius XII's agonies and hesitations, more akin to Paul VI's than to his own certainties. The popular view of Pius XII embraced respect, admiration, and high intellectual regard. He spoke on every topic imaginable, and like Wojtyla considered himself both a linguist and a philosopher. However, he never called a Church council and never had to deal with the unleashed forces of dissent that so perplexed Paul VI.

Reform has its own hope and its own dynamics, sparking an exuberance that comes from upending the old order of things. But restoration has its own model as well, and it is based on a romantic interpretation of the past. Wojtyla seems to be pleading for such a restoration of the papacy of Pius XII, but without the arched pomp that the latter engaged in. Wojtyla believes that if one can strip the papacy of its pretentious symbols and be more accessible to the media, then one can restore the Church and the papacy to the era of unquestioning obedience.

Once when he was discussing possible bishop candidates for the United States, he took off his papal ring and uncharacteristically slammed his hand on the table, saying, "No, we need stronger men there." Strength, fortitude, authority, heroism — such is the worldview of John Paul II. As for himself, he once reflected, "I have received more graces than battles to fight."[49]

But the forces of dissent are powerful in the Roman Catholic Church, and they arise from complex causes that have little in common with the dreams of restoration. It is not a failure of will that the Church is facing; it is profound economic, social, and cultural changes. Pope John felt that intuitively; Paul clearly articulated it in the beginning. Wojtyla is denying it. In defense of the conservative position, however, one can ask if the Catholic Church lost so much after Vatican II, how can one say that more accommodation with the world will now work? The progressive response is that if the Church cannot change, it will not survive; and the rejoinder is obvious — if it changes, can it survive with its integrity intact? That is the central dilemma facing John Paul II's entire papacy, and his answer is very clear: the Church will remain conservative in dogma and practice, but try to reach out to the concerns of the world by emphasizing social justice, while not compromising basic tenets of the faith. Under such a prescription, the universal Catholic Church may be reduced to a smaller but harder core, militant and obedient faithful.[50]

Understanding this formulation should not lead one to the simplistic conclusion that the state of the Catholic Church is simply a conservative Polish pope versus a progressive reforming faithful. The history of the modern Church involves the basic problem of providing leadership in an organization that lives not by production or consumption, but by ideas, beliefs, and symbols of the most important and intimate experiences of our brief lives.

One can see this difficulty in Wojtyla's convoluted dealings with the Latin American Church. Organizationally, the Catholic Church is essentially a bureaucracy, headed by Italians (until recently), funded by Americans and Germans, trying increasingly to convert restless peoples in the Third World. It is in Latin America, Africa, and also Asia, where the populations are increasing substantially, that the Church must focus — thus Vatican II's emphasis on evangelicalism. The great opponents of Catholicism as expressed in John Paul II's speeches, are materialism, secularism, commercialism, and sexual exploitation. Catholics, however, have always lived beside decadence, corruption, and hedonism, and the Church continues to survive. The real ideological challenge to Catholicism today is Islam, and the most profound problem facing the Church is the condition of teeming and poverty-stricken masses across the nonindustrial southern hemisphere, many of them practicing or nominal Catholics. The challenges are then more basic, more demographic, more explosive than many people realize.[51]

The Protestant Reformation came about not just because of the failings of priests and popes, but also because of the long-term consequences of the plagues that killed off the local clergy and left people unchurched. In a similar situation, in the United States Catholicism has become more secularized in large part because of the dearth of vocations, especially of nuns who once controlled rather ably the schools and the hospitals — the beginning and the end of life. The Vatican's increasing alienation from many women has had deleterious consequences far beyond making American feminists unhappy. It very well may be that the Catholic Church will lose many women, in the same way that it lost many of the industrial workers in Europe in the nineteenth century. At times, though, John Paul seems to sense that he has gone too far; in March 1996, for example, he urged that women, especially religious, be given greater power in the Church, but stopped short of talking about the priesthood.

In 1996, a Vatican spokesman had to admit that the Czech Church in 1970 during the Cold War had ordained several women and some married men because of the severe shortage of clergy at the time. The ordinations were simply dismissed by the Vatican as "invalid," and those individuals were not reordained in 1992 when the Communist regime was over.

The world Karol Wojtyla was born in was the aftermath of the profound breakup of the Great War, where old patterns of deference based on class, authority, and religion which had persisted since the Middle Ages were destroyed.[52] The postwar period was unable to heal those wounds, and the Second World War advanced the chaos even further. The Catholic Church reentered politics to stabilize some of the countries in Western Europe, but it must be remembered that it was basically the Catholic countries that fell to totalitarianism — Italy, Spain, Portugal, Vichy France, Austria, and the Catholic parts of Germany. Small wonder that Pius XII had a difficult time condemning the Fascist regimes in World War II; so many of his coreligionists lived in those lands.

Still the Roman Catholic Church was remarkably resourceful in both wars through its humanitarian efforts and was solidly committed to defending its own religious liberty after the last conflict, becoming aligned by necessity with the United States. All of those dramatic expressions — the 1920s, the war years, the Cold War period — are part of Wojtyla's background, just as the Napoleonic regime was a looming presence in the tenures of Pius VI and Pius VII in the late eighteenth and early nineteenth centuries.

Although those wars of the twentieth century are over, the consequences have continued to be unsettling. The Catholic Church is mainly success-ful where its beliefs are supported by strong families, dependably funded Catholic schools, and a popular culture that respects tradition and piety. The economics of the postwar industrial states and their effects have upset the props of the first two; the communications revolution with its pervasive commercialism has up-ended the last.

LIBERATION THEOLOGY

Pope John Paul II started his reign with a clear, confident agenda of restora-tion. In Latin America he moved from the very beginning to clamp off the growth of so-called liberation theology. But the animosity he created and his own intelligent reappraisal led him to reassess what he at first believed and what the conservatives told him about that region of the world.

His predecessor, Paul VI, had gone to Medellín in 1968 and given his guarded support to what turned out to be the beginnings of a very radical turn to the left. Paul VI, for all his subtleties, clearly placed the tradition-bound Roman Catholic Church on the side of the poor. In his encyclical *Populorum Progressio* and his letter *Octogesima Adveniens,* he embraced the Third World and pledged that the Church "cannot plead for the status quo." The synods held in Rome in 1971 and 1974 further supported the transformation of unjust economic and political systems. Thus the Church, especially in Latin America, developed a "preferential option for the poor" and denounced the "institutionalized violence" of oligarchical rule as "a social sin."[53]

Although Paul spoke out against identifying the Church with any po-litical party or ideology, still elements of the clergy became radicalized and numerous murders and tortures of priests and nuns ensued in Latin America. The People of God often became organized in ecclesiastical base communities, the Bible became a tract for revolution, and Jesus was cel-ebrated as the greatest revolutionary of them all, whose Gospels were interpreted in neo-Marxist rhetoric. The conservative Church, once aligned so closely with the Latin American ruling classes in the 1940s and 1950s, was becoming increasingly committed to the poor and the dispossessed. John Paul I had indicated a desire to visit Latin America, seeking to repli-cate the trip of his immediate predecessor. Now it fell to Wojtyla to take his place, and the consequences would be clearly troubling to the progressive wing of the Church.

Before John Paul II arrived, there were reports that he had already con-demned "liberation theology," which in fact was not true. Actually his views, which seemed so confusing at the time, were rather clear upon closer scrutiny. He opposed priests and nuns getting involved in politics, arguing that their true vocation was to teach the word of God, but he was also very much on the side of land reform, a just wage, and democratic changes. His attitudes toward Marxism were honed in his own long-time battle against the Communist state in Poland, and the last thing he was amenable to was any attempt to encourage a Christian synthesis with that atheistic philosophy. The Gospels' radicalism came from true liberation, which he maintained was the freedom to know and to appreciate God's workings. He also had some concerns about the nonhierarchical or horizontal Church that some radical theologians had advocated.

The pope also must have worried about the toll that revolutionary activities were taking on the Catholic Church in Latin America. By the end of the 1970s more than 850 priests and nuns had been martyred in that region. So when the Latin American Episcopal Conference (CELAM) and others met at Puebla de los Angeles, Mexico, in 1979, the pope faced a very difficult situation.

Initially the pope was advised by Sebastiano Cardinal Baggio of the Congregation for Bishops and Colombian Archbishop Alfonso López Trujillo, both of whom warned that base communities were threatening the authority of local bishops and had to be abolished. Puebla must correct the abuses of Medellín, the new pope was counseled.[54]

But the pope, for reasons of his own, turned away from such an irrevocable and drastic step that would have condemned the directions of much of his Latin American Church. He vigorously supported the search for social justice, which he was always comfortable with, but criticized the assertion that Christ was a political figure, a revolutionary, or a subversive. Still the conservatives did not get a specific statement of condemnation, although they would work in the Curia to get censures of liberation theologians. As for the progressives, they were rather demoralized by the pope's lack of fervor in their cause.[55]

One of the figures in the more radical wing of the church in Latin America was Archbishop Oscar Romero of El Salvador, who was actually a rather quiet, nonpolitical prelate at the beginning of his tenure. But swept up in the civil war taking place in his nation and the murders of clergy, he became an articulate spokesman for social justice and human rights. In May 1979, he visited the pope and asked John Paul to condemn the murders of priests and others by Salvadoran death squads. The pontiff instead recommended "great balance and prudence," and asked that Romero stay with defending basic principles rather than incurring risk by making specific accusations. Still the pope insisted on the need for "courage and boldness."

After another visit by the archbishop in January 1980, John Paul II expressed his personal sympathies for the plight of the Church in Latin America and was deeply concerned about the possibilities of more bloodletting and retribution from the left. Several months later, on March 24, 1980, Romero was murdered by agents of the military intelligence command as he said Mass in the chapel of a hospital. It was a modern St. Stanislaus; it was another St. Thomas à Becket in the making. The Catholic Church thus added another martyr to its long rolls.[56]

The Polish born Wojtyla was himself a courageous man, not above using the fault lines of politics to advance the interests of the Church in his native country. To be successful there, one had to have a near monolithic Church willing to face the clumsy Communist client state that was indirectly under the control of the Soviet Red Army. But Latin America is very different. That region is infected with Marxist guerrillas, decadent military or oligarchical regimes, and very weak nascent democratic states. And the level of poverty there was not being alleviated in many areas by social reforms or state planning. Poland for all its economic problems is still not a Third World country.

The religious faith in his land was and is conservative and pietistic. While the hierarchy, including Wojtyla, was on the right side of the river called Vatican II, in Latin America the Church was faced with aggressive Protestant evangelical sects, articulate Marxist ideologues, and revolutionary happenings. The Church moved quickly from being a prop of the local and national oligarchies to becoming in some nations the very vanguard of revolution. As in Poland the hierarchy looked to the Church for solace, but with John Paul the more radical Catholics seemed at times to find more of a critic than an advocate. That discomfort was accentuated by the pope's disastrous visit to Nicaragua and the Curia's attacks upon liberation theologians. Thus the revolutionary Church of Latin America found danger at home and censure in Rome.

To John Paul the situation in Latin America was symptomatic of a larger problem — the unraveling of discipline in the Church since Vatican II. From his very disciplined perspective he saw such dislocations everywhere: the liberation theologians of Latin America, the advocates of syncretism in Africa, the easy ways of theologians and bishops in the United States and liberal Western Europe, the laxity of the Jesuits, and the general confusion of so many professors of Catholic theology.

Not since Pius X had a pope sought to exercise such authority over the way the faithful lived, thought, and prayed. Gone were the smiling tolerance of John XXIII and the nuanced hesitations of Paul VI. Their successor believed that by a determined exercise of his indomitable will and extremely charismatic personality he could restore the Roman Catholic Church, preserve its ancient doctrines, and prepare it for the third millennium. Will and faith and leadership by only one dedicated man could make the difference. It was an extraordinary agenda and as expected — it partially failed.

John Paul had read and understood the words of the liberation theologians, although he may not have empathized with all their sentiments and their neo-Marxist vocabulary. Those theologians advocated basic Church communities, *comunidades eclesiales de base,* which had been defined as families that lived together and consider what they could do in common according to the spirit of the Gospel. The leftist Brazilian priest and theologian Leonardo Boff argued that "a commitment to faith must have its political manifestation." Thus it was understandable how some conservatives — Church leaders and secular politicians — saw these communities as having subversive implications.[57]

The Church, especially in Brazil, was in the decade from 1968 to 1978 under considerable attack, with a long list of assaults and murders of its clergy. In El Salvador the Inter-American Human Rights Commission concluded that the Catholic Church was being "systematically persecuted." In Colombia, Camilo Torres, a priest and a guerrilla, was killed. Other priests were engaged in similar human rights activities in Colombia, Nicaragua, and Argentina. At first the Church was just a haven for hope; then it became an agent of social and political change.[58]

As noted, before Wojtyla came to Latin America, he was approached by conservative prelates, arguing that he had to stop the abuses of the liberation theologians and revolutionary priests. He was himself, of course, orthodox, but still he was cognizant of the fact that, in his own words, "the future of the Church will be decided in Latin America."

On the evening before his arrival, the Sanctuary of the Virgin of Guadalupe in Mexico City was already attracting people waiting for the pontiff's visit. When the pope finally arrived in Mexico, he kissed the soil and welcomed the religious who were dressed in simple civilian black outfits. Mexican law prohibited priests and nuns from wearing their religious garb in public — a part of the country's long tradition of anticlericalism. The road to the city was thronged with cheering crowds extending as far as eighty miles, with people crying out "Viva el Papa," and scattering flowers and confetti along the way. In Zócalo Square, originally laid out by the Spanish conqueror Hernando Cortés, over two hundred thousand people waited, many of them dressed in rags and frayed clothing. "You are Peter," some chanted as he passed by; and above the cathedral square was a huge banner that tellingly read, "Marxismo no."

True to his conservative leanings, the new pope criticized theological deviations and reiterated the need for fidelity to the Catholic creed and to his own office. Later at the airport he was presented with a blanket full of roses, the sign of the Dark Virgin of Guadalupe. According to religious legend, an Indian, Juan Diego, wanted to have a shrine built at Tepeyac, where he claimed he first saw the Virgin. When the local Catholic bishop demanded proof of her visitation, Mary returned and had Diego pick roses from a nearby mountain. At the bishop's palace the Indian offered up his blanket, which had enfolded in it an imprint of the Virgin. For the pontiff, what he saw in that nation must have seemed a great resemblance in piety to Our Lady of Czestochowa whom he deeply revered. Everywhere John Paul II celebrates easily the special blessings of Mary.

At one point the virile and handsome pope stopped a cheering group of nuns, chastising them, "Remember you are the mystical brides of Christ." And he also insisted in his addresses that political action and radical ideologies were not a substitute for prayer, an obvious swipe at liberation theology. John Paul pointedly remarked, "You are priests and members of religious orders, not social or political leaders.... Let us have no illusion that we will serve the Gospel if we 'dilute' our charisma by showing an exaggerated interest in temporal problems."

The trip to Latin America was a distasteful chore in some ways — for the pope appeared to many as a rigid conservative, although a person with a committed sense of social justice. In a visit to Brazil in 1980, John Paul showed his personal sympathies by insisting, "The Church is on the side of the poor, and that is where she must stay." Later on March 9, 1983, in a very poor and exploited Haiti, the pontiff blurted out, "Things must change here." Addressing a group of students in that nation, he pleaded for a just society and recalled, "In my youth I lived these same convictions.... As a young student I proclaimed them with the voice of literature and art." Still he was not portrayed as a friend of the progressive impulses unleashed by Vatican II in Latin America. In that sense reality and appearance were indeed one.[59]

POLAND — MOTHER OF ALL POLES

But his second major trip was a return of the heart, an odyssey back to his beloved Poland. To the relief of the Communist regime, then headed by party boss Edward Gierek, the pope insisted that his visit was to be a religious and not a political event. The government added to that theme by saying that it was the Polish episcopacy, not the state, that had invited him.

But in that nation, the political implications soon mixed with the spiritual, exactly the sort of behavior that John Paul II warned against elsewhere. Indeed his attitudes and activities have been contradictory; while he has urged priests and bishops to stay out of politics in their own nation, Karol Wojtyla has been deeply enmeshed in political action, public policy debates, and even partisan intrigue in his own nation before and especially after his election.

In 1970 Gomulka had been displaced after violent riots in the Baltic area, and the party put in Gierek, who promised some accommodation with the Catholic Church. By 1973, however, the state demanded a unified socialist education system that made it impossible for children to attend church for religious instruction. The bishops denounced that step as a violation of freedom of conscience and proclaimed the new laws not bind-

270 / Vicars of Christ

ing on the faithful. In 1976, steep increases in the cost of food led to greater unrest, and the Church supported the right to protest. In addition, Cardinal Wojtyla publicly denounced discrimination against Catholics in filling various offices and positions and maintained that atheism was not a legitimate political philosophy.[60] Before he became pope, Wojtyla also encouraged the so-called flying university to hold classes on church property, and he vigorously criticized antichurch propaganda. Most importantly, Wojtyla took to task state censorship, saying with other Polish bishops that "the spirit of freedom is the proper climate for the full development of a person."[61]

Now the situation facing the Marxist state was quite different. The government permitted the pope to return — what else could a Polish regime do in reality? But he wished to go to Krakow in May to celebrate the nine hundredth anniversary of the martyrdom of St. Stanislaus. As has been noted, that legendary bishop had been killed for criticizing the wicked ways of a Polish king, and as with the death of Thomas à Becket in Britain, the king's knights had rid the monarch of that troublesome man.* The symbolism was too powerful for the Communist party, and so they postponed the pope's visit until the next month, June 1979 — a delay that probably meant more to the party cadres than to anyone else.

The Communist regime also prohibited the pope from visiting Piekary near the Silesian capital of Katowich, the site of a popular annual pilgrimage by Catholic men at the end of the month of May. The government was worried about the Church's growing influence among the workers of that region. Instead the pope could celebrate Mass at the more important shrine of Czestochowa on June 5, and workers would be shipped in from parts of Silesia to attend.

In addition, he was not allowed to say Mass in the new church at Nowa Huta, the site of Wojtyla's successful battle against government directives opposing the construction of new churches. Before he came in May, an explosion ripped off the leg on a statue of Lenin — a portent of events to come. Then on a cloudless June 2, the pope's Alitalia Boeing 727 landed at Warsaw airport. Government officials had carefully kept the airport crowd size as small as they could. Greeting the pontiff were the thin Cardinal Wyszyński, dressed in a black cassock, and high-ranking officials of the Polish nation led by president Henryk Jablonski, accompanied by a military band and guard of honor. The cardinal prelate entered the plane first and privately greeted his younger colleague. Some time later John Paul II emerged and dropped to his knees to kiss Polish soil. To the surprise of Vatican observers, the Communist leader delivered a warm welcome, calling

---

*An angry Pope Gregory VII excommunicated the king, and he was forced into exile. Every succeeding king of Poland had to walk barefoot in sackcloth and kneel at the saint's tomb to ask for forgiveness for Boleslaw's evil deed.

the pope several times "Your Holiness," not exactly an accepted Communist salutation. He was praised as his proud nation's son, embraced by Poland, the "Mother of All Poles." John Paul was deeply moved and extended his own warm greetings as well.

The first stop was Victory Square for an open air Mass before three hundred thousand people. It was there that the Russians had built an Orthodox church in the nineteenth century; it was there that Czar Nicholas I had created a parade ground for his troops; and it was there that the Germans had constructed a monument to their successful 1939 invasion. Overlooking that square stood an imposing oak cross. Addressing the crowd, the vigorous pope remarked, "The pope can no longer remain a prisoner of the Vatican; he had to become Peter the pilgrim once more."

John Paul went on to other ceremonies and services. At one point he visited Gniezno, the ancient see of the Polish primates, where the earliest Polish kings were crowned and prayed at the tomb of St. Adalbert, who was a missionary to the Baltic peoples and who was killed by Prussian pagans. The pope also stressed the saint's Czechoslovakian background, as he trumpeted the theme that he was not just a Polish pope, but a Slavic one as well. He sang with the crowds, embraced the enthusiasm of the young, and reached deeply into the chords of piety.

At the great folk shrine of Polish Catholicism, Czestochowa, the crowd held up signs proclaiming the coming of the six-hundredth anniversary in 1982 of the Black Madonna's visitation. The Poles believed that the Virgin Mary saved Poland from invading Swedish armies in the battle of Czestochowa in 1655. At that site a small number of monks and knights forced the Swedes to retreat. The town has a revered monastery on a hill called Jasna Góra ("Luminous Mountain"), which is the site of the shrine of the Black Madonna. The famed portrait of the Madonna housed there is an icon that has become darkened over the centuries and is supposed to have been painted by St. Luke the Evangelist on a wooden plank that was the actual table of the Holy Family in Nazareth. In 1430 a Hussite soldier scarred the face of the portrait with a saber.

The pope greeted the massive crowds with a simple exclamation — "I am here." They responded with the song "Sto Lat, Sto Lat" ("May he live a hundred years"). The pope toyed with the crowd, saying, "If this pope lives all those years, your grandchildren will be coming to see him, and what can be done with such an old pope? I can see only one solution: he'll have to run away and live in a monastery." Shades of Paul VI's melancholy thoughts, and on such a fine occasion.

John Paul cited the Virgin Mary's role in Polish history and life, saying, "She is present here in some strange way." When he was entertained by a young woman musician, he engagingly remarked, "I had to come to Poland to learn to sing again." The pontiff later talked to a meeting of bishops at a local monastery and gave his views on the uneasy relationship between the church and state, as he urged authentic dialogue and a respect for the rights of all citizens. It was estimated that three and a half million people saw him at Czestochowa alone, and some twelve million people, or one-third of the total population, came out to visit him while he was in Poland.

On another occasion he reiterated his earlier position that the priesthood is a gift to God, a gift forever. He noted in passing, "It has been suggested that the pope was trying to impose the Polish model of priesthood on whole world." But he observed that only with a life consecrated to the Church could the Church survive in "today's secularized world." At the Catholic University in Lublin, which he knew so well, he celebrated the development of human potential, and then observed that universities around the world seemed to be undergoing "some kind of deformation."

Coming back to Krakow, the pope praised his old associations and sadly remarked, "I have discovered in Rome that it is not easy to leave Krakow behind." He continued, "My heart has not ceased to be united with you, with this city, with this patrimony, with this 'Polish Rome.' " That night he sought to retire from the hectic pace and stayed at the archbishop's palace on Franciszkanska Street, where he had once lived. But the crowds would not let him go. He teased them, "Do you intend to sleep tonight?" And they shouted back, "No." The pontiff countered, "Well I am going to bed because tomorrow I have got to walk on my feet, not my eyelashes." Then he said the Angelus with them and a prayer for the dead and closed the window tightly.

On the sixth day of his visit, he returned to his birth place at Wadowice, where he met his old teacher of religion and acknowledged the parish of his family. Then he went on to the death city of Auschwitz, called in Polish Oswiecim, which is now a gruesome museum and still has the wrought iron lettering over the gates that reads, "Arbeit macht frei" — "Work will make you free." Some four million people from twenty-eight countries and fifty nationalities had been exterminated in the Auschwitz and the neighboring Birkenau (Brezinka) complexes.

One of the priests murdered there, Father Maximilian Kolbe, had traded his life for that of a Polish father of ten children and had been beatified by the Roman Catholic Church in 1971. The pope knew Auschwitz well, having been there before, and he walked quietly to Block Eleven, Cell 18, and prayed at the site of Kolbe's internment. Outside was Franciszek Gajowniczek, the man for whom the priest had traded his life on July 30, 1941. Near the camp the pope saw the railroad cars that had led countless people to their death, the international monument to the victims of Fascism, and a large canopy with a cross that carried a coil of barbed wire and a striped flag with the letter P for prisoner and the designation 16670, Kolbe's camp number.

The Polish pontiff had referred to Auschwitz as the "Golgotha of our times," and he called Abraham the father of all. He specifically cited the people of Yahweh and insisted that no one should indifferently pass by the memorial tablets written in Polish, Russian, and Hebrew. He reminded listeners that six million Poles had died in this war — one-fifth of our "people"; he repeated Paul VI's powerful admonition at the United Nations against war, and then he left the crowd in tears. Pointedly, John Paul observed, "Responsibility for war rests not only with those who directly cause the war, but also with those who do not do everything in their power to prevent it."

The next day was more upbeat as the pontiff visited the mountains that he so loved. There he appeared at Our Lady of Ludzmierz, another Marian shrine. Colorful costumes of the mountain people dotted the crowd. Later that day he went back to Krakow and renewed old acquaintances with academics and clergy. He addressed a large audience of students, talking of his much valued ties to youth and contradicting those who saw them as materialistic and seduced by the consumer society. Sometime in the early morning, he walked incognito along the streets of Krakow to remember once again its sights and sounds.

Then on June 9 the pope finally got permission to go to Nowa Huta, the sterile state community planned without a Church — the city of the Communist future, it was said. Karol Wojtyla had fought a long battle to erect a church there, and he consecrated it in 1977. The Communists finally agreed that he could celebrate a Mass, not at that church, but at a Franciscan church nearby — another empty party prohibition.

The Polish trip ended with the pontiff unexpectedly embracing Polish president Jablonski on both cheeks, and whispering good wishes for his mother to him. Then remarkably Jablonski kissed the pope's hands. The picture of those events raced across the nation's newspapers. Thus it was that Karol Wojtyla, the one-time factory worker, seminarian in exile, quiet intellectual, and reluctant prelate came home to his beloved Poland. For him it was a sentimental journey; for the Communist state it was the beginning of the end.

The Soviet leaders had been less sanguine about the whole visit. When the Polish episcopate issued the invitation to the pope, the Russian premier Leonid Brezhnev warned Gierek, "I advise you not to receive him because it will cause you much trouble." He cited with approval Gomulka's refusal in 1966 to give Paul VI a visa for the Christian millennium celebration. But as Gierek knew, there was now a Polish pope. And besides he himself had been graciously received by Paul VI back on December 1, 1977.[62]

The pope's visit resurrected a true sense of pride among the Polish people. Clearly their allegiances were more with the Catholic Church than with the Communist state. A little more than a year later, the Gierek government raised food prices by 80 percent and unrest boiled over. At the Lenin shipyard at Gdansk, the workers led by a thirty-six-year-old electrician named Lech Walesa staged a sit-down strike. From those activities Solidarity and Rural Solidarity were born, and the Communist government's eventual demise was in sight. The Church, after some hesitation, supported the unions, and the Gierek regime was replaced by another Communist government, headed by Stanislaw Kania. Polish dissidents demanded and eventually got the right to strike, a relaxation of censorship, an end to Communist monopoly on the press, a five-day work week, more economic reforms and worker self-government, and some autonomy for the universities. Then in December 1981, the pendulum swung again to a crackdown on dissidents after the concerned Soviet government insisted that the Polish regime restore order to its homeland. Security forces began a series of arrests, transportation was disrupted, and communications were cut off. The new authority was called the Military Council of National Salvation and was headed by General Wojciech Jaruzelski, who declared martial law and announced that a "state of war" existed.

On June 16, 1983, with martial law still in effect, the pope revisited his homeland. The pontiff was received by warm crowds again, but the context was more somber. Wojtyla the patriot appealed to the people with figures of Polish history and recounted the nation's long history of torment and troubles, as if saying this too will pass away. Subtly he spoke of the "solidarity" of the Church with the people, and it was taken by the cheering crowds and the regime as a code word for solidarity with the union. The Communist government angrily accused John Paul of political activity, and indeed in Ponzan before moving on to dedicate another new church at Nowa Huta the pontiff paid tribute to those who had died in 1956 during riots over escalating prices.

The pope had met with Walesa, and the Vatican newspaper *l'Osservatore Romano* informed its readers that the pope had distanced himself from the labor leader in return for concessions from the Polish regime, including ending military rule. Clearly Walesa was offered up as a sacrifice. A distraught John Paul II fired the editor, but in fact the substance of the story was correct.[63]

Four years later he returned to Poland again and once more expressed his solidarity with his homeland. The pope again met with union leader Lech Walesa, and the pontiff also visited a suburban church where Father Jerzy Popielusko had been assigned. In 1984 that priest was murdered by the secret police because of his support of the Solidarity movement. The pope prayed at his grave and placed yellow and white flowers, the colors of the Vatican city-state, on it.

The government eventually realized that it needed Solidarity's cooperation, and with Moscow's consent it sought to work with the union to better economic conditions. Free elections were held and Solidarity won handily. The Catholic Church was granted total freedom, and Józef Cardinal Glemp approved of the formal separation of church and state in Poland.

THE SLAVIC POPE

Watching these events was a major admirer of the pope, the new American president Ronald Reagan, who suggested that CIA Director William Casey establish some closer ties with the Vatican on the Polish question. Reagan had been deeply moved by John Paul's reception in 1979 in his homeland. Rumor had it that in December 1980 the pope had already sent Leonid Brezhnev a letter warning him that if the Soviet premier decided to invade Poland, the pope himself would return and rally the people to resist the occupation. If true, it was an extraordinary communication.

In 1979, the pope had also appointed a cardinal *in pectore* (in secret), and word spread throughout Lithuania that it was their imprisoned archbishop. The Soviet press at that time called the pope's views "an infection" and accused the Vatican of trying to "extend its religious influence over the republic." In January 1981 Lech Walesa had visited the pontiff in Rome and was hosted by Luigi Scricciollo, a spokesman for the Italian Labor Conference. Walesa may have misplaced his trust, for the Italian intelligence agencies believed that Scricciollo was a source for Bulgarian intelligence and a conduit to the Communist regime.

Casey, a devout Roman Catholic himself, went to Rome to seek to establish some ties with the Vatican, or at least to exchange information. His request for a formal meeting was denied, however, and Vatican Secretary of State Cardinal Casaroli refused even to see him privately. Meanwhile, the U.S. government quietly moved to dry up investments that might help the Polish government, and the regime began to totter economically. Then in July 1981, the Reagan administration offered Poland $740 million in aid aimed at promoting reform and protecting Solidarity. In addition, the American labor movement, through the AFL-CIO, was providing advice, training, and financial support to Solidarity.

After the military takeover in Poland and with the pope's near assassination fresh in his mind, Cardinal Casaroli finally agreed to meet with Casey. The Church, he insisted, could not play a covert role with the intelligence agency or serve as a cover for CIA operatives, but it would provide information and facilitate contacts within Poland. Admiral John Poindexter, a National Security Council staff person and later himself director of the CIA, summarized the relationship: "Clearly in terms of gathering information as to what was happening and from the standpoint of talking to Solidarity and other supporters of Western objectives in Poland, the Vatican was very helpful." The Church was not a partner, but had "mutual objectives in Poland." The agency gave the Catholic Church a code name in its own jargon — "the Entity."

The Israeli intelligence services and the French counterespionage units were also involved in helping to provide information and protecting some Solidarity activists. CIA funds were transferred in and out of accounts to help Solidarity publish and distribute literature and to buy electronic transmitters. The Solidarity movement, though, was infiltrated with spies in the service of the military government, while the CIA in turn penetrated the Polish regime at least as high as the deputy minister of defense.

In 1982, Reagan, having recovered from an assassination attempt on his life, had promised to keep the pope informed of his administration's actions toward Poland. Casey was later to bring John Paul information about what was being done to help Solidarity, but what specifics he gave are not public. In 1996 a major biography of the pope maintained, undoubtedly with some exaggerations, that the pontiff was deeply involved in directing Solidarity, met personally with Casey, and in return avoided criticizing the Reagan administration's policies in Nicaragua and its decision to upgrade nuclear weaponry in NATO.

By July 1984, Jaruzelski's government tried to reach some accommodation with the dissidents and declared an amnesty, but his efforts were only partially successful. The KGB and Soviet intelligence officers had since John Paul's election watched the Vatican closely. One report concluded, "the antisocialist bias of the Vatican's activities have [sic] become particularly marked with the arrival on the papal throne of John Paul II." The KGB also charged that "the Vatican's principal interest is concentrated on the most 'promising' countries of Eastern Europe, from its point of view, Poland, Hungary, and Yugoslavia." By 1985 the Soviet Union would be headed by a new sort of leader, Mikhail Gorbachev, whose liberalization policies would lead to a democratization of Poland and the ultimate demise of the Soviet empire. As for the Vatican, it sought to get the United States administration to end economic sanctions against Poland, arguing in the words of the pope that the people had suffered enough. Walesa and other Solidarity leaders agreed, but the sanctions continued until January 1987.[64]

Pope John Paul moved quickly in the late 1980s and early 1990s to regularize relations with Poland, Hungary, the former Soviet Union states, Czechoslovakia, Romania, Bulgaria, and Albania. In 1985 he had issued an encyclical, *Slavorum Apostoli,* which praised the Slavic peoples and their common roots. Once again a pope paraded out Saints Cyril and Methodius — the two Greek monks who had transported Christianity to the Slavic peoples a millennium ago. They were saints in the undivided Church, that is before the split with Eastern Christianity in 1054.

In 1985 the Communist regime in Czechoslovakia had prevented John Paul from going to that nation. By 1990 the world had changed, and playwright and President Václav Havel remarked that he himself had been a prisoner of the state six months ago and now he was there to greet the first Catholic pontiff in history to visit his homeland. The pope in his youth had lived near the Czech border and acknowledged their common heritage, exclaiming, "Here are our roots." When he was asked by a reporter to characterize the collapse of Marxism throughout Eastern Europe, he confidently said that it was just "another Tower of Babel."

FACING THE SOVIET STATE

After his first visit to Poland, the Soviet leadership had ordered a top secret worldwide smear campaign against the pope and the Vatican's foreign policies. On November 13, 1979, the Secretariat of the Central Council approved a six-point program which was also signed by men who would become future premiers of the Soviet Union: Yuri Andropov, Konstantin Chernenko, and Mikhail Gorbachev.

The plan included the mobilization of Communist parties of Lithuania, Latvia, Ukraine, and Byelorussia, and also the news agency Tass, Soviet television, the Academy of Sciences, and other organizations that were to begin a propaganda campaign against the pontiff. The second point in the proposal urged an exchange of information and propaganda with various other Communist parties, especially in states with large Catholic populations.

The Ministry of Foreign Affairs was instructed to stress the Soviet Union's commitment to world peace, and the Ministry and the KGB secret police were told to upgrade their efforts in the struggle against the Vatican's Eastern European diplomacy. The fifth point enumerated in the plan had the KGB publicizing through the media in various countries claims that the Vatican's policies were harmful and that the pope was dangerous to his own Church. Special channels were to be employed in both Western and Socialist countries to spread that alarm. Lastly the Academy of Sciences was to organize more studies on the benefits of scientific atheism.

The new pope was portrayed by the Soviet leaders as using religion in an ideological struggle against socialism and of having encouraged the activities of what it called "disloyal priests." The Marxist state was pledged to encourage what it saw as tendencies in the Catholic Church that opposed the anti-Communist foreign policies of the Vatican. Oddly enough, this particular proposal did not mention Poland and the special consequences that a collapse of that Soviet puppet regime would bring. Later it would be charged that the party leadership had approved more than simply a propaganda offensive against the pope. As John Paul II prophetically observed to Archbishop Romero, political activity, especially in nondemocratic states, can exact from the Church a terrible price — including the blood of martyrs.[65]

It seems ironically fated that the other important political figure who would cross the pope's diplomatic horizon also would be a Slav, Mikhail Gorbachev. And in some ways, he shared some characteristics with John Paul: he came to power at the early age of fifty-four, had advanced rapidly through the aid of powerful mentors, was deemed charismatic, and sought to channel directly the powerful forces of democratization sweeping through an authoritarian organization.

Mikhail Sergevich Gorbachev was born in 1931 in the Stavropl territory of the Soviet Union. He studied law at Moscow State University, joined the Young Communist organization, and in 1971 was elected to the powerful Central Committee. He was appointed secretary of agriculture in 1978, the traditional elephant burial ground for ambitious Soviet bureaucrats, but he succeeded in staying viable and became the youngest person promoted to the Politburo. In March 1985 he was named the leader of the Soviet Union, the youngest man to hold that position since Joseph Stalin. In 1988 he became Soviet president, its chief of state.

As soon as he took office, he announced that he was intent on nothing less than a major overhaul of Soviet society. He called his policies *glasnost* (opening up) and *perestroika* (restructuring). He sought to overcome the increasingly obvious consequences of seventy years of Communist political oppression and economic stagnation by a profound transformation of the Soviet system. Gorbachev adopted modified open elections, and advocated a modernization program to achieve a more flexible economic system — giant steps that would challenge total party control then held by the bureaucratic cadre and its props, the internal secret police and the Red Army.

While all his reforms at home did not satisfy the expectations that they aroused, still Gorbachev's initiatives were well received by Western foreign leaders, especially Prime Minister Margaret Thatcher in Britain. Even Presidents Ronald Reagan and George Bush entered into important arms limitations agreements that partially eliminated the nuclear arms race and led to disarmament on an unparalleled scale. Gorbachev also took the popular step of removing Soviet troops in Afghanistan by early 1989, thus ending one of the major points of contention with the West.

He met with John Paul, and there seemed to be a real understanding of the magnitude of the changes that the Soviet Union was facing, as they both seemed to enter into a sort of mutual admiration society. For some reason, Gorbachev publicly commented that he had informed the pope that he had been baptized as a Christian in the Russian Orthodox faith. The pope correctly remarked that the Soviet leader's whole problem was to find a way "to change the system without changing systems," and privately he expressed the hope that the president could keep the Soviet Union together. Gorbachev permitted a lessening of Soviet pressure on its satellites, including the pope's beloved Poland. There the Communists finally allowed free elections, which Solidarity handily won.

As is so often true, the tides of revolution overwhelm the forces of reform, especially in recent history. Modern reformers raise expectations that they cannot fulfill in time and are too often replaced by the forces of chaos and then repression. The course of modern revolution is the course of eighteenth-century France and not colonial United States. After the great uprising for liberation comes too often deep discontent, terror, and repression.

Although these two Slavic leaders lived in different worlds, both faced similar difficulties. By 1990 John Paul was still dealing with the problems of trying to mobilize the Church against the loosening tendencies unleashed by Vatican II. He was permitting crackdowns and admonitions, although generally to no avail. Vatican II had raised expectations in his own authoritarian system. But in the Soviet Union Gorbachev was facing even more serious problems at home because of the worsening economy. He insisted that the state had to remain socialist, that Communism could function with "a human face." He was being challenged not just by reactionary elements, but also by democratic forces, led ironically by Boris Yeltsin, a flamboyant demagogue who had been a harsh Communist apparatchik at one time. As matters worsened, Yeltsin was elected the first president of the Russian Republic, still encased however in the Soviet system.

Gorbachev faced continued old-line Communist opposition, and on August 19, 1991, those elements staged an inept coup to remove him while he was on vacation. Yeltsin rallied the people of Moscow, other cities followed in support, and the coup remarkably failed within seventy-two hours. Quickly Gorbachev was restored, the Communist Party officially banned, and the Baltic states given their independence. By December 1991, however, the Soviet Union just collapsed. Eleven of the remaining republics formed the Commonwealth of Independent States, but Gorbachev was the president of no remaining nation, and thus went into retirement on Christmas Day. Later he observed, "Everything that happened in Eastern Europe those last few years would have been impossible without the presence of this pope."[66]

John Paul must have watched the mind-boggling events with incredible attention. He knew the politics of Eastern Europe as well as anyone, but no one could have expected what happened. The Vatican diplomats and the Western intelligence agencies never predicted the demise of the Soviet Union so quickly. To some of the Catholic faithful, it seemed as if the Virgin's predictions came true, and only a few years after John Paul's final dedication, with other bishops, of Russia to the cause of Mary on March 25, 1984. The formidable empire crumbled like pie crust — to paraphrase Lenin's remarks. The pope, however, refused to see those occurrences as an act of God. Communism fell because of its own injustices, he concluded. As for his own role, the pope judged, "I didn't cause this to happen. The tree was already rotten. I just gave it a good shake and the rotten apple fell."

The peculiar events that took place later, especially in 1995, added another twist. Repudiated Communist Party adherents in Poland helped elect a president, Alexsandr Kwaswienski, who defeated Lech Walesa, the Solidarity hero. And Communists in Russia began to make remarkable inroads into the democratic parliament. In once tightly ruled Tito's Yugoslavia, the demise of the Communist state there led to enormous ethnic violence, especially genocidal attacks in Bosnia. The pope deplored such misery once again. What could one make of what had taken place in such a short period of time? The pope had laid aside his own admonitions that the Church should not be involved in secular politics, and now he was seeing that the ways of mammon were not only sometimes evil, but increasingly fickle.

And as Poland was experiencing the problems of democratization, the role of the Church itself in that state began to lessen. There was an official separation of church and state, an increase in the number of divorces, and even reports of greater acceptance of abortion.

A disillusioned pope watched as his own countrymen insisted on keeping abortion legal. He sadly remarked, "I was offended by the Poles. But I'm getting over it." There was less talk about the so-called Third Rome, the role of Moscow in Christendom. The pope had always believed that "the light comes from the east," but it did not. There was also less rhetoric about the triumph of a Slavic pope and less success in promulgating the goals of reuniting an activist and diverse Roman Catholic Church with what was an increasingly ossified Eastern Orthodox set of national communities. The pope warned these newly freed nations that they must avoid the perils of the West, the emphasis upon profit, the rampant personal liberty, and especially the excesses of consumerism. But to many the appeal of the West was not just its eighteenth-century Enlightenment legacies, its liberal political rhetoric, or its sophisticated financial institutions, but the creature comforts that it brought to people so long denied the most basic elements of life. Thus once again the pope seemed to be out of tune with the movement which, in this case, he himself had help to father — the demise of the Marxist-Leninist states of Eastern Europe.

In reflecting on the strength of his own Polish Catholic Church, John Paul had often praised the unity of that congregation, the importance of tradition, authority, and obedience to the bishops and to Rome. But those conditions were not present in other Eastern European nations, or at times even in Poland. In many ways the pontiff lived in a pre–Vatican II world. And early in his pontificate, he seemed to believe that if he wished it to be so and said it, the Church in very different lands would restore the hierarchical model. But that was not to be.

REASSERTING DOGMATIC AUTHORITY

It was that assumption that led the pope to turn the synods from consultative assemblies to another forum for implementing his will and his view of the Church. It was that assumption that led him to assert in the most vigorous, and at times intolerant, ways the magisterium — the teaching authority the Church — which in reality became the teaching authority of the pope exercised over national congregations of bishops and over Church theologians.

John Paul II has been an incredibly prolific pope in his written pronouncements — rivaling Pius XII, the last traditionalist in that office. Very early in his reign, he issued his first encyclical, *Redemptor Hominis,* obviously written by the pope himself and not by a collection of Curial theologians and experts. Because of his very different personalist philosophical bent and his Polish background and language, the messages are rather complex, if not convoluted. For example, that first letter was seen as a critique of atheism, a real preoccupation with this pope, who had lived almost all of his life behind two iron curtains of totalitarianism. But was it also, some people asked, a critique of interfaith ecumenism?

John Paul II is fascinated by the benchmark year 2000 and hopes to be the pope of the third millennium of Christianity. Yet he uses at times the creaky Marxist vocabulary of alienation to talk about the sophisticated ills of people today. Because he is so very bright, so full of ideas, it appears that John Paul has abandoned the slow, cumbersome processes characteristic of collegiality. Again like Pius XII, he knows that he can do it faster and say it better, which in many cases is true. For example, he accepts in principle Vatican II's formulation of a common priesthood of the faithful, but his real interest is in the traditional sacramental priesthood of men. Referring to priestly vows, he has abandoned the more flexible policies of Pope Paul and has concluded, "One must think of all these things, especially in moments of crisis, and not have recourse to a dispensation, understood as an 'administrative instruction,' as though in fact it were not on the contrary a matter of a profound question of conscience and a test of humanity." The response of many liberal Catholics in France, Spain, and Germany was critical toward the pope's "Letter to Priests." One theologian, Hans Küng, actually attacked the pope for "violating the human right to marriage."

On one level the pope insisted in November 1979 to a gathering of cardinals that the main task of his pontificate would be to implement Vatican II. Later he called a synod to give its participants a very candid and depressing review of Vatican finances, asked for their advice on how to reform the Curia, and discussed the relationships between the Church and culture, especially the gap between science and faith — two carryover topics from the Council. He is in so many ways, though, a son of that Council, and its broad reach makes it possible for him to travel and be noticed, that is, to become in the end, pope.

But he has criticized false notions of liberty and renewal and has opposed any reinterpretations of traditional dogma. And his strong assertion of Catholic identity has made ecumenism less possible. As John Paul has said, he opposes reducing dogmatic concerns to "a common minimum" —

a strategy used sometimes in interfaith dialogues, especially in their initial stages. The pontiff's very intense devotion to Mary, which some attribute to being a substitute for the human mother he lost so early, also discourages new approaches to Protestant Christianity, which often has no strong traditions of worship and respect in that area.[67]

He has resolutely moved against theological dissidents as well. For some time the Vatican had been looking closely at the work of one of Catholicism's best known theologians, Edward Schillebeeckx, a Flemish Dominican who taught at a Catholic university in the Netherlands. Even before John Paul's tenure, Schillebeeckx's work on Jesus had raised conservative eyebrows, especially when those unorthodox views in his complex books received wide currency. One of his volumes aimed to show how Jesus was experienced by his contemporaries — an approach that stressed his humanity rather than his divinity, the latter of which the theologian did not deny.[68] Especially troubling to the Vatican was his view that in cases of extreme necessity the Christian community could provide itself with extraordinary ministers for consecrating the Eucharist. In December 1979, he was summoned to Rome to appear before two judges and a defense lawyer appointed by the Congregation.

At about the same time the Congregation moved against Hans Küng, a Swiss theologian teaching at the University at Tübingen in West Germany. Among other controversial pronouncements, Küng has argued that the notion of Jesus as the Son of God is really not to be taken literally. Also he directly challenged the concept of infallibility, concluding that the Church, not the pope, was infallible and only in the sense that the Church persists in the truth of Jesus Christ. He further cited historical examples of alleged papal heresies that later were appropriately rejected by councils, and he agreed with another author's conclusions that Pius IX was mentally unbalanced at the time of the first Vatican Council, having allegedly threatened the bishops into making their infallibility proclamation.

In October 1979, Küng publicly attacked the new pope, picturing him as having repudiated the directions of the Second Vatican Council with its emphasis on freedom, ecumenism, and collegiality. Consequently Küng would be stripped of his authority to teach as a Catholic theologian but allowed to stay on at the university in another department.[69] Thus his claim to be a Catholic theologian was denied to a man who once was brought to Rome and celebrated as one of the *periti,* or experts. At the same time, the Congregation was also reviewing the writings of American Catholic author David Tracy and the Latin American Leonardo Boff, one of the fathers of liberation theology. Overall the Congregation's sanguine view was that the faithful "have a sacred right to receive the word of God, uncontaminated, and so they expect vigilant care should be exercised to keep the threat of error from them."[70]

In August 1979, the Congregation for the Doctrine of the Faith condemned a book on human sexuality written by a half dozen members of the Catholic Theological Society of America, and in September the pope went after the Jesuits. In October the Holy See informed a Jesuit priest, Robert Drinan of Massachusetts, that he could not seek reelection to the U.S. Congress for a sixth term.[71]

Two additional episodes that received widespread publicity were the expulsion of Rev. Charles Curran from his teaching position at Catholic University in Washington, D.C., and the controversial treatment of Archbishop Raymond Hunthausen of Seattle. Curran had speculated that sexual morality had to be viewed within broader contextual frameworks than the ones then current in Vatican theology, and his views over the years generated substantial concern in the Curia and with traditional Catholics. He indicated that masturbation, for example, was not really sinful or important. He also argued that while homosexual actions were wrong, such acts might be the only way for some to achieve a degree of humanity and sexuality. He advocated a "theology of compromise" toward those acts as well as toward premarital sex. In addition, he suggested that contraception was acceptable.

In his writings he was also tolerant of artificial insemination and sterilization. More pointedly, Curran refused to accept the view that abortion was synonymous with murder, and had gone on record supporting the *Roe v. Wade* decision in which the Supreme Court established a national policy in America permitting abortions within limits. His dissenting views included a more liberal attitude toward divorce as well, and he maintained that questions of morality were part of the "noninfallible" magisterium of the Church, that is, they were open to dissent.

Curran had been under close scrutiny before. As early as April 1967 he was fired from Catholic University because of his statements on abortion, but a strike by students and faculty forced the administration to reinstate him. The next year he helped lead a petition drive among Catholic theologians who opposed publicly the pope's birth control encyclical. Once again the faculty supported the dissidents and Curran remained.

But in March 1986 Curran and Joseph Cardinal Ratzinger met in Rome, and the matter remained unresolved. By later summer of 1986, he was again dismissed from his position in the university, and over three hundred fellow theologians protested the Vatican's condemnation. Finally the university trustees offered him an opportunity to teach elsewhere, but not in the graduate school in theology. Later he left for other institutions outside of the Church's purview.[72]

Also controversial was the Vatican's treatment of one of its own bishops, Archbishop Hunthausen, who had a reputation as a liberal who supported pacifism and refused at one time to pay part of his income taxes as a protest against defense spending. The Vatican was bombarded with conservative Catholic protests which accused him of general permissiveness in running his diocese. It was alleged, for example, that he had allowed a special Mass for homosexuals in the cathedral, had expressed his sympathy for them, and had tolerated weird liturgies featuring clowns, balloons, and dancing at a funeral. In addition he had granted an imprimatur to a book on sexual morality that was somewhat outside of the Church's orthodox views.

Finally in late summer of 1986, Hunthausen was instructed to turn over his decision-making authority in the areas of the treatment of former priests, the training of new priests, marriage regulations, the moral supervision of homosexuals, and the management of health care facilities in the diocese to a new auxiliary bishop, Donald Wuerl. The result was an enormous outcry in the diocese and outside for what was perceived as a insult to the bishop and also to the Church in that region. Even the Canon Law Society questioned whether his treatment did not violate Church law. The Vatican was forced this time to back down, and a three-bishop commission was appointed to examine the various charges. By 1987 Rome reinstated the archbishop's authority, but it named a coadjutor bishop with whom he should consult. Traditional Catholics and clergy waited anxiously for his coming retirement.[73]

The leading agent in these condemnations was Cardinal Ratzinger of Bavaria, a once well regarded liberal who had cooperated with the progressive *periti* at Vatican II. He had been an articulate critic of the Holy Office — the precursor to his own Congregation — saying its behavior was detrimental to the Catholic faith. However, reacting to the student unrest of the 1960s and post–Vatican II excesses, he felt that discussions had often led to "lies" and that the age-old truths of the Church were being threatened by the turn that the legacy of the Council had taken. Pope Paul had named him archbishop of Munich and Freising, and he met Karol Wojtyla at an episcopal synod a year before the latter's election.

As he admitted, he became more conservative after 1968 as he saw that the consequences of the Council were leading to an unraveling of the Church. What the popes and the Council Fathers expected, he said, was a new Christian unity; instead what they got was dissension that seemed to pass from self-criticism to self-destruction. He advocated "restoration" as a way to achieve a new balance and not as a turning back. It would be, he insisted, a recovery of lost values within a new totality, and he cited St. Charles Borromeo, who helped to rebuild the Catholic Church after the Council of Trent without retreating back to the Middle Ages.

The real crisis of the Church was above all else a crisis of priests and religious orders, he publicly argued. Traditional pillars of ecclesiastical reform — the great religious orders — had vacillated, lost vocations, and experienced identity crises. In addition, bishops in episcopal conferences often accepted group decisions instead of being strongly persistent in their convictions, Ratzinger explained.

He then went on to speak of the major challenge before the Church, one of teaching moral theology. Like Wojtyla he had serious reservations about the cultural influences of the West, noting that "economic *liberalism* creates its exact counterpart, *permissivism,* on the moral plane." Theologians must choose between opposing modern society or opposing the magisterium of the Church. In women's religious orders, there was a "feminist mentality," especially in North America. Only those who had lived in cloistered contemplative orders had withstood the *Zeitgeist* because of their sheltered life and their clear sense of mission.

In other instances, John Paul himself took the lead in dealing with discipline problems in his Church. In January 1980 the pope invited the Dutch bishops to Rome to end their divisions and to bring to heel one of the most unorthodox churches in his realm. Unlike Paul he was clearly not willing to accept their unruliness. Meeting behind closed doors, the bishops ended up accepting the pope's criticisms and his prescriptions. They went home and curtailed liturgical innovations, ecumenism, intercommunion, and the use of pastoral workers instead of priests. They also terminated appeals by bishops for a relaxation of priestly celibacy. The Dutch Church was brought in line, but deep resistance toward the pope by elements of the faithful was apparent in his later visit to that nation. The normal indices of Church participation also began to decline in the Netherlands. Thus it appeared that the progressive bishops were meeting the aspirations of what represented a large segment of their church.[74]

Having finished that business, the pope called the Ukrainian bishops to the Vatican to resolve several longstanding problems. In 1949 the Ukrainian Catholic Church with ties to Rome was declared illegal by the Soviet Union, and its archbishop, Jósef Slipyi, was shipped to Siberia for eighteen years. Finally Pope John XXIII's appeals to Premier Nikita Khrushchev to have him released were successful. The archbishop was later made a cardinal and lived in exile in Rome. Slipyi on his own decided to declare himself a patriarch, a step Pope Paul disapproved, and he went on to criticize the pope's overtures toward Eastern European Communist governments as "an obscene insult to the blood of martyrs of the Gulag Archipelago."[75]

John Paul persuasively informed a suspicious Slipyi that he supported the right of religious freedom, including in the Ukraine, and that the Ukrainian Catholics were invited to give him a name for assistant bishop who would end up being the successor to the cardinal. The local synod chose a successor, and the pope had patched over an old quarrel.

Not all areas of contention lent themselves to such easy solution. Two of John Paul's predecessors, Pius XII and Paul VI, both had reservations about the Jesuits at times, but they were still admirers of the order. During Vatican II, Jesuits such as Bea, Rahner, and John Courtney Murray, among others, helped to set the impressive agenda; later, though, some members

286 / Vicars of Christ

of the order were rather vocal in their reservations about Paul's encyclical on birth control.

Beginning in 1965, a Basque named Don Pedro Arrupe had led the order and advocated an opening to the left, which included democratization of the Jesuits and an emphasis on its social calling. Conservatives saw that as a betrayal of its historic religious apostolate in favor of social activism, rabble-rousing, and Marxism. Paul began to become concerned about the order's loss of identity and whether it was laicizing itself by becoming simply a humanitarian agency. In September 1973, Paul wrote a letter to General Superior Arrupe, condemning the intellectual and disciplinary tendencies he felt would injure the order. He also opposed the attempts to end the differences in the organization between priests and nonpriests and a proposal to allow Jesuits the right to object to certain commands, including those from the pope himself. He directly intervened when conservatives told him that there might even be a possibility that the Jesuits at their general conference would be moving toward ending their traditional fourth vow — that of strict obedience to the pope.

It is with this background that John Paul II acted quickly and sternly in dealing with the Jesuits. When Arrupe decided to resign, the pope refused to accept his resignation, arguing that under the order's bylaws such a decision required his prior approval. Arrupe stayed, but afflicted later by a stroke, he was finally permitted to resign, and he moved to name one of his lieutenants, American Vincent O'Keefe, to the position of vicar general until a General Congregation could elect a successor.

The pope then surprised the Jesuits and decided to stop any such appointment. In a deliberate slap at the Society, the pope named his own "personal delegate" vested with full powers to lead and personally control the order. Later, in September 1983, the Jesuits elected Father Peter Hans Kollenbach as successor to Arrupe. Kollenbach proved to be a moderate and judicious leader, as he toned down but kept the basic thrust of the Decree Four statement. John Paul, who has had no real close experience with religious orders or the Society of Jesus, may have overreacted as he took the next logical step to Paul's warnings and applied shock therapy to a proud and often haughty company of men. In any case, after the controversy settled down, he went on to praise the Jesuits for their "docile harmony with the directives of the magisterium." As for Arrupe, he had candidly indicated to the Society that the last three popes had serious reservations with the directions the Jesuits were going — directions he himself favored. It seemed to some that the conservative Polish pope was more at home with conservative organizations such as Opus Dei, an association that Pope Paul had kept at arm's length, than with the long established religious orders, which included not just the Jesuits but the Dominicans and Franciscans as well.[76]

THE ASSASSINATION ATTEMPT

Pope John Paul II is and has been a leader of surety and tenacious purpose, but on May 13, 1981, he experienced an event that had profound personal impact on him, threatening his life, deepening his already intense spirituality, and turning him even more to the protection of the Blessed Virgin Mary. As the late afternoon sun was setting, the pope was riding through the crowds in St. Peter's Square. At a range of less than ten feet, Mehmet Ali Agca fired a Browning 9 directly at the vulnerable pontiff.

Two bullets entered the pope, one penetrating his abdomen and the second hitting his right forearm and injuring the second finger of his left hand. A nun from Bergamo, Sister Letizia, had deflected the aim of the professional assassin by pulling on his jacket, and thus probably saved John Paul's life. The pope sank down in the vehicle into the arms of one of his aides, losing blood profusely and exhibiting on his face a strange mixture of pain and tranquility as he prayed. In the hospital, he kept repeating, "Mary, my mother, Mary, my mother," as he came perilously close to death.[77]

Overnight the vigorous pope appeared less triumphalistic and desperately human and mortal. Once he had observed that when he was young sick people used to intimidate him.[78] He was now to come to understand that his pontificate was to be closely linked to martyrdom and to suffering, and that he was spared to lead the Church hopefully into its third millennium, while he was destined to endure more pain. In his hospital room he contemplated the intercession of Mary, and then later read the collected information on the apparitions at Fatima, Portugal.

He had been informed, as had others, by the last living Fatima child, the nun Sister Lucy, that the Virgin's request had still not been met. She had mandated that Russia had to be dedicated to her, and that dedication had to be done by the pope *in concert* with the Catholic Church's other bishops. This he would do, as he prayed publicly for the conversion of Russia. At the time it seemed far-fetched, for the Western intelligence agencies reported the continuing strength of the Soviet regime.

It has been speculated that the professional assassin who wounded the pope was hired by the Bulgarian secret police on behalf of the Russian KGB. The Soviet leaders had begun a campaign to discredit the pope and had been especially wary of his activities with the Ukrainians and of course with the Poles. The argument made in some quarters was that the Russians had ordered the pope's murder and used their allies to pull the trigger. However, the opening of some historical archives in previously Communist countries has not lent any verification to that charge. After his recuperation, John Paul visited his assailant, then in a Roman prison, and in one of the most impressive photos of our time, the world saw the pope, as if almost hearing a confession, listening intently to Agca. Lip readers claimed that the assassin asked him how he was still alive, and the pope responded that another hand had directed matters. Then John Paul bluntly asked the assailant who had sent him. The latter's responses to the pontiff's questions are not recorded, although he had said that John Paul knows everything about the episode.[79]

The pope, who had experienced such a lamentable young adulthood, once again knew pain and loneliness but also a sense of being saved specifically by God's direct intercession. That experience probably added to his heroic sense of mission, his willingness to ask more of his fellow co-religionists than they were sometimes willing to give, and enhanced his view of the Blessed Virgin's watchful care. Later he sent one of the bullets that had wounded him to Fatima to be placed in a crown on a statue of Mary. Privately he observed of the new bulletproof, glass-enclosed popemobile, "All these precautions are useless. As soon as I go out, dressed in white from head to foot, I'm a target they can't possibly miss."[80]

The pope had rushed his recovery and had to return to the hospital and deal with a serious infection. But gradually he seemed physically mended, and he continued to devote himself to a more intensive role in the life of Polish national politics, as he came to embrace even more the Solidarity movement and Walesa. The pope, who had disapproved of liberation politics in Latin America, ended the career of a Jesuit liberal congressman from Massachusetts, and pushed against the Church's involvement in partisan battles, became in many ways a participant in the end of the Polish Communist state. That demise was the preface to the real curtain riser — the total collapse of the Soviet system. The Slavic pope would play a critical role, as did the United States administration, in that turn of events. Even more importantly, the ethnic tensions and economic problems would unravel the then reforming Communist state headed up by Mikhail Gorbachev.

For over a century there had been prophecies of a Slavic pope, but this one's impact on geopolitics in that area was truly beyond expectations. Thus Karol Wojtyla became even more than he imagined, a man of great destiny striding the world stage. In some strange way the pope who so rejected the extremes of the West seemed to take solace at first in the view that Moscow, the so-called Third Rome, would play a special role in the changing nature of faith and religious allegiances in the third millennium.[81] It was an Eastern Europe romance, one that misjudged the nature of contemporary Russians and one that denigrated the true importance of the industrialized West in the world of ideas and ideologies.

THE HEROIC POPE

The pope demanded more of his faithful, but the people of North America and Western Europe were weary of such sacrifices. They had been through two terrible World Wars and a Great Depression. They intended to enjoy prosperity and peace — and yes, wallow a bit in their consumer products. That self-indulgence bothered the pontiff, and he reached out to the children of the next generation, as he pleaded for faith and justice. Rather remarkably they seemed attuned to his admonitions and to his extraordinary charisma. They responded in lively ways to his personal appearances, but as a group they still prized their possessions and their sexual and creative freedom. Thus the great contradiction of public attitudes in the United States and elsewhere toward this pope.

That same dimension can be seen in the pope's treatment of Catholic universities. Since the late 1970s, Catholic educators in the United States, led by the respected president of Notre Dame University, Father Theodore Hesburgh and Jesuit priest Robert Henle of Georgetown, departed from the Vatican's attempts to control Catholic colleges and universities. They argued that such a step threatened the tradition of trustee control (important to American concepts of incorporation), raised problems for academic accreditation, and might present hurdles in receiving federal aid. So they insisted on delaying revisions. Finally in 1990 the pope issued a new apostolic constitution, *Ex Corde Ecclesiae,* which sought to impose a unified charter that would place Catholic institutions of higher education under local bishops. In November 1996, the American bishops brokered a compromise with major Catholic university leaders.[82]

John Paul had moved easily with academic and intellectuals throughout most of his adult life, and he had been an articulate spokesman for freedom of expression. He argued that the Church in the modern world was really the champion of reason, freedom, and progress. Rather remarkably, he also insisted in 1979 that the Curia reopen the Church's condemnation of Galileo Galilei, and he finally rehabilitated that controversial astronomer in 1992. Galileo had been originally brought to trial before the Inquisition in 1633 and threatened with torture if he did not recast his view that the earth revolved around the sun, a view advanced earlier by the Polish scientist Copernicus. Wojtyla had been an admirer of Copernicus and lamented the consequences of Galileo's trial, which established the popular view that faith and science were inherently in conflict.[83] Later, in October 1996, the pontiff lent his support to the theory of human evolution as well.

The pope also reinvigorated the Pontifical Academy of Sciences and had its members focus on informing national leaders of the horrors of nuclear weapons.[84] In the industrial city of Turin, the pope in April 1980 once again criticized both liberalism and Marxism, and his views seemed to be remarkably similar to the longstanding complaints of the European Catholic right that somehow the West had taken a wrong turn back at the Enlightenment. Behind it all in the pope's eyes was the menace of aggressive atheism and its war on God. Later, in 1981, he spoke of the need for "those great souls" in history, individuals committed to respecting the faith. Addressing the crowd, the pontiff exhorted simply, "Europe needs Christ!"

But it would be a mistake to view John Paul as a simple conservative. In fact, his statements are very critical of capitalism and its emphasis on unbridled wealth and consumerism. His first encyclical, *Redemptor Hominis,* was an affirmation of the dignity of workers written by the only pope who has ever worked in an industrial setting. Still, while he supported the struggle for justice, he opposed class warfare and hatred of others, a clear critique of Marxism.

On March 19, 1981, he addressed a group of factory workers north of Rome and insisted, "Be assured that the pope is with you, that the pope is on your side, whenever justice has been violated, peace is threatened, or the due rights of anyone and the common good need to be encouraged." He then walked with the workers, ate, and drank wine with them. The pope answered their questions, listened to their grievances, and remembered his own times as a worker during World War II. When a television reporter observed to someone that this was the first time that a pope had eaten with the workers, the pontiff overheard the remark. Quietly he responded, "And that's not the only novelty of this pontificate."

To mark the ninetieth anniversary of Leo's *Rerum Novarum,* John Paul II issued in September 1981 his encyclical *Laborem Exercens.* In it he supported joint ownership of the means of work, stressed the need for unions to be nonpolitical, and reiterated once again the idea of a Catholic social doctrine.[85]

THE RESTIVE NEW WORLD

But his idea of social doctrine was very different from that taking place in Third World countries. As noted, the Vatican, with the pope's concurrence, had moved against the leaders of the liberation theology movement in Latin America. The Congregation sent the Peruvian bishops a letter listing objections to the writings of the theologian Gustavo Gutiérrez. The bishops were, however, divided, and Gutiérrez was invited to Rome for some private consultations. Then the Congregation went after the Brazilian Franciscan, Leonardo Boff. Instead of presenting his case to the bishops, the Congregation also called him to Rome. Two Brazilian bishops, however, went with him in a show of support. In March 1985, the Vatican issued a document answering Boff's criticisms, and in May he was prohibited from publishing or teaching for a period of time. Later the scrutiny continued, and a frustrated Boff left the priesthood altogether.[86]

In addition, back in 1983, John Paul had made a controversial trip to Nicaragua, a visit that became the nadir of his travels. The Nicaraguan revolution had expelled the Somoza family, which for several generations had impoverished that tiny nation. Coming to power was a group of

Castro-like Marxist guerrilla fighters called the Sandinistas. What made that situation difficult for the Vatican was that five of its major political leaders were Catholic priests, the most visible being the minister of culture, Ernesto Cardenal. Cardenal was a committed revolutionary and poet, and an associate of the gentle Trappist monk, Thomas Merton. He was to comment, somewhat sarcastically, that the pope was correct, clergy should not be involved in politics. "I used to be a poet. I became a priest, and the love of God led me to revolution. I have never gone in for politics."[87]

The position of the Vatican was that priests could not hold public office, and that if they did, they could not then exercise priestly functions until they resigned. The pope at first insisted that he would not visit that nation until that "irregularity" was resolved, but he decided on the trip anyhow. When he arrived at the airport, he publicly chastised Ernesto Cardenal while the priest knelt to receive the pontiff's blessing. John Paul uncharacteristically shook his finger at him angrily and insisted that he had to normalize his status.

Later in front of a large crowd, the pope ended up in a shouting match with hecklers, probably planted there by the Sandinistas. When some people chanted, "We want peace!" the pontiff shouted back, "Silence," three times. In his visit he avoided mentioning the attacks of the anti-Sandinista Contras, who were heavily funded then by the Reagan administration, and he demanded that Catholics support their bishops.[88]

It was an extremely distasteful episode and was probably instigated by the Sandinista regime. Later the Vatican insisted that the priests still in the government had to resign. One finally left the priesthood and became laicized, one left the Jesuits, and two were suspended from their priestly functions. Much later, however, in early 1996, the pope visited Nicaragua again. By then the Sandinistas had been voted out by the people, and the pope was greeted by enthusiastic crowds. In place of the strident guerrilla leader President Daniel Ortega, who had once greeted the pontiff in military greens, the new president was Violeta Chamorro, elected in 1990. She embraced John Paul and kissed his head as if she were welcoming a long lost uncle. As the pope proceeded down the major highway, lo and behold there was a billboard from previous president Ortega celebrating John Paul's visit. The pope had insisted that the Church be separated from the regime, and it appeared that in the longer perspective he was once again correct.[89] In October 1996, Ortega again ran for president — this time on a platform emphasizing God, forgiveness, and private enterprise. He lost a second time.

John Paul has made his position over the years very clear: the Church "does not need to have recourse to ideological systems in order to love, defend, and collaborate with liberation of the human being." As for liberation theology, one comes away with two very different impressions of that development. There is a genuine sense of righteousness against exploitation and a charming resurrection of the powerful image of Jesus' thirst for justice sake. But the theology overall seems to be rather shallow, intellectually ragged, and often a collection of socialist slogans loosely wrapped in religious garb. By 1996, John Paul was simply dismissing liberation theology as irrelevant, and Cardinal Ratzinger was focusing his concerns on moral relativism.

Karol Wojtyla, the scholar of Marxism, probably has a better command of that ideology than did either its priest-advocates in Latin America or the Communist party bosses in Eastern Europe. Still the basic and primary problems of poverty, exploitation, and government violence remained, and even the liberation theologians acknowledged that John Paul addressed those issues as well as they did. In fact two such theologians, Leonardo and Clodovis Boff, noted that while the pontiff put distance between himself and their rhetoric, he shared many of their legitimate concerns.[90]

It may be thought that, once again, John Paul reacted too swiftly and too abruptly to a very complex problem in the Third World, where he himself had said the future of the Catholic Church would be decided. By April 1986, the Vatican issued an "Instruction on Christian Freedom and Liberation" which took a more benign view, although in a somewhat abstract sense, of the liberation theology movement. In the same month the pope had a friendly three-day meeting with the Brazilian bishops. The restrictions on Leonardo Boff, who had humbly observed the Vatican's limitations on his freedom, were at first lifted, although the criticisms were to be resurrected later.[91] Looking back at the pope's confusing journey into Latin American ecclesiastical controversies, one can appreciate more fully Pope Paul VI's careful nuanced style; sometimes vigor and assertiveness are not always unalloyed virtues. At times John Paul seems to be too preoccupied with reining in deviating intellectual constructs, such that he gives the impression of a lack of sympathy to the very movements with which he himself is genuinely aligned. Unlike John XXIII, he cannot seem to turn away from setting everything right; unlike Paul VI, he cannot live in a world with ambiguities.

Soon after his first Polish trip, the pope also visited another historically Catholic country, Ireland. Again John Paul warned against the prevailing materialism, self-indulgence, and consumerism so much a part of Western society in his view. At one point in Galway, he overlooked a crowd of two hundred thousand people on a racetrack and cried out, "Young people of Ireland, I love you." Across the isle, the pope spoke out against moral shortcuts, the preoccupation with comfort, wealth, and pleasure, and the need to remember the Kingdom of God. He supported the traditional bans on divorce and abortion and strongly opposed sectarian hatred in that island. In English, the pontiff proclaimed, "Violence is evil,... violence is unacceptable as a solution to problems,... violence is unworthy of man, . . . violence is a lie" — references to the bloody wars so common in Ireland's life.

But as in Italy, Ireland would show signs of moving away from the traditions of the faith. In 1995, that nation voted for a statute permitting divorce. That outcome was allegedly due in part to the revelations about a bishop living with his long-time mistress. Across the English Channel, in early 1996, even the saintly Mother Teresa approved of a divorce for the much publicized and estranged prince and princess of Wales. A continuous stream of soap opera headlines, taped lovers' conversations, and public confessions of infidelity on both their parts had taxed even her legendary patience. Thus at times the pope during his term in office has had to face continuing deviations from the deposit of the faith — even among the usually faithful. He was especially embarrassed when the conservative cardinal he appointed to the see in Vienna, Hermann Grör, had to be replaced after accusations of pedophilia were made.[92]

Nowhere were the corrosive evidences of consumerism, hedonism, and excessive freedom more apparent in the pope's eyes than in the United States. There too the effects of Vatican II and the birth control encyclical had contributed to a general loss of faith, to confusion in the seminaries, and to a massive decline in vocations. The pope was to observe that the Americans were nice people, but when it came to matters of religion, they sometimes followed outdated European trends. The pontiff sarcastically observed on one occasion that they had yet to "get past Bultmann" — a reference to the unorthodox biblical scholar of the early twentieth century.

Generally American Catholic attitudes reflected those of their fellow countrymen rather than traditional papal admonitions. For example, at the time of the pope's visit in October 1979, 66 percent of Catholics approved of birth control, 63 percent of divorce, 53 percent wished for priests to be allowed to marry, and 51 percent tolerated abortion on demand. The Church the pope saw was not one militant Church, but a host of groups often speaking past each other. John Paul was concerned about the lack of Church discipline and the supposed weakness of some of his bishops, and he moved to change those directions.[93]

On his first visit his reception was enormously positive. In Boston, for example, the city and neighborhoods turned out in force, even in the rain, and the pope graciously remarked, "America the beautiful, even when it rains." A six-foot poster in Boston quoted his words at his inauguration, "Be not afraid to open the door wide for Christ." In New York City he addressed the United Nations General Assembly, where he pleaded for peace and insisted on the inalienable rights of every human being. That evening he said Mass before seventy-five thousand people in Yankee Stadium and spoke against "the frenzy of consumerism."

The next morning at Madison Square Garden, a youth concert exploded with football chants, "Rack 'em up, stack 'em up, bust 'em in two — Holy

Father, we're for you." And the pope began to sing along, "Whoa — hoo — whoa — ." In Harlem he consoled his predominantly black audience saying, "If we are silent about the joy that comes from knowing Jesus, the very stones of our cities will cry out. For we are an Easter people and alleluia is our song!"[94]

In Philadelphia, he reaffirmed his belief that "the priesthood is forever," and in Washington, D.C., on September 7, 1979, he had to face the forces of feminism within his own Church. Sister Mary Theresa Kane, the head of the Leadership Conference of Women Religious, in an address to Pope John Paul spoke of "the intense suffering and pain that is part of the life of many women in the U.S. Church." She insisted that in supporting dignity for people, the Church must open up its own ministries to all as well. Later the pope argued that women were excluded from the priesthood, not because the Church was making a statement about human rights or because of any exclusion of women from the mission of the Church. Rather the exclusion was due to historical tradition: Christ had not included any women in the first twelve Apostles. John Paul went on to praise the Blessed Virgin Mary, noting that while she was not incorporated into the hierarchical constitution of the Church, "yet she makes all hierarchy possible."[95]

Later in other countries the pope would face the same criticism from other women religious. For example, on June 3, 1980, John Paul met a crowd of five thousand French nuns at the motherhouse of the Sisters of Charity where the miraculous medal was struck by Catherine Labouré in 1830. There Sister Daniéle Souillard spoke of the need to abandon the traditional garb of nuns in order to pursue their professional work. The pope had insisted that the nuns should "never be ashamed to recognize your identity as women consecrated to the Lord." But some of the religious thought the admonition ill-advised if not trivial.

A third example occurred on November 20, 1980, in Germany, where Barbara Engl, president of the Munich Association of Catholic Youth, was critical of the pope's homily on Satan. She contended that young people felt the Church was more concerned with perpetuating divisions with the Evangelical Church than in promoting unity. She also indicated that there was a real need for priests and chaplains, and that the celibacy ban made little sense as did the limits on women's ministry.

The pope did not respond immediately, but in April 1980 he had praised St. Catherine of Siena, the sometime advisor and sometime harsh critic of popes. He called attention to the fact that "her feminine nature was richly endowed with fantasy, intuition, sensibility, an ability to get things done, a capacity to communicate with others, a readiness for self-giving and service."[96] Thus the pope's attitudes toward women remained both respectful and traditional, seeing them primarily as helpmates. In 1995 the Congregation for the Doctrine of the Faith insisted that the pope's ban on women as ministers had the force of an infallible declaration, increasing in some a sense of second-class membership in a Church dedicated ironically to the special intercession of the Virgin Mary.

The most doctrinaire of the pope's addresses in the United States came at a Chicago seminary to 350 American bishops. There he proceeded to outline the sacred deposit of Christian doctrine that had to be safeguarded and taught. He extolled Pope Paul VI's encyclical *Humanae Vitae* and asked the bishops to give witness to the truth, thereby serving all of humanity. He went on to indicate that it was the laity's right to receive "the word of God in its purity and integrity as guaranteed by the magisterium of the universal Church."[97]

Later he observed that he was not offended to be called a conservative, for "the pope is not here to make changes, but to conserve what he has received with his charge." Thus, to the pope, Catholicism remained a fairly rigid belief system with a strong disciplinary code. Even though many Catholics disagreed with the message, as has been noted, they still loved the messenger. Throughout his visits to the United States over the years, the public responses, especially among the young, has been extremely positive and respectful.

After a year in office, John Paul was praised by *Time* magazine which called him "John Paul, Superstar."[98] In the article, that journal of opinion indicated that the pope lifted people above the drabness of their own lives and showed them that they are capable of expressing better emotions and performing better deeds than they may have thought. Later, in 1995, the pope was proclaimed the "Man of the Year" for many of the same reasons.

John Paul's commitment to traditional Catholic dogma and its distinctive mission had another side effect. The day after his election, John Paul indicated that he was committed to overcoming the obstacles to Christian unification — a preoccupation of both John XXIII and Paul VI. But almost immediately he seemed less interested in such efforts, especially as it dealt with the churches in the West. He was not influenced much by the Anglican/Roman Catholic International Commission and its discussions on the nature of the ministry. In Washington, D.C., for example, he said to an interfaith group, "Recognition must be given to the deep divisions which still exist over moral and ethical matters. The moral life and the life of faith are so deeply united that it is impossible to divide them."[99]

He clearly rejected ecumenism as a limited collaboration and insisted the churches should avoid reducing matters to a doctrinal minimum or the lowest common denominator. The Congregation for the Doctrine of the Faith had warned against glossing over problems inherent in any discussions of reunification and ecumenism, and John Paul concurred with that view. Still the pope spoke of "the great common treasury" of the various Christian faiths, and in November 1980 the pope visited West Germany and faced directly some difficult Protestant authorities and clergymen. Instead of confronting them and stressing their doctrinal and historical differences, John Paul referred to the Epistle to the Romans, which Martin Luther had called "the heart of the New Testament." He even quoted Luther approvingly in that regard, a neat rhetorical trick indeed.[100]

Still, his interests in interfaith efforts were more oriented toward the Eastern Orthodox, as he continued his appeal as a Slavic pope to the peoples of the East. As early as February 1980, he talked of "the rearticulation of the ancient traditions of the East and West." As Pope Paul VI recognized, however, the papacy itself was a major obstacle — if not the major obstacle — for all non-Catholic Christians. John Paul spoke of the Petrine ministry before, in October 1978, and stressed its relationship to the Church's internal unity and the need to guarantee its special mission. In his eyes, as in Paul's, only the pontificate could accomplish those objectives. The addition of the doctrine of infallibility in the late nineteenth century and newly promulgated Marian doctrines of the Immaculate Conception and the Assumption also added to the problems of interfaith unity as all recognized.

As the years passed, John Paul continued to insist on dogmatic rigor. When the pope came back to the United States in 1987, some of the American bishops tried to explain the differences between European and American cultures. Joseph Cardinal Bernardin told the pope, "It is important to know that many Americans, given the freedom they have enjoyed for than two centuries, almost instinctively react negatively when they are told they must do something. As a result the impression is sometimes given that there is a certain rebelliousness in American Catholics, that they want to 'go it alone.' " He then went on, "When someone questions how a truth might be better articulated or lived today, he or she is sometimes accused [by the Vatican] of rejecting the truth itself or portrayed as being in conflict with the Church's teaching authority. As a result, both sides are locked in what seems to be adversarial positions. Genuine dialogue becomes almost impossible. They must be able to speak to one another in complete candor, without fear."

Archbishop Rembert Weakland of Milwaukee tried to explain even further: "The faithful are now more inclined to look at the intrinsic worth of an argument proposed by the teachers in the Church than to accept it on the basis of the authority alone." But the pope insisted, "It is sometimes claimed that dissent is totally compatible to being 'a good Catholic' and poses no obstacle to the reception of the sacraments. This is a grave error. Dissent from Church doctrine remains what it is, dissent; as such it may not be proposed or received on an equal footing with the Church's authentic teaching."[101]

The pope did what one would expect he would do in dealing with the American Church. In 1980 he installed a Vatican papal nuncio in Washington, Archbishop Pio Laghi, to look closely at new appointments to that hierarchy, and he placed in high-profile American dioceses — Boston, New

York, Washington, and Los Angeles — men who he knew shared his views and his insistence upon orthodoxy. Rumor has it that the new apostolic delegate was being given five years "to clean up the American Church." In 1985, he good-naturedly remarked, "They just gave me five more years."[102]

In order to guarantee orthodoxy throughout the Church, the Vatican led by Cardinal Ratzinger pushed for a new oath of fidelity, reminiscent of the Modernist hysteria of Pius X. The new oath was to be effective March 1, 1989. All parish priests, rectors, professors of theology in seminaries, and rectors of Catholic universities, as well as teachers of subjects dealing with faith and morals were to take a pledge. It read as follows: "I firmly embrace and retain all and everything which is definitely proposed in doctrine about faith and morals by the Church. In addition, I adhere by religious assent of the will and intellect to the teachings which either the Roman Pontiff or the College of Bishops declare when they exercise the authentic magisterium, even if they do not intend to proclaim them by definitive act." The Vatican gave its final judgment on any dissent from that instruction, saying that if Catholic theologians could not agree then they should in conscience be quiet or "suffer for the truth in silence and prayer."

THE DISSENTING FAITHFUL

The pope also decided to reach some conclusion in dealing with rebellion on the right. He had tried desperately, as had Paul, to deal with Archbishop Marcel Lefebvre, who at the age of eighty-two had moved to ordain four hundred bishops from his followers, individuals committed to the Tridentine Latin rite and to the Church before Vatican II. He had named his seminary in a Swiss mountain valley at Econe "The Priestly Fraternity of St. Pius X." By voiding an earlier agreement with the Vatican, Lefebvre in turn incurred automatic excommunication. Before a congregation of five thousand supporters, he reasserted his continuous opposition to the changes that had taken place since the last Council. Three years later he died of cancer, still unrepentant, and the pope issued a statement saying that he had hoped for a moment of repentance and would have been willing to lift the excommunication decree if there had been any sign of reconciliation. The pope, in a gesture to traditional Catholics, did permit the Latin rite to be celebrated if the local bishop concurred, as long as it was not seen as a repudiation of the changes of Vatican II. When the vernacular Mass was criticized for not being very contemplative because of its excessive dialogue and lack of mystery, the pontiff simply remarked, "The Word is also a mystery."[103]

Sometimes John Paul himself seemed to be uncomfortable with the extent to which he felt he had to go to protect orthodoxy. After his confrontation with the Dutch bishops and their decision to support him over the wishes of most of their faithful, the pope was to realize the consequences of his tough stand. In 1985, he made a trip through the Benelux countries, and in the Netherlands; the streets were almost deserted, in marked contrast to almost every other area to which he had gone. When there was strong protest against the pope's decision about nominating a new local bishop against the wishes of the faithful, he tried to explain his thoughts on the matter, saying, "In all sincerity, the pope attempts to understand the life of the Church and the appointment of every bishop. He gathers information and advice in accordance with ecclesiastical law and custom. You will understand that opinions are sometimes divided. In the last analysis, the pope has to make the decision. Must the pope explain his choice? Discretion does not permit him to do so." On another occasion, he argued, "You cannot take a vote on truth. You cannot pick or choose."

The pope's recalcitrance in consulting with clergy in individual countries led him into another firestorm when he invited Kurt Waldheim to the Vatican in June 1987. That invitation raised an avalanche of protest from Jews because of questions that had been raised about Waldheim's Nazi past, which had recently been discovered. The Vatican's answer in response was that the pope had an absolute right to invite whomever he wished to the Vatican, and that Waldheim then was the president of Austria. Later as proof began to mount about Waldheim's complicity in some of the worst crimes of the twentieth century, the Vatican for unexplained reasons gave him a knighthood, the Order of Pius X, almost as if to insist that it had no intention to listening to other people's judgments or the outcries from Jews and Christian alike.[104]

In his dealings with the African Church, the pope sounded a sense of alarm as well. His predecessor, Paul VI, had asked for an African Christianity, and indeed that was being worked out to the chagrin of many traditionalists in the Vatican. The successes of early Christianity were due in part to its remarkable ability to synthesize, to borrow, to adapt, and to twist pagan, Jewish, Greek, and Middle Eastern customs and cultic devotions into Christian channels. Where the Church failed, as when it placed constraints on the Jesuits in China, it had refused to adapt its religion to local customs and vocabularies.

At Vatican II, Cardinal Wojtyla had voted for enculturation, and as late as 1995 argued in favor of it, citing once again the failures in China, where the Church had refused to compromise with that nation's revered customs. In May 1980, however, he had visited that continent with a very different message. In Zaire, to the disappointment of many Catholics, he refused to attend a Mass featuring dancing and drums. He argued that the dangers of Africanization were especially apparent in worship, because there had to be "a substantial unity with the Roman rite." The pope appeared to be saying that there was really only one ritual, and that that was rooted in European tradition.

His real concern may have been expressed in his remarks to young married couples in Kinshasa, when he seemed to indicate that if Africa Africanized the Mass, they would wish to Africanize their marriage customs as well, which would include trial marriage and polygamy. He insisted that monogamy was not a European but a Semitic idea, and that Africans were perfectly capable of that commitment. Being a Christian meant being converted, that is, changing customs, he insisted.

Six months later at a General Synod, forty African bishops continued to advocate that the Church should approve of African marriage customs according to which marriage unfolds progressively and is not fully sealed until the birth of the first child. In an environment in which sensuality seemed to be less repressed than in the West (or at least so it is usually assumed), the pope faced another dilemma. It was reported that a considerable number of Catholic priests lived in various states of intimacy with women companions — another topic about which John Paul felt strongly. Thus even in the newly converted missionary fields, the pope saw the same challenges and the chaos due to a lack of discipline, loose ties of Church unity, and above all a failure of nerve.[105]

The pope was in a peculiar position. He was a son of the Council and in fact was genuinely committed to its implementation. But he and his closest advisors, such as Ratzinger, had to believe that its alleged effects were often disastrous for the Catholic Church, at least within the traditional framework. Still, in a sense of collegiality, he called general synods, including one on the role of the family in the modern world. One hundred and sixty-one bishops were elected by their peers to attend. This time, though, the agenda would be structured, as were the results.

The problem, of course, was that *Humanae Vitae* had hemmed in the basic contexts of the debate. The tone of the conference was set when the pope hailed a Chilean mother of seventeen children as a heroine. To listen to the married couples invited to the synod, one would assume that everyone accepted Paul's ill-fated encyclical on birth control.

The pope was generally quiet during the synod, but his views were well known to all. And on October 8, he had told a general audience in St. Peter's Square that husbands who looked at their wives with "concupiscence" had committed adultery in their hearts. That view, explainable within the context of his philosophical statements, drew sharp and often humorous commentaries — adding to the criticism that a celibate clergy including its pope really knew very little about the allures of sex. But John Paul was unbending. He had expressed his frustrations with American bishops earlier when he pointed to their 1968 pastoral letter on birth control and demanded, "Here's your own doctrine. When are you going to start insisting on it?" That tone continued to be evident in his treatment of the topic of sexual morality over the years.[106]

Thus those delegates to the synod who asked for a reexamination of the Church's teaching on sexuality got nowhere, as would be expected. As noted, during the synod John Paul decided to rehabilitate Galileo, who had himself been censured centuries before by the Holy Office for his views on the movement of the planets. Would a future pope, it was asked, change the Church's views on contraception also, coming to see the advances of science and reproductive technology in a different light?

Lastly, in dealing with the topic of divorced Catholics raised at the synod, the pope insisted that those who remarried could receive communion only if they abstained from sex. Critics charged again that physical contact and not spiritual renewal was becoming the continuing preoccupation of the Vatican. One well-known conservative American monsignor, George Kelly, bluntly observed in 1981 that the Church "lost its people to contraception, and in a very few years." As for the pope, he dismissed a close friend's criticism of the contraception ban, concluding, "I can't change what I've been teaching all my life."[107]

By the mid- and late 1980s the overall contours of the Wojtyla papacy were set. Despite his insistence that he was dedicated to implementing the Council's decrees, it was clear that he saw his papacy as a time of restoration, of a return to traditional values and discipline. He not only insisted on preserving the deposit of the faith, as all popes are sworn to do, but he also moved beyond that obligation. John Paul came close to aligning the teaching proclamations of his papacy with the near status of being infallible.

Infallibility is a loose and historically unclear formulation which itself has never been fully defined, even at Vatican I. At times it seems that with mounting opposition to his restoration ideology, John Paul has insisted on raising the ante and by doing so has made the Church and the papacy more vulnerable in the long run to attack, both inside and outside the fold. Even the extreme Pius IX never went that far. One good example is the Congregation for the Doctrine of the Faith's edict in 1995 that the exclusion of women from the priesthood was an infallible declaration. If that were so, some asked, why has it never been enunciated before by any pope, even by the most conservative ones. Infallibility was being used to quell debate rather than simply to preserve the faith.[108] And a few months later, the pope defensively stressed the need to open leadership positions up to religious women — excluding, however, the ministry of the priesthood.

The call to dialogue that this pope so celebrates, the invitation to intellectual freedom over which Cardinal Wojtyla so lacerated the Polish regime, were casualties of the march toward restoration. The second trend of this papacy is the increasingly frantic pace of the pope, almost as if he believes the alleged prophecy of Padre Pio that he would both be pope and also live an endangered life. He has faced enormous cheers in America, hostile reactions in the Netherlands, and nasty episodes in Nicaragua, but he continues on. Across the globe the pope has brought his message, and nowhere has he been more insistent than in his denunciations of abortion.

THE CULTURE OF LIFE

Abortion, of course, is not new in Western history. The classical Greeks and Romans practiced it, as did other cultures, but by the twentieth century the techniques of medical technology became more sophisticated and also safer in allowing women abortion as an option. In the United States the issue came to a head rather late in a Supreme Court case, which is the usual way that Americans deal with intractable issues — that is, by turning them into legal controversies. That decision in *Roe v. Wade* (1973) led to a Solomonic verdict that abortion was permitted in the first three months, was generally prohibited in the last three, and was a judgment call in the second trimester. No one was totally happy with the compromise. The Court based its verdict on biological views of the human fetus's viability rather than on any metaphysical or spiritual basis, as one would expect in a pluralistic society such as the United States.[109]

The difficulty is that the definitions of viability at conception or potentiality are very complex, and it is impossible to conduct public policy based on the latest monograph from a research laboratory. At times John Paul seemed to accept the biological basis for his condemnation, as when he had to acknowledge that medieval theologians such as the great Aquinas had said that human life does not begin until the "quickening period," or up to fifteen weeks or so after conception. The pope pointed out quite correctly that such observations were based on an obsolete view of biology.

He reflected that "in the Middle Ages, it was thought that the developing being passed through a vegetable phase, then into an animate phase, and so forth, thus the responsibility for interrupting a pregnancy might not have seemed so serious to tender consciences as one might have believed that they were only putting an end to a plant or to an animal. Today that sort of rationalizing is no longer possible. The human being exists from the moment of conception. Modern medicine uses other ways to express that, but as for us we say that even an embryo, a baby is already marked with the image of God."[110]

The pope then explained that some people oppose abortion but support artificial contraception. "But to permit the use of artificial contraceptives is the same as to open the way for abortion, because the moral attitude is what counts in this instance. Human life is an absolute value, tied up with the creative power of God. It is not manipulatable."

But the positions of some Vatican theologians are more complex. The view or usual stereotype is that the Church believes that life begins at the very moment of conception — long before any definition of viability such as pain or neurological reactions are apparent to observers. Some theologians in the Congregation for the Doctrine of the Faith, however, have argued that the ontological status of the embryo has no bearing on the propriety of abortion. Respect for human life is called for from the moment that the process of gestation begins, and human biological life has value and must be protected whether it is considered to have a spiritual soul or not.[111]

That view is a little different from the general pronouncements of the pope. Those theologians are saying that the prohibition against abortion from the moment of conception is "an intuition of faith." Those views free the questions of morals from the latest findings of laboratory scientists, but they also introduce elements of ambiguity that are less than persuasive in a pluralistic society.

Taking the advice of Cardinal Bernardin in the United States and others, the pope expanded his abhorrence of abortion into a full-length encyclical titled *Evangelium Vitae*. Arguing against abortion, birth control, capital punishment, and modern war, the pope proposed instead a seamless garment, a tapestry of respect for the culture of life against the culture of death. It is a powerful document even for those who may have reservations about its absolutist tone.[112]

The pope's commitment is not limited just to teaching the faith on the issue. The Vatican, in an old-time display of international power politics, made common cause with Islamic regimes in order to oppose a U.N. conference in Cairo, Egypt, meant to support reproductive freedom and worldwide abortion on demand. The Moslem theologians and many Protestant fundamentalists have opposed abortion as well, although John Paul II has become the single most articulate spokesperson against that accelerating practice. The archbishop of New York, John Cardinal O'Connor, observed, "I see an alliance forming between the Catholic Church and the Muslim world against the West. It would really change an awful lot."

A THIRD MILLENNIUM

The pope has continued his frantic pace on into his seventies. In addition to his travels, generally four major journeys a year, he continues to put forth a steady stream of letters and pronouncements. In 1983, he completed John XXIII's work by promulgating a new code of canon law. In 1985, he celebrated the twenty-fifth anniversary of Vatican II in his own way. In 1991, he used the occasion of a Church synod to celebrate the collapse of Communism. In 1992, a new catechism of the Catholic Church came out in Italy and France, and was followed in 1994 by a best-selling English edition for Britain and the United States. He attended a colorful international interfaith conference at Assisi in 1986 and expressed a desire to hold another at Jerusalem. In 1992, he issued an encyclical called *Veritatis Splendor*, which reiterated traditional Catholic moral theology and called for disciplinary action against dissident theologians. On October 19, 1994, John Paul became the first sitting pope to write a book, *Crossing the Threshold of Hope,* and two years later, after his sixth operation, he published his autobiography.

As noted, in September 1994, he spearheaded international opposition to abortion at the Cairo Conference on Population and Development, and sitting in a hospital bed on May 22, 1994, the pope signed an apostolic letter, *Ordinatio Sacerdotalis,* that said women could never be priests. A year later his Congregation for the Doctrine of the Faith raised that prohibition to an infallible pronouncement. In a radio address heard in Communist China on January 14, 1995, the pope offered to acknowledge that nation's officially sponsored Church if it recognized the pope's authority over China's Catholics. In November 1996, after a serious operation and a short recuperation, he met with Fidel Castro and planned a visit to Cuba. The aging dictator exclaimed how as a boy he never dreamed he would visit a pope and dine with cardinals.

Still, at times the usually sensitive and humane pope seems to become cavalier in his treatment of dissent. When on one occasion he was asked to reconsider seriously the question of a married clergy and female ministers, he recited the World War I tune, "It's a long way to Tipperary." It was an uncharacteristically flippant tone for a serious prelate to take.

There was also the way he dealt with Jacques Gaillot, the Catholic bishop of the diocese of Évreux in Normandy, a gentle and low-keyed individual who dresses in common street clothes. Gaillot had taken to television to talk about the problems of the dispossessed, supported the distribution of condoms to combat AIDS, and advocated a married priesthood, among other views. The pope agreed that he should be shipped to a Sahara desert site called Partenia in Southern Algeria, where there were few real Catholics left.

It was a cynical display of papal authority. But true to our times, the bishop turned Partenia into "a virtual diocese" — one linked to the Internet. Thus the bishop's views were available to anyone with a computer connected to the World Wide Web! The bishop would answer questions, accept e-mail, and give out his unorthodox views while living in the comforts of France. When the bishop saw the pope again, John Paul asked him, "Why are you so *métitaque?*" Gaillot responded, "I am just trying to be like you."[113]

Popes live in real time too, and this pope was prone to slow down as the ailments of advancing age caught up. In 1994, he lamented, "I'm a poor wretch." At times he even seemed frail, his hands shaking, his eyes glazed, and his legendary strength being sapped. In addition to his wounds in 1981 and the subsequent viral blood disorder right after the shooting, John Paul has also been plagued with other ailments. In 1992, he had removed a large intestinal tumor, described as non- or pre-cancerous; in 1993, he had a shoulder injury after he tripped on a carpet; in 1994, he had a partial hip replacement after he broke his thighbone in a bathroom fall; in 1996 he had an appendectomy and was diagnosed with Parkinson's disease.

After his election, he had answered the complaints of some in the Vatican about the costs of building a swimming pool at Castel Gandolfo. He responded that the pool was cheaper than a new conclave! Into his seventies he still cut a graceful figure as a skier and kept up an exhausting pace, wearying his younger associates. As John Paul exhibits more signs of deterioration, however, there is speculation about what characteristics the next pope should have. Usually the pattern was to tilt to the other side — but this pope was a philosopher, a poet, a theologian, a pastor, and a diplomat. Which was the path to the future? The *New York Times* laid out a list of cardinals that were probable "papable," and they all characteristically praised the pontiff and celebrated his good health. As for John Paul he insisted that with God's permission he would lead the Church into the third millennium, the beginning of a new time of the faith coming under the aegis of the Slavic pope. It seems his destiny.

When he was young he had been seen as a special, but never a pampered child. His uniqueness comes from a very real and true sense that he is a survivor — of a family that died around him, of a genocidal war and brutal occupation, of youthful accidents, of Communist terror and intermittent persecution, of a near assassination. Whatever he tries his hand at, he has succeeded brilliantly. Popes rarely come to that office with such a record of genuine achievements, especially from a far-off nation. Apologists of the pope see his election as a special sign of the Holy Spirit's inspiration for a Church in crisis.

Once there he seemed clear on his agenda, but at times even he appears to have reservations that the conservatives were too willing to write off large segments of Catholics for a leaner, more militant Church. He prefers exhortation and example, and in those regards he has no peer. And at times he must be weary of the ways of restoration himself. In fact at times his efforts have been remarkably innovative and unpredictable. He has made special efforts to reach out to Jews, Muslims, Anglicans, Lutherans, and especially Orthodox Christians — showing that he is in many ways the heir to John XXIII and Paul VI. His Assisi meeting with religious of many faiths and sentiments was the most graphic testimony to those sympathies.

Despite his views on an exclusive male priesthood, the pope has apologized to women for past slights. Indeed he is preparing an apology for the sins committed by members of his Church in the past centuries. That initiative was poorly received by the College of Cardinals in June 1994, but it is an extraordinary proposal by any pope. The pontiff observed, "The Church too must make an independent review of the darker side of its history."

On a personal level, Wojtyla is a man known for being mild-mannered, remarkably charitable, and almost nonjudgmental of people and their failings. He is uninterested in material possessions, including his own clothes, almost to the embarrassment of his friends. His companions are his books, his world ideas, and he is above all a skilled listener. The burdens of the papacy have turned him into a very different symbol for millions. John Paul II will never be called "good Pope John." He will be enshrined as a charismatic and formidable reactionary figure who began in earnest the process of reining in the Church and spurning the excesses of the modern world. He will be seen as having turned away from the spirit of Vatican II, while repeating the expressions of its rambling documents and religious clichés.

As noted, millions disliked the message, but they still love the messenger. As noted, *Time* magazine, one of the major props of the superficial communications revolution in the United States, named him in 1995 the "Man of the Year." Why? Because he has the courage of his convictions in a world where such a characteristic was rare. He is not a deal maker, an equivocator, an old-time Vatican diplomat. He has proclaimed, "We must never separate ourselves from the Cross. Never."[114] Although he must have had his own doubts at times, he has insisted on protecting the traditional doctrines of his Church and of his right as pope to exercise its magisterium, its teaching responsibilities. His message as he nears the end of the century is the same as the one he proclaimed at his inauguration: "Non abbiate pavra," "Be not afraid." It was to be the hallmark, not just of his pontificate, but of his entire extraordinary life.

CONCLUSION

Since the end of the Papal States, the modern popes have recast their views of the sacred office they hold and of the relationship of the Church — the barque of St. Peter — to the city of man. The papacy for centuries was indeed involved in secular politics, international diplomacy, common intrigue, and ordinary administration. But swept up in the torrents of the Enlightenment, revolutions, and nationalism, the Papal States became an anachronism. The popes were dependent on the armies and the influence of the Catholic protector states, but by the mid-nineteenth century such commitments were threadbare. The temporal power of the papacy became the final casualty of the late growth of the Italian nationalist spirit.

The reaction of Pius IX was a mixture of arrogance, resignation, and pietism. If he could not rule a corner of the world, he insisted on turning his energies toward changing the international Church into a virtual fortress of dogma, tradition, and faith. His reign was the longest in the history of the office, over thirty-one years, and he had time left to not only witness the end of the Papal States, but also to move the Catholic Church into its most defensive strategy since before the Council of Trent.

He, not the world, insisted that the pope become a prisoner of the Vatican. It was a misguided attempt to gain sympathy and hopefully to bring about a restoration of the temporal authority of his office. Twice in recent memory, once in his own recall in 1850, and earlier in Pius VII's return from exile in 1814, that approach had borne fruit. But instead the once pleasant Pio Nono became a fossil in his own garden. The man who had tried liberalism became the very image of the reactionary pontiff living in the Vatican museums. His style of leadership moved to an intense devotionalism that led to *his* Vatican Council that in turn accepted the doctrine of papal infallibility. He would lose the temporal patrimony that he inherited, but he would prevail in the arena where the papacy still commanded the troops, named the generals, and defined the terrain.

Near the end of his life, he was asked to reassess his prison status, but no, the old man said, that would have to be left to his successor. The cardinals, nearly all appointees of the long-lasting Pius, were astute enough to recognize that a very different papacy was needed, and they turned to an aging aristocrat who ran his own court and even issued what were sort of his own encyclicals. Leo XIII was meant to be a transitional figure — the passage between the failing policies of Pio Nono and some new man who would carry the Church forward at a later date. Instead he lasted twenty-five years, second in duration to his predecessor. One cardinal at the time remarked, "We thought we elected a Holy Father, what we got was an eternal father."

The old pontiff survived into his nineties and never rebuffed a challenge. He is supposed to have approached the end of his years lamenting that he did not have more time to finally reconcile the age-old conflicts between the Scriptures and science! Leo, when he was younger, had proven to be less than an adroit diplomat, but he learned with age. He was sweepingly comprehensive in his diplomatic interests with friends and foes alike, matched wits with Bismarck, pleaded for reconciliation with France, recognized belatedly the uniqueness of the American Church, and stitched together concordats and agreements all over the globe.

Leo remained physically inside the gates, but his agents were robust and peripatetic figures in the parlors of international diplomacy. As for his historical reputation, he caught the scent of social change and sought to deal with the immense dislocations of industrialization. It has been said that the Church lost the workers in the nineteenth century. Leo now gave the Church a new social gospel in his landmark encyclical *Rerum Novarum*. There is a quaint tone to it today, but it is still the most famous papal letter ever issued, a bold attempt to meld the archaicism of medieval economics to the brutal Dickensian world of regulated time and cheap labor. The aura of a pope dealing with such gruesome social conditions was more important than his observations about guilds and fair wages.

The next conclave had enough of the Leonine preoccupation with the world and his subtle diplomacy. The cardinals wanted a pious man — a pastoral soul, one tender and prayerful. Out of those instincts emerged the only pope-saint of recent times, Pius X. His leadership style was dichotomous. He prompted a childlike love of prayer, contemplation, the rosary, and frequent communion. And he epitomized in the process the best qualities of the Italian folk Church. Pius addressed the souls of the young and the desires of many for a faith grounded in mystery, ritual, and sacred tradition.

But Pius X also presided over a minor reign of terror that allowed the worst impulses of an Inquisition-marked Church to flourish in some corners. He permitted, if not encouraged, attacks on the clergy and on the hierarchy of his own churchmen, bearing witness to the fact that isolated, inner-directed institutions can become both fanatical and petty in the service of noble ideas. The politics of character assassination and the zeal to compile anonymous dossiers registered sour notes that paralleled the piety of a simple priest housed too often alone within the Vatican walls.

Upon his death, once again a conclave appointed by one pope and governed by his rules faced the need to choose a very different sort of pontiff. The cardinals acknowledged that they faced the brink of a great war and turned to a protégé of Leo and his secretary of state, Merry del Val. He was a smallish man with at times a waspish tongue and a slight limp, but Benedict XV emerged as a true diplomat-pope. Even in the face of the demands of the Italian state that Benedict and the Vatican must be ignored by its allies, he still became one of the most important humanitarian figures born of that brutalizing conflict. Benedict refused to take sides, refused to accept the assumptions of the propaganda efforts spun by each alliance. He clearly had his favorites and was troubled deeply by Italy's march into the ranks of war. But if God Himself believes in the corporal acts of mercy, then his pope, who threw his weight on the side of those activities, must secure a just reward on judgment day.

And equally important for the legacy of the Church, Benedict with a sharp eye for talent set the stage directly and indirectly for the future of that Church by picking out men of talent who went on to become successor popes. He plucked Ratti out of the Vatican Library to go to Poland. It was the apprenticeship of Pius XI. He would break through the shy asceticism of the Roman Pacelli and place him into the German provinces. It was the apprenticeship of Pius XII. Through his secretary of state Gasparri, two other unlikely diplomat popes were set on the honora causa of ecclesiastical ascendancy. Roncalli was identified first as a promising bureaucrat for missionary efforts, and later as a diplomat to the far reaches of Bulgaria. The sickly, diffident Montini would be quickly recalled from the cold plains of Poland to become during the next war and beyond the most accomplished Curialist of them all.

Benedict assumed few of the airs of authority, but he was clear in his own mind where the Church had to go. He stopped the hysteria of the Modernist witch hunt, saying simply that to be called a Christian and a Catholic was honor enough. No more loyalty oaths were needed. And he insisted on using his good offices internationally to ameliorate some of the worse conditions of the conflict.

In the process he too stayed within the Vatican walls, but he was a true follower of Leo. His diplomacy strengthened the Catholic Church because his objectives were not to restore the Papal States, but to comfort the ailing soul of Western civilization. Ironically, he is little remembered today even within his own Church. Perhaps it was his diminutive stature, for leadership is both symbolic and charismatic. Perhaps it was that the great leaders of World War I were soon eclipsed by their counterparts in a far worse conflict. So Benedict was like Woodrow Wilson and Lloyd George, who look pale now beside Franklin Delano Roosevelt and Winston Churchill.

He groomed a successor who advanced to the papacy quicker than could have been imagined or was probably desirable. Pius XI came out of a scholarly, temperate, quiet lifestyle, but once on the Throne of Peter he was authoritarian, irascible, and highly idiosyncratic in his governing of the Church. He disliked consultation and refused at times even to go through the motions of listening. He ended the isolation of the papacy by feasting with Mussolini and his Fascist thuggery. In a world of totalitarianism he tried to contain those evils by concordats with dictators, and they betrayed him as he probably foresaw in his darker moments they would. Pius XI's leadership skills were rarely influenced by the need to exhibit sensitivity. He commanded, others obeyed. He died on the eve of telling the full truth about the Nazi and Fascist regimes, bluntly and without reservation, to the awful world that was emerging.

His successor was inevitable — a skilled diplomat, the son of a great family of Vatican retainers, and a decent and pious man. Pacelli, who called himself Pius XII, would not know peace. The skills of negotiation and bargaining meant little as World War II enveloped. He emulated Benedict at first: the Vatican must be above the fray. Pius, however, soon became a great ally of the West, condemning the consequences of Nazism and Fascism, but subtly avoiding them by name.

Such restraint was branded later as cowardice, but he was no coward. He might have misjudged or even been timid at times, but Pius opened up too many doors for the persecuted to be castigated as an ally of the dictators' causes. His leadership style was more of a refined version of his predecessor's haughty authoritarianism. Agents and visitors knelt in his august presence, and he too was not an admirer of collegiality or consultation.

He boldly became involved in the Cold War and tried to recast the papacy as a center for strong leadership on an endless series of questions that entertained the modern imagination. He sought not only to recast dogma, but also to become a moral communicator on the postwar world and its anxieties. In the process, Pius XII seemed to many then and later the very epitome of what a pope should be. He was ascetic, holy, decent, and morally committed.

But as he grew older he seemed to forget that leaders have to be concerned about the bureaucratic structures that support their institutions. Critical appointments were neglected, important decisions postponed, outstanding problems left festering. Pius was a morally autonomous man, but he was too disengaged to breathe life into his Church's operations. Under his eloquent facade was a papal administration characterized at times by neglect and genuine lack of interest.

Once again, the cardinals looked for a transitional figure between the High Church atmosphere of Pacelli and some unnamed man in the future. They could not determine who that would be, for Pius had groomed no successor, nor would anyone dare stand up as Pecci had done in his own local diocese before he became Leo XIII. So they chose an amiable old duffer from a prestigious see who had compiled a respectable diplomatic record abroad and who had few enemies — and for better or for worse, he created a revolution.

It has been said that conservatives are more successful in bringing about profound changes than self-styled radicals. There have been few radicals or even progressives in the history of the papacy, although there have been very successful reform popes, starting with Gregory the Great in the fourth century. But reform popes, and especially Church councils, do their work in order to condemn various heresies that crop up. They are then, by their very nature, defensive endeavors meant to cleanse periodically the Roman Catholic Church or to wage war against the errors of the world of which there are legions.

But John XXIII did not proclaim such a mission. The purpose of Vatican II was to make the Church relevant to the contemporary world, to open up the windows of the Church and let the outside light in. No longer was the pope a prisoner of the Vatican — either in theory or in practice. No longer was the Church to be a fortress; rather it was like all of us — a mere pilgrim on the road.

What exactly John had in mind is unclear. His leadership style was somewhat laissez-faire and diffident at times. He was by nature a remarkably nonjudgmental and tolerant man, and his advanced years had taught him that so much that annoys and aggravates fades away in time. He made a career of getting along — with even the most unusual people. John had pacified the Bulgarians, humored the Turks, pleased Charles de Gaulle, and above all put up with Pius XI and Pius XII and the suspicious Curia. In every position he took, he was initially underestimated for he was both ambitious and yet not a self-promoter.

What popes who were his patrons saw in him is unclear. Perhaps he was just one of the boys in the Curia bureaucracy — an enjoyable, humorous, nonintellectual Italian who made one feel comfortable and superior socially to be around. John in his early career had been cited as coming too close to Modernism, and he never ventured into the wilds of theology again. Instead his faith was a simple love and recitation of the practices and the creed of his youth. While the Vatican, for example, would worry whether the Jesuit Pierre Teilhard de Chardin was a pantheistic heretic, John simply wondered why the paleontologist-theologian could not be satisfied with the catechism. It seems naive, but in part he was correct. In the crisis moments of one's brief life, the faithful have recourse in the end to the simple prayers taught at a mother's knee rather than the nuances of speculative theology. It is not boorish to recognize the central importance in life of sentiment, tradition, and memory. Reason is still alive in that neighborhood, but it does not reign supreme and alone.

John loved the Church and believed in the guiding power of the Holy Spirit. Although he may have had occasional doubts about the Council he himself abruptly called, he still believed that it would not err. He was in that view a traditionalist. And he was a traditionalist in many other ways as well — in his respect for liturgical Latin, in his reaffirmation of celibacy, and in his commitment to shrines, feast days, and saints.

Quite probably he thought that the mere calling of a council would establish his worth, his immortality on earth as pope. John seemed at first satisfied with the conservative Curia drafts with their same old responses. But soon he insisted on a more positive view toward the contemporary world, thereby emboldening the progressives in the Council. He protected at times the dissident theologians by refusing to follow the Curia's censures, opened up the Vatican's diplomacy to a rapprochement with the Communist world, and intervened rarely but decisively at times for the progressive Council Fathers.

Those Fathers were generally in the first session as conservative dogmatically as the Curia, but they too often had champed at the bit against the zeal, arrogance, and insensitivities of the Church bureaucrats. At first, though, the Council could be seen as a conflict between the center and the Western European periphery, the Roman Curia versus the outlying provinces — usually those from Protestant or near-Protestant lands such as Belgium, Germany, Netherlands, and Austria.

The progressives became encouraged by John's tone, and the Council began to reject the Curia drafts in session one. There was also the media, and some of the progressive bishops manipulated public perceptions into a good guy–bad guy battle that made it easy for the public to comprehend a very complicated session. But the core theology of the session was still set along traditional lines. Only when John was gone and the bishops and their theologians regrouped did the thrust of the Council change.

But that would be after John's passing. In a few short years he had laid the groundwork, unknowingly, for some major changes that he would have enjoyed and welcomed, and also for departures from the Church's orthodoxy that he would have abhorred. Such is the nature of revolutions — especially intellectual revolution — for ideas cannot be contained any more than the destiny of troops or the temper of assemblies commanded.

The Church reexamined its dogma, its liturgy, and its hospitality toward the world. The Council reaffirmed the basic dogmas of the faith, as of course all knew it would, but the consequences of the Council were more far-reaching than the modest compromise documents that marked its deliberations. That spirit of self-examination became critical and corrosive, almost destructively so, and it led to an unraveling of accepted patterns of obedience, deference, and piety.

The greatest casualties were not the laity, but the religious, the foot soldiers of the Church militant. It is hard to pronounce the Council an unrivaled success after thirty years retrospective, for the toll it took was heavy and extensive. Conservatives argued that the Church embraced the secular realm and that the world won. Good Pope John called the Council too quickly — without focusing the issues clearly; later Paul let it go on too long and thus left the Church vulnerable to the noxious fumes of secularism, liberalism, and misguided experimentation. What started out as an optimistic venture in faith became a theater for the ecclesiastically bored, marginally orthodox theologians, and trendy religious. In the process the laity were disturbed, confused, and scandalized. Unfortunately for the progressive view of the Council, the slippage in the normal standards of Church orthodoxy — baptism, marriage, vocations, financial support — dropped so quickly and severely that it is hard in retrospect to judge Vatican II as a great triumph for the Church.

Surely though it gave Catholics in the modern world important and overdue statements on such issues as anti-Semitism, civil liberties, and world peace. It seemed to recognize the needs of the diverse peoples of God living in the complex city of man, but it is hard to agree that John's legacy left the Catholic Church stronger in the short run. On the other hand, though, the Church lives in the long run historically.

John's leadership still was so at variance with the traditions of the papacy, especially since Pio Nono, that the other segments of the Church government had a difficult time fitting in or readjusting. They wanted a rejuvenation of the Church, especially after the stupor of the last days of Pius XII, but they did not wish any general upheaval. We all enjoy revolutions as long as we are personally left alone. John did not seek to do more than set the tone of openness; unlike other popes he really did let events take the whip hand at first. And because he tolerated all so easily, he was loved more than feared. His authority gave way to genuine affection — to the stereotype of "Good Pope John." Whether that leadership style would have continued if he had lived longer is not clear. Still he could win over the fiercest religious partisan by simply embracing him and repeating that he was "Joseph, your lost brother." And he melted the hearts of a Communist premier's family when he pledged to pray for their children.

John's successor inherited his partially formed dream of a council, even though he himself originally would have preferred that such a council not be called. Actually Paul VI was a progressive at heart, a professional Curial bureaucrat who was influenced by the winds of diverse philosophies and world events. He was a reflective, almost timid person, a gentle soul indeed who was genuinely uncomfortable in having to rein in the unorthodox and repeating over and over again the more traditional formulations of the faith. Still it was Paul who reformed the Curia more than any pope in modern memory had dared, it was Paul who abandoned Latin for the vernacular, it was Paul who balanced the dynamism of the later Council sessions with the uneasiness of traditional Catholicism.

He was his own severest critic, saying that he had not provided the leadership that his Church needed. But in fact, his balancing, his equivocations, his delays may have allowed for some decent time for changes to become institutionalized. He prevented any severe lurchings to the extremes, and because of that straddling Paul may have prevented schisms and full-blown reactions.

His major encyclical, *Humanae Vitae,* was so criticized that he was clearly affected by its poor reception. His tolerance of both Suenens and Lefebvre won him little respect, for his papacy lacked boldness and vigor. But he was the first pope — indeed a true Paul — to travel the world, and this added a new dimension to papal leadership. He became a pilgrim for peace and social justice. With those changes, he opened the Church to bold experimentation especially in Africa and Latin America — occurrences that troubled the conservative Curia, the world he himself had come out of. By the end of his term, Paul was clearly marking time — praying for a decent end to his wearying stewardship.

His successor came from the leftist working-class movement in Italy, and his attitudes in part reflected that populist sentiment. John Paul I loved the poor more than the pretensions of the Church, yet he was a conservative cleric — more than Paul VI was, and it was under him that that mix would have had to work itself out. Would he support the reaction of the traditional right which had educated him and which had formed his character? Or would he have been a bold man willing to sell the Vatican jewels to befriend the poor? We shall never know if he would have been an ecclesiastical reactionary betraying Vatican II, or a stirring tribune of the dispossessed of the world.

From the beginning there was no doubt about his successor's views, even within a month's time. John Paul II was a foreign prelate who made his reputation with bold ideas, conservative rhetoric, and very clear notions of papal authority. He was never seen as a strong hands-on administrator either in Poland or in Rome. He is a leader who appeals over the heads of the Curia, the bishops, the synods, to the common people from whence he sprang. His leadership is a unique mixture of old-time charisma, new technological presence, traditional dogma, and incredible will power. If he had any doubts about the efficacy of his papacy and its style, he has rarely expressed them.

Surely he must be seen as knowledgeable as Paul VI about the limits of his power, the moral apathy of the world, the weaknesses of his own institutional Church. He believes, however, that by a concerted display of personal commitment he can return the Roman Catholic Church to its patterns of deference, authority, and creedal integrity. Building on Paul VI's travels, he has brought his electrifying personality and steadfast faith all over the world — into the marketplaces, the dens of thieves, the death camps of our times. His leadership is so powerful and so unique that it is charismatic in both the media hype and in the classical definitions of such a rare presence.

He and his associates have sought to restore the control of the center over the periphery of the Church — over the bishops, the theologians, the political leaders, and the national conferences. At times his enthusiasm has led to abrupt judgments from which he has had to retreat, to absolute policies in areas that demanded more subtlety and skill.

But such subtlety and skill have been displayed in foreign policy. John Paul II has played a major role in raising the consciousness and spirits of his Polish compatriots to stand up against the Communist regime and indeed to be not afraid. His diplomatic efforts have reflected his long-term confidence in the justice of that cause and in the primacy of the Roman Catholic Church across the globe.

Thus in the late nineteenth and in the twentieth century, the papacy exhibited a variety of leadership styles and personal demeanors. Central to the office is a deep sense of doctrinal continuity, of preserving the magisterium and the deposit of the faith. The popes, except in part for John XXIII, were "traitors to the world." They did not accept its allures, celebrate its charms, await its public approval.

The papacy in the past had been bound up with secular politics and temporal power, especially during the Renaissance. That link had helped corrupt the Church, for, as Jesus Christ himself had remarked, one cannot serve two masters. The failure of Pius IX to retain his patrimony — the Papal States — forced the Church to become more international, more multicultural, and yet more inner-directed. At first that led to bouts of self-righteousness and excessive pietism, reaching its apex in St. Pius X's and Pius XII's reigns, in which the Church seemed to become more vulnerable institutionally as its popes became more holy publicly.

It is commonplace over the last several centuries to read eulogies and obituaries for the Roman Catholic Church, smugly written accounts on why it must die. At times the Church has survived in spite of its popes, and at times it is the people who have safeguarded the faith more than the higher clergy.[1] But in the period that we have observed here, the papacy has surely done what its proponents have credited it with: it has provided a sense of unity and doctrinal continuity during one of the most explosive and violent centuries in the annals of humankind. It has done so in part because of the very guardedness that its pontiffs have shown toward the prevailing moods, the giddy trends, and the uncertain sentiments of the world.

NOTES

Preface

1. Michael Grant, *St. Peter* (New York: Scribner, 1995), part 4 on the Apostle in Rome.

2. J. N. D. Kelly, *The Oxford Dictionary of Popes* (Oxford: Oxford University Press, 1986). The remark on "heretical" popes is based on Kelly's discussions of some early popes, and also on Bernhard Schimmelpfennig, *The Papacy* (New York: Columbia University Press, 1992), 67–69, although this view is by no means accepted by all Church historians. See also E. R. Chamberlin, *The Bad Popes* (New York: Barnes & Noble, 1969).

Introduction

1. *From Max Weber: Essays in Sociology,* ed. H. H. Gerth and C. Wright Mills (New York: Oxford University Press, 1946), 78–79.

2. Avery Dulles, *Models of the Church* (Garden City, N.Y.: Doubleday, 1974).

3. Erik H. Erikson, *Identity: Youth and Crisis* (New York: Norton, 1968) and *Childhood and Society* (New York: Norton, 1950).

4. Edwin A. Weinstein, *Woodrow Wilson: A Medical and Psychological Biography* (Princeton: Princeton University Press, 1981).

Chapter One / Pius IX: The First Modern Pope

1. Karl Otmar von Aretin, *The Papacy and the Modern World* (New York: McGraw-Hill, 1970), 78–79; E. E. Y. Hales, *Revolution and Papacy, 1769–1846* (London: Eyre and Spottiswoode, 1960); John Martin Robinson, *Cardinal Consalvi, 1737–1824* (New York: St. Martin's Press, 1987), introduction.

2. J. Derek Holmes, *The Triumph of the Holy See* (Shepherdstown, W. Va.: Patmos Press, 1978), 101–2. The long criticism is in E. L. Woodward, "The Diplomacy of the Vatican under Popes Pius IX and Leo XIII," *Journal of the British Institute of International Affairs* 3 (May 1924): 121. One profile of Metternich is in E. L. Woodward, *Three Studies in European Conservatism* (London: Constable, 1929), part 1.

3. E. E. Y. Hales, *Pio Nono: A Study in European Politics and Religion in the Nineteenth Century* (New York: P. J. Kenedy, 1954), 27.

4. G. F.-H. and J. Berkeley, *Italy in the Making* (Cambridge: Cambridge University Press, 1968), 3:3.

5. Hales, *Pio Nono*, xi.

6. On the French Revolution and Napoleon: Thomas S. Bokenkotter, *A Concise History of the Catholic Church*, rev. ed. (New York: Image Books, 1990), chap. 24. On the power of the papacy: René Fülöp-Miller, *Leo XIII and Our Times* (New York: Longmans, Green, 1937), 32. On the Congress of Vienna: Harold Nicholson, *The Congress of Vienna: A Study in Allied Unity: 1812–1822* (New York: Harcourt, Brace, 1946), Henry A. Kissinger, *A World Restored; Metternich, Castlereagh, and the Problems of Peace, 1812–1822* (New York: Grosset & Dunlap, 1964); and Robinson, *Cardinal Consalvi*, chap. 5.

7. On the Organic Articles, John McManners, *Church and State in France, 1870–1919* (New York: Harper & Row, 1972), 4; *The New Catholic Encyclopedia* (New York: McGraw-Hill, 1967), 10:754.

8. Friedrich Nippold, *The Papacy in the 19th Century* (New York: G. P. Putnam's Sons, 1900), 23–28; J. B. Bury, *History of the Papacy in the 19th Century: Liberty and Authority in the Roman Catholic Church*, aug. ed. (New York: Schocken, 1964); Martin, *Cardinal Consalvi*, passim.

9. Nippold, *The Papacy*, 53–55.

10. Hales, *Pio Nono*, 60–63.

11. Denis Mack Smith, *Mazzini* (New Haven: Yale University Press, 1994).

12. Hales, *Pio Nono*, 67–68.

13. Ibid., 71.

14. Ibid., 90.

15. Nippold, *The Papacy*, 102.

16. Denis Mack Smith, *Cavour* (New York: Knopf, 1985); William Roscoe Thayer, *The Life and Times of Cavour*, 2 vols. (Boston: Houghton, Mifflin, 1911).

17. Hales, *Pio Nono*, 121.

18. Ibid., 158–62.

19. Smith, *Cavour*, 78–79. The background on the marriage is in ibid., 142–43, and Thayer, *Cavour*, 1: 531–32.

20. Hales, *Pio Nono*, 178 and xii.

21. Ibid., 199–202.

22. Ibid., 206–11.

23. Ibid., 227.

24. Ibid., 244.

25. Ibid., 252.

26. Ibid., 256–58.

27. Ibid., 261.

28. Emil Ludwig, *Bismarck, the Story of a Fighter* (New York: Blue Ribbon Books, 1927), 412–22; Otto Pflanze, *Bismarck and the Development of Germany* (Princeton: Princeton University Press, 1990), vol. 2, chap. 7.

29. Hales, *Pio Nono*, 137–48; Kelly, *Oxford Dictionary*, 310.

30. Hales, *Pio Nono*, 278; forty-five French bishops were absent when the vote on papal infallibility came up: see McManners, *Church and State in France*, 1.

31. Hales, *Pio Pino*, 290–95; Nippold, *The Papacy*, 155.

32. Nippold, *The Papacy*, 159–61; Johann Joseph Ignor von Döllinger, *Letters from Rome on the Council by Quirinus*, 2 vols. (New York: DaCapo Press, 1973); Wilfred Ward, *The Life and Times of Cardinal Wiseman*, 2 vols. (New York: Long-

mans, Green, 1900), chap. 30; *The Roman Question: Extracts from the Dispatches of Odo Russell from Rome, 1858–1870,* ed. Noel Blakiston (London: Chapman and Hall, 1962).

33. Hales, *Pio Nono,* 299–306; Edward Cuthbert Butler, *The Vatican Council, 1869–1870, Based on Bishop Ullathorne's Letters* (Westminster, Md.: Newman Press, 1962).

34. Hales, *Pio Nono,* 320–21, and Pflanze, *Bismarck,* chap. 7.

Chapter Two / Leo XIII: The Soul of the Industrial State

1. Joseph E. Keller, *The Life and Acts of Pope Leo XIII* (New York: Benziger Brothers, 1879); Eduardo Soderini, *The Pontificate of Leo XIII* (London: Burns, Oates and Washbourne, 1934), vol. 1, chaps. 1–3; William J. Kiefer, *Leo XIII: A Light from Heaven* (Milwaukee: Bruce, 1961); Justin McCarthy, *Pope Leo XIII* (New York: Frederick Warne, 1896). Hartwell dela Garde Grissell, *Sede Vacante: Being a Diary Written during the Conclave of 1903 . . .* (London: James Parker, 1903), 2, argues incorrectly that there is no ceremony of striking the dead pope's forehead.

2. René Fülöp-Miller, *Leo XIII and Our Times* (New York: Longmans, Green, 1937), 53–54.

3. Those observations are in ibid., 56–60.

4. "Leo XIII," *The New Catholic Encyclopedia* (New York: McGraw-Hill, 1967), 8:647–49.

5. Soderini, *The Pontificate of Leo XIII,* 1:71–72.

6. Ibid., 81.

7. Lillian Parker Wallace, *Leo XIII and the Rise of Socialism* (Durham, N.C.: Duke University Press, 1966), 80.

8. Ibid., 74.

9. Ibid., 87; Eduardo Soderini, *Leo XIII, Italy and France* (London: Burns, Oates and Washburne, 1935), part 1.

10. Soderini, *The Pontificate of Leo XIII,* 108–9, 151; on Pius IX, see Fülöp-Miller, *Leo XIII,* 82.

11. Ibid., 113–20; *Leo XIII and the Modern World,* ed. Edward T. Gargan (New York: Sheed and Ward, 1961).

12. Otto Pflanze, *Bismarck and the Development of Germany* (Princeton: Princeton University Press, 1990), vol. 2, passim; Lillian Parker Wallace, *The Papacy and European Diplomacy, 1869–1878* (Chapel Hill: University of North Carolina Press, 1948), chaps. 6 and 7.

13. H. W. L. Freudenthal, "Kulturkampf," *The New Catholic Encyclopedia,* 8:167–69; Wallace, *Leo XIII and the Rise of Socialism,* 131.

14. Soderini, *Leo XIII, Italy and France,* part 1; S. William Halperin, "Leo XIII and the Roman Question," in *Leo XIII and the Modern World,* 101–26; Humphrey Johnson, *The Papacy and the Kingdom of Italy* (London: Sheed and Ward, 1926), chap. 3; and S. William Halperin, "Italian Anti-Clericalism 1871–1914," *Journal of Modern History* 19 (March–December 1947): 18–34.

15. Bismarck's award is discussed in Wallace, *Leo XIII and the Rise of Socialism,* 134; Halperin, "Leo XIII and the Roman Question," 117; Francesco Crispi, *The Memoirs of Francesco Crispi* (New York: Hodder and Stoughton, 1912), 2:

393–94; Arturo Carlo Jemolo, *Church and State in Italy 1850–1950* (Oxford: Basil Blackwell, 1960), chap. 3; S. William Halperin, *The Separation of Church and State in Italian Thought from Cavour to Mussolini* (New York: Octagon Books, 1965); and Wallace, *Leo XIII and the Rise of Socialism,* 17. Between 1881 and 1891, Leo contacted the governments of Austria and Spain at least five times about leaving Rome. See Philip Hughes, *Pope Pius the Eleventh* (New York: Sheed and Ward, 1937), 56.

16. Eric McDermott, S.J., "Leo XIII and England," in *Leo XIII and the Modern World,* 127–58.

17. Ibid., 131.

18. Ibid., 136.

19. Ibid., passim, and John Jay Hughes, *Absolutely Null and Utterly Void* (Washington: Corpus Books, 1968).

20. Wallace, *Leo XIII and the Rise of Socialism,* 66–67, 103.

21. Ibid., 286; Soderini, *Leo XIII, Italy and France,* part 2.

22. Wallace, *Leo XIII and the Rise of Socialism,* 291–300; Soderini, *Leo XIII, Italy and France,* part 2; John McManners, *Church and State in France, 1870–1914* (New York: Harper & Row, 1972).

23. Halperin, "Leo XIII and the Roman Question," 108–9; John J. Robinson, *Born in Blood: The Lost Secrets of Freemasonry* (New York: M. Evans, 1989); Robinson argues that the Masons are the heirs of the Knights Templar in Britain who fled arrest and torture mandated by Pope Clement V and the king. They became a secret society of mutual protection that attracted great revolutionaries such as George Washington, Sam Houston, Garibaldi, and Símon Bolívar. See especially on Leo, 307–11 and 345–59. This book has been called to my attention by Michael Nugent of the IBEW, Washington, D.C.

24. J. N. D. Kelly, *The Oxford Dictionary of Popes* (New York: Oxford University Press, 1986), 311–13. The "Civitas Leonina" refers to the area surrounded by a strong wall in the neighborhood of the Vatican and St. Peter's as far as the Castel Sant'Angelo, on the right side of the Tiber. Toward the middle of the ninth century Leo IV had enclosed that area, and it was a separate administrative unit until Sixtus V incorporated the district at the end of the sixteenth century as the fourteenth "rione," called Borgo. See Daniel A. Binchy, *Church and State in Fascist Italy* (Oxford: Oxford University Press, 1941), 256, and E. R. Chamberlain, *The Bad Popes* (New York: Barnes and Noble, 1969), 8–9.

25. Thomas C. McAvoy, "Leo XIII and America," in *Leo XIII and the Modern World,* 157–80.

26. Ibid., 163–63.

27. Especially informative on Leo's thoughts in this area are articles by John Courtney Murray, S.J., "Leo XIII on Church and State: The General Structure of the Controversy," *Theological Studies* 14 (1953): 1–30; "Leo XIII: Two Concepts of Government," *Theological Studies* 14 (1953): 551–67; and "Leo XIII: Two Concepts of Government, II. Government and the Order of Culture," *Theological Studies* 15 (1954): 1–33.

28. Ray Allen Billington, *The Protestant Crusade, 1800–1860: A Study in the Origins of American Nativism* (New York: Macmillan, 1938); J. P. Dolan, *The*

American Catholic Experience: A History from Colonial Times to the Present (New York: Doubleday, 1985).

29. Thomas T. McAvoy, *The Great Crisis in American Catholic History, 1895–1900* (Chicago: H. Regnery, 1957); Henry J. Browne, *The Catholic Church and the Knights of Labor* (New York: Arno Books, 1976).

30. Marvin R. O'Connell, *John Ireland and the American Catholic Church* (St. Paul: Minnesota Historical Society Press, 1988), chaps. 13–16.

31. Ibid.; McAvoy, "Leo XIII and America," passim; John Tracy Ellis, *The Life of James Cardinal Gibbons* (Milwaukee: Bruce, 1952), vol. 2, chap. 16, is on "Americanism"; James Gibbons, *A Retrospective of Fifty Years* (New York: Arno Press, 1972).

32. Quote is from O'Connell, *John Ireland*, 462–63; John C. Fenton, "The Teachings of the Testem Benevolentiae," *American Ecclesiastical Review* 129 (1953): 124–33. The full text is an appendix in McAvoy, *The Great Crisis.*

33. McAvoy, "Leo XIII and America," 176. On one of the consequences of the development of the Catholic Church in the United States, see Thomas F. O'Dea, *American Catholic Dilemma* (New York: Sheed and Ward, 1958); and Gerald P. Fogarty, *The Vatican and the American Hierarchy from 1870 to 1965* (Wilmington, Del.: Michael Glazier, 1985), 190–94; James M. O'Toole, *Militant and Triumphant: William Henry O'Connell and the Catholic Church in Boston, 1859–1944* (Notre Dame, Ind.: University of Notre Dame Press, 1992), 104.

34. Raymond H. Schmandt, "The Life and Work of Leo XIII," in *Leo XIII and the Modern World*, 15–50; Soderini, *Pontificate of Leo XIII*, 130–33.

35. Thomas Bokenkotter, *A Concise History of the Catholic Church*, rev. ed. (New York: Image Books, 1990), 300–301.

36. Wallace, *Leo XIII and the Rise of Socialism*, chaps. 7 and 10.

37. *The Papal Encyclicals 1878–1903*, comp. Claudia Carlen Ihm (Wilmington, N.C.: McGrath, 1981), 241–61. A more convenient edition is *The Church Speaks to the Modern World*, ed. Etienne Gilson (New York: Image Books, 1954), chap. 8.

38. Leo had problems with party rivalries, see Michael P. Fogarty, *Christian Democracy in Western Europe, 1820–1953* (Notre Dame, Ind.: University of Notre Dame Press, 1957), 10. In France the encyclical intensified the Catholic factionalism, see Parker Thomas Moon, *The Labor Problem and the Social Catholic Movement in France: A Study in the History of Social Politics* (New York: Macmillan, 1921), 172–93; the American experience is explored in Aaron I. Abell, "The Reception of Leo XIII's Labor Encyclical in America," *Review of Politics* 7 (October 1945): 464–95.

39. Wallace, *Leo XIII and the Rise of Socialism*, 40; Soderini, *The Pontificate of Leo XIII*, 139.

40. Schmandt, "The Life and Work of Leo XIII," 19; a more critical judgment of Leo than mine is in E. L. Woodward, "Diplomacy of the Vatican under Popes Pius IX and Leo XIII," *Journal of the British Institute of International Affairs* 3 (May 1924): 113–38.

Chapter Three / Pius X: Moods of Piety and Moods of Repression

1. Carlo Falconi, *The Popes in the Twentieth Century, from Pius X to John XXIII* (Boston: Little, Brown, 1967), 2; they also misplaced Leo's ring at first;

see Hartwell dela Garde Grissell, *Sede Vacante: Being a Diary Written during the Conclave of 1903 . . .* (London: James Parker, 1903), 2.

2. Falconi, *Popes in the Twentieth Century,* 7; Emil Schmitz, *Life of Pius X* (New York: American Catholic Publication Society, 1907); Frances A. Forbes, *Life of Pius X* (London: R. & T. Washbourne, 1919).

3. Girolamo Dal-Gal, *Pius X, The Life-Story of the Beatus: The New Italian Life of Pius X* (Westminster, Md.: Newman Press, 1954), 120.

4. Igino Giordani, *Pius X: A Country Priest* (Milwaukee: Bruce, 1954); René Bazin, *Pius X* (London: Sands, 1928); an interesting pictorial biography is Leonard Von Matt and Nello Vian, *St. Pius X* (Chicago: Henry Regnery, 1955), 5.

5. Dal-Gal, *Pius X,* chaps. 2 and 3; Andrew W. Canepa, "Pius X and the Jews: A Reappraisal," *Church History* 61 (September 1992): 362–72.

6. Francis X. Seppelt and Klemens Löffler, *A Short History of the Popes* (St. Louis: B. Herder, 1932), 498.

7. Dal-Gal, *Pius X,* 128–29; on his sisters: Katherine Burton, *The Great Mantle: The Life of Giuseppe Melchiore Sarto, Pope Pius X* (New York: Longmans, Green, 1950), 167.

8. Seppelt and Löffler, *A Short History,* 498.

9. Eduardo Soderini, *The Pontificate of Leo XIII* (London: Burns, Oates and Washbourne, 1934), 1:91.

10. Pierluigi L. Occelli, *St. Pius X* (London: St. Paul Publications, 1954), 140–42; Burton, *Great Mantle,* 152.

11. Burton, *Great Mantle,* 158, chap. 13; Giordani, *Pius X,* chap. 21; Bazin, *Pius X,* 302–40; Falconi, *Popes in the Twentieth Century,* 58–72.

12. See above pp. 53 and 60 on Leo's remarks on reconciling science and the Scriptures.

13. *New Catholic Encyclopedia* (New York: McGraw-Hill, 1967), 9:991–95.

14. Antonio Fogazzaro, *The Saint* (New York: G. P. Putnam's, 1906).

15. Michael Davies, *Partisans of Error* (Long Prairie, Minn.: Neumann Press, 1983), 94–101, contains the syllabus *Lamentabili Sane.*

16. *The Papal Encyclicals, 1903–1939,* comp. Claudia Carlen Ihm (Wilmington, N.C.: McGrath, 1981), 71–97.

17. *The New Catholic Encyclopedia,* 9:995.

18. Falconi, *Popes in the Twentieth Century,* 37–38; a more supportive view of the Modernist handling is in Auguste Pierre Laveille, *A Life of Cardinal Mercier* (New York: Century, 1928), chap. 7.

19. Falconi, *Popes in the Twentieth Century,* 43.

20. Peter Hebblethwaite, *Pope John XXIII: Shepherd of the Modern World* (Garden City, N.Y.: Doubleday, 1985), chap. 4; on Vatican II, see Davies, *Partisans of Error,* passim.

21. Falconi, *Popes in the Twentieth Century,* 54.

22. Burton, *Great Mantle,* 158.

23. I am indebted to Dr. James Brennan, dean of the Graduate School at Loyola University of Chicago, for this insight. Also see Burton, *Great Mantle,* 180–81.

24. Burton, *Great Mantle,* 179; *New Catholic Encyclopedia,* 12:1051–52; and 11:410; Michael Fogarty, *Christian Democracy in Western Europe, 1820–1953* (Notre Dame, Ind.: University of Notre Dame Press, 1957).

25. André Jardin and André-Gean Tudesq, *Restoration and Reaction, 1815–1848* (Cambridge: Cambridge University Press, 1983); Maurice Agulhon, *The Republican Experiment, 1848–1852* (Cambridge: Cambridge University Press, 1983); Alain P. Lessis, *The Rise and Fall of the Second Empire, 1852–1871* (Cambridge: Cambridge University Press, 1987); Jean-Marie Mayeur and Madeleine Rebrioux, *The Third Republic From Its Origins to the Great War, 1871–1914* (Cambridge: Cambridge University Press, 1987); Ross William Collins, *Catholicism and the Second French Republic, 1848–1852* (New York: Octagon Books, 1980); John McManners, *Church and State in France, 1870–1914* (New York: Harper & Row, 1972); Maurice J. M. Larkin, "The Church and the French Concordat, 1891–1902," *English Historical Review* 81 (October 1966): 717–39.

26. McManners, *Church and State,* 138; Joseph N. Moody, "The Dechristianization of the French Working Class," *Review of Politics* 20 (January 1958): 46–69.

27. McManners, *Church and State,* 165.

28. Ibid., 169.

29. *New Catholic Encyclopedia,* 11:411; Burton, *Great Mantle,* 205, 157.

30. F. A. Forbes, *The Life of Pius,* 173; Burton, *Great Mantle,* 216–17.

31. Burton, *Great Mantle,* 164; Rafael Merry del Val, *Memories of Pius X* (Westminster, Md.: Newman Press, 1951), 63; F. A. Forbes, *Rafael, Cardinal Merry del Val* (New York: Longmans, Green, 1932); Marie C. Buehrle, *Rafael, Cardinal Merry del Val* (Houston: Lumen Christi Press, 1980).

32. Falconi, *Popes in the Twentieth Century,* 289; Kenneth L. Woodward, *Making Saints: How the Catholic Church Determines Who Becomes a Saint, Who Doesn't, and Why* (New York: Simon and Schuster, 1996).

33. Occelli, *St. Pius X,* chap. 14; Dal-Gal, *Pius X,* chap. 10; Merry del Val, *Memories of Pius X: A Symposium on the Life and Work of Pius X* (Westminster, Md.: Newman Press, 1951), chaps. 13 and 14.

34. John Dominic Crossan, *The Historical Jesus: The Life of a Mediterranean Jewish Peasant* (San Francisco: HarperCollins, 1991); Morton Smith, *Jesus the Magician* (New York: Harper & Row, 1978); John P. Meier, *A Marginal Jew: Rethinking the Historical Jesus* (New York: Doubleday, 1994).

Chapter Four / Benedict XV and the Mad Dogs of War

1. On Pius X's preoccupation with internal affairs, see Carlo Falconi, *The Popes in the Twentieth Century* (Boston: Little, Brown, 1967), 91. Also of interest is Humphrey Johnson, *Vatican Diplomacy in the World War* (Oxford: Basil Blackwell, 1933), 8–10. My note on the origins of the family name is from William Barry, "Benedict XV: Pontiff of Peace," *Dublin Review* 170 (April–June 1922): 162. The French press at first celebrated Cardinal Della Chiesa's alleged Francophile tendencies.

2. Henry E. G. Rope, *Benedict XV: The Pope of Peace* (London: John Gifford, 1941), Book 1. The Consalvi quote is on p. 33; J. Van den Heuvel, *The Statesmanship of Benedict XV* (New York: Benziger Bros., 1923), 16–17.

3. Walter H. Peters, *Life of Benedict XV* (Milwaukee: Bruce, 1959), 32–35.

4. Rope, *Benedict XV,* 30.

5. Peters, *Life of Benedict XV,* 39.

6. Rope, *Benedict XV,* 43.

7. Barry, "Benedict XV," 164; Peters, *Life of Benedict XV,* 45–48; Falconi, *Popes in the Twentieth Century,* 100, on quasi-secular Catholic journalism.

8. Peters, *Life of Benedict XV,* 68; William Henry O'Connell, *Recollections of Seventy Years* (Boston: Houghton Mifflin, 1934), 341–42.

9. Peters, *Life of Benedict XV,* 75–83; William Teeling, *Pope Pius XI and World Affairs* (New York: Frederick A. Stokes, 1937), 93. Published also under the title: *The Pope in Politics* (London: Lovat Dickson, 1937).

10. Peters, *Life of Benedict XV,* 90–92.

11. Ibid., 101.

12. Arturo Carlo Jemolo, *Church and State in Italy, 1850–1950* (Oxford: Basil Blackwell, 1960), 103.

13. The discussion of the origins and extent of World War I is taken in abbreviated form from my book *The Ferocious Engine of Democracy* (Lanham, Md.: Madison Books, 1995), 2:64–68. The sources are: A. J. P. Taylor, *Illustrated History of the First World War* (New York: G. P. Putnam's Sons, 1964); Keith Robbins, *The First World War* (New York: Oxford University Press, 1985); Winston S. Churchill, *The Unknown War: The Eastern Front* (New York: Charles Scribner's Sons, 1931); George F. Kennan, *The Fateful Alliance* (New York: Pantheon, 1984); Norman Stone, *The Eastern Front, 1914–1917* (New York: Charles Scribner's Sons, 1975); Denna F. Fleming, *The Origins and Legacies of World War I* (New York: Doubleday, 1968); Fritz Fischer, *Germany's Aims in the First World War* (New York: W. W. Norton, 1967); Luigi Albertini, *The Origins of the War of 1914,* 3 vols. (New York: Oxford University Press, 1952–57); Graydon A. Tunstall, Jr., *Planning for War against Russia and Serbia: Austro-Hungarian and German Military Strategies, 1871–1914* (New York: Columbia University Press, 1993); John M. Blum, *Woodrow Wilson and the Politics of Morality* (Boston: Little, Brown, 1956); Sidney B. Fay, *The Origins of the World War* (New York: Macmillan, 1930); and Patrick Devlin, *Too Proud to Fight: Woodrow Wilson's Neutrality* (New York: Oxford University Press, 1975).

14. *The Papal Encyclicals, 1903–1939,* comp. Claudia Carlen Ihm (Wilmington, N.C.: McGrath, 1981), 3: 143–51. Also of use is *His Holiness Pope Benedict XV on the Great War,* ed. Gabriel Martyn (London: Burns & Oates, 1916); and Falconi, *Popes in the Twentieth Century,* 115, and Robert Dell, "The Vatican and the War," *Fortnightly Review* 103 (February 1915): 286–95.

15. Peters, *Life of Benedict XV,* 113.

16. Ibid., 114; Denis Gwynn, *The Vatican and the War in Europe* (London: Burns, Oates and Washbourne [1940]), chaps. 2, 3, 4.

17. Peters, *Life of Benedict XV,* 114.

18. Ibid., 115; Henry L. Dubly, *The Life of Cardinal Mercier, Primate of Belgium* (London: Sands, 1928), part 2; Augusta Pierre Lavielle, *A Life of Cardinal Mercier* (New York: Century, 1928), chaps. 7, 8, 9.

19. Van den Heuvel, *The Statesmanship of Benedict XV,* 33.

20. Peters, *Life of Benedict XV,* 121.

21. Jemolo, *Church and State in Italy,* 163.

22. Denis Mack Smith, *Mussolini* (New York: Knopf, 1982), chap. 3; Martin Clark, *Modern Italy 1871–1982* (London: Longman, 1984), chap. 9.

23. Peters, *Life of Benedict XV*, 127–38.

24. Johnson, *Vatican Diplomacy*, 18, 36; Clark, *Modern Italy*, 182.

25. Johnson, *Vatican Diplomacy*, 20–21.

26. Anthony Brennan, *Pope Benedict XV and the War* (Westminster: P. S. King & Son, 1917), 5–6; see also a summary of Friedrich Ritter von Lama's work in *Peace Action of Pope Benedict XV* (Washington, D.C.: Catholic Association for International Peace, 1936), and Diplomaticus [pseud.], *No Small Stir* (London: Society of SS. Peter & Paul, 1917).

27. Johnson, *Vatican Diplomacy*, 21–21. For a different view see Algeron Cecil, "Vatican Policy in the Twentieth Century," *Journal of the British Institute of International Affairs* 4 (January 1925): 1–29.

28. Peters, *Life of Benedict XV*, 140–41.

29. Johnson, *Vatican Diplomacy*, 24–25; Peters, *Life of Benedict XV*, 143.

30. Peters, *Life of Benedict XV*, 153–57.

31. Rope, *Benedict XV*, 135–44.

32. Ibid., 153.

33. The speculations are from Johnson, *Vatican Diplomacy*, chap. 6.

34. Donald A. MacLean, *The Permanent Peace Program of Pope Benedict XV* (New York: Catholic Association for International Peace, 1931), 5.

35. Peters, *Life of Benedict XV*, 192–93.

36. Johnson, *Vatican Diplomacy*, 13–19.

37. Peters, *Life of Benedict XV*, 181–85.

38. Ibid., 181; Daniel A. Binchy, *Church and State in Fascist Italy* (Oxford: Oxford University Press, 1941), 307.

39. Peers, *Life of Benedict XV*, 169–70, 177.

40. Ibid., 193–94.

41. Clark, *Modern Italy*, 189; Peters, *Life of Benedict XV*, 195.

42. Peters, *Life of Benedict XV*, 195–97.

43. Ibid., 197. On other initiatives toward a variety of ethnic and national groups see Monsignor Batiffol, "Pope Benedict XV and the Restoration of Unity," *Constructive Quarterly* 6 (1918): 209–25; Philip Hughes, *Pope Pius the Eleventh* (New York: Sheed and Ward, 1937), chap. 3; "Pope Pius XI," *New Catholic Encyclopedia* (New York: McGraw-Hill, 1967), 11:411–14. For a more critical view of Vatican diplomacy during this time, see Sergio I. Minerbi, *The Vatican and Zionism: Conflict in the Holy Land, 1895–1925* (New York: Oxford University Press, 1990).

44. Tad Szulc, *Pope John Paul II: The Biography* (New York: Scribner, 1995), 13–14.

45. Albertini, *Origins of the War*, passim.

46. Peters, *Life of Benedict XV*, 228–29.

Chapter Five / Pius XI and the New Men of Violence

1. Robert R. Palmer, *A History of the Modern World* (New York: Knopf, 1956), 757; Elizabeth Wiskemann, *Europe of the Dictators, 1919–1945* (New York: Harper & Row, 1966), chaps. 1–3.

2. Palmer, *History of the Modern World*, 760; Anthony Rhodes, *The Vatican in the Age of Dictators, 1922–1945* (New York: Holt, Rinehart & Winston, 1974),

162; *The Columbia History of Eastern Europe in the Twentieth Century*, ed. Joseph Held (New York: Columbia University Press, 1992).

3. Erick Hobsbawm, *The Age of Extremes: A History of the World 1914–1991* (New York: Pantheon, 1994), 122–35.

4. Rhodes, *Vatican*, 90–95.

5. Dimitri Volkogonov, *Lenin: A New Biography* (New York: Free Press, 1995); Rhodes, *Vatican*, 133.

6. [William Cecil James Wicklow] Lord Clonmore, *Pope Pius XI and World Peace* (New York: E. P. Dutton, 1938), 62.

7. Tad Szulc, *Pope John Paul II: The Biography* (New York: Scribner, 1995), 13–14. Different views of who stayed in Warsaw have been given. The Italian and Danish ambassadors may have stayed also; for the larger number of ambassadors, see William Teeling, *Pope Pius XI and World Affairs* (New York: Frederick A. Stokes, 1937), 72.

8. Hobsbawm, *Age of Extremes*, 50, 87. When he visited London, Ratti saw the tradition of keeping to the *left* of the road, which started with Pope Boniface VIII in 1300, to cope with the traffic during the papal jubilee in Rome. From Teeling, *World Affairs*, 59.

9. Denis Gwynn, *The Vatican and the War in Europe* (London: Burns, Oates, and Washbourne [1940]), 89. On the League of Nations see Peter Hebblethwaite, *Paul VI: The First Modern Pope* (New York: Paulist Press, 1993), 124.

10. Wicklow, *World Peace*, 32–45.

11. Rene Fontenelle, *His Holiness Pope Pius XI* (London: Metheun, 1938); Philip Hughes, *Pope Pius the Eleventh* (New York: Sheed and Ward, 1937), 19; Achille Ratti, *Essays in History* (Freeport, N.Y.: Books in Libraries, 1967).

12. Hughes, *Pope Pius the Eleventh*, 67; Carlo Falconi, *The Popes in the Twentieth Century* (Boston: Little, Brown, 1967), 171.

13. Falconi, *Popes in the Twentieth Century*, 159; Hughes, *Pope Pius the Eleventh*, chap. 11.

14. Rhodes, *Vatican*, 19; Hughes, *Pope Pius the Eleventh*, chap. 1.

15. Fontenelle, *His Holiness*, 25.

16. Ibid., 21; Falconi, *Popes in the Twentieth Century*, 178.

17. Fontenelle, *His Holiness*, 29–31; Paul I. Murphy, *La Popessa* (New York: Warner Books, 1983), 153, claims that the conclave picked Camillo Cardinal Laurenti, who supposedly turned down the papacy in 1922.

18. Teeling, *World Affairs*, 17; Fontenelle, *His Holiness*, 37–38; Falconi, *Popes in the Twentieth Century*, 153–54.

19. Rhodes, *Vatican*, 19; Falconi, *Popes in the Twentieth Century*, 216–17; Hebblethwaite, *Paul VI*, 118.

20. Robert Sencourt, *Genius of the Vatican* (London: Jonathan Cape, 1935); Daniel A. Binchy, *Church and State in Fascist Italy* (Oxford: Oxford University Press, 1970), 73, 82.

21. Binchy, *Church and State*, 82–86; Rhodes, *Vatican*, 162; Hughes, *Pope Pius the Eleventh*, 173.

22. Benito Mussolini, *My Autobiography* (Westport, Conn.: Greenwood Press, 1970; originally published in 1928).

23. Denis Mack Smith, *Mussolini* (New York: Knopf, 1982), 15, 35; also of in-

terest Christopher Hibbert, *Benito Mussolini: The Rise and Fall of Il Duce* (Boston: Little, Brown, 1962); S. William Halperin, *The Separation of Church and State in Italian Thought from Cavour to Mussolini* (New York: Octagon Books, 1971), chap. 5; George Seldes, *Sawdust Caesar: The Untold Story of Mussolini and Fascism* (New York: Harper & Bros., 1935); Herbert Finer, *Mussolini's Italy* (New York: Archon Books, 1964), part 2.

24. Wicklow, *World Peace,* 78; on the various sources of support for Fascism, see Donald H. Bell, *Sesto San Giovanni: Workers, Culture and Politics in an Italian Town, 1880–1922* (New Brunswick, N.J.: Rutgers University Press, 1986). The conditions of Italy are also outlined in Martin Clark, *Modern Italy 1871–1982* (New York: Longman, 1988), chap. 10.

25. Smith, *Mussolini,* 42–56.

26. Sencourt, *Genius of the Vatican,* 208.

27. Harold Nicolson, *Diplomacy* (New York: Harcourt, Brace, 1939), chaps. 2 and 5.

28. Binchy, *Church and State,* 100.

29. Ibid., 106.

30. Gwynn, *The Vatican and War in Europe,* 98.

31. Teeling, *World Affairs,* 129.

32. Binchy, *Church and State,* 139; Teeling, *World Affairs,* 236.

33. Binchy, *Church and State,* 140; Rhodes, *Vatican,* 28; Hughes, *Pope Pius the Eleventh,* 198, on the Mafia and Freemasons; Alexander Stille, *Excellent Cadavers: The Mafia and the Death of the First Italian Republic* (New York: Pantheon, 1995); and Murphy, *La Popessa,* 187–89, which claim that the Vatican may have worked with the White House to get sanctuary in Italy for Mafia crime boss Charles "Lucky" Luciano.

34. Binchy, *Church and State,* 158; Rhodes, *Vatican,* 46; Luigi Sturzo, *Church and State* (London: Centenary Press, 1939), chaps. 14 and 15; John F. Pollard, *The Vatican and Italian Fascism 1929–32* (Cambridge: Cambridge University Press, 1985); Avro Manhattan, *The Vatican in World Politics* (New York: Gaer Associates, 1949).

35. Binchy, *Church and State,* 174; Rhodes, *Vatican,* 40.

36. Binchy, *Church and State,* 258–61; *Documents on International Affairs, 1929,* ed. John W. Wheeler-Bennett (Oxford: Oxford University Press, 1930), 216–41, for texts of the treaty, financial convention, and concordat. See also *Survey of International Affairs, 1929,* comp. Arnold J. Toynbee (Oxford: Oxford University Press, 1930), part 5; Mario Falco, *The Legal Position of the Holy See before and after the Lateran Agreements* (Oxford: Oxford University Press, 1935); Benedict Williamson, *The Treaty of Lateran* (London: Burns, Oates, and Washbourne, 1929).

37. Binchy, *Church and State,* 220–26; and Gwynn, *The Vatican and War,* 120.

38. Binchy, *Church and State,* 270–71, 195.

39. Ibid., 186.

40. Ibid., 205–6; Smith, *Mussolini,* 162.

41. Binchy, *Church and State,* 207–10.

42. Ibid., 323–33; Giovanni Gentile, *The Reform of Education* (New York: Harcourt, Brace, 1922); Giovanni Gentile, *Theory of Mind as Pure Act* (New York: Macmillan, 1922); Giovanni Gentile, *Genesis and Structure of Society* (Urbana:

University of Illinois Press, 1960); Merritt Moore Thompson, *The Educational Philosophy of Giovanni Gentile* (Los Angeles: University of Southern California Press, 1934); Roger Holmes, *The Idealism of Giovanni Gentile* (New York: Macmillan, 1937); Henry Stilton Harris, *The Social Philosophy of Giovanni Gentile* (Urbana: University of Illinois Press, 1960); Lorenzo Minio-Palvello, *Education in Fascist Italy* (Oxford: Oxford University Press, 1946); William A. Smith, *Giovanni Gentile on the Existence of God* (Louvain: Editions Nauwelaerts, 1970).

43. *The Papal Encyclicals, 1903–1939*, comp. Claudia Carlen Ihm (Wilmington, N.C.: McGrath, 1981), 525–36.

44. Binchy, *Church and State*, 341.

45. Ibid., 408–9; Tracy H. Koon, *Believe, Obey, Fight: Political Socialization of Youth in Fascist Italy, 1922–1943* (Chapel Hill: University of North Carolina Press, 1985) on the political socialization of youth in fascist Italy.

46. Binchy, *Church and State*, 409–13.

47. Ibid., 490–96.

48. Ibid., 514.

49. Ibid., 517–22.

50. *Papal Encyclicals*, 445–58.

51. Binchy, *Church and State*, 545.

52. Rhodes, *Vatican*, 70; Teeling, *World Affairs*, 139.

53. Francis A. Ridley, *The Papacy and Fascism: The Crisis of the Twentieth Century* (London: M. Secker Warburg, 1937), part 3, and Geoffrey T. Garratt, *Mussolini's Roman Empire* (Indianapolis: Bobbs-Merrill, 1938), 15.

54. Binchy, *Church and State*, 64–42; Rhodes, *Vatican*, 76.

55. Rhodes, *Vatican*, 77.

56. Binchy, *Church and State*, 649–50. On Mussolini and Islam, see Teeling, *World Affairs*, 143.

57. Teeling, *World Affairs*, 158; Binchy, *Church and State*, 295–308.

58. George Seldes, *The Vatican: Yesterday, Today, Tomorrow* (New York: Harper & Bros., 1934), 307.

59. Wicklow, *World Peace*, 108.

60. *Papal Encyclicals*, 415–44.

61. Wicklow, *World Peace*, 114–22.

62. *Papal Encyclicals*, 537–54.

63. Wicklow, *World Peace*, 217–18; Stewart A. Stehlin, *Weimar and the Vatican 1919–1933: German-Vatican Diplomatic Relations in the Interwar Years* (Princeton: Princeton University Press, 1983), chap. 7.

64. Rhodes, *Vatican*, 175.

65. Ibid., 169; Teeling, *World Affairs*, 116; Gwynn, *The Vatican and War*, chap. 8.

66. Rhodes, *Vatican*, 175.

67. William Teeling, *Crisis for Christianity* (London: Religious Books Club, 1939), 100–7; Rhodes, *Vatican*, 179–80.

68. *New Catholic Encyclopedia* (New York: McGraw-Hill, 1967), 11:414.

69. Rhodes, *Vatican*, 183–200; 150–51.

70. Wicklow, *World Peace*, 176.

71. Hughes, *Pope Pius the Eleventh*, 301–2.

72. Rhodes, *Vatican*, 207–8.

73. Falconi, *The Popes in the Twentieth Century*, 194.

74. Rhodes, *Vatican*, 114–30; Paul Preston, *Franco: A Biography* (New York: Basic Books, 1994); Michael Curtis, *Three against the Third Republic: Sorel, Barres, and Maurias* (Princeton: Princeton University Press, 1959).

75. Rhodes, *Vatican*, 105; Hughes, *Pope Pius the Eleventh*, 290. The poet T. S. Eliot was an admirer of Maurras and defended him after the pope's condemnation. But after Maurras's support of Vichy France, he concluded that the pope's views were sounder than he thought originally; in Louis Menard, "Eliot and the Jews," *New York Review of Books*, June 6, 1996, 43, 39.

76. Wicklow, *World Peace*, 180–210. On Pius's comment on Maurras, see Rhodes, *Vatican*, 106.

77. Wicklow, *World Peace*, 231–34; *Papal Encyclicals*, 391–414.

78. Wicklow, *World Peace*, 280–86; Rhodes, *Vatican*, 98–102.

79. Hughes, *Pope Pius the Eleventh*, chap. 7; Benedict Williamson, *The Story of Pope Pius XI* (New York: P. J. Kenedy & Sons, 1931), chap. 9.

80. Rhodes, *Vatican*, 161; Teeling, *World Affairs.* 157–61; *New York Times*, February 10, 1939, 1+; Gerald P. Fogarty, *The Vatican and the American Hierarchy from 1870 to 1965* (Wilmington, Del.: Michael Glazier, 1985), 243+, indicates that Bishop Gallagher supported Coughlin, denies that the Vatican had spoken to him directly, and observes that Coughlin continued his attacks until the Justice Department stopped some of his activities. It is clear that the apostolic delegate and several of the hierarchy used this conflict against the radio priest.

81. Rhodes, *Vatican*, 71; Hansjakob Stehle, *Eastern Politics of the Vatican, 1917–1979* (Athens: Ohio University Press, 1981), 67.

82. His criticisms of the concordats are in John P. McKnight, *The Papacy: A New Appraisal* (New York: Rinehart, 1952), 257; *New York Times*, February 10, 1939, 1+; Rhodes, *Vatican*, 20.

Chapter Six / Pius XII and the Spiritual Twilight of the West

1. Anthony Rhodes, *The Vatican in the Age of the Dictators, 1922–1945* (New York: Holt, Rinehart & Winston, 1974), 221; Carlo Falconi, *The Popes in the Twentieth Century* (Boston: Little, Brown, 1967), 235; Domenico Tardini, *Memories of Pius XII* (Westminster, Md.: Newman Press, 1961), 109.

2. John P. McKnight, *The Papacy: A New Appraisal* (New York: Rinehart, 1952), 218.

3. Ibid., 220–21, 230; Thomas B. Morgan, *The Listening Post: Eighteen Years on Vatican Hill* (New York: G. P. Putnam's Sons, 1944), chap. 13, records that Pacelli was first an aide to Merry del Val and accompanied him to London to pay the Vatican's respects after the death of Queen Victoria.

4. Rhodes, *The Vatican*, 221.

5. Ibid., 222–23; McKnight, *The Papacy*, 257, 291; Tardini, *Memories*, 73.

6. Rhodes, *The Vatican*, 223; also of use: *The Persecution of the Catholic Church in the Third Reich: Facts and Documents* (New York: Longmans, Green, 1940), for the earlier record of violations of the concordat.

7. Ibid., 224–26; Tardini, *Memories*, 39.

8. Oscar Halecki and James F. Murray, Jr., *Pius XII: Eugenio Pacelli, Pope of Peace* (New York: Farrar, Straus and Young, 1954), 93; Edward L. Heston, *The Holy See at Work* (Milwaukee: Bruce, 1950), 270–84; Paul I. Murphy, *La Popessa* (New York: Warner Books, 1983), 153, claims that before the final vote Pacelli refused to accept his election by the conclave. There is some speculation that the volume is partially fiction.

9. Peter Hebblethwaite, *Paul VI, the First Modern Pope* (New York: Paulist Press, 1993), chap. 16.

10. Rhodes, *Vatican,* 230–32; Michael Bloch, *Ribbentrop* (New York: Crown, 1992), on the pope and Secretary of State Cardinal Maglione, 275.

11. *The Papal Encyclicals 1939–1958,* comp. Claudia Carlen Ihm (Wilmington, N.C.: McGrath, 1981), 5–22.

12. Rhodes, *Vatican,* 242–46; Jan Olav Smit, *Angelic Shepherd: The Life of Pope Pius* (New York: Dodd, Mead, 1951), 221.

13. James MacGregor Burns, *Roosevelt: The Soldier of Freedom* (New York: Harcourt, Brace, Jovanovich, 1970), 411; and Michael P. Riccards, *The Ferocious Engine of Democracy: The American Presidency, 1789–1989* (Lanham, Md.: Madison Books, 1995), vol. 2, chap. 4.

14. Rhodes, *Vatican,* 249; I prefer the translation in Falconi, *Popes in the Twentieth Century,* 261; Murphy, *La Popessa,* 196.

15. Isaac Deutscher, *Stalin: A Political Biography* (New York: Oxford University Press, 1949), chap. 12; Walter Laqueur, *Stalin: The Glasnost Revelations* (New York: Charles Scribner's Sons, 1990), chap. 11.

16. *Wartime Correspondence between President Roosevelt and Pope Pius XII,* ed. Myron C. Taylor (New York: DeCapo Press, 1975), 61–62; John S. Conway, "Myron C. Taylor's Mission to the Vatican, 1940–1950," *Church History* 44 (March 1975): 85–99.

17. Gerhard L. Weinberg, *A World at Arms: A Global History of World War II* (New York: Cambridge University Press, 1994), chap. 8.

18. Halecki, *Pius XII,* 178; Rhodes, *Vatican,* 275.

19. Halecki, *Pius XII,* 179; Denis Mack Smith, *Mussolini* (New York: Knopf, 1982), chap. 16; Umberto Eco, "Ur-Fascism," *New York Review of Books,* June 22, 1995, 12+.

20. Halecki, *Pius XII,* 181.

21. Ibid., 184.

22. Ibid., 194; Susan Zuccotti, *The Italians and the Holocaust: Persecution, Rescue, and Survival* (London: Peter Halban, 1987), 130, argues that the pope still did not properly denounce the deportation of Roman Jews; also see Murphy, *La Popesa,* 226. Journalist Nicola Grazioli in 1995 maintained that in the closing months of the war the Vatican drafted a plan to expand its territory to include a stretch of land reaching to the sea. Pius XII and his close aides in 1944 envisioned enlarging the city-state to take in a corridor to the Tyrrhenian Sea about twelve miles to the southwest. The pope is reported to have sought that strip as a way of getting compensation for the battle of Portia Pia in 1820 when the Vatican ended up losing most of its territory. Supposedly an influential cleric stopped the plan.

23. Halecki, *Pius XII,* 195–201; Elizabeth Wiskemann, *Europe of the Dicta-*

tors, 1919–1945 (New York: Harper & Row, 1966), chap. 15; James Hennessey, "American Jesuit in Wartime Rome," *Mid-America* (July 1974), 32–58.

24. McKnight, *The Papacy*, 237.

25. Rhodes, *Vatican*, 239.

26. Ibid., 258–62; McKnight, *The Papacy*, 235.

27. Rhodes, *Vatican*, 264.

28. Saul Friedlander, *Pius XII and the Third Reich: A Documentation* (New York: Knopf, 1966), 262–65; Guenter Lewy, *The Catholic Church and Nazi Germany* (New York: McGraw-Hill, 1964); Avro Manhattan, *The Vatican in World Politics* (New York: Gaer Associates, 1949), chap. 9–11.

29. Rhodes, *Vatican*, 273–74.

30. *Papal Encyclicals 1939–1958*, 37–64.

31. Hebblethwaite, *Paul VI*, 74–78, 165–69.

32. Gordon Zahn, *German Catholics and Hitler's Wars* (New York: Sheed and Ward, 1962); Lewy, *The Catholic Church and Nazi Germany*, passim; Rhodes, *Vatican*, 290–94.

33. Rhodes, *Vatican*, 296–97; Robert Cecil, *The Myth of the Master Race: Alfred Rosenberg and Nazi Ideology* (New York: Dodd, Mead, 1972).

34. Arno J. Mayer, *Why Did the Heavens Not Darken? The "Final Solution" in History* (New York: Pantheon Books, 1988); Lucy S. Dawidowicz, *The War against the Jews, 1933–1945* (New York: Holt, Rinehart and Winston, 1975); Martin Gilbert, *The Holocaust: The Jewish Tragedy* (New York: Holt, Rinehart and Winston, 1986); Paul Hilberg, *The Destruction of the European Jews*, rev. ed., 3 vols. (New York: Holmes and Meier, 1985); Martin Gilbert, *Auschwitz and the Allies* (New York: Holt, Rinehart and Winston, 1981); *FDR and the Holocaust*, ed. Verne W. Newton (New York: St. Martin's Press, 1996); Frederick B. Chary, *The Bulgarian Jews and the Final Solution, 1940–1944* (Pittsburgh: University of Pittsburgh, 1972); J. H. Crehan, "The Papacy and the Polish Holocaust," *The Month* (November 1967): 253–59. Dean James F. Brennan, of Loyola University, has called my attention to the tolerant attitude of Poles, especially some of their kings, toward Jews going back to the Spanish Inquisition.

35. Rolf Hochhuth, *The Deputy* (New York: Grove Press, 1964).

36. Carlo Falconi, *The Silence of Pius XII* (Boston: Little, Brown, 1970), passim; Tardini, *Memories*, passim. On Montini's exile, I have benefitted from an anonymous source.

37. Guido Gonello, *The Papacy and World Peace: A Study of the Christmas Messages of Pope Pius XII* (London: Hollis and Carter, 1945).

38. Hebblethwaite, *Paul VI*, 169.

39. Falconi, *Silence*, 47–59.

40. Ibid., 59–61; Peter Hebblethwaite, *Pope John XXIII: Shepherd of the Modern World* (New York: Doubleday, 1985), 192–93.

41. Falconi, *Silence*, 86–88.

42. Ibid., 72; Smit, *Angelic Shepherd*, chaps. 12–13.

43. Falconi, *Silence*, 86–88.

44. Rhodes, *Vatican*, 339–47; Alexander Ramati, *While the Pope Kept Silent: Assisi and the Nazi Occupation* (London: George Allen & Unwin, 1978); Jonathan

Steinberg, *All or Nothing: The Axis and the Holocaust, 1941–1943* (New York: Rutledge, 1990), part 1, phase 1.

45. Falconi, *Silence,* 15; *l'Osservatore Romano,* April 9, 1959.

46. McKnight, *The Papacy,* 298; Michael Fogarty, *Christian Democracy in Western Europe, 1820–1953* (Notre Dame, Ind.: University of Notre Dame, 1957), chap. 23; on Sicily, Murphy, *La Popessa,* 233–36, and on his subordinates, 247–51.

47. McKnight, *The Papacy,* 304–6.

48. Ibid., 359, 310–11; Stella Alexander, *The Triple Myth: A Life of Archbishop Alojzije Stepinac* (New York: Columbia University Press, 1987).

49. McKnight, *The Papacy,* 312.

50. Ibid., 316; Arturo Carlo Jemolo, *Church and State in Italy, 1850–1950* (Oxford: Basil Blackwell, 1960), chap. 7.

51. McKnight, *The Papacy,* 340.

52. John Cooney, *The American Pope: The Life and Times of Francis Cardinal Spellman* (New York: Times Books, 1984), passim; Gerald P. Fogarty, *The Vatican and the American Hierarchy from 1870 to 1965* (Wilmington, Del.: Michael Glazier, 1985).

53. On aerial bombing, see Richard Rhodes, "The General and World War III," *The New Yorker* 71 (June 19, 1995): 47–59; on McCarthy: Thomas C. Reeves, *The Life and Times of Joe McCarthy; A Biography* (New York: Stein and Day, 1982), and David M. Oshinsky, *Conspiracy So Immense: The World of Joe McCarthy* (New York: Free Press, 1983).

54. Cooney, *American Pope,* 255–56; Murphy, *La Popessa,* 290–92.

55. Falconi, *The Popes in the Twentieth Century,* 297–98.

56. Smit, *Angelic Shepherd,* 165–69. Pius considered for a while calling Hitler "a killer of mankind" and denouncing specifically the concentration camps. Then he expressed doubts about FDR's veracity on these issues, due to Roosevelt's supposed prior knowledge of the Japanese attack on Pearl Harbor. In addition, Pius also apparently considered and then rejected excommunicating Hitler, who in the early part of his life was a Catholic. See Murphy, *La Popessa,* 211.

57. Smit, *Angelic Shepherd,* 175–77.

58. Ibid., 264–65.

59. Ibid., 272–73.

60. Falconi, *The Popes in the Twentieth Century,* 280.

61. Murphy, *La Popessa,* 292–93; Malachi Martin, *The Decline and Fall of the Roman Church* (New York: G. P. Putnam's Sons, 1981), 261–66; Tardini, *Memories,* 76, 83.

62. Murphy, *La Popessa,* passim; Tardini, *Memories,* 175.

63. Falconi, *The Popes in the Twentieth Century,* 300.

64. Hebblethwaite, *Pope John XXIII,* 270–71.

Chapter Seven / John XXIII and the Promise of Aggiornamento

1. Paul Hoffman, *O Vatican!: A Slightly Wicked View of the Holy See* (New York: Congdon & Weed, 1984), 19–27; Carlo Falconi, *The Popes in the Twentieth Century* (Boston: Little, Brown, 1967), 304–7; Barrett McGurn, *A Reporter Looks at the Vatican* (New York: Coward-McCann, 1962).

2. Francis J. Webber, "Pope Pius XII and the Vatican Council," *American Benedictine Review,* 21, 421–24; William A. Purdy, *The Church on the Move: The Characters and Policies of Pius XII and John XXIII* (New York: John Day, 1966).

3. Peter Hebblethwaite, *Paul VI, the First Modern Pope* (New York: Paulist Press, 1993), chap. 18.

4. Vittorio Gorresio, *The New Mission of Pope John XXIII* (New York: Funk & Wagnalls, 1970), 51. Roncalli was actually baptized Giuseppe Angelo; see Alden Hatch, *A Man Called John: The Life of Pope John XXIII* (New York: Hawthorn Books, 1963), 25. The only other patriarchs in the West are the bishop of Rome and the bishop of Lisbon.

5. Pope John XXIII, *Journal of a Soul* (New York: McGraw-Hill, 1965); Louis Michaels, *The Stories of Pope John: His Anecdotes and Legends* (Springfield, Ill.: Templegate, 1964), 15.

6. Richard James Cushing, *Call Me John* (Boston: St. Paul Editions, 1963), passim; Zsolt Aradi, *Pope John XXIII: An Authoritative Biography* (New York: Farrar, Straus and Cudahy, 1959).

7. Lawrence Elliott, *I Will Be Called John: A Biography of Pope John XXIII* (New York: E. P. Dutton, 1973), 15.

8. Ibid., 16; Meriol Trevor, *Pope John* (New York: Doubleday, 1967), chap. 1.

9. Cushing, *Call Me John,* 82; Zsolt Aradi, *John XXIII: Pope of the Council* (London: Burns & Oates, 1961), 4; Pope John XXIII, *Pope John XXIII: Letters to His Family* (New York: McGraw-Hill, 1970), 4; Ernesto Balducci, *John, "The Transitional Pope"* (New York: McGraw-Hill, 1965).

10. Hatch, *A Man Called John,* 47; Elliott, *I Will Be Called John,* 21; Giacomo Lercaro and Gabriele De Rosa, *John XXIII: Simpleton or Saint?* (Chicago: Franciscan Herald Press, 1965), part 2.

11. Peter Hebblethwaite, *Pope John XXIII: Shepherd of the Modern World* (Garden City, N.Y.: Doubleday, 1985), 54.

12. Hannah Arendt, *Men in Dark Times* (New York: Harcourt, Brace, Jovanovich, 1968), 68; E. E. Y. Hales, *Pope John and His Revolution* (London: Catholic Book Club, 1965), part 1; Giancarlo Zizola, *The Utopia of Pope John XXIII* (Maryknoll, N.Y.: Orbis Books, 1978).

13. Elliott, *I Will Be Called John,* 92.

14. Hebblethwaite, *Pope John,* 63–78.

15. Hatch, *A Man Called John,* 67; Elliott, *I Will Be Called John,* 83.

16. Hebblethwaite, *Pope John,* 113–15.

17. Elliott, *I Will Be Called John,* 96.

18. Cushing, *Call Me John,* 41.

19. Hebblethwaite, *Pope John,* 121–29; Elliott, *I Will Be Called John,* 106.

20. Elliott, *I Will Be Called John,* 101–3.

21. Ibid., 115; Hebblethwaite, *Pope John,* 138–40.

22. Hebblethwaite, *Pope John,* 133–36; Hebblethwaite, *Paul VI,* 104.

23. Hebblethwaite, *Pope John,* 143; Leone Algisi, *John the Twenty-Third* (London: Catholic Book Club, 1963), chap. 6.

24. Cushing, *Call Me John,* 43; Gorresio, *New Mission,* 72.

25. Hebblethwaite, *Pope John,* 149–52.

26. Elliott, *I Will Be Called John,* 156.

27. Hebblethwaite, *Pope John,* 169.

28. Ibid., 188.

29. Ibid., 195. On the Jews and the Good Friday prayer, see Elliott, *I Will Be Called John,* 284.

30. Hatch, *A Man Called John,* 126; Pope John XXIII, *Mission to France: 1944–1953* (New York: McGraw-Hill, 1966).

31. Cushing, *Call Me John,* 48; Paul Johnson, *Pope John XXIII* (Boston: Little, Brown, 1974), passim; Hales, *Pope John and His Revolution,* 18, claims that the demand was for the removal of *thirty-three* bishops.

32. Elliott, *I Will Be Called John,* 199; Hebblethwaite, *Pope John,* 218.

33. Hebblethwaite, *Pope John,* 227; Algisi, *John Twenty-Third,* chaps. 8–10.

34. Hebblethwaite, *Pope John,* 238; Algisi, *John Twenty-Third,* chap. 11.

35. Hebblethwaite, *Pope John,* 249.

36. Hatch, *A Man Called John,* 148.

37. Hebblethwaite, *Pope John,* 265.

38. Bernard R. Bonnot, *Pope John XXIII: An Astute Pastoral Leader* (Staten Island, N.Y.: Alba House, 1979), 6.

39. Elliott, *I Will Be Called John,* 243.

40. Hebblethwaite, *Pope John,* 286. A very different and more positive view of Cossa is presented in Nicola Fusco, *John Is His Name: A Survey of the Popes by That Name* (New York: Society of St. Paul, 1959), 11.

41. Hebblethwaite, *Pope John,* 291; Algisi, *John Twenty-Third,* chap. 13.

42. Hebblethwaite, *Pope John,* 293.

43. Ibid., 294–300; Michaels, *Stories of Pope John,* 61.

44. Cushing, *Call Me John,* 58; Elliott, *I Will Be Called John,* 272; Ernesto Balducci, *John "the Transitional Pope"* (New York: McGraw-Hill, 1965), 24; Michaels, *Stories of Pope John,* 34.

45. Hebblethwaite, *Pope John,* 310–24; Gorresio, *The New Mission,* chap. 10.

46. Paul I. Murphy, *La Popessa* (New York: Warner Books, 1983), 304.

47. Hebblethwaite, *Pope John,* 326–30.

48. Elliott, *I Will Be Called John,* 268.

49. Murphy, *La Popessa,* 229; Elliott, *I Will Be Called John,* 188.

50. Hebblethwaite, *Pope John,* 339–40.

51. Ibid., 348.

52. Ibid., 350.

53. Ibid., 361–68; Hales, *Pope John and His Revolution,* part 4.

54. Johnson, *Pope John,* 178–79.

55. Hebblethwaite, *Pope John,* 427–28; Gorresio, *The New Mission,* chap. 8.

56. Elliott, *I Will Be Called John,* 276.

57. Norman Cousins, *The Improbable Triumvirate: John F. Kennedy, Pope John, Nikita Khrushchev* (New York: W. W. Norton, 1972), passim; Roland Flamini, *Pope, Premier, President: The Cold War Summit That Never Was* (New York: Macmillan, 1980); Michael J. Cimerola, "The Vatican and the Soviet Union: The Impact of Pope John," M.A. thesis, George Washington University, 1976.

58. Cushing, *Call Me John,* 65; *The Papal Encyclicals 1958–1961,* comp. Claudia Carlen Ihm (Wilmington, N.C.: McGrath, 1981), 5:107–29; *The Encyclicals and Other Messages of John XXIII* (Washington, D.C.: TPS Press, 1964).

59. Hebblethwaite, *Pope John,* 229; Gorresio, *The New Mission,* 135.

60. Hebblethwaite, *Pope John,* 230; Gorresio, *The New Mission,* chap. 7.

61. *Mater et Magistra,* ed. Donald R. Campion and Eugene K. Culhane (New York: America Press, 1961); Peter Rega, *John XXIII and the Unity of Man* (Westminster, Md.: Newman Press, 1966); John F. Cronin, *The Social Teaching of Pope John XXIII* (Milwaukee: Bruce, 1963); Hebblethwaite, *Pope John,* 389, 378; Hales, *Pope John and His Revolution,* part 2.

62. Hebblethwaite, *Pope John,* 368.

63. Ibid., 270.

64. Ibid., 370–71.

65. Hans Küng, *The Council, Reform and Reunion* (New York: Sheed and Ward, 1961), published originally as *Konzil und Wiedervereingung.* Also see his later *The Council in Action* (New York: Sheed and Ward, 1963); and Robert B. Kaiser, *Pope, Council, and World; The Story of Vatican II* (London: Burns and Oates, 1963).

66. Gorresio, *The New Mission,* chap. 9, 383–84; Augustin Bea, *The Unity of Christians* (New York: Herder and Herder, 1963), chap. 5, and his *Ecumenism in Focus* (London: Geoffrey Chapman, 1969).

67. Hebblethwaite, *Pope John,* 411–12.

68. Ibid., 414.

69. Ibid., 416.

70. Gorresio, *The New Mission,* 92–93.

71. Hales, *Pope John and His Revolution,* 97.

72. George Bull, *Vatican Politics at the Second Vatican Council 1962* (New York: Oxford University Press, 1966), chaps. 1 and 2.

73. Harold Macmillan, *Winds of Change, 1914–1939* (New York: Harper & Row, 1966).

74. The following section on the first session of Vatican II relies heavily on Xavier Rynne, *Letters from Vatican City: Vatican II, First Session, Background and Debates* (New York: Farrar, Straus, 1963). This section draws on 70–71. Also: Hales, *Pope John and His Revolution,* part 3; Henri Fesquet, *The Drama of Vatican II: The Ecumenical Council, June, 1962–December, 1965* (New York: Random House, 1967), 3–102; Bernard Häring, *The Johannine Council: Witness to Destiny* (New York: Herder and Herder, 1963); Carlo Falconi, *Pope John and the Ecumenical Council: A Diary of the Second Vatican Council, September–December 1962* (Cleveland: World, 1964); Antoine Wenger, *Vatican II: Volume I: The First Session* (Westminster, Md.: Newman Press, 1966).

75. Hebblethwaite, *Pope John,* 435.

76. Rynne, *Letters,* 87–97.

77. Ibid., 100–109.

78. Ibid., 114–29. On the canon of the Mass, see Gorresio, *The New Mission,* 287.

79. Rynne, *Letters,* 141–42.

80. Bonnot, *Pope John XXIII,* 255.

81. Hebblethwaite, *Pope John,* 450–52; Elliott, *I Will Be Called John,* 281; Hatch, *A Man Named John,* 247.

82. Rynne, *Letters,* 201–18.

83. Michaels, *Stories of Pope John,* 40; *The HarperCollins Encyclopedia of Catholicism,* ed. Richard P. McBrien (New York: HarperCollins, 1995), 710.

84. Hebblethwaite, *Pope John,* 448.

85. Gorresio, *The New Mission,* 91; Howard Gardner, *Leading Minds: An Anatomy of Leadership* (New York: Basic Books, 1995), chap. 9; Hales, *Pope John and His Revolution,* 126; Eugene C. Bianchi, *John XXIII and American Protestants* (Washington, D.C.: Corpus Books, 1968), chap. 6; a more human picture is presented in Curtis Bill Pepper, *An Artist and the Pope* (New York: Grosset & Dunlap, 1968); Loris Capovilla, *The Heart and Mind of John XXIII: His Secretary's Intimate Recollection* (New York: Hawthorn, 1964); Michaels, *The Stories of Pope John XXIII,* passim.

86. Falconi, *Popes in the Twentieth Century,* 364.

87. Lercaro and De Rosa, *John XXIII: Simpleton or Saint?* part 1 deals with Roncalli in historical perspective. A critical judgment of the Council as a majestic gamble that failed is Malachi Martin, *Three Popes and the Cardinal* (New York: Farrar, Straus and Giroux, 1972).

Chapter Eight / Paul VI: The Perils of Aggiornamento

1. Peter Hebblethwaite, *Paul VI: The First Modern Pope* (New York: Paulist Press, 1993), 8; this is the most comprehensive biography of Paul and my account is indebted to both its chronology and some of its opinions; Wilton Wynn, *Keepers of the Keys: John XXIII, Paul VI, and John Paul II, Three Who Changed the Church* (New York: Random House, 1988), 24; and Alden Hatch, *Pope Paul VI* (New York: Random House, 1966), 192.

2. John C. Clancy, *Apostle for Our Time: Pope Paul VI* (New York: P. J. Kenedy, 1963), 144–49; *Correspondence, John XXIII* (New York: Herder and Herder, 1965).

3. Wynn, *Keepers of the Keys,* 46; Jean Guitton, *The Pope Speaks: Dialogues of Paul VI with Jean Guitton* (New York: Meredith Press, 1968), part 1; Hatch, *Pope Paul VI,* 192.

4. Hatch, *Pope Paul VI,* chaps. 2 and 3; Corrado Pallenberg, *Pope Paul VI,* rev. ed. (New York: G. P. Putnam's Sons, 1968), chaps. 1–4; Roy MacGregor-Hastie, *Pope Paul VI* (London: Frederick Muller, 1964), passim; William E. Barrett, *Shepherd of Mankind; A Biography of Pope Paul VI* (Garden City, N.Y.: Doubleday, 1964), Book I; Jose Luis Gonzalez and Teofilo Perez, *Paul VI* (Boston: St. Paul Editions, 1964).

5. Owen Chadwick, *The Christian Church in the Cold War* (New York: Penguin Books, 1991), chap. 1.

6. Francis X. Murphy, "A Brief Biography of Paul VI," in *Paul VI: Critical Appraisals,* ed. James Andrews (New York: Bruce, 1970), 140; Archbishop Angelo dell'Acqua said during Pius's illness in 1954 that Montini was running the Church; see Hatch, *Pope Paul VI,* 99.

7. Wynn, *Keepers of the Keys,* 26–28; Hatch, *Pope Paul VI,* 104, 107; Malachi Martin, *Three Popes and the Cardinal* (New York: Farrar, Straus and Giroux, 1972), 8.

8. Clancy, *Apostle for Our Time,* 117; James F. Andrews, "The Pope in an Age

of Insecurity," in his *Paul VI: Critical Appraisals,* 7–27; Hatch, *Pope Paul VI,* 118; Guitton, *The Pope Speaks,* 58.

9. Hebblethwaite, *Paul VI,* 318.

10. Alberto Melloni, "Pope John XXIII: Open Questions for a Biography," *Catholic Historical Review* 72 (January 1986): 51–67.

11. Clancy, *Apostle for Our Time,* 189–90; Hatch, *Pope Paul VI,* 147. After the conclave one cardinal is supposed to have said of Montini's election, "We have John with Pacelli's brains" (Hatch, *Pope Paul VI*), 149. On new rules of election, see Celestine Bohlen, "New Rules for Electing Pope Stress Secrecy," *New York Times,* February 25, 1996, 4. Since 1945 the rules required that a candidate had to get a majority of two-thirds plus one of those voting.

12. Hebblethwaite, *Paul VI,* 328–29.

13. Carlo Falconi, *Pope John and the Ecumenical Council: A Diary of the Second Vatican Council, September–December 1962* (New York: World, 1964). On "docility," see Aelred Graham, *Zen Catholicism* (New York: Crossroad, 1963), 46; Giancarlo Zizola, *The Utopia of Pope John XXIII* (Maryknoll, N.Y.: Orbis Books, 1978).

14. Rather useful are twelve pamphlet portraits of cardinals in *The Men Who Made the Council,* ed. Michael Novak (Notre Dame, Ind.: University of Notre Dame Press, 1964). See also the anthology by Walter M. Abbott, *Twelve Council Fathers* (New York: Macmillan, 1963).

15. Hebblethwaite, *Paul VI,* 2–25; Guitton, *The Pope Speaks,* 11, 110–12.

16. I have followed closely the account of Xavier Rynne [Francis X. Murphy] in summarizing the proceedings of Vatican II. See also Henri Fesquet, *The Drama of Vatican II: The Ecumenical Council, June, 1962–December, 1965* (New York: Random House, 1967); *Vatican Council II,* ed. Austin Flannery (Northport, N.Y.: Costello, 1987); *The Documents of Vatican II* (New York: Herder and Herder, 1966). Relevant here is Rynne, *The Second Session: The Debates and Decrees of Vatican Council II, September 29 to December 4, 1963* (New York: Farrar, Straus, 1964), 10–33.

17. Rynne, *Second Session,* 37.

18. Ibid., 158; George Bull, *Vatican Politics and the Second Vatican Council, 1962–5* (New York: Oxford University Press, 1966), chap. 5; Wynn, *Keepers of the Keys,* 50; Augustin Bea, *Ecumenism in Focus* (London: Geoffrey Chapman, 1969).

19. Michael Serafian, pseud. [Malachi Martin], *The Pilgrim* (London: Farrar, Straus, 1964), 159; Hugh Morley, *The Pope and the Press* (Notre Dame, Ind.: University of Notre Dame Press, 1968); Edward L. Heston, *The Press and Vatican II* (Notre Dame, Ind.: University of Notre Dame Press, 1967).

20. Rynne, *Second Session,* 62–63.

21. Ibid., 88; Hans Küng, *Infallible? An Inquiry* (Garden City, N.Y.: Doubleday, 1971). A more moderate view is Yves Congar, *Diversity and Communion* (London: S.C.M. Press, 1984).

22. Rynne, *Second Session,* 99, 100, 104, 111, 117.

23. Ibid., 117–18; Paula Butturini, "Vatican Move Raises Question," *Boston Globe,* November 23, 1995, 2.

24. Hebblethwaite, *Paul VI,* 358–65.

25. *Pope Paul VI in the Holy Land* (New York: Herder and Herder, 1964) is the source for this section. Also see Hebblethwaite, *Paul VI*, 372–75; and Hatch, *Pope Paul VI*, 166–67; George Cornell, *Voyage of Faith: The Catholic Church in Transition* (New York: Odyssey, 1966), 144–46.

26. Cornell, *Voyage of Faith*, 72, 85; Hebblethwaite, *Paul VI*, 350, 375–77; on the papacy as an obstacle, 350; E. J. Stormon, *Towards the Healing of Schism: The Sees of Rome and Constantinople: Public Statements and Correspondence between the Holy See and the Ecumenical Patriarchate, 1958–1984* (New York: Paulist Press, 1987).

27. Hebblethwaite, *Paul VI*, 381–82.

28. Xavier Rynne, *The Third Session: The Debates and Decrees of Vatican Council II, September 14 to November 21, 1964* (New York: Farrar, Straus & Giroux, 1965), 3–7.

29. Ibid., 25–33, 128.

30. Ibid., 141; Hatch, *Pope Paul VI*, 195; *Augustin Cardinal Bea: Spiritual Profile: Notes from the Cardinal Diary*, ed. Stjepan Schmidt (London: Geoffrey Chapman, 1971).

31. Rynne, *The Third Session*, 184–89.

32. Hebblethwaite, *Paul VI*, 403–6; Bull, *Vatican Politics*, 63.

33. Hebblethwaite, *Paul VI*, 408–12; Hatch, *Pope Paul VI*, 210–11; Cornell, *Voyage of Faith*, 52.

34. Hebblethwaite, *Paul VI*, 423–27.

35. Xavier Rynne, *Fourth Session* (New York: Farrar, Straus and Giroux, 1966), chap. 2.

36. Bill Adler, *Pope Paul in the United States: His Mission for Peace on Earth, October 4, 1965* (New York: Hawthorn Books, 1965); *An Instrument of Your Peace: The Mission for Peace by Pope Paul VI and His Momentous Visit to America* (New York: Commemorative Publications, 1965); Joseph Califano, *The Triumph and Tragedy of Lyndon Johnson: The White House Years* (New York: Simon and Schuster, 1991), 71–73.

37. Rynne, *Fourth Session*, 56, 73–75.

38. Ibid., 137–47.

39. Ibid., 149.

40. Ibid., 163.

41. See "Nostra Aetate," http://list.serv.American.edu/catholic/church/VaticanII/nostra-aetate.html.

42. Rynne, *Fourth Session*, 201–34.

43. Hebblethwaite, *Paul VI*, 436–59; Cornell, *Voyage of Faith*, 3; Tad Szulc, *Pope John Paul II* (New York: Scribner, 1995), chap. 15.

44. Hebblethwaite, *Paul VI*, 462–65; Owen Chadwick, *Michael Ramsey: A Life* (Oxford: Clarendon Press, 1990), chap. 13.

45. John T. Noonan, Jr., *Contraception: A History of Its Treatment by the Catholic Theologians and Canonists* (New York: New American Library, 1965), part 1.

46. Hatch, *Pope Paul VI*, 222, on "Vatican roulette" characterization; John N. Kotre, *Simple Gifts: The Lives of Pat and Patty Crowley* (New York: Andrews and McMeel, 1979), chap. 9.

47. Szulc, *Pope John Paul II,* 253.

48. Dan Sullivan, "A History of Catholic Thinking on Contraception," in *What Modern Catholics Think about Birth Control: A New Symposium,* ed. William Birmingham (New York: New American Library, 1964), 28–72; Noonan, *Contraception,* parts 1 and 2; Charles F. Curran, "Natural Law and Contemporary Moral Theology," in his edited *Contraception: Authority and Dissent* (New York: Herder and Herder, 1969), 151–75. The antiwomen quotes are from Sullivan; William E. May, *Contraception: Humanae Vitae and Catholic Sexual Thought* (Chicago: Franciscan Herald Press, 1984) reports that the majority report was written between June 4 and 9, 1964.

49. "Humanae Vitae," in *The Papal Encyclicals 1958–1981,* comp. Claudia Carlen Ihm (Wilmington, N.C.: McGrath, 1981), 5:223–36; Joseph A. Selling, "The Reaction to Humanae Vitae: A Study in Special and Fundamental Theology," 2 vols., S.T.D. dissertation, Catholic University of Louvain, 1978; *The Teaching of Humanae Vitae: A Defense* (San Francisco: Ignatius Press, 1988); John Mahoney, *The Making of Moral Theology: A Study of the Roman Catholic Tradition* (Oxford: Clarendon Press, 1987), chap. 2; *Human Sexuality, New Directions in American Catholic Thought: A Study,* ed. Anthony Kosnik (New York: Paulist Press, 1977); Norman St. John-Stevas, *The Agonizing Choice: Birth Control, Religion and the Law* (London: Eyre and Spottiswoode, 1971); Janet E. Smith, *Humanae Vitae: A Generation Later* (Washington, D.C.: Catholic University Press, 1991); Robert Blair Kaiser, *The Politics of Sex and Religion: A Case History in the Development of Doctrine, 1962–1984* (Kansas City, Mo.: Leaven Press, 1985); *The Birth Control Debate,* ed. Robert C. Hoyt (Kansas City, Mo.: National Catholic Reporter, 1968); John Paul II, *Reflections of Humanae Vitae: Conjugal Morality and Spirituality* (Boston: St. Paul's Editions, 1984); Andrews, "The Pope in an Age of Insecurity," 30; Jay P. Dolan, *The American Catholic Experience: A History from Colonial Times to the Present* (Notre Dame, Ind.: University of Notre Dame Press, 1992), 435–38; George Gallup, Jr., and Jim Castelli, *The American Catholic People: Their Beliefs, Practices, and Values* (Garden City, N.Y.: Doubleday, 1987), 52, 55, 56, 62, 93, also indicates that only 60 percent believe the pope is infallible under certain circumstances.

50. Andrew Greeley and Mary Greeley Durkin, *How to Save the Catholic Church* (New York: Viking, 1984), indicates that nine out of ten Catholics do not accept the birth control ban with four out of five weekly communicants dissenting. The decline of vocations is in Dolan, *American Catholic Experience,* 435–38.

51. Yves Congar, *Challenge to the Church: The Case of Archbishop Lefebvre* (Huntington, Ind.: Our Sunday Visitor, 1976); Joseph A. Jungmann, *The Mass of the Roman Rite: Its Origins and Development,* 2 vols. (Westminster, Md.: Christian Classics, 1986); Eugene Kennedy, *Tomorrow's Catholics, Yesterday's Church: The Two Cultures of American Catholicism* (New York: Harper & Row, 1988); Annibale Bugnini, *The Reform of the Liturgy 1948–1975* (Collegeville, Minn.: The Liturgical Press, 1990); Peter Hebblethwaite, *The Runaway Church: Postconciliar Growth or Decline* (New York: Seabury Press, 1975), chap. 2.

52. A more sympathetic view is given in the judicious volume Thomas Bokenkotter, *A Concise History of the Catholic Church,* rev. ed. (New York: Image Books, 1990), chap. 34.

53. Hebblethwaite, *Paul VI*, 475–76; on St. Peter Celestine V, see J. N. D. Kelly, *The Oxford Dictionary of Popes* (New York: Oxford University Press, 1986), 206–8.

54. Some of the popular histories of the Jesuits loosely call them an "order," that is, a group of people who live under a religious rule like the Benedictines. I have used that nomenclature as well as "Society" which is its actual title. For a critical review of the Council see Avery Dulles, "Vatican II and the American Experience of Church," in *Vatican II: Open Questions and New Horizons,* ed. Gerald M. Fagin (Wilmington, Del.: Michael Glazier, 1984); 38–57; *Vatican II: Assessments and Perspectives, Twenty-Five Years After (1962–1987),* ed. Rene Latourelle, 3 vols. (New York: The Paulist Press, 1988).

55. Hebblethwaite, *Paul VI*, 479; a different view of Paul's achievements is contained in Michael Novak, *The Open Church: Vatican II, Act II* (New York: Macmillan, 1964); he has since become a major figure praising the ethical implications of moving toward capitalism and celebrating the profit motive in his *Spirit of Democratic Capitalism* (Lanham, Md.: Madison Books, 1991). See also *The Gospel of Peace and Justice: Catholic Social Teaching since Pope John,* ed. Joseph Gremillion (Maryknoll, N.Y.: Orbis Books, 1976); on Medellín: Penny Lernoux, *People of God: The Struggle for World Catholicism* (New York: Viking Books, 1989), 25–26.

56. Hebblethwaite, *Paul VI*, 495–97; Bokenkotter, *A Concise History,* 377–80; Raymond Hedin, *Married to the Church* (Bloomington: Indiana University Press, 1995); Thomas C. Fox, *Sexuality and Catholics* (New York: George Braziller, 1995), chap. 6; Lawrence K. Altman, "Study Challenges Beliefs on Conception," *New York Times,* December 7, 1995), A 28; on Nigeria see Salvatore J. Adams, "The Anguish of the Pope," in Andrews, ed., *Paul VI,* 39.

57. *Gay Priests,* ed. James Wolf (San Francisco: Harper and Row, 1989), 60, found that 48.5 percent of priests and 55.1 percent of current seminarians were judged by others to be gay, although the methodology of this study leaves much to be desired; see *The Vatican and Homosexuality: A Reaction to the "Letter to the Bishops of the Catholic Church on the Pastoral Care of Homosexual Persons,"* ed. Jeannine Gramick and Pat Furey (New York: Crossroad, 1988), for a larger context arising from the 1986 letter on the topic of homosexuality; Philip Jenkins, *Pedophiles and Priests: Anatomy of a Contemporary Crisis* (New York: Oxford University Press 1996); James F. Clarity, "Ireland's Catholic Hierarchy Confronts Sex Abuse of Children," *New York Times,* October 19, 1995, A11; Annie Murphy and Peter de Rosa, *Forbidden Fruit: The True History of My Secret Love Affair with Ireland's Most Powerful Bishop* (Boston: Little, Brown, 1993).

58. Bokenkotter, *A Concise History,* 385–86; Hebblethwaite, *Paul VI,* 490–91.

59. Hebblethwaite, *Paul VI,* 500–506; Califano, *The Triumph and Tragedy of Lyndon Johnson,* 326–27; *American Catholics and Vietnam,* ed. Thomas E. Quigley (Grand Rapids, Mich.: Williams B. Eerdmans, 1968).

60. On the Suenens controversy see José de Broucker, *The Suenens Dossier: The Case for Collegiality* (Notre Dame, Ind.: Fides, 1970); Elizabeth Hamilton, *Cardinal Suenens: A Portrait* (London: Hodder and Stoughton, 1975); Léon-Joseph Suenens, *Coresponsibility in the Church* (New York: Herder and Herder, 1968).

61. Hebblethwaite, *Paul VI,* 523–34.

62. Ibid., 536–38.

63. Ibid., 543–52.

64. Ibid., 585–93; Edward D. O'Connor, *Pope Paul and the Spirit: Charisms and Church Renewal in the Teaching of Paul VI* (Notre Dame, Ind.: Ave Maria Press, 1978); Léon-Joseph Suenens, *A New Pentecost?* (New York: Seabury Press, 1975).

65. Hebblethwaite, *The Runaway Church*, 86; Hebblethwaite, *Paul VI*, 595–603; Giuseppe De Rosa, "Learning the Hard Way: The Referendum on Divorce in Italy," *The Month* (August 1974): 668–71.

66. Hebblethwaite, *Paul VI*, 610–11.

67. Richard Hammer, *The Vatican Connection* (New York: Holt, Rinehart & Winston, 1982), chaps. 16–18; a more general treatment is Avro Manhattan, *The Vatican Billions: Two Thousand Years of Wealth Accumulation from St. Peter to the Space Age* (London: Paravision Books, 1972). The figure of $200 million may be exaggerated. Thirty million is also noted, and the role of Tisserant and other Vatican officials may not be supported by other sources. See Luigi DiFonzo, *St. Peter's Banker* (New York: Franklin Watts, 1983); Nick Tosches, *Power on Earth* (New York: Arbor House, 1986); Rupert Cornwell, *"God's Banker"* (New York: Dodd, Mead, 1983); Charles Raw, *The Moneychangers* (London: Harvill, 1992); Larry Gurwin, *The Calvi Affair: Death of a Banker* (London: Macmillan, 1983); and Manfred Ketrs de Vries, "Leaders on the Couch: The Case of Roberto Calvi," *Research and the Development of Pedagogical Materials* (Fontainebleau, France: Insead, 1990).

68. Lernoux, *People of God*, 302–24; in 1984 Pope John Paul II has allowed the celebration of the Tridentine Mass under certain strictly controlled circumstances.

69. Hebblethwaite, *Paul VI*, 627.

70. Ibid., 628–32; Malachi Martin, *The Jesuits: The Society of Jesus and the Betrayal of the Roman Catholic Church* (New York: Simon and Schuster, 1987).

71. Hebblethwaite, *Paul VI*, 7, on the Hamlet–Don Quixote quote; 670–73 on Lefebvre.

72. Bugnini, *Reform of the Liturgy*, passim.

73. On modern man remark: Andrews, "The Pope in the Age of Anxiety," 23; Leonard Sciascia, *The Moro Affair and the Mystery of Majorana* (Manchester: Carcanet, 1987).

74. Hebblethwaite, *Paul VI*, 710.

Chapter Nine / John Paul II: The Uneasy Agenda of Restoration

1. Francis X. Murphy, *The Papacy Today* (New York: Macmillan, 1981) 141.

2. Ibid., chap. 7; Albino Luciani, *Illustrissimi: Letters from John Paul I* (Bedford, England: Mount, 1978); Peter Hebblethwaite, *The Year of Three Popes* (New York: Collins, 1978), chaps. 5–9; Andrew Greeley, *The Making of the Popes 1978: The Politics of Intrigue in the Vatican* (Kansas City: Andrews and McMeel, 1979); Malachi Martin, *The Decline and Fall of the Roman Church* (New York: G. P. Putnam's Sons, 1981).

3. Trevor Hall and Kathryn Spink, *Pope John Paul II: A Man and His People* (New York: Exeter, 1985), 7; David Remmick, "The Pope in Crisis," *New Yorker*, October 17, 1994, 50–64.

4. Hall, *Pope John Paul II*, 8.

5. David A. Yallop, *In God's Name: An Investigation into the Murder of Pope John Paul I* (New York: Random, 1984), and the rejoinder, John Cornwell, *Thief in the Night: The Death of John Paul I* (New York: Viking, 1989).

6. Peter Hebblethwaite, "John Paul I" in *Modern Catholicism: Vatican II and After*, ed. Adrian Hastings (New York: Oxford University Press, 1991), 444–46.

7. Tad Szulc, *Pope John Paul II* (New York: Scribner, 1995), 273; Nicholas Cheetham, *Keepers of the Keys: A History of the Popes from St. Peter to John Paul II* (New York: Scribner, 1983), chap. 25; Adam Bujak, *John Paul II* (San Francisco: Ignatius Press, 1992); Jef de Roeck, *John Paul II: The Man from Poland* (London: Geoffrey Chapman, 1979); George Huntson Williams, *The Mind of John Paul II: Origin of His Thought and Action* (New York: Seabury Press, 1981); and Carl Bernstein and Marco Politi, *His Holiness: John Paul II and the Hidden History of Our Time* (New York: Doubleday, 1996).

8. Szulc, *Pope John Paul II*, 272; Bernstein and Politi, *His Holiness*, 159, 166.

9. Ibid., 274.

10. Ibid., 141, says that Wojtyla met Padre Pio in the 1940s, but in *The Pope from Poland: An Assessment*, ed. John Whale (London: Collins, 1980), 260, the time is placed in the 1960s, and it was predicted by Pio that he would have a short papacy terminated by violence.

11. George Blazynski, *Pope John Paul II: A Man from Poland* (New York: Dell, 1979), 3.

12. Peter Hebblethwaite, *Pope John Paul II and the Church* (Kansas City, Mo.: Sheed and Ward, 1995), 12; Hall, *Pope John Paul II*, 14.

13. Szulc, *Pope John Paul II*, 271–81; Blazynski, *Pope John Paul II*, 106.

14. Mieczyslaw Malinski, *Pope John Paul II: The Life of Karol Wojtyla* (New York: Seabury Press, 1979), 4.

15. Szulc, *Pope John Paul II*, 79, 283; Blazynski, *Pope John Paul II*, 3; Bernstein and Politi, *His Holiness*, 370.

16. Szulc, *Pope John Paul II*, 17, 117; John Paul II, *"Be Not Afraid": John Paul II Speaks Out on His Life, His Beliefs, and His Inspiring Vision for Humanity* (New York St. Martin's Press, 1984), 13–14; Blazynski, *Pope John Paul II*, 33, indicates that his mother died of a heart ailment; while Mary Craig, *Man from a Far Country: A Portrait of Pope John Paul II* (London: Hodder & Stoughton, 1982), 3, indicates that she died in childbirth and that the other female child who died after living only one day was born three years before Karol; Bernstein and Politi, *His Holiness*, says that his mother was a seamstress (28).

17. Hall, *Pope John Paul II*, 16; Bernstein and Politi, *His Holiness*, 55.

18. Malinski, *Pope John Paul II*, 48.

19. Craig, *Man from a Far Country*, 24; Malinski, *Pope John Paul II*, 37; Pope John Paul II, *A Gift and a Mystery* (New York: Doubleday, 1996), 5–6.

20. Hall, *Pope John Paul II*, 17–18. On Wojtyla's underground activity, see Blazynski, *Pope John Paul II*, 49, substantiated by Dr. Joseph L. Lichten, the representative of the Anti-Defamation League of B'nai B'rith in Rome; a denial is in Bernstein and Politi, *His Holiness*, 60.

21. Szulc, *Pope John Paul II*, 101–3.

22. Blazynski, *Pope John Paul II*, 51. Wojtyla has said that it was Cardinal

Sapieha who opposed his joining the Carmelites, in John Paul II, *"Be Not Afraid,"* 32; and Pope John Paul II, *Gift and Mystery,* 24–25.

23. Blazynski, *Pope John Paul II,* 58.

24. Szulc, *Pope John Paul II,* 147.

25. Craig, *Man from a Far Country,* 40.

26. Karol Wojtyla, "The Acting Person" in *Analecta Husserliana* (Boston: D. Reidel, 1979), vol. 10; Kevin Wildes "In the Name of the Father," *New Republic,* December 26, 1994, 21–25.

27. Szulc, *Pope John Paul II,* 155–56; Craig, *Man from a Far Country,* 52.

28. The best known of Wojtyla's verse plays is *The Jeweler's Shop: A Meditation on the Sacrament of Matrimony Passing on Occasion into a Drama* (New York: Random House, 1980; appeared first in December 1960). A collection of his verse in English is *The Place Within* (New York: Random House, 1982).

29. Szulc, *Pope John Paul II,* 171.

30. Szulc, *Pope John Paul II,* 19, 181; Malinski, *Pope John Paul II,* 42, says erroneously that the pontiff had a mild form of leukemia.

31. Szulc, *Pope John Paul II,* 95, 190. Later *l'Osservatore Romano* listed Wojtyla as having published five books, forty-four philosophical pieces, twenty-seven essays, and a variety of poetry.

32. Andrew N. Woznicki, *A Christian Humanism: Karol Wojtyla's Existential Personalism* (New Britain, Conn.: Mariel Publications, 1980), 62; Malinski, *Pope John Paul II,* 113; Ronald Modras, "The Moral Philosophy of Pope John Paul II," *Theological Studies* 41 (December 1980): 683–97; Bernstein and Politi, *His Holiness,* 133, 144.

33. Karol Wojtyla, *Love and Responsibility,* rev. ed. (New York: Farrar, Straus, Giroux, 1995).

34. Craig, *Man from a Far Country,* 59; Bernstein and Politi, *His Holiness,* 88.

35. Szulc, *Pope John Paul II,* 205–12, 223.

36. Ibid., 218.

37. Blazynski, *Pope John Paul II,* 170.

38. Szulc, *Pope John Paul II,* 253–55; Robert McClory, *Turning Point: The Inside Story of the Papal Birth Control Commission and How Humanae Vitae Changed the Life of Patty Crowley and the Future of the Church* (New York: Crossroad, 1995).

39. Blazynski, *Pope John Paul II,* 83.

40. Malinski, *Pope John Paul II,* chap. 19.

41. Hall, *Pope John Paul II,* 33; Bernstein and Politi, *His Holiness,* 102.

42. Craig, *Man from a Far Country,* 83.

43. Szulc, *Pope John Paul II,* 243–44; Bernstein and Politi, *His Holiness,* 107, 162.

44. Karol Wojtyla, *Sign of Contradiction* (New York: Seabury Press, 1979); Malinski, *Pope John Paul II,* 42; Bernstein and Politi, *His Holiness,* 482.

45. John Paul II, *"Be Not Afraid,"* passim; André Frossard, *Portrait of John Paul II* (San Francisco: Ignatius Press, 1990), 15.

46. Peter Hebblethwaite, *Paul VI* (New York: Paulist Press, 1993), 7; James F. Andrews, "The Pope in an Age of Insecurity," in *Paul VI: Critical Appraisals,* ed. James F. Andrews (New York: Bruce, 1970), 14–15; Peter Hebblethwaite, *The Run-*

away Church (New York: Seabury Press, 1975); George A. Schlichte, *Politics in the Purple Kingdom: The Derailment of Vatican II* (Kansas City, Mo.: Sheed & Ward, 1993).

47. Peter Hebblethwaite, *Introducing John Paul II: The Populist Pope* (London: Collins, 1982), 54; Bernstein and Politi, *His Holiness*, 482.

48. Hebblethwaite, *Introducing*, 21; Whale, *The Pope from Poland*, 27; Bernstein and Politi, *His Holiness*, 424.

49. On the romantic tradition, see John Paul II, *Crossing the Threshold of Hope* (New York: Knopf, 1995), 120; John Paul II, *"Be Not Afraid."*

50. Szulc, *Pope John Paul II*, 23.

51. Peter Hebblethwaite, *The Next Pope* (San Francisco: HarperSanFrancisco, 1995).

52. Arno Mayer, *The Persistence of the Old Regime: Europe in the Great War* (New York: Pantheon, 1981); "Pope Sees Larger Role for Nuns," *Washington Post*, March 29, 1995, 2, from Reuters News Service. Information on women priests in Czechoslovakia was carried on the Associated Press wire and reported in the United States in November 1995.

53. Penny Lernoux, *People of God: The Struggle for World Catholicism* (New York: Viking, 1989), 24–28.

54. Szulc, *Pope John Paul II*, 325.

55. The respected historian Jaroslav Pelikan in his *Jesus through the Centuries: His Place in the History of Culture* (New Haven: Yale University Press, 1985), argues that the images of Jesus have changed immensely over the years.

56. Szulc, *Pope John Paul II*, 327.

57. Whale, ed., *The Pope from Poland*, 65–86.

58. Ibid.; David Willey, *God's Politician: John Paul at the Vatican* (Boston: Faber and Faber, 1992), chap. 6.

59. Phillip Berryman, *The Religious Roots of Rebellion: Christians in Central American Revolutions* (Maryknoll, N.Y.: Orbis, 1984), 275; John Paul II, *"Be Not Afraid,"* 142; Hall and Spink, *Pope John Paul II*, 331.

60. Hall, *Pope John Paul II*, 31; Willey, *God's Politician*, chap. 1.

61. Whale, ed., *The Pope from Poland*, 112.

62. On the pope's visits to Poland see Szulc, *Pope John Paul II*, chap. 23; and Whale, ed., *The Pope from Poland*, passim. The quote on the war is in Whale's volume, 165.

63. Willey, *God's Politician*, 40–43. A postscript on Poland is Jane Perlez, "Shrinking Gap between Church and State," *New York Times*, July 17, 1995, A3.

64. The ties to the Reagan administration are presented in Bernstein and Politi, *His Holiness*, passim; Peter Schweizer, *Victory: The Reagan Administration's Secret Strategy That Hastened the Collapse of the Soviet Empire* (New York: Atlantic Monthly Press, 1994).

65. Szulc, *Pope John Paul II*, chap. 21.

66. Frossard, *Portrait of John Paul II*, 105; Remmick, "The Pope in Crisis," 54; Bernstein and Politi, *His Holiness*, 351 and 476.

67. Whale, ed., *The Pope from Poland*, 117–19, 229–31; John Paul II, *Crossing the Threshold of Hope*, 130–31; Bernstein and Politi, *His Holiness*, 494.

68. Edward Schillebeeckx, *Jesus: An Experiment in Christology* (New York: Vintage, 1981); Bernstein and Politi, *His Holiness,* 48.

69. Peter Hebblethwaite, *The New Inquisition? Schillebeeckx and Küng* (London: Collins, 1980); *Contraception: Authority and Dissent,* ed. by Charles E. Curran (New York: Herder and Herder, 1969); John A. Coleman, *An American Strategic Theology* (New York: Paulist Press, 1982); Eugene Kennedy, "A Dissenting Voice: Catholic Theologian David Tracy," *New York Times Magazine,* November 9, 1986, 21+.

70. Hebblethwaite, *Introducing,* 69.

71. Louis Baldwin, *The Pope and the Mavericks* (Buffalo, N.Y.: Prometheus Books, 1988), 45.

72. Ibid., 71–99.

73. Ibid., 101–3; Kenneth A. Briggs, *Holy Siege: The Year that Shook Catholic America* (San Francisco: HarperSanFrancisco, 1992).

74. Craig, *Man from a Far Country,* 197–98; Joseph Ratzinger and Vittorio Messori, *The Ratzinger Report: An Exclusive Interview on the State of the Church* (San Francisco: Ignatius Press, 1985). See also his more moderate and scholarly *Church, Ecumenism and Politics: New Essays in Eccesiology* (New York: Crossroad, 1988).

75. Craig, *Man from a Far Country,* 158.

76. Jean Lacouture, *Jesuits: A Multibiography* (Washington, D.C.: Counterpoint, 1995), chaps. 16–17; Malachi Martin, *The Jesuits: The Society of Jesus and the Betrayal of the Roman Catholic Church* (New York: Simon and Schuster, 1987), part 4; Henry Kamm, "The Secret World of Opus Dei," *New York Times Magazine,* January 8, 1984, 38+; Bernstein and Politi, *His Holiness,* 422.

77. Szulc, *Pope John Paul II,* 355–67.

78. Frossard, *Portrait of John Paul II,* 68.

79. Paul B. Henze, *The Plot to Kill the Pope* (New York: Scribner, 1983); Claire Sterling, *The Time of the Assassins* (New York: Holt Rinehart & Winston, 1985). An unproven tale is that the pope and Leonid Brezhnev actually met on a Soviet warship in the Mediterranean; see Luigi Forni, *The Dove and the Bear* (Kent, England: Midas Books, 1983.) Brezhnev said, "All that stuff about communism is a tall tale for popular consumption. After all, we can't leave the people with no faith. The church was taken away, the czar was shot, and something had to be substituted. So let the people build communism" (*Washington Post Book World,* July 9, 1995, 3). On Fatima, see Timothy Tindal-Robertson, *Fatima, Russia and Pope John Paul II: How Mary Interviewed to Deliver Russia from Marxist Atheism May 13, 1981–December 15, 1991,* 2d ed. (Devon: Augustine, 1992).

80. Frossard, *Portrait of John Paul II,* 58.

81. Hansjakob Stehle, *Eastern Politics of the Vatican 1917–1979* (Athens: Ohio University Press, 1981), chap. 9.

82. George A. Kelly, *The Battle for the American Church Revisited* (San Francisco, Ignatius Press, 1995), chap. 6; Andrew Greeley, *The Catholic Myth: The Behavior and Beliefs of American Catholics* (New York: Scribner, 1990).

83. James Reston, *Galileo: A Life* (New York: HarperCollins, 1994), passim.

84. Hebblethwaite, *Introducing,* 89–91; Gordon Thomas and Max Morgan-Witts, *Averting Armageddon* (Garden City, N.Y.: Doubleday, 1984); *Catholics and*

Nuclear War: A Commentary on the Challenge of Peace, the U.S. Catholic Bishops Letter on War and Peace, ed. by Philip J. Murnion (New York: Crossroad, 1983).

85. Hebblethwaite, *Introducing,* 99–113.

86. Phillip Berryman, *Liberation Theology: Essential Facts about the Revolutionary Movement in Latin America — and Beyond* (Philadelphia: Temple University Press, 1987), 109.

87. Whale, ed., *The Pope from Poland,* 93.

88. Berryman, *Liberation Theology,* 108; Humberto Belli, *Breaking Faith: The Sandinista Revolution and Its Impact on Freedom and Christian Faith in Nicaragua* (Westchester, Ill.: Crossway Books, 1985); Robert Kagan, *A Twilight Struggle: American Power and Nicaragua* (New York: Free Press, 1996).

89. Julia Preston, "Pope Returns in Jubilation and Triumph to Nicaragua," *New York Times,* February 8, 1996, A14; Larry Rohter, "Church Bombings Worry Nicaragua as Papal Visit Nears," *New York Times,* January 21, 1996, 3.

90. Some of the major works on liberation theology that I have reviewed are: Leonardo Boff and Clodovis Boff, *Salvation and Liberation* (Maryknoll, N.Y.: Orbis, 1984); Gustavo Gutiérrez, *A Theology of Liberation: History, Politics, and Salvation* (Maryknoll, N.Y.: Orbis, 1988); Leonardo Boff, *Ecclesiogenesis: The Base Communities Reinvent the Church* (Maryknoll, N.Y.: Orbis, 1986); *Liberation South, Liberation North,* ed. Michael Novak (Washington: American Enterprise Institute, 1981), especially Juan Luis Segundo, "Capitalism-Socialism: A Theological Crux," 7–23; Richard Shaull, *Heralds of a New Reformation: The Poor of South and North America* (Maryknoll, N.Y.: Orbis, 1984); José P. Miranda, *Marx and the Bible: A Critique of the Philosophy of Oppression* (Maryknoll, N.Y.: Orbis, 1974).

91. Berryman, *Liberation Theology,* 110.

92. Craig, *Man from a Far Country,* 166–70; Norman St. John-Stevas, *Pope John Paul II: His Travels and Mission* (London: Faber and Faber, 1982), 45; Bernstein and Politi, *His Holiness,* 510.

93. Ibid., 173–77.

94. Hebblethwaite, *Introducing,* 115–16.

95. Ibid., 117–21.

96. Craig, *Man from a Far Country,* 178–79.

97. Ibid., 181; Frossard, *Portrait of John Paul II,* 90.

98. Hebblethwaite, *Introducing,* 142.

99. Ibid., 149–53.

100. Willey, *God's Politician,* 85–86.

101. Kelly, *The Battle,* 9.

102. Willey, *God's Politician,* 90–92; Frossard, *Portrait of John Paul II,* 113.

103. Willey, *God's Politician,* 88; Remmick, "The Pope in Crisis," 52. The Vatican would have usually given Waldheim the higher Order of the Golden Spur rather than the lesser Order of Pius X. Roberto Suro, "John Paul Holds Waldheim Meeting," *New York Times,* June 26, 1987, 1+.

104. Willey, *God's Politician,* chap. 7.

105. Janet E. Smith, *Humanae Vitae: A Generation Later* (Washington, D.C.: Catholic University Press, 1991); John Paul II, *Reflections on Humanae Vitae: Conjugal Morality and Spirituality* (Boston: St. Paul's Editions, 1984).

106. Robert Blair Kaiser, *The Politics of Sex and Religion: A Case History in the Development of Doctrine, 1962–1984* (Kansas City, Mo.: Leaven Press, 1985), chaps. 11–12; Bernstein and Politi, *His Holiness,* 83.

107. Peter Steinfels, "Vatican Says the Ban on Women as Priests Is 'Infallible' Doctrine," *New York Times,* November 19, 1995, 1+; Peter Steinfels, "Wariness Greets Vatican Doctrinal Claim," *New York Times,* November 22, 1995, 24. The pronouncement followed the revelation that in 1970 women were ordained in Communist Czechoslovakia when the Church was forced underground. See the Associated Press report for November 13, 1995, and also Paula Butturini, "Vatican Move Raises Questions," *Boston Globe,* November 23, 1995, 2. Also relevant is Richard P. McBrien, "Ten Points on Infallibility," *Catholic Free Press,* April 12, 1993, 4.

108. James J. McCartney, *Unborn Persons: Pope John Paul II and the Abortion Debate* (New York: Peter Lang, 1987), 83–84.

109. Frossard, *Portrait of John Paul II,* 80–81.

110. McCartney, *Unborn Persons,* 83–84.

111. Pope John Paul II, *The Gospel of Life (Evangelicum Vitae)* (New York: Random House, 1995).

112. Bernstein and Politi, *His Holiness,* 526; Hebblethwaite, *Next Pope,* passim; Roberto Suro, "12 Faiths Join Pope to Pray for Peace," *New York Times,* October 28, 1986, 3; John Paul II, *Crossing the Threshold of Hope;* on women, see "Pope Sees Larger Role," 2. On China, Alan Cowell, "Pope Offers the Chinese a Deal on the Church's Role," *New York Times,* January 15, 1995, 3; on irresponsible behavior, Bernstein and Politi, *His Holiness,* 521.

113. Adam Gopnik, "A Virtual Bishop," *New Yorker,* March 18, 1996, 59–63.

114. Frossard, *Portrait of John Paul II,* 111; Bernstein and Politi, *His Holiness,* 114.

Conclusion

1. John Henry Newman, *On Consulting the Faithful in Matters of Doctrine* (New York: Sheed and Ward, 1961), contains the judgment that during the Arian heresy "the Catholic people, in the length and breadth of Christendom, were the obstinate champions of Catholic truth, and the bishops were not.... We are obliged to say that the governed were preeminent in faith, zeal, courage, and constancy.... The great evangelical lesson [is] that, not the wise and powerful, but the obscure, the unlearned, and the weak constitute her real strength" (109–10).

INDEX

Gracias, Valerian, 217
Grant, Ulysses S., 78
Gregory I, St. ("Gregory the Great"),
   viii, 185, 192, 211, 310
Gregory VII, St. (Hildebrand), 15, 37,
   133, 270
Gregory XV (Alessandro Ludovici),
   202
Gregory XVI (Bartolomeo Alberto
   Cappellari), 5–8, 12–13, 32, 50,
   58, 130
Grente, Georges, 178
Grey, Edward, 79
Grör, Hermann, 293
Grosz, Josef, 154, 155
Gutiérrez, Gustavo, 290

Hales, E. E. Y., 20, 24
Halifax, Edward Frederick Lindley
   Wood, 1st Earl of, 40–41, 126
Halter, Marek, 251
Hammar, Richard, 240
Häring, Bernhard, 212
Havel, Václav, 276
Hebblethwaite, Peter, 184, 204
Hecker, Isaac, 48
Heenan, John, 219
Henle, Robert, 289
"Henri V," Count of Chambord,
   42–43, 131
Henry IV, 37
Henry VIII, 40
Hermaniuk, Maxim, 206
Herriot, Édouard, 171
Herzog, Isaac, 148, 155
Hesburgh, Theodore, 289
Heydrich, Reinhard, 144, 251
Hindenburg, Paul von, 79, 86
Hitler, Adolf, 88, 97, 106–7, 118,
   120–23, 132, 134, 136, 142,
   144–46, 149, 170
Hlond, August, 149
Hobsbawm, Eric, 96–97
Hochhuth, Rolf, 145
Hoover, Herbert, 98, 127
Horthy de Nagybánya, Miklós, 151

Hotzendorf, Conrad von, 79
Humanae Vitae, 235, 259, 295, 299,
   313
Humani Generis, 171, 177, 185
Hume, Basil, 255
Hunthausen, Raymond, 283, 284
Hus, John, 98

Immaculate Conception, 25, 27, 229,
   235, 296
Immortale Dei, 43
Infallibility, 19, 26–28, 30, 36–38,
   45, 53, 59, 61, 190, 193, 209, 229,
   235, 300
Ingarden, Roman, 252
Iniquis Afflictisque, 127
Innitzer, Theodor, 122
Innocent I, St., 161
Innocent III (Lotario di'conti di Segni),
   49, 183
Innocent V (Pierre of Tarentaise), 161
Innocent VII (Cosimo Gentile de'
   Migliorati), 73
Inter Sodalicia, 93
Ireland, John, 47

Jablonski, Henryk, 270, 273
James II, 10
Jan III Sobieski, 92
Jansenism, 65
Jaruzelski, Wojciech, 274, 276
Jesuits (Society of Jesus), 11, 18, 27,
   37, 228, 241, 286
John of the Cross, St., 251–52
John XXIII (Angelo Roncalli), 1, 3,
   60, 64, 85, 95, 133, 143, 148, 150,
   187, 163–200, 204, 209, 212, 218,
   223, 228, 232, 234–35, 245, 255–
   56, 258–59, 262–63, 267, 285,
   292, 302, 304–5, 308, 310–12,
   314
John XXIII — antipope (Baldassarre
   Cossa), 175
John Paul I (Albino Luciani), 94,
   245–48, 259, 265, 313

ABOUT THE AUTHOR

MICHAEL P. RICCARDS is currently the president of Fitchburg State College in Massachusetts. He has been president of St. John's College in Santa Fe and Shepherd College in West Virginia. Dr. Riccards has been a Fulbright Fellow to Japan and a National Endowment for the Humanities Fellow at Princeton University. He is the author of a two-volume history of the American presidency, *The Ferocious Engine of Democracy.*